Alice in Murderland

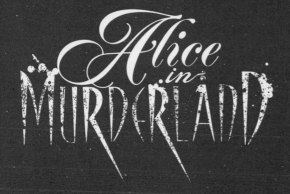

10

Kaori Yuki

Characters & Story

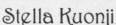

Stella Kuonji
Fourth daughter of the Kuonji family. Was taken in by the Kuonjis, along with eldest brother, Zeno. Loves Zeno.

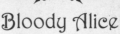

Bloody Alice
Another personality residing within Stella that appears when she loses all reason.

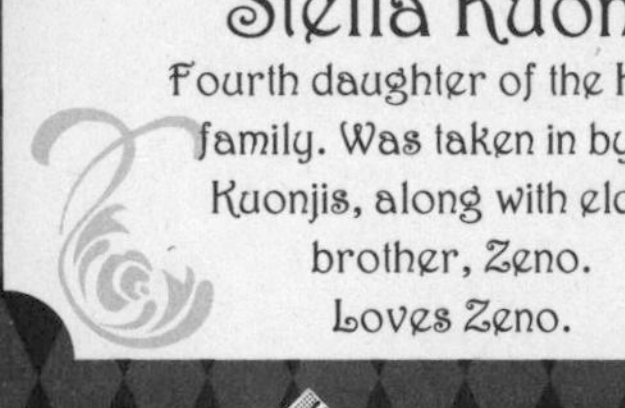

Tsukito
Grandson of Kokonoe, the chief of the Black Rabbit bodyguards. The true Zeno was a personality inside of Tsukito.

Olga
Head of the Kuonji Group and matriarch of the family.

Kokonoe
Chief of the Black Rabbit bodyguards tasked with protecting the nine siblings.

The Kuonji Siblings

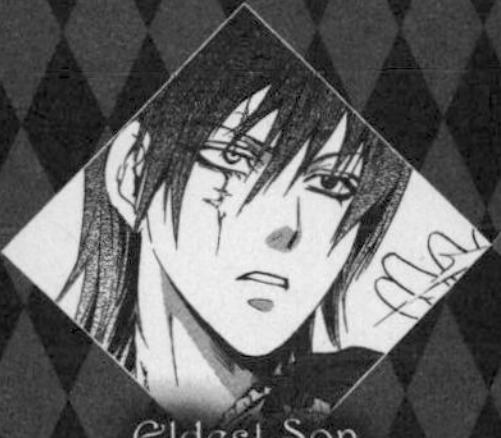

Eldest Son

Zeno

Previously thought to be Stella's beloved big brother, but actually an impostor who replaced him five years ago.

DEAD!

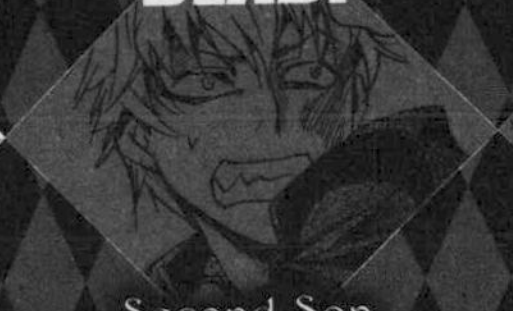

Second Son

Sid

The culprit behind a wave of local murders. Killed by Stella after her transformation into "Bloody Alice."

DEAD!

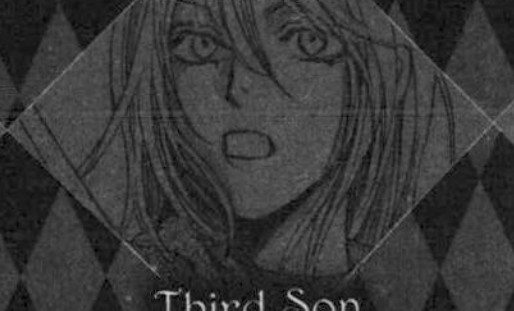

Third Son

Sol

Maré's older twin. Fought Stella to avenge his younger brother Maré and lost. In the end, he chose to die.

DEAD!

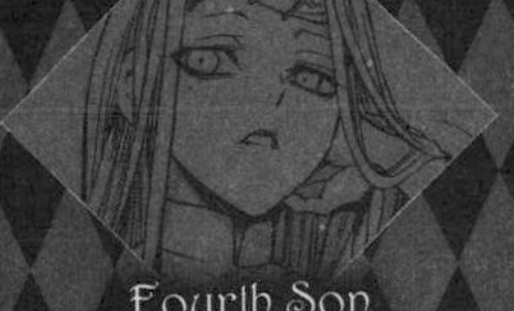

Fourth Son

Maré

Sol's younger twin. He and Stella had an antagonistic relationship, and he died at the end of their showdown.

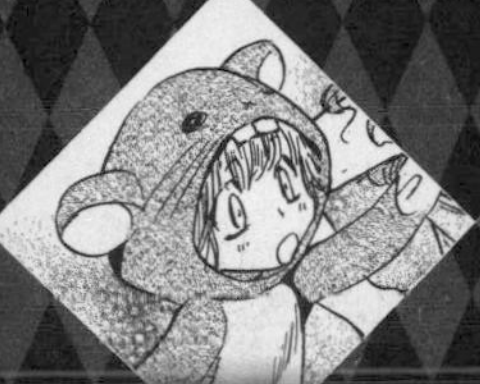

Fifth Son

Melm

The youngest of all the Kuonji siblings. Had been in Claire's care due to his youth.

DEAD!

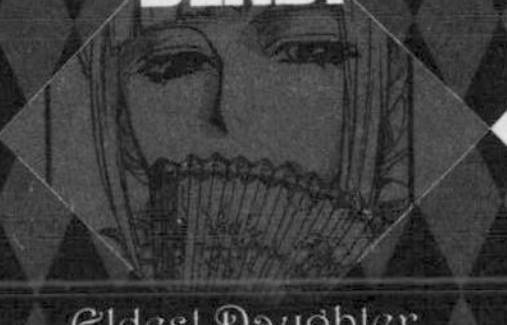

Eldest Daughter

Ibara

The best fighter among the siblings. She challenged Stella to a one-on-one fight, and Alice crushed her heart, killing her.

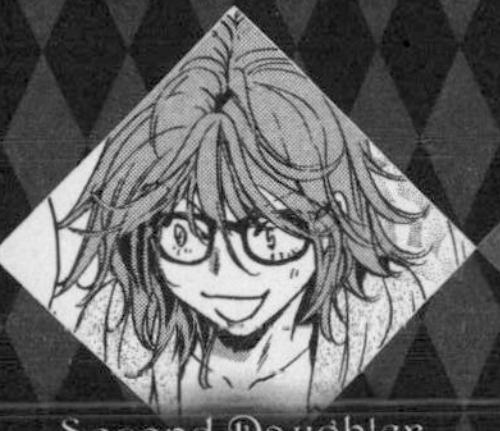

Second Daughter

Miser

Reptile *otaku*. Plots to make her escape from the Kuonji house with her boyfriend, Io, and Stella.

DEAD!

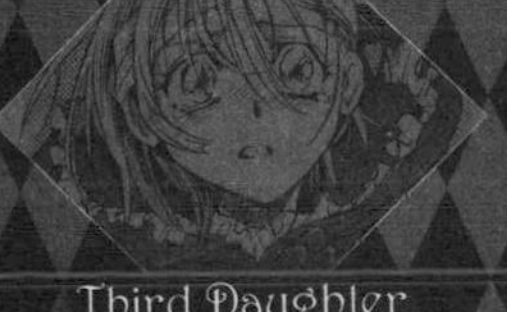

Third Daughter

Claire

Closest to Stella of all the siblings. Was finished off by eldest son, Zeno, after her showdown with Stella.

Story

Stella, fourth daughter of the Kuonji family, world leaders of industry, finds that she must engage in a battle royale with her siblings for the sake of her eldest brother, Zeno. As a succession of challenges comes from her siblings and numerous clashes of life or death unfold, Stella fights alongside "Bloody Alice," her second battle-awakened personality. With just three siblings left—Miser, Melm, and Stella—mother Olga imposes a rematch on the remaining sisters, but Miser and Stella decide to hatch an escape instead. While going through the motions of battle to satisfy their mother during their fight, the sisters successfully cause Olga to hallucinate Miser's death at Stella's hands. And once Miser has reunited with her boyfriend, Io, the trio attempt to carry out their escape, only to be caught by the ever-watchful Olga. How far will Stella now go to save her sister...!?

Key Words

Secret of Elysium • A mysterious ability passed down through the Kuonji line that grants the wielder power over life and death, as well as immortality.

Bandersnatch • The true form of the members of the Kuonji family. Attempts to grow the number of people infected with its blood and steals the souls of others for family sustenance.

Murderland Rules • The nine brothers and sisters must kill one another until only one is left standing. The game must be completed within one year, by Zeno's twentieth birthday. The lone survivor will become head of the family, inheriting the Kuonji Group and all its assets.

Black Rabbits • Bodyguards who may be used by the siblings as pawns. There are special methods by which this manipulation can be accomplished.

Alice in Murderland

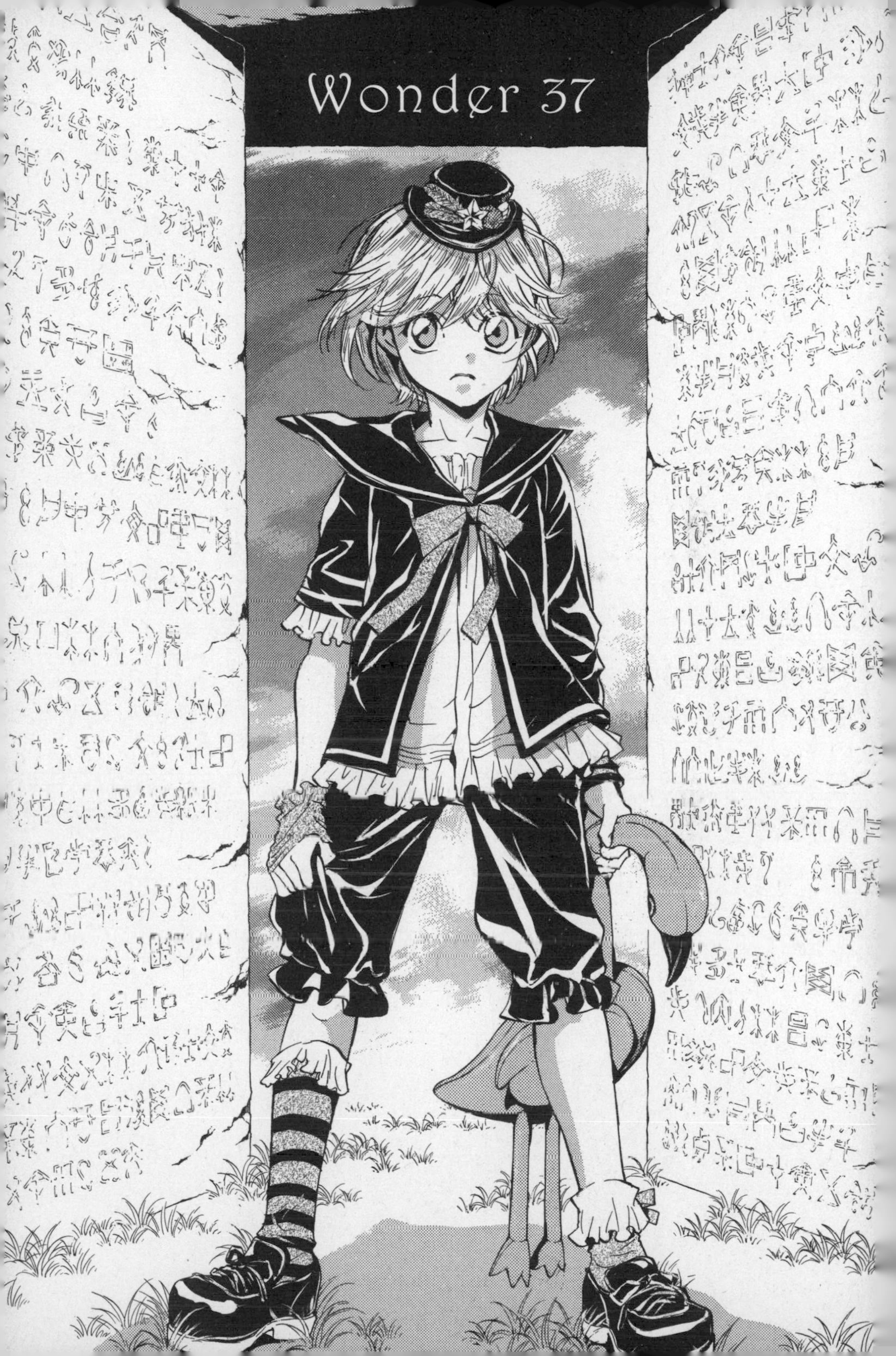
Wonder 37

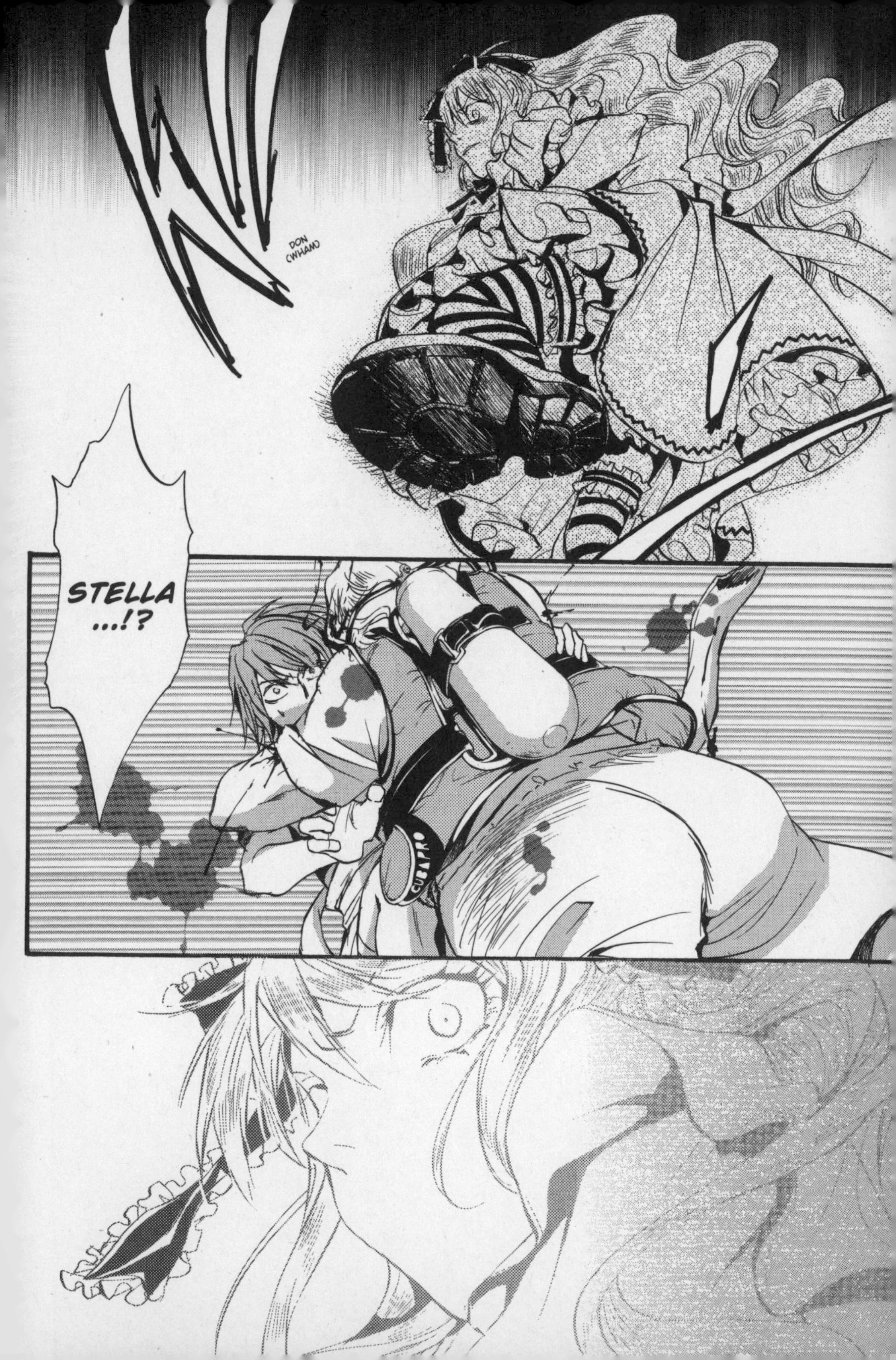
DON
(WHAM)
STELLA ...!?

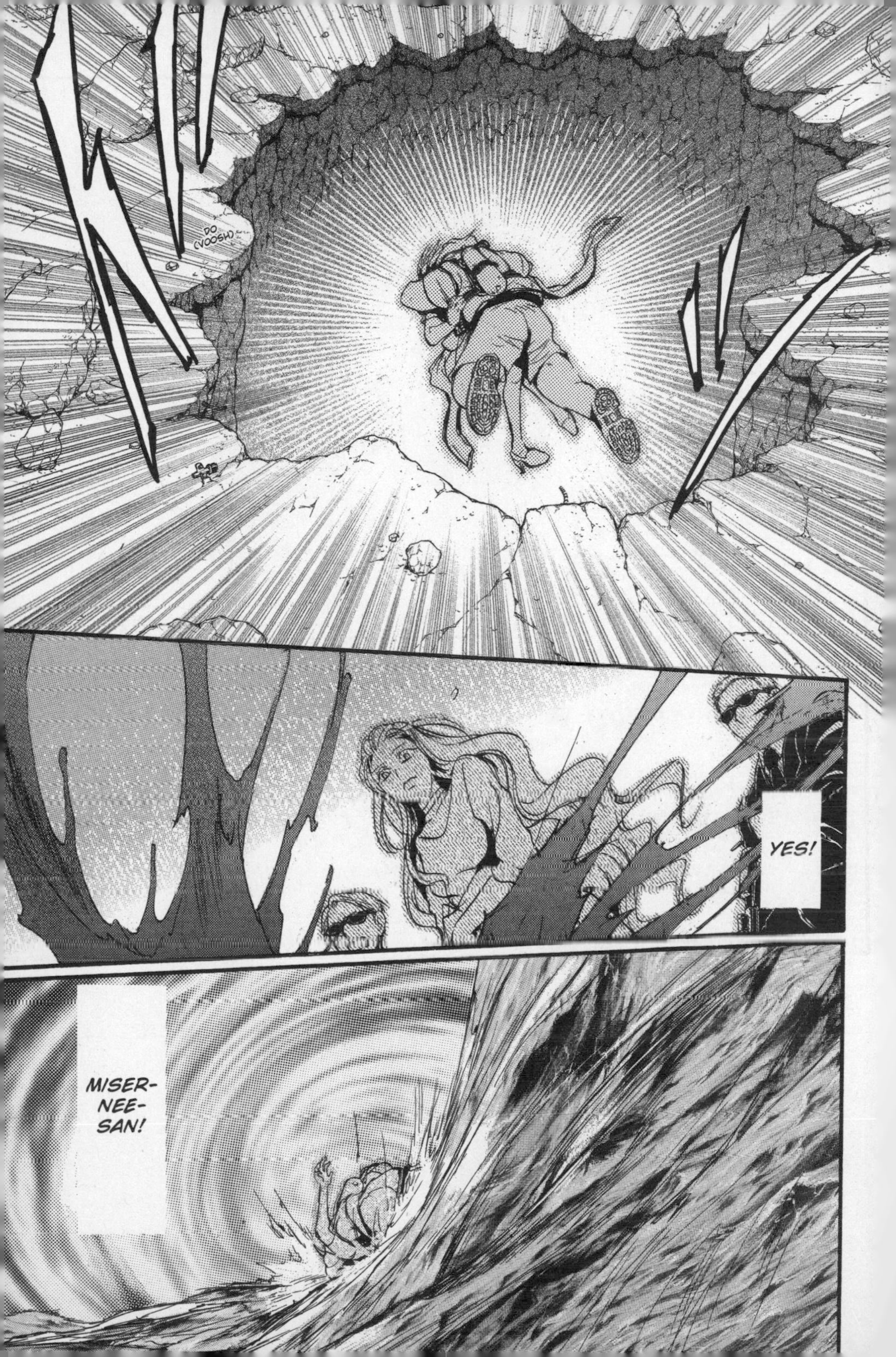
DO (VOOSH)
YES!
MISER-NEE-SAN!

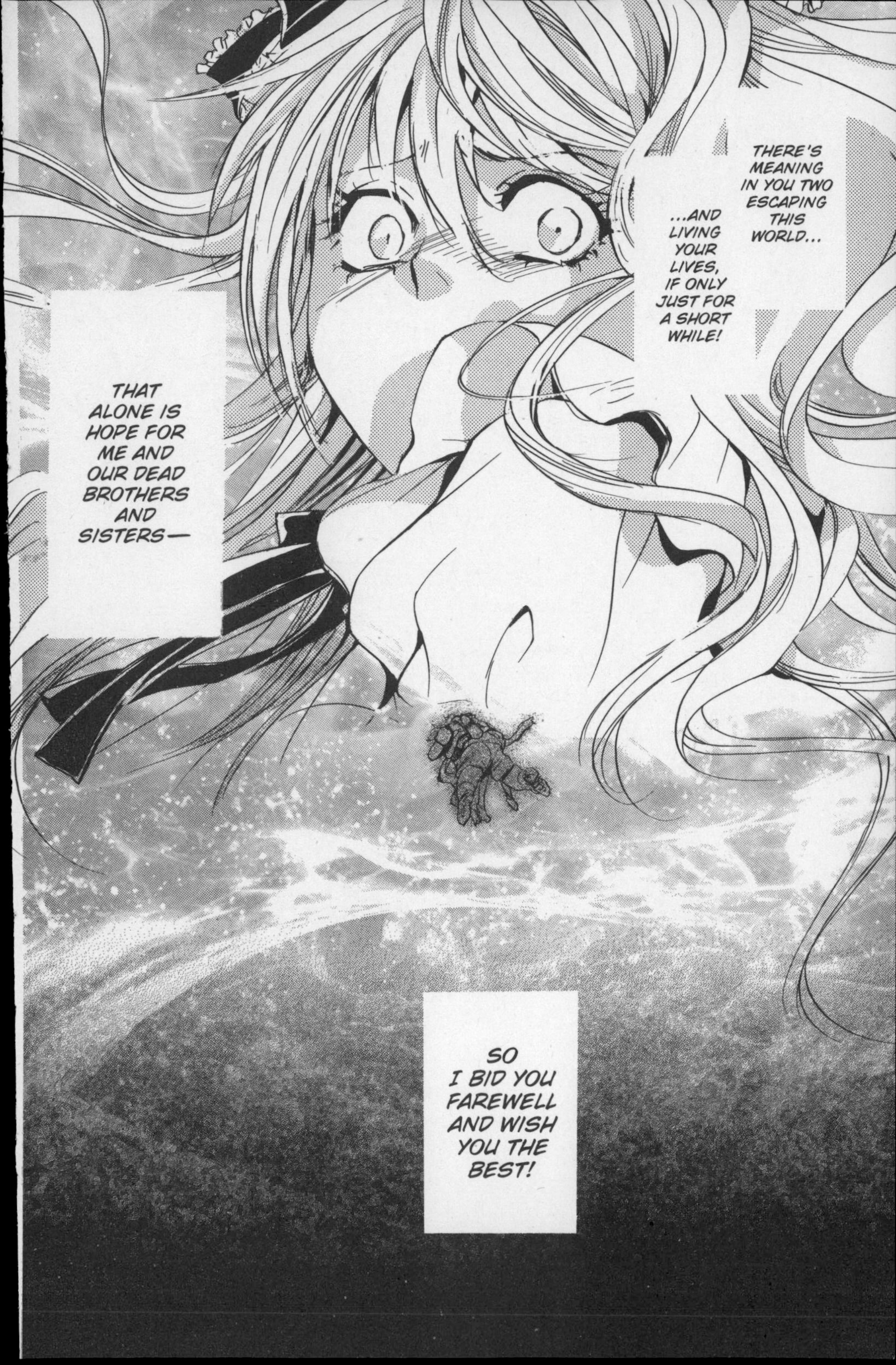
THERE'S MEANING IN YOU TWO ESCAPING THIS WORLD...
...AND LIVING YOUR LIVES, IF ONLY JUST FOR A SHORT WHILE!
THAT ALONE IS HOPE FOR ME AND OUR DEAD BROTHERS AND SISTERS—
SO I BID YOU FAREWELL AND WISH YOU THE BEST!

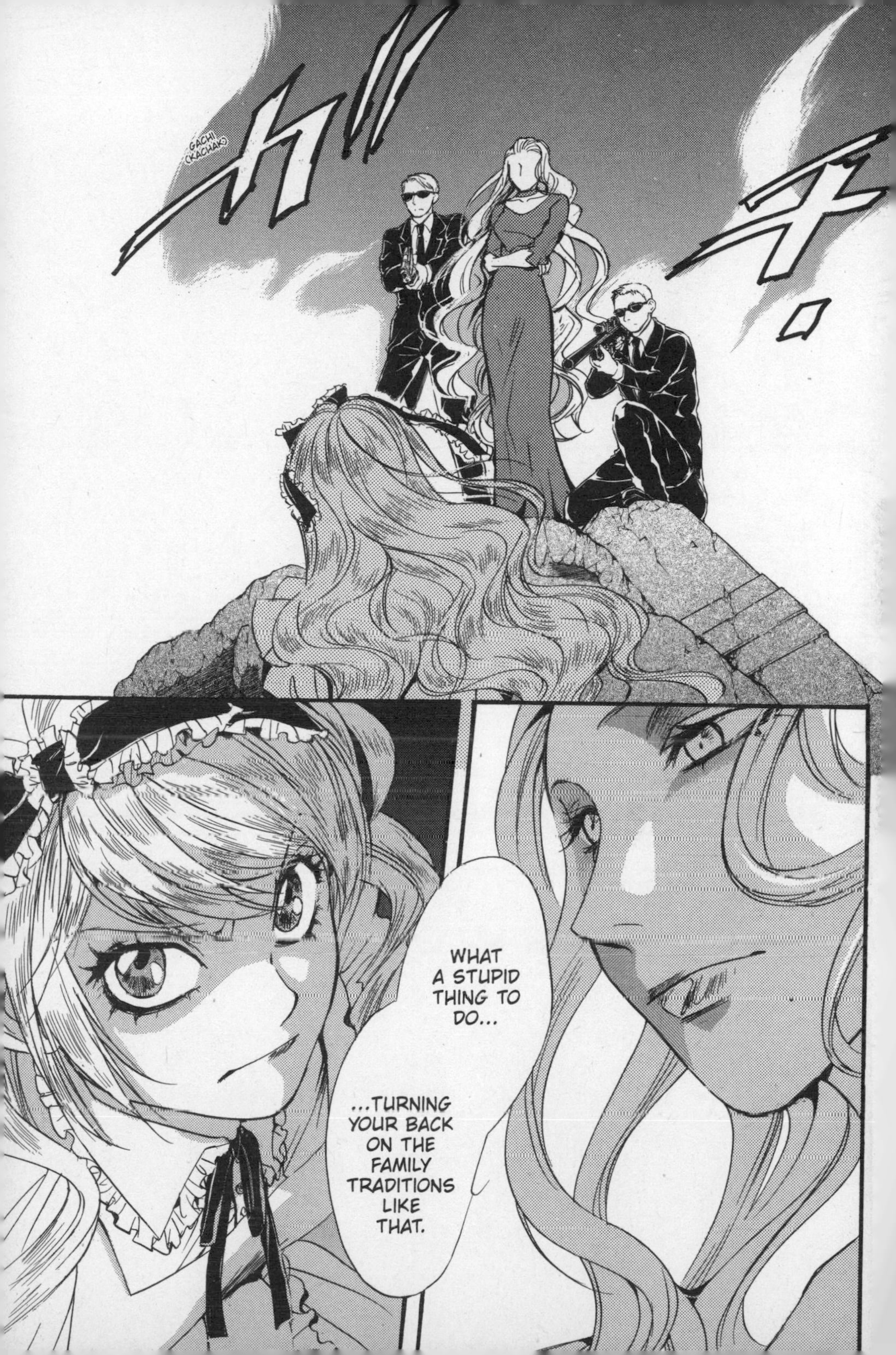
GACHI (KACHAK)
WHAT A STUPID THING TO DO...
...TURNING YOUR BACK ON THE FAMILY TRADITIONS LIKE THAT.

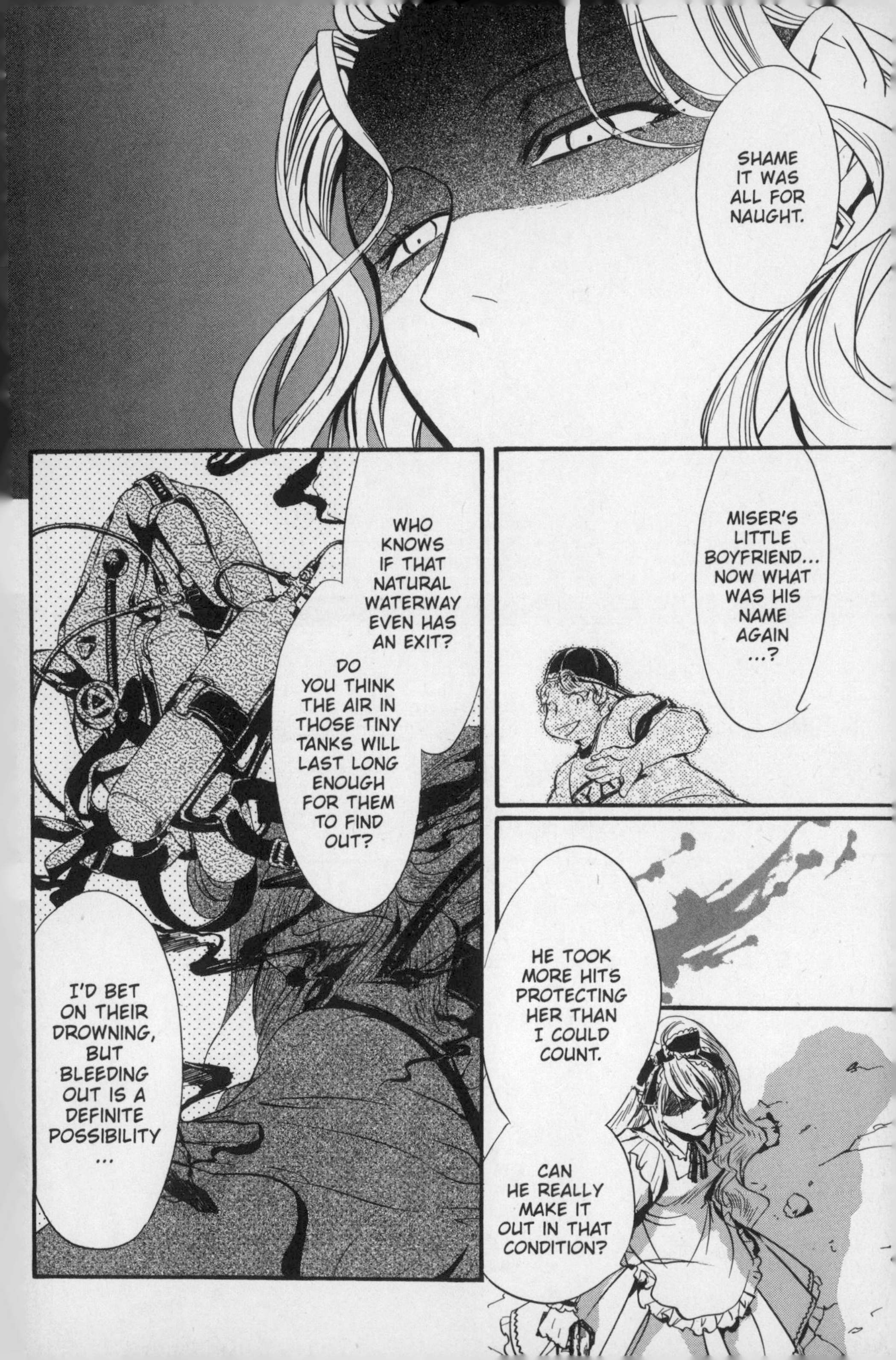
SHAME IT WAS ALL FOR NAUGHT.
MISER'S LITTLE BOYFRIEND... NOW WHAT WAS HIS NAME AGAIN ...?
HE TOOK MORE HITS PROTECTING HER THAN I COULD COUNT.
CAN HE REALLY MAKE IT OUT IN THAT CONDITION?
WHO KNOWS IF THAT NATURAL WATERWAY EVEN HAS AN EXIT?
DO YOU THINK THE AIR IN THOSE TINY TANKS WILL LAST LONG ENOUGH FOR THEM TO FIND OUT?
I'D BET ON THEIR DROWNING, BUT BLEEDING OUT IS A DEFINITE POSSIBILITY ...

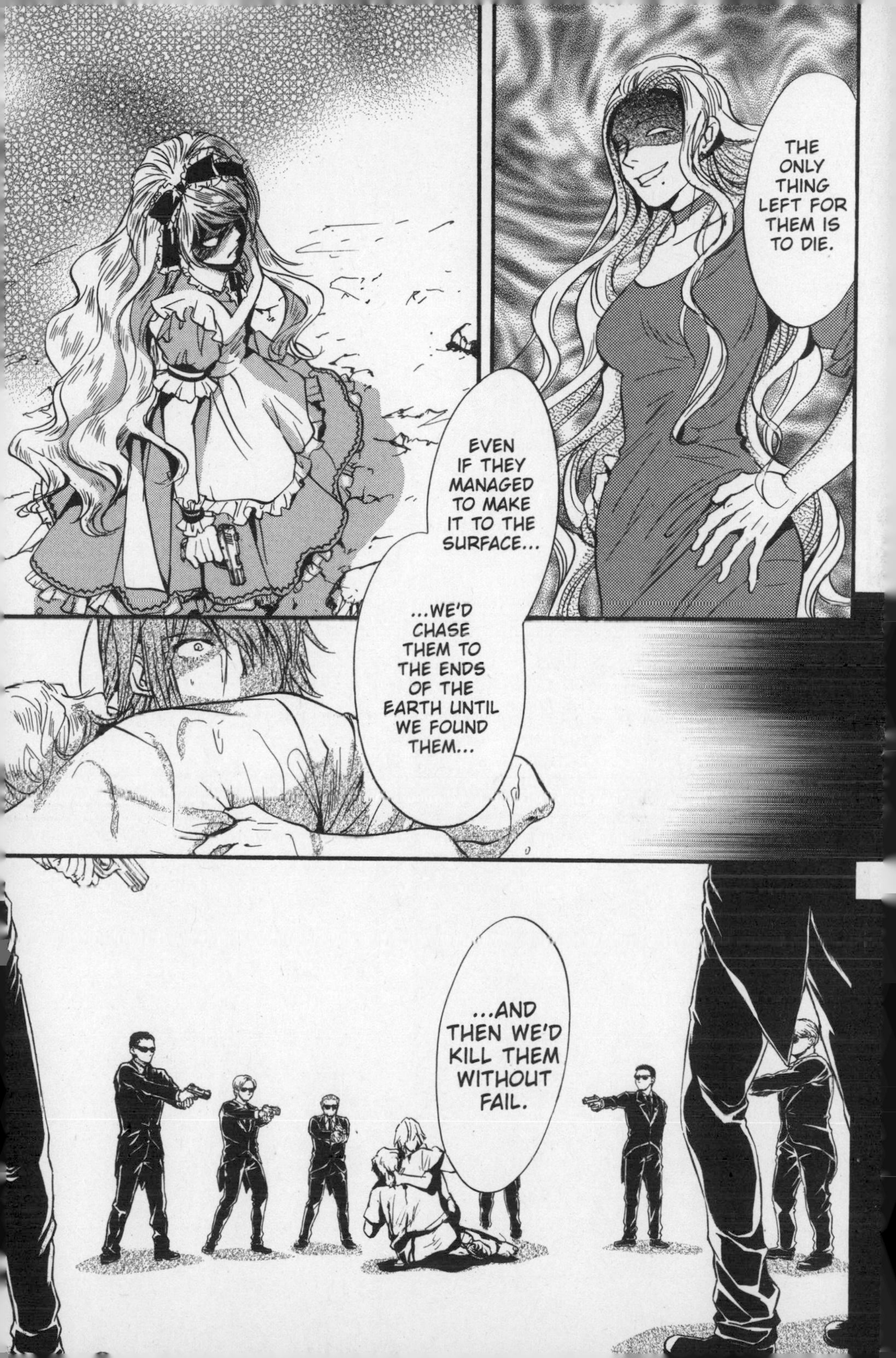
THE ONLY THING LEFT FOR THEM IS TO DIE.
EVEN IF THEY MANAGED TO MAKE IT TO THE SURFACE...
...WE'D CHASE THEM TO THE ENDS OF THE EARTH UNTIL WE FOUND THEM...
...AND THEN WE'D KILL THEM WITHOUT FAIL.

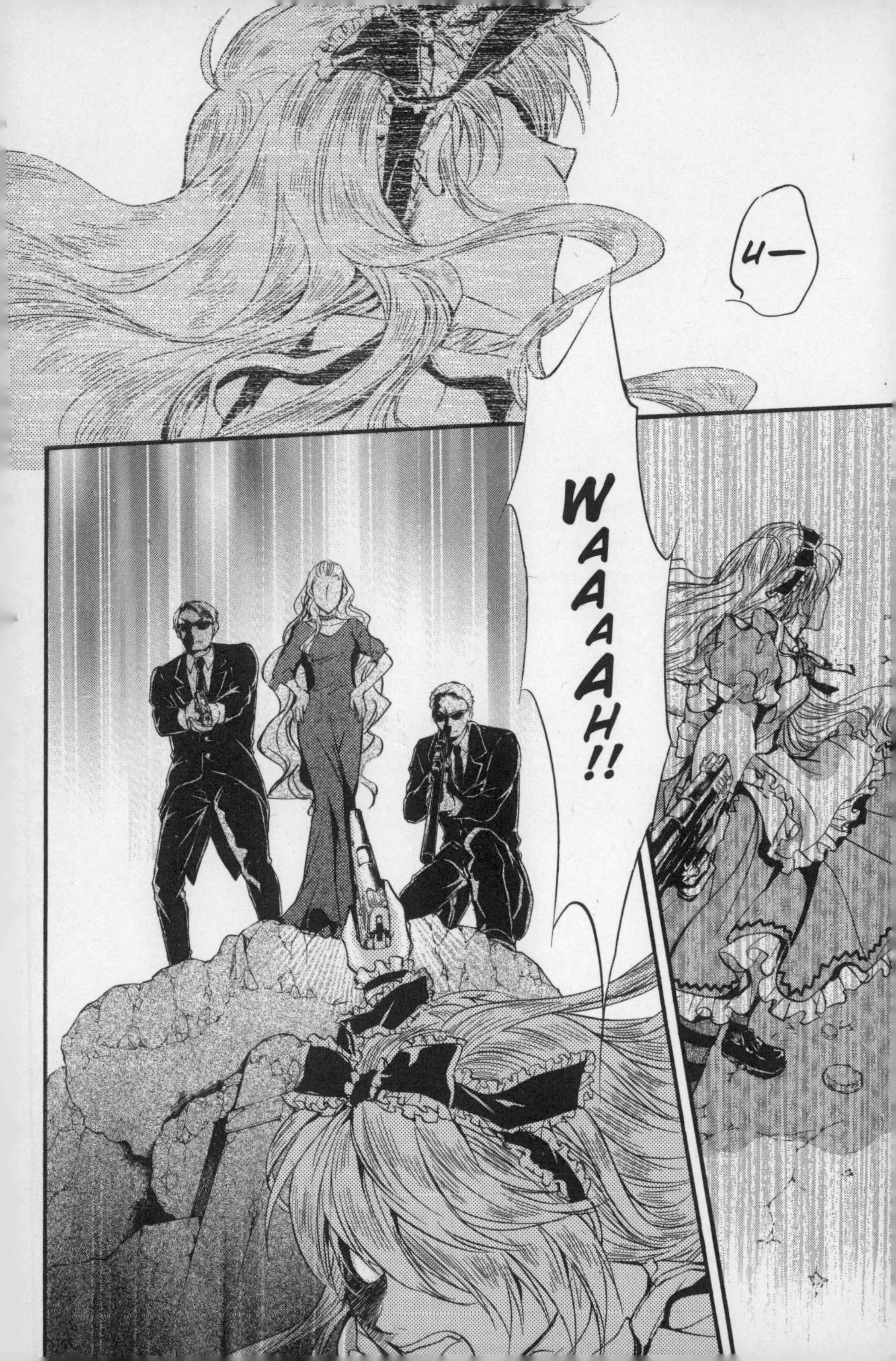

U—
WAAAAAH!!

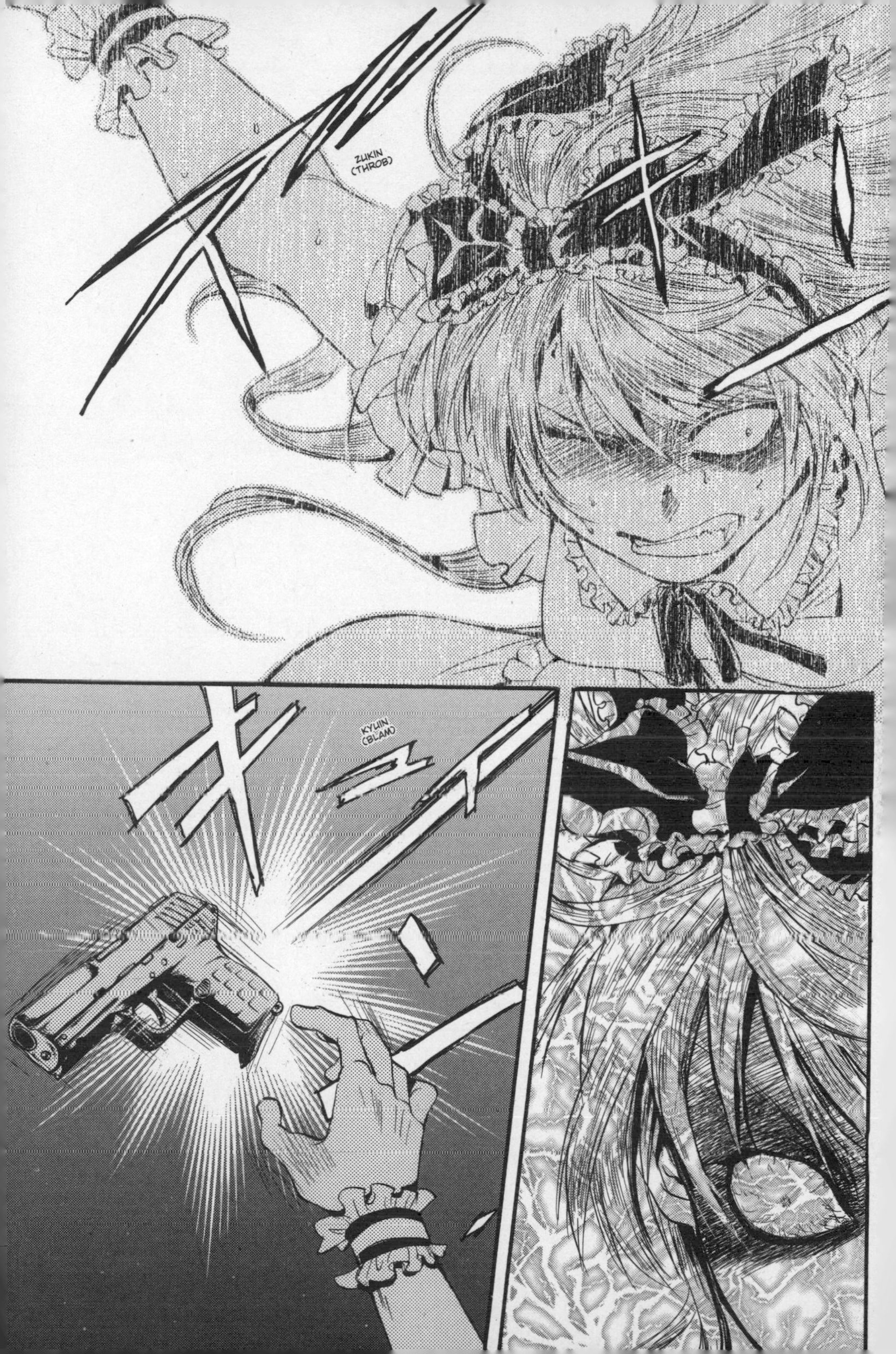
ZUKIN (THROB)
KYUIN (BLAM)

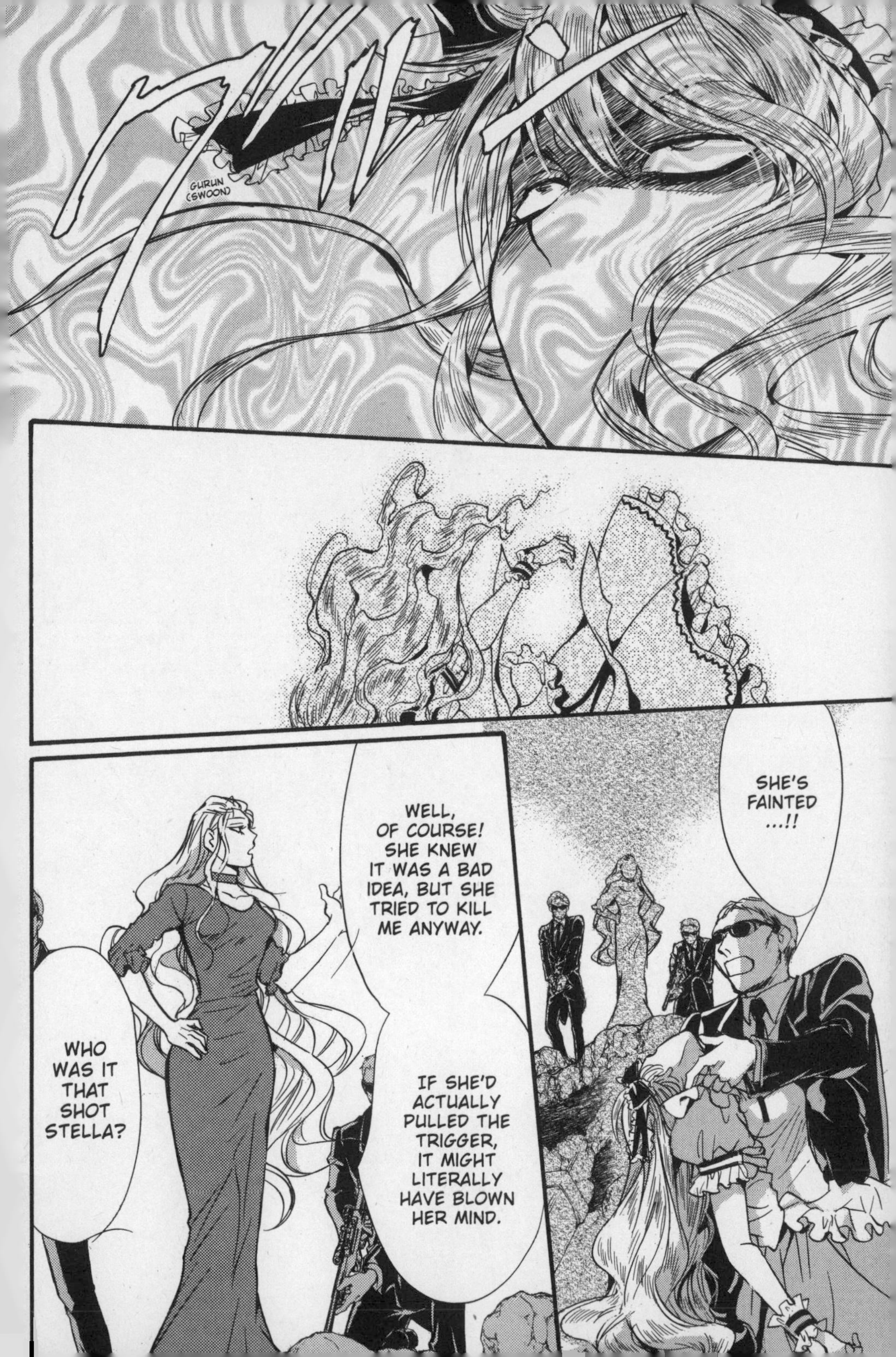
GURUN (SWOON)
SHE'S FAINTED ...!!
WELL, OF COURSE! SHE KNEW IT WAS A BAD IDEA, BUT SHE TRIED TO KILL ME ANYWAY.
IF SHE'D ACTUALLY PULLED THE TRIGGER, IT MIGHT LITERALLY HAVE BLOWN HER MIND.
WHO WAS IT THAT SHOT STELLA?

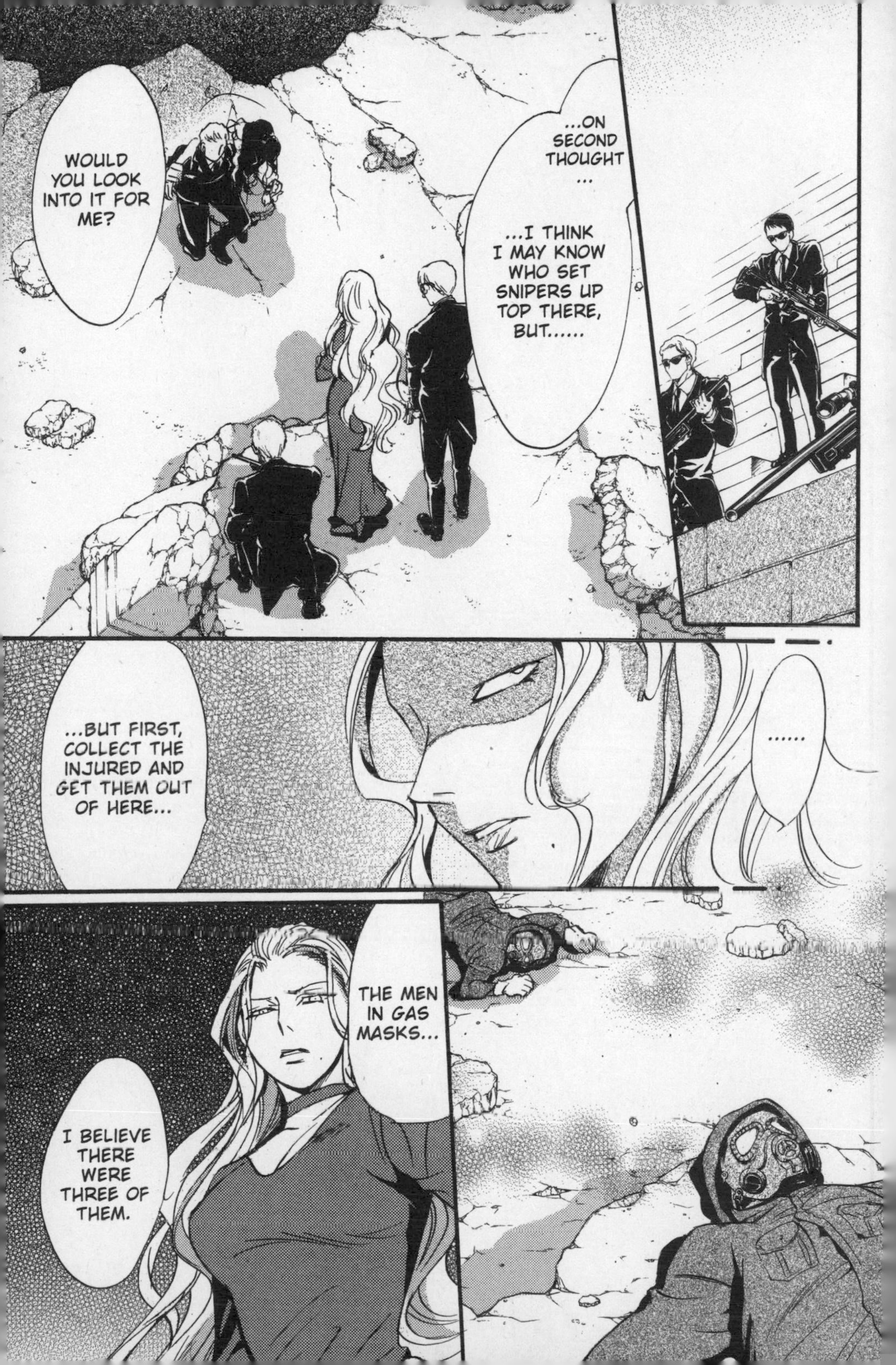
...ON SECOND THOUGHT ...
...I THINK I MAY KNOW WHO SET SNIPERS UP TOP THERE, BUT......
WOULD YOU LOOK INTO IT FOR ME?
......
...BUT FIRST, COLLECT THE INJURED AND GET THEM OUT OF HERE...
THE MEN IN GAS MASKS...
I BELIEVE THERE WERE THREE OF THEM.

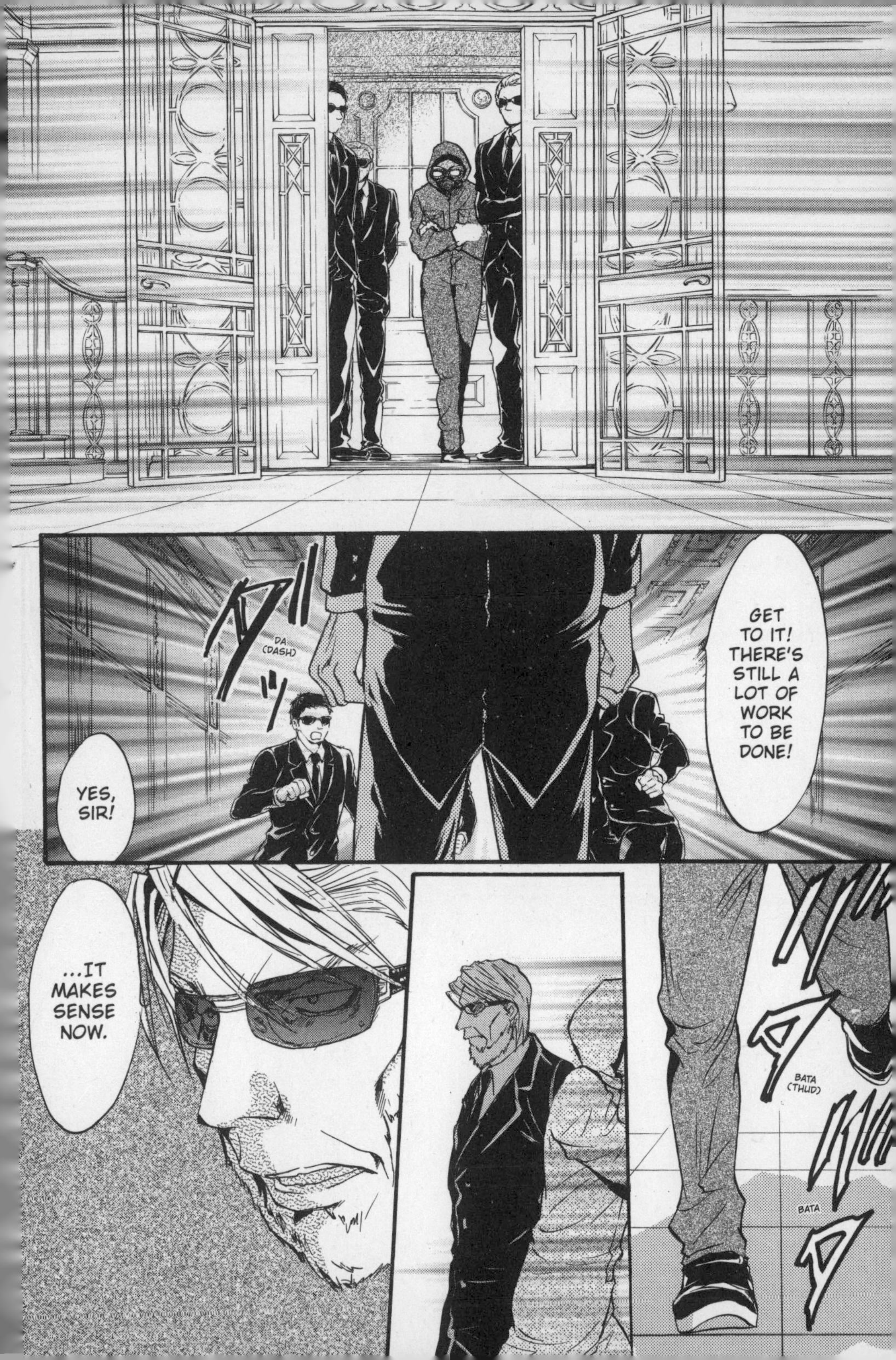
GET TO IT! THERE'S STILL A LOT OF WORK TO BE DONE!
DA (DASH)
YES, SIR!
BATA (THUD)
BATA
...IT MAKES SENSE NOW.

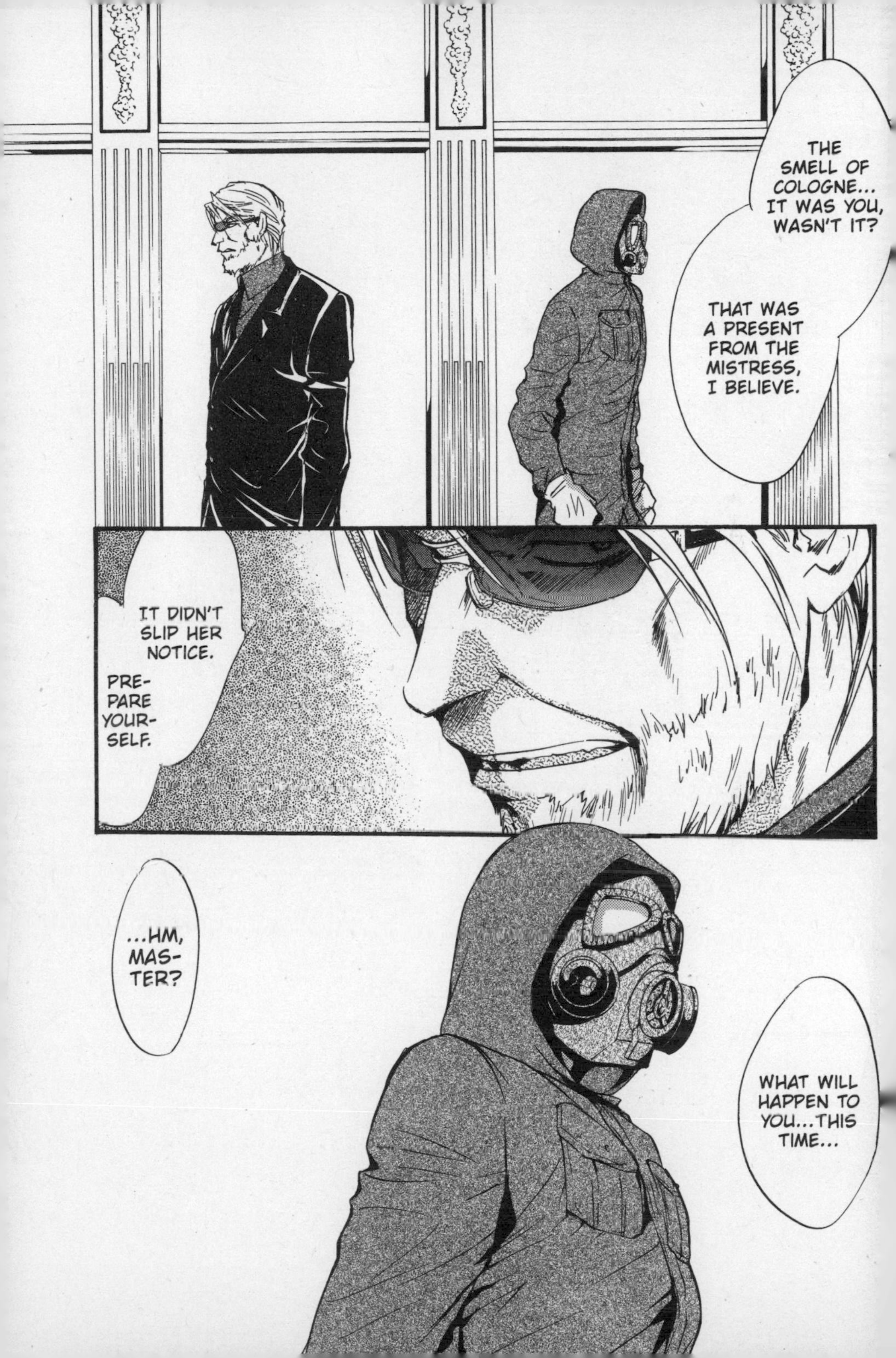
THE SMELL OF COLOGNE... IT WAS YOU, WASN'T IT?
THAT WAS A PRESENT FROM THE MISTRESS, I BELIEVE.
IT DIDN'T SLIP HER NOTICE.
PRE-PARE YOUR-SELF.
WHAT WILL HAPPEN TO YOU...THIS TIME...
...HM, MAS-TER?

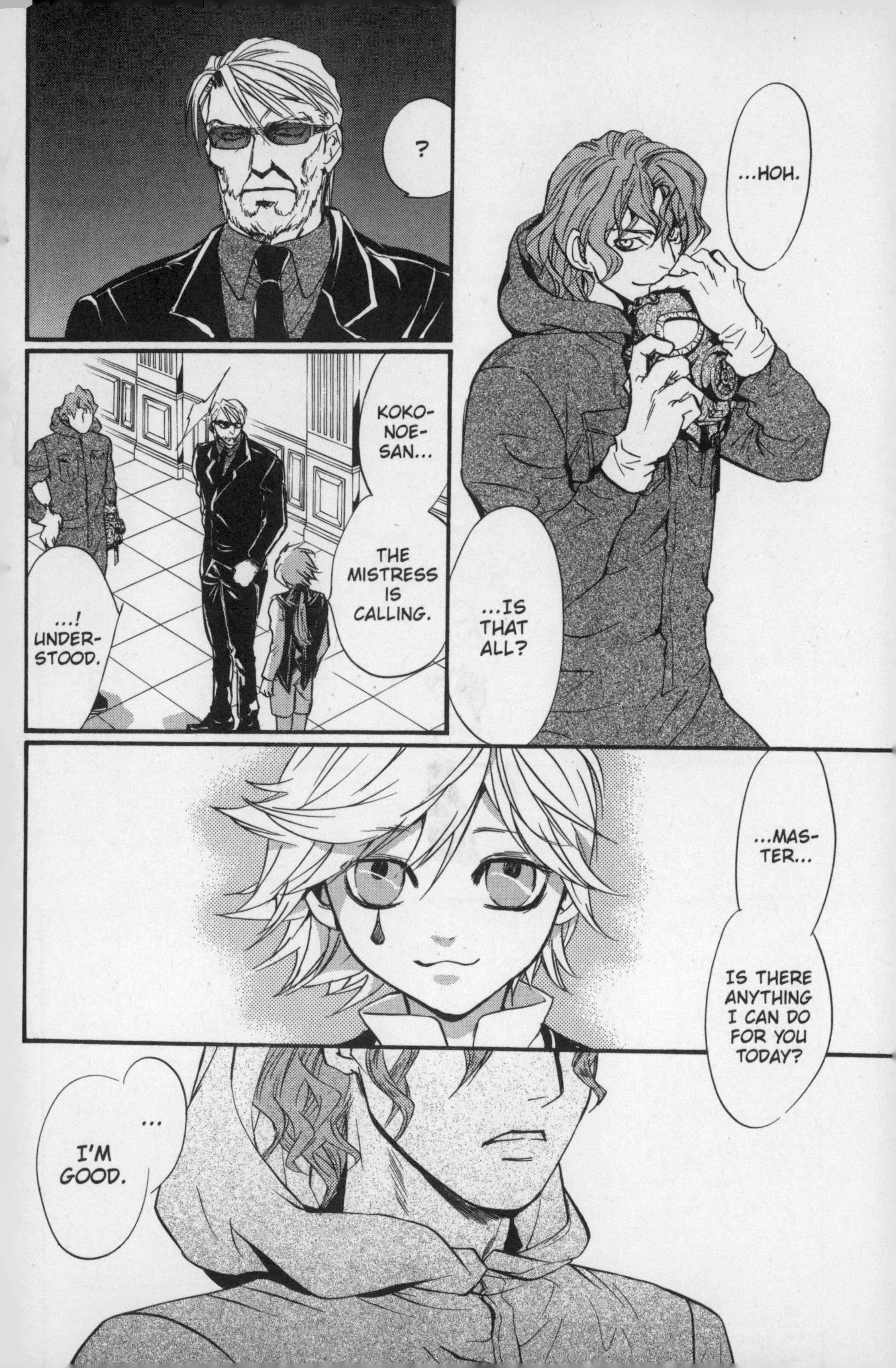

...HOH.
...IS THAT ALL?
?
KOKO-NOE-SAN...
THE MISTRESS IS CALLING.
...! UNDER-STOOD.
...MAS-TER...
IS THERE ANYTHING I CAN DO FOR YOU TODAY?
... I'M GOOD.

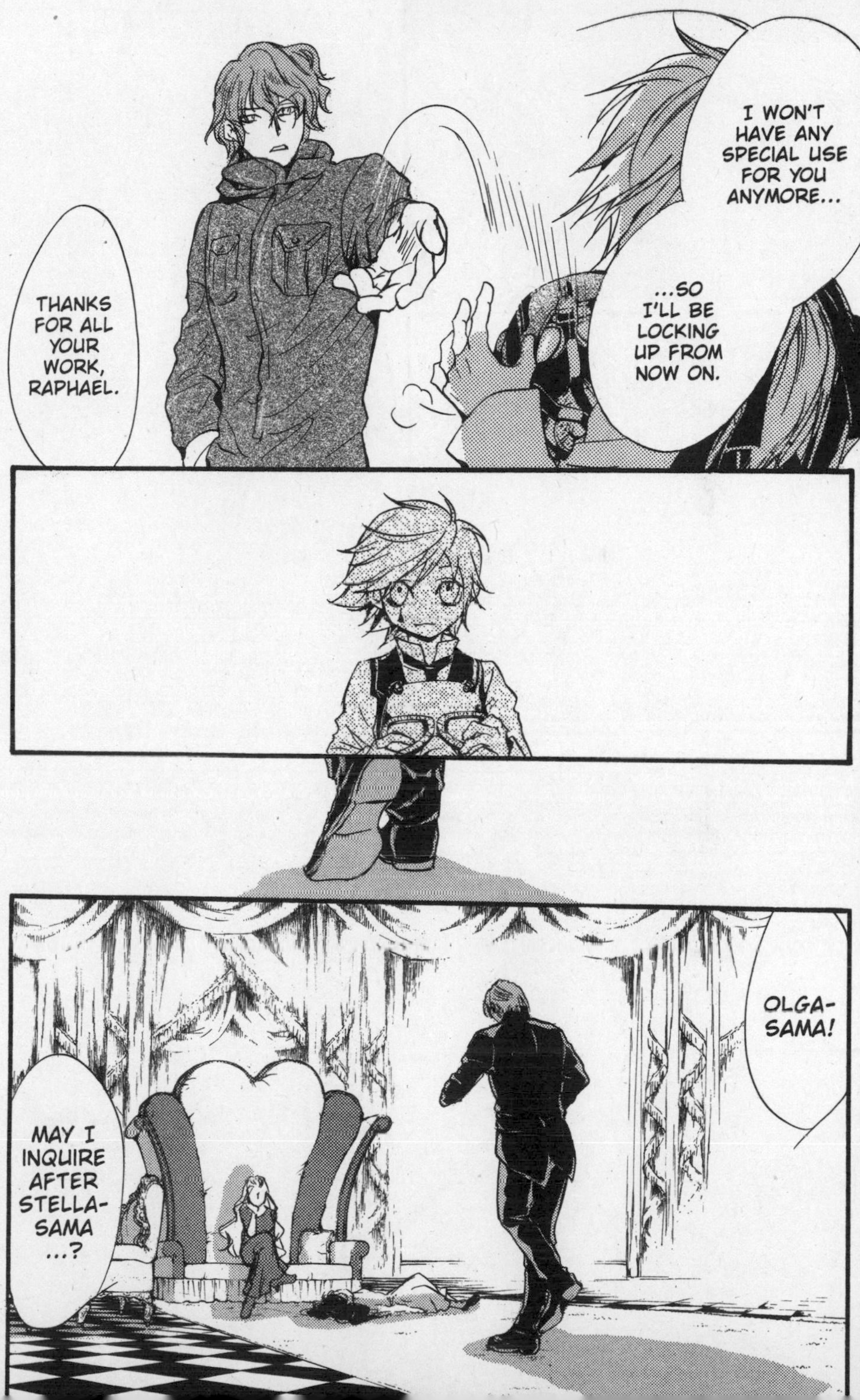
I WON'T HAVE ANY SPECIAL USE FOR YOU ANYMORE...
...SO I'LL BE LOCKING UP FROM NOW ON.
THANKS FOR ALL YOUR WORK, RAPHAEL.
OLGA-SAMA!
MAY I INQUIRE AFTER STELLA-SAMA...?

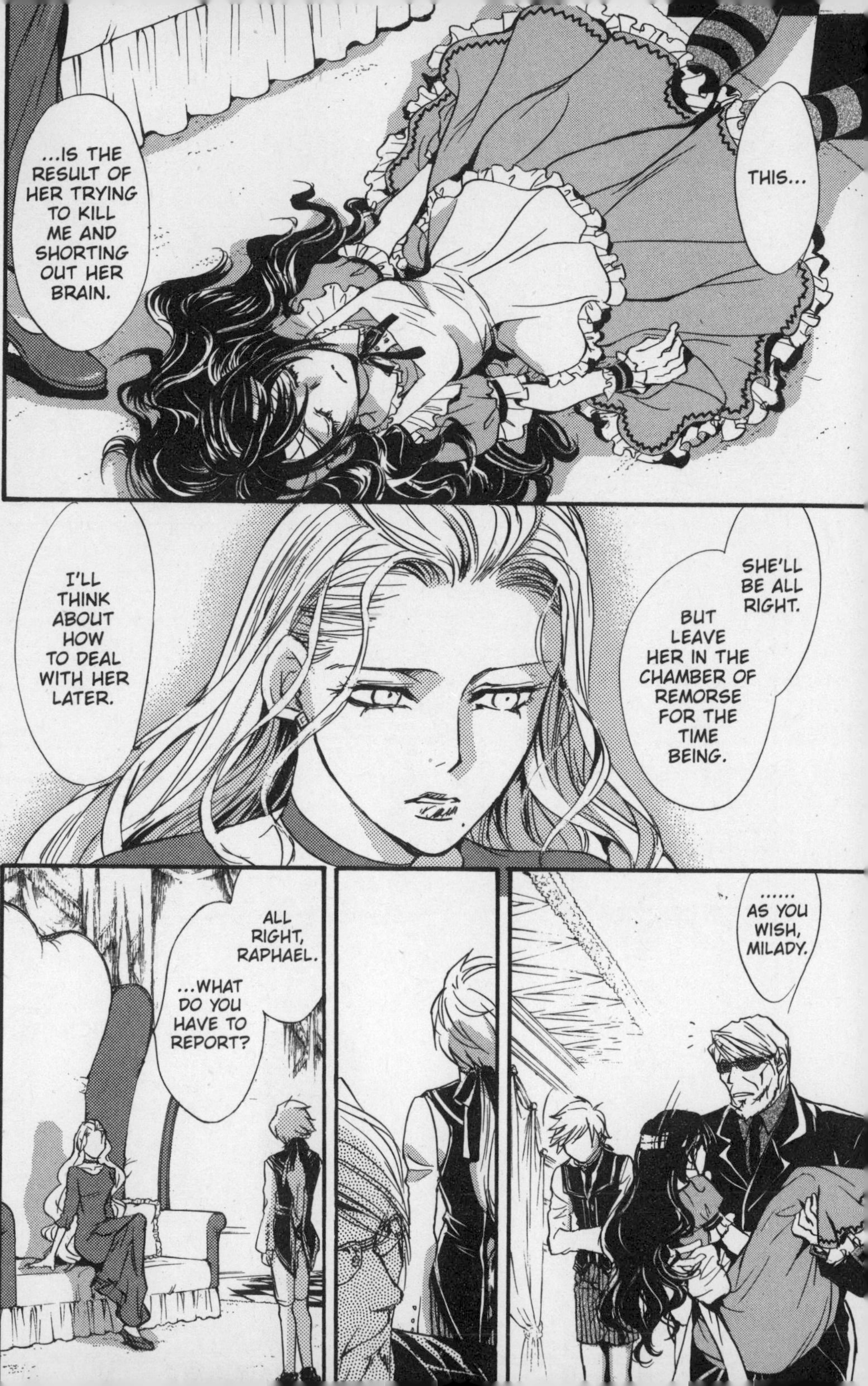
THIS...
...IS THE RESULT OF HER TRYING TO KILL ME AND SHORTING OUT HER BRAIN.
SHE'LL BE ALL RIGHT.
BUT LEAVE HER IN THE CHAMBER OF REMORSE FOR THE TIME BEING.
I'LL THINK ABOUT HOW TO DEAL WITH HER LATER.
...... AS YOU WISH, MILADY.
ALL RIGHT, RAPHAEL.
...WHAT DO YOU HAVE TO REPORT?

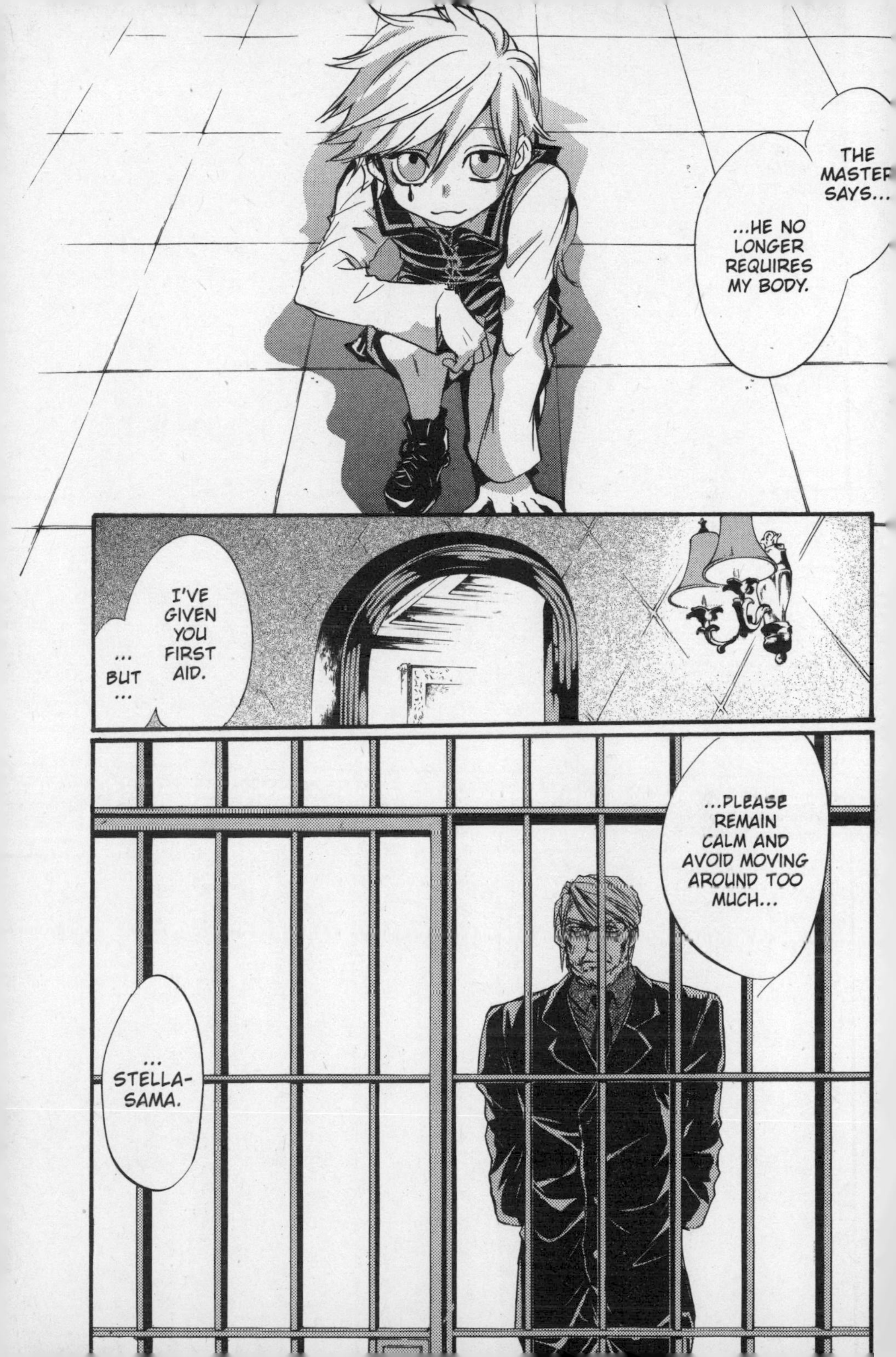
THE MASTER SAYS...
...HE NO LONGER REQUIRES MY BODY.
I'VE GIVEN YOU FIRST AID.
...BUT...
...PLEASE REMAIN CALM AND AVOID MOVING AROUND TOO MUCH...
...STELLA-SAMA.

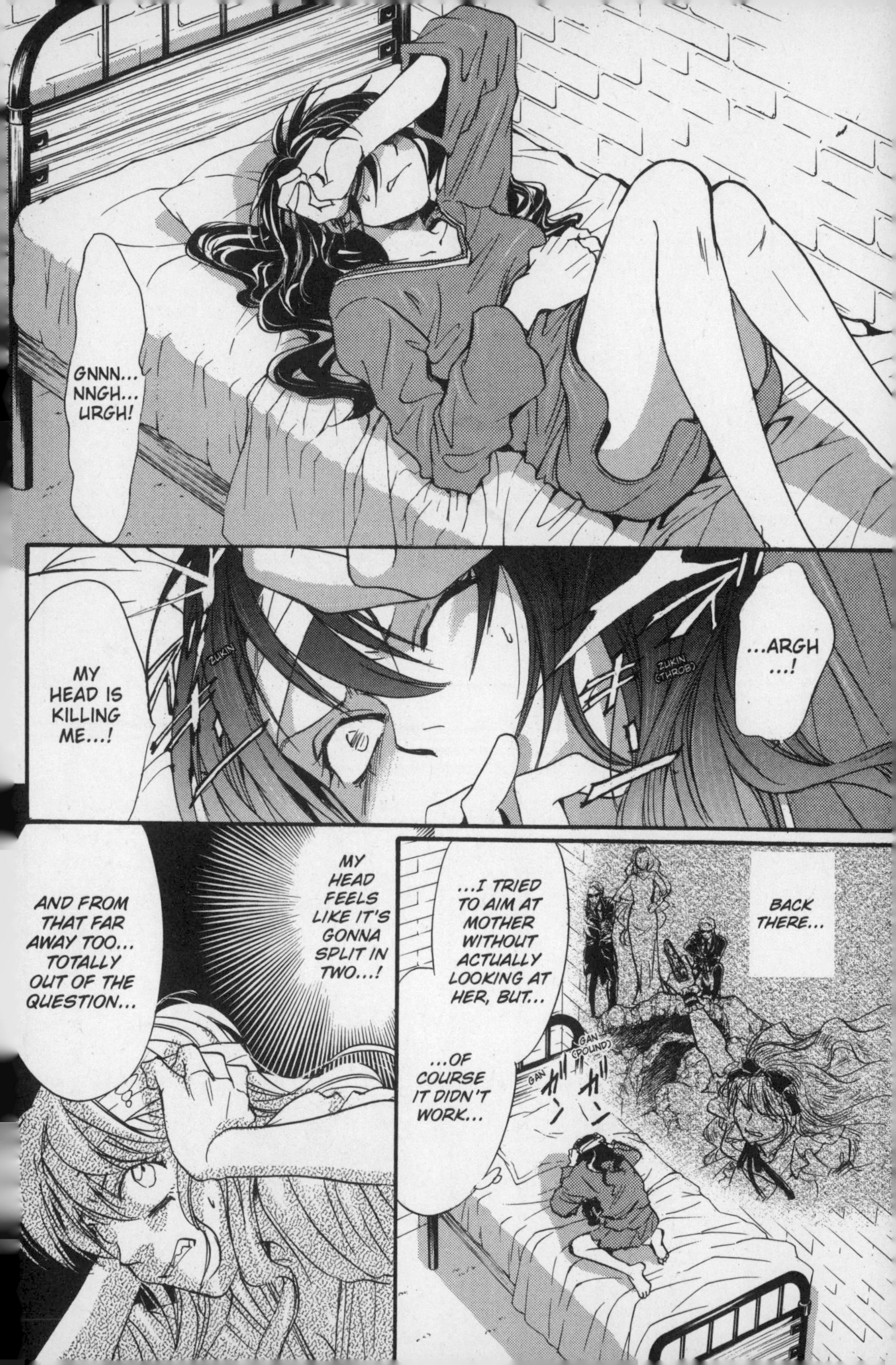
GNNN... NNGH... URGH!
...ARGH ...!
ZUKIN (THROB)
ZUKIN
MY HEAD IS KILLING ME...!
BACK THERE...
...I TRIED TO AIM AT MOTHER WITHOUT ACTUALLY LOOKING AT HER, BUT...
GAN (POUND)
GAN
...OF COURSE IT DIDN'T WORK...
MY HEAD FEELS LIKE IT'S GONNA SPLIT IN TWO...!
AND FROM THAT FAR AWAY TOO... TOTALLY OUT OF THE QUESTION...

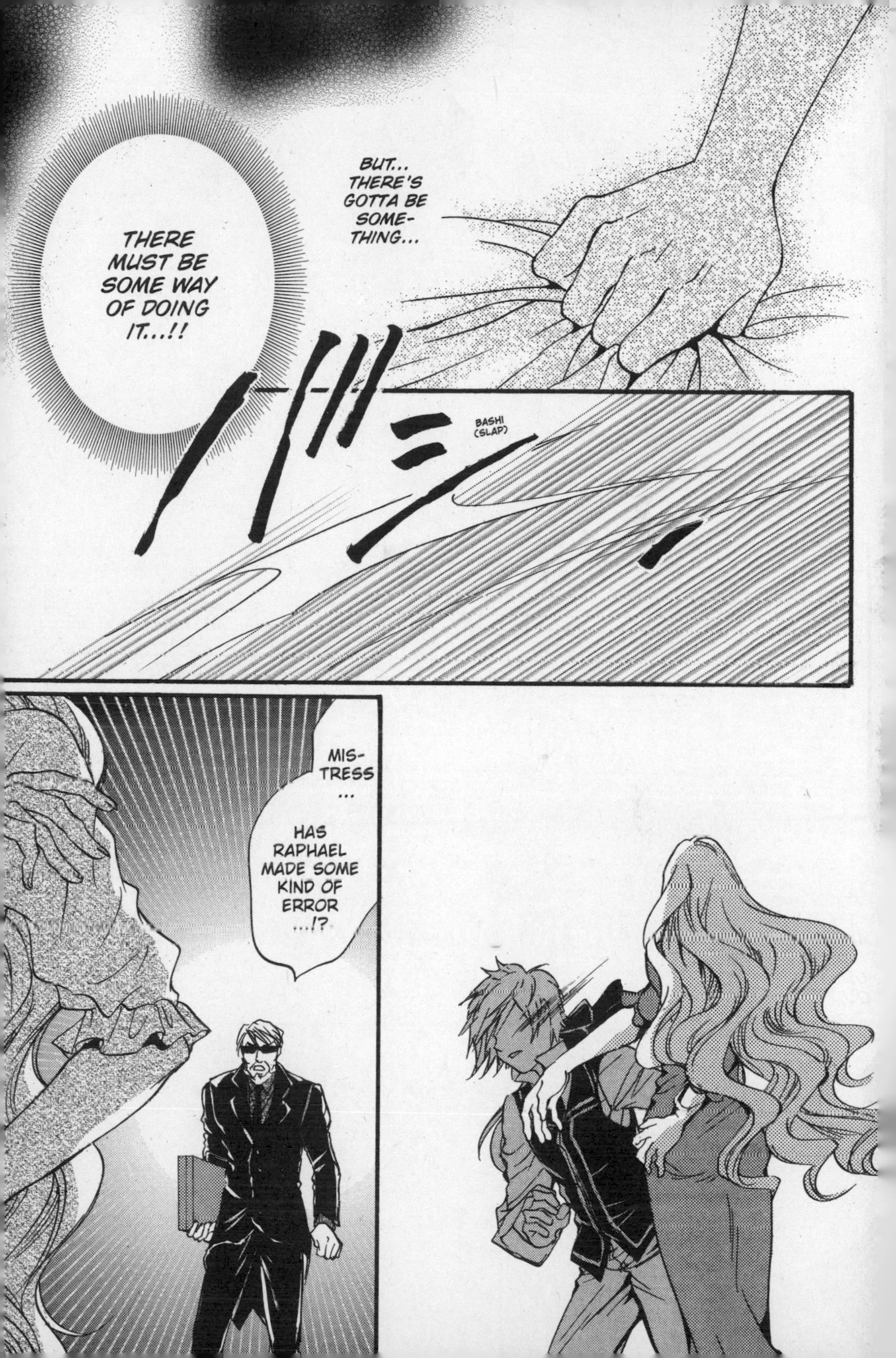
BUT... THERE'S GOTTA BE SOME-THING...
THERE MUST BE SOME WAY OF DOING IT...!!
BASHI (SLAP)
MIS-TRESS ...
HAS RAPHAEL MADE SOME KIND OF ERROR ...!?

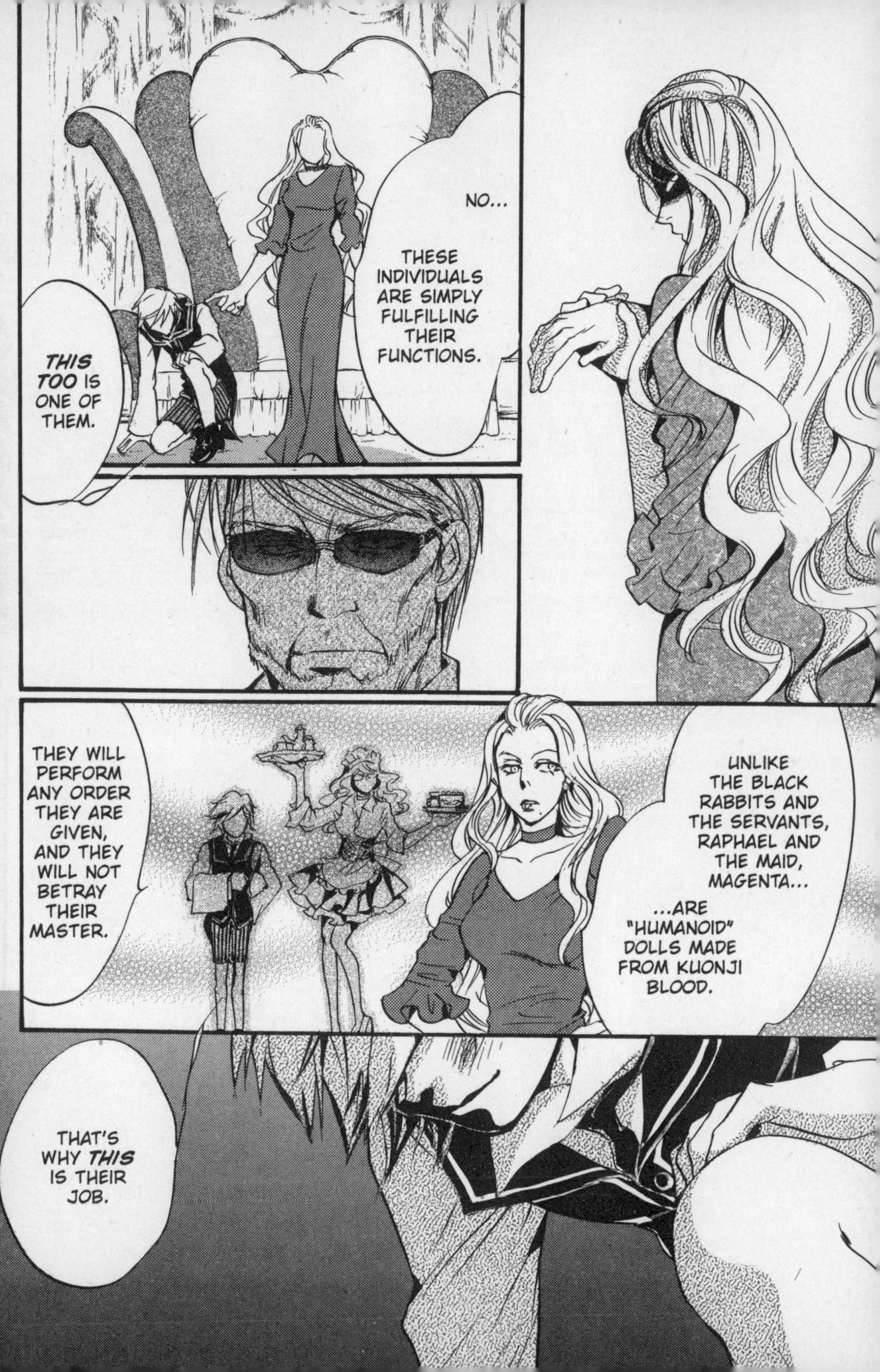
NO...
THESE INDIVIDUALS ARE SIMPLY FULFILLING THEIR FUNCTIONS.
THIS TOO IS ONE OF THEM.
UNLIKE THE BLACK RABBITS AND THE SERVANTS, RAPHAEL AND THE MAID, MAGENTA...
...ARE "HUMANOID" DOLLS MADE FROM KUONJI BLOOD.
THEY WILL PERFORM ANY ORDER THEY ARE GIVEN, AND THEY WILL NOT BETRAY THEIR MASTER.
THAT'S WHY *THIS* IS THEIR JOB.

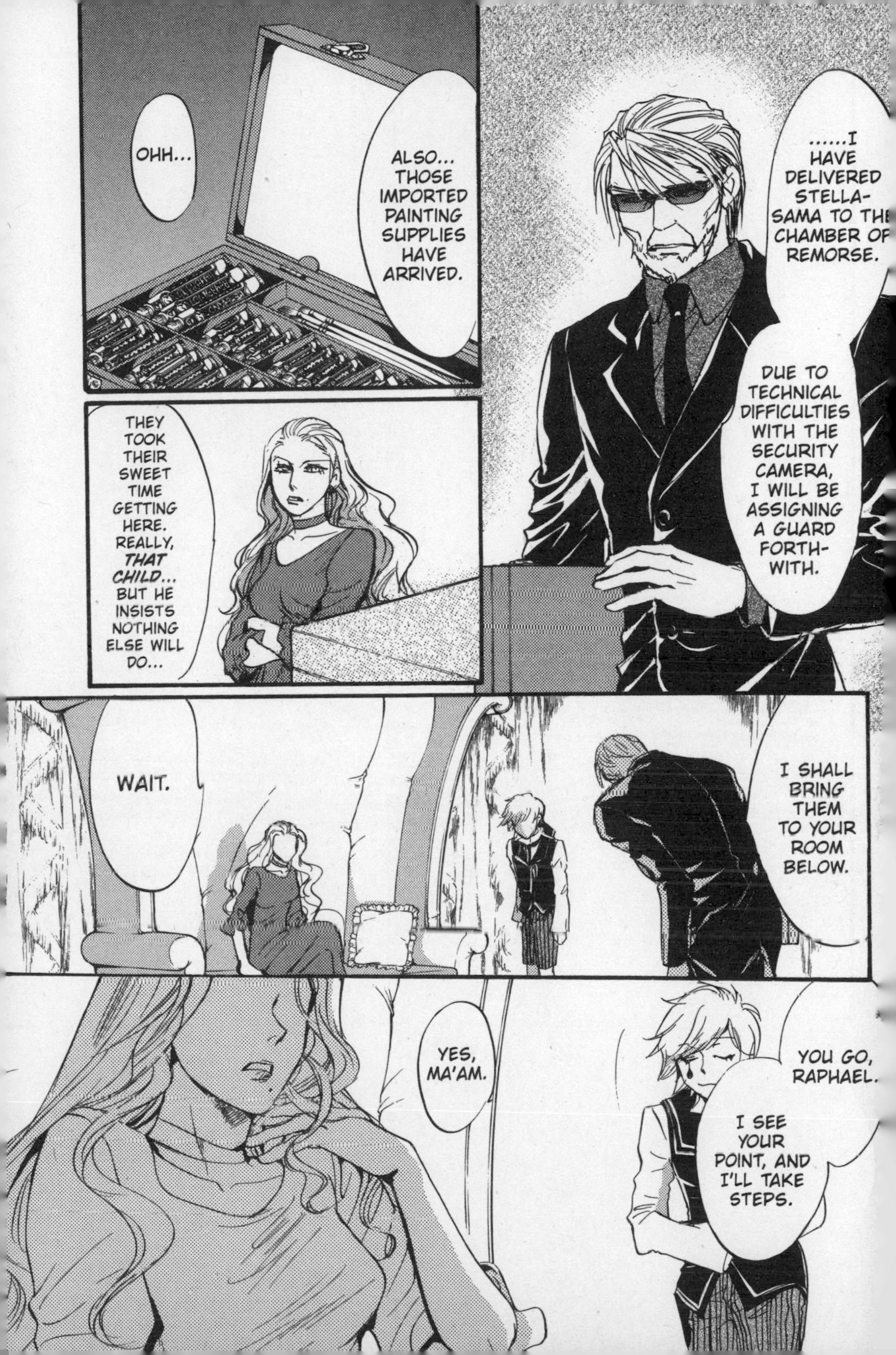
......I HAVE DELIVERED STELLA-SAMA TO THE CHAMBER OF REMORSE.
DUE TO TECHNICAL DIFFICULTIES WITH THE SECURITY CAMERA, I WILL BE ASSIGNING A GUARD FORTH-WITH.
ALSO... THOSE IMPORTED PAINTING SUPPLIES HAVE ARRIVED.
OHH...
THEY TOOK THEIR SWEET TIME GETTING HERE. REALLY, *THAT CHILD*... BUT HE INSISTS NOTHING ELSE WILL DO...
I SHALL BRING THEM TO YOUR ROOM BELOW.
WAIT.
YOU GO, RAPHAEL.
I SEE YOUR POINT, AND I'LL TAKE STEPS.
YES, MA'AM.

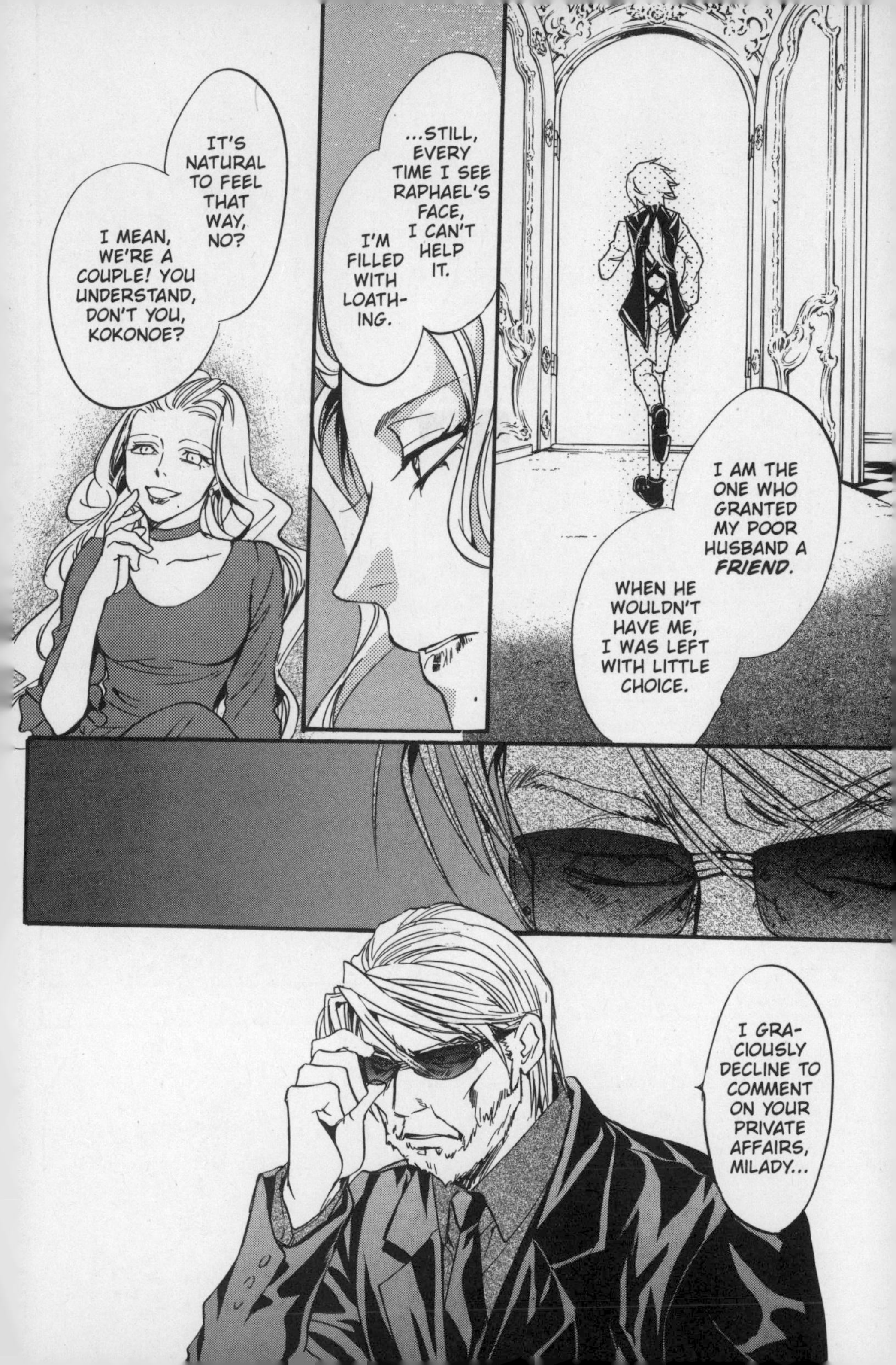
I AM THE ONE WHO GRANTED MY POOR HUSBAND A *FRIEND*.
WHEN HE WOULDN'T HAVE ME, I WAS LEFT WITH LITTLE CHOICE.
...STILL, EVERY TIME I SEE RAPHAEL'S FACE, I CAN'T HELP IT.
I'M FILLED WITH LOATHING.
IT'S NATURAL TO FEEL THAT WAY, NO?
I MEAN, WE'RE A COUPLE! YOU UNDERSTAND, DON'T YOU, KOKONOE?
I GRACIOUSLY DECLINE TO COMMENT ON YOUR PRIVATE AFFAIRS, MILADY...

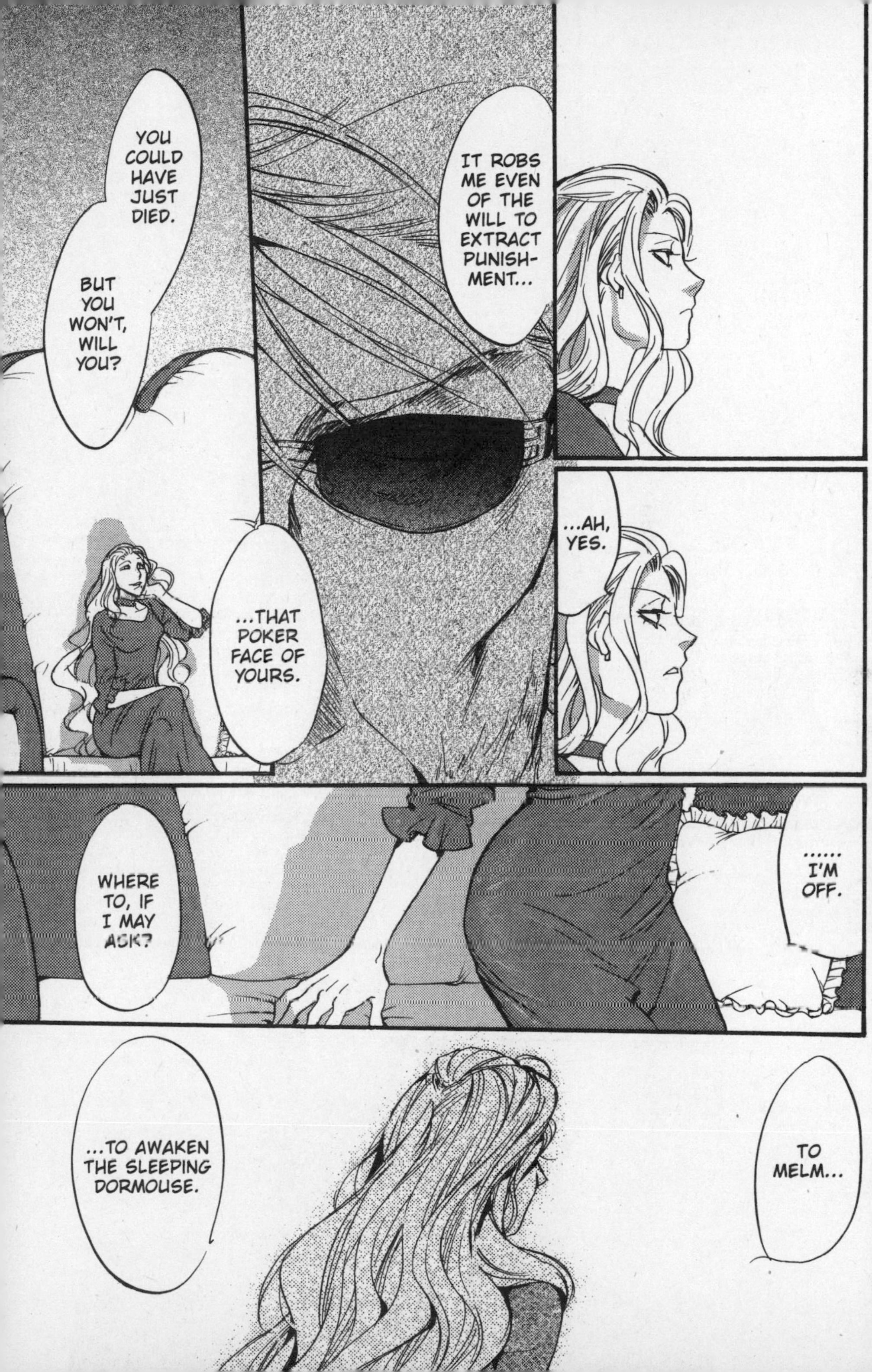
...AH, YES.
IT ROBS ME EVEN OF THE WILL TO EXTRACT PUNISH-MENT...
...THAT POKER FACE OF YOURS.
YOU COULD HAVE JUST DIED.
BUT YOU WON'T, WILL YOU?
......I'M OFF.
WHERE TO, IF I MAY ASK?
TO MELM...
...TO AWAKEN THE SLEEPING DORMOUSE.

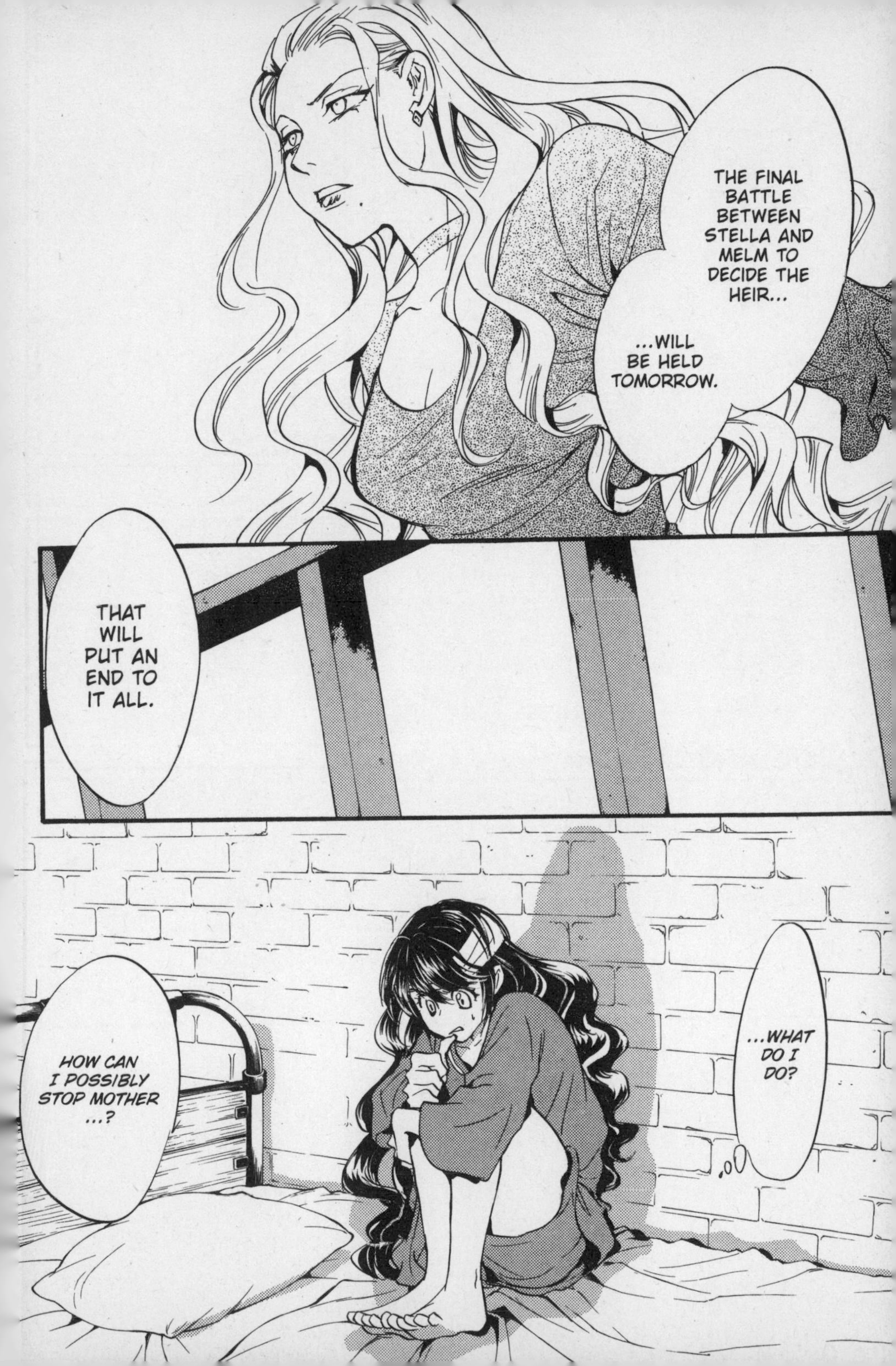
THE FINAL BATTLE BETWEEN STELLA AND MELM TO DECIDE THE HEIR...
...WILL BE HELD TOMORROW.
THAT WILL PUT AN END TO IT ALL.
...WHAT DO I DO?
HOW CAN I POSSIBLY STOP MOTHER ...?

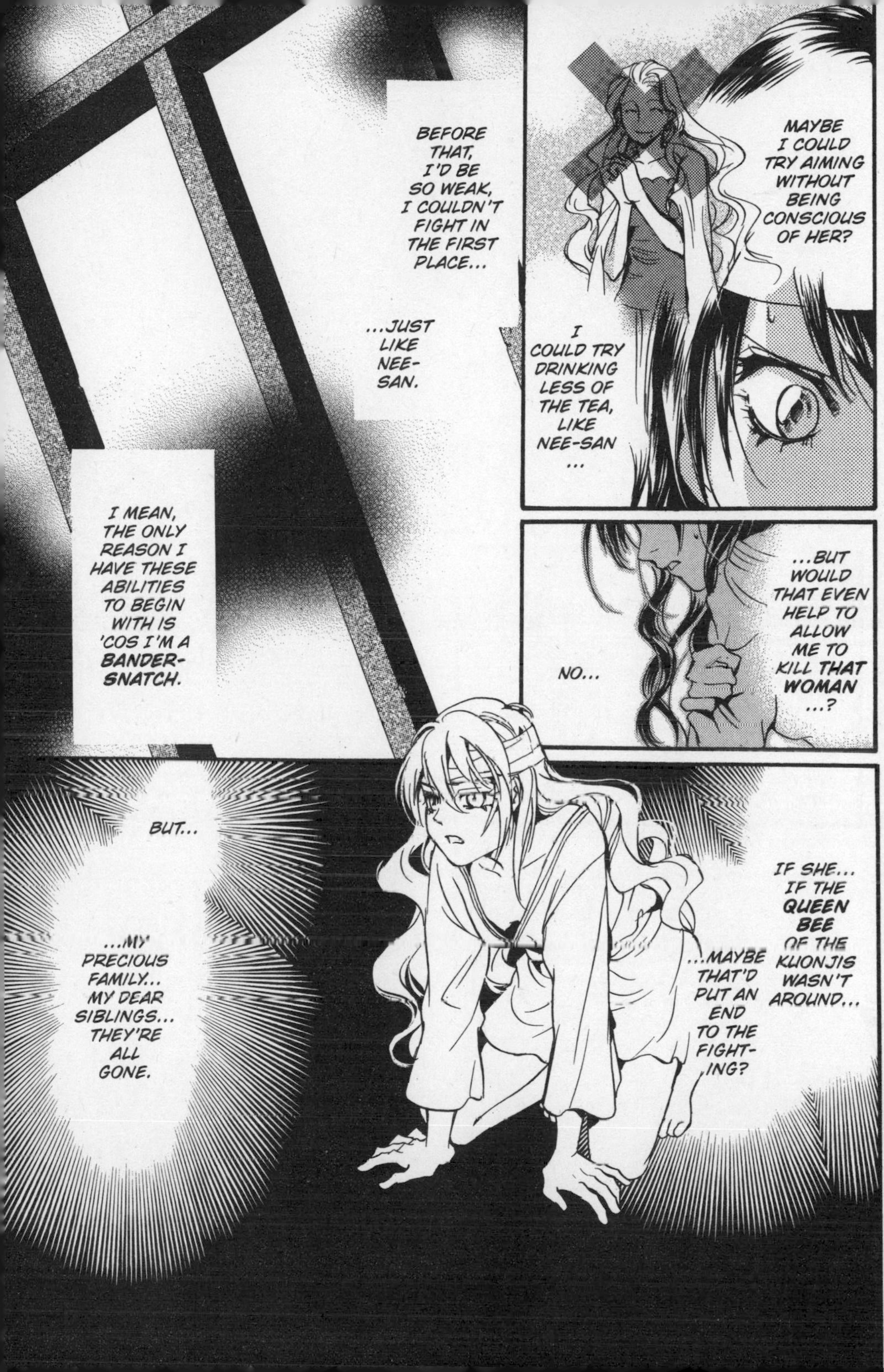
MAYBE I COULD TRY AIMING WITHOUT BEING CONSCIOUS OF HER?
I COULD TRY DRINKING LESS OF THE TEA, LIKE NEE-SAN...
...BUT WOULD THAT EVEN HELP TO ALLOW ME TO KILL THAT WOMAN...?
NO...
BEFORE THAT, I'D BE SO WEAK, I COULDN'T FIGHT IN THE FIRST PLACE...
...JUST LIKE NEE-SAN.
I MEAN, THE ONLY REASON I HAVE THESE ABILITIES TO BEGIN WITH IS 'COS I'M A BANDERSNATCH.
IF SHE... IF THE QUEEN BEE OF THE KUONJIS WASN'T AROUND...
...MAYBE THAT'D PUT AN END TO THE FIGHTING?
BUT...
...MY PRECIOUS FAMILY... MY DEAR SIBLINGS... THEY'RE ALL GONE.

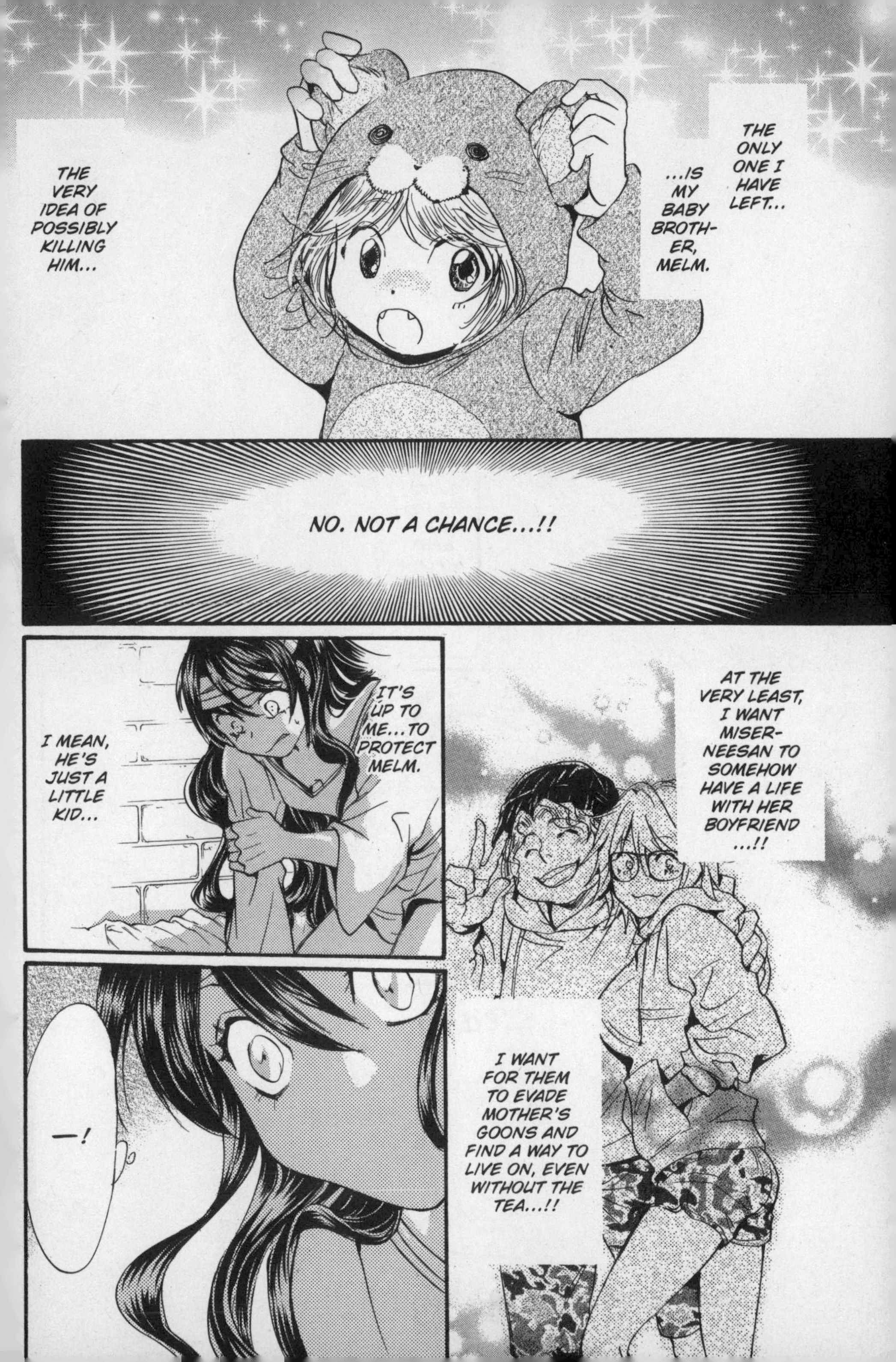
THE ONLY ONE I HAVE LEFT...
...IS MY BABY BROTH-ER, MELM.
THE VERY IDEA OF POSSIBLY KILLING HIM...
NO. NOT A CHANCE...!!
AT THE VERY LEAST, I WANT MISER-NEESAN TO SOMEHOW HAVE A LIFE WITH HER BOYFRIEND ...!!
I WANT FOR THEM TO EVADE MOTHER'S GOONS AND FIND A WAY TO LIVE ON, EVEN WITHOUT THE TEA...!!
IT'S UP TO ME...TO PROTECT MELM.
I MEAN, HE'S JUST A LITTLE KID...
—!

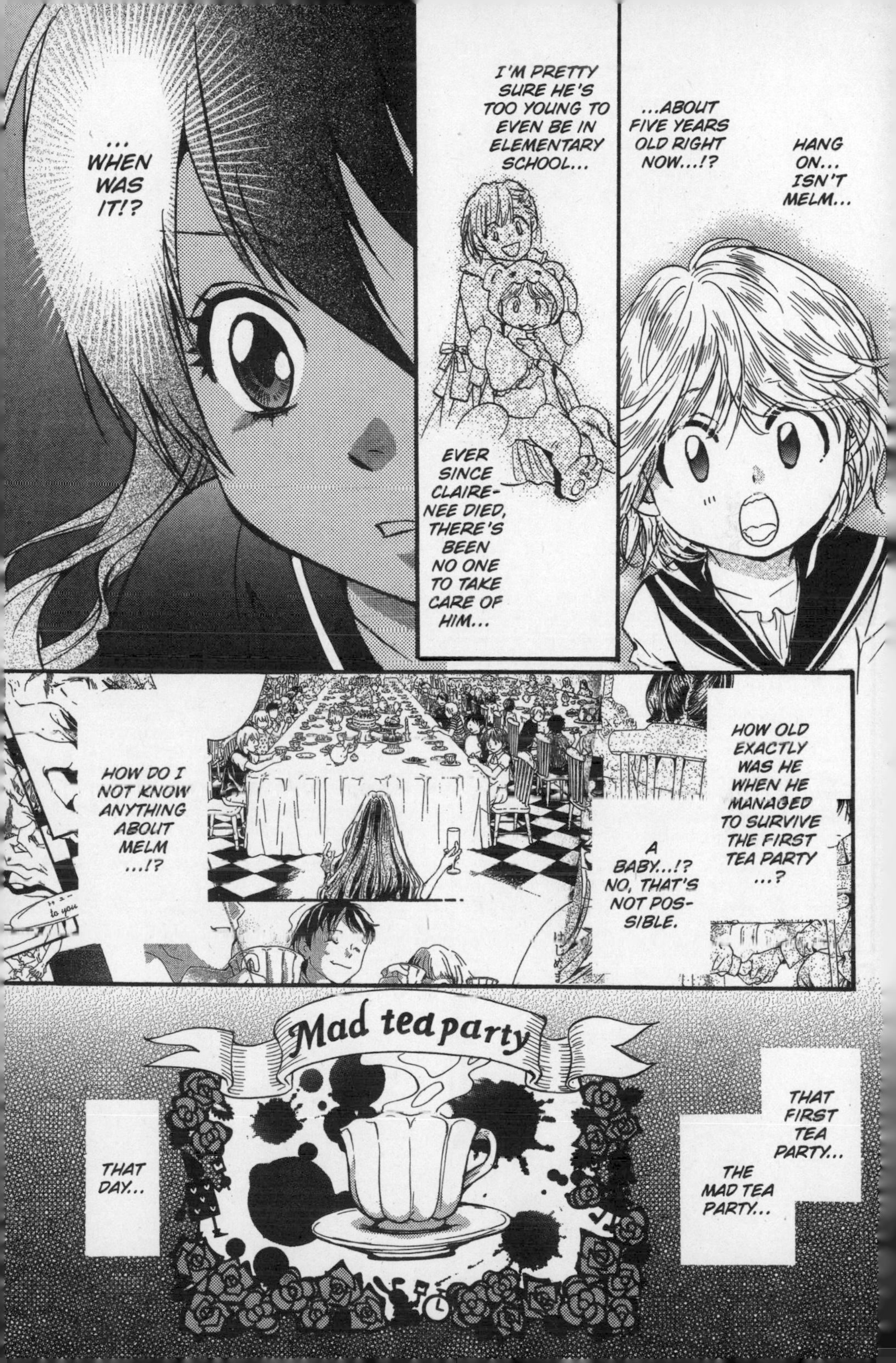
HANG ON... ISN'T MELM...
...ABOUT FIVE YEARS OLD RIGHT NOW...!?
I'M PRETTY SURE HE'S TOO YOUNG TO EVEN BE IN ELEMENTARY SCHOOL...
EVER SINCE CLAIRE-NEE DIED, THERE'S BEEN NO ONE TO TAKE CARE OF HIM...
...WHEN WAS IT!?
HOW OLD EXACTLY WAS HE WHEN HE MANAGED TO SURVIVE THE FIRST TEA PARTY...?
A BABY...!? NO, THAT'S NOT POS-SIBLE.
HOW DO I NOT KNOW ANYTHING ABOUT MELM...!?
THAT FIRST TEA PARTY...
THE MAD TEA PARTY...
Mad tea party
THAT DAY...

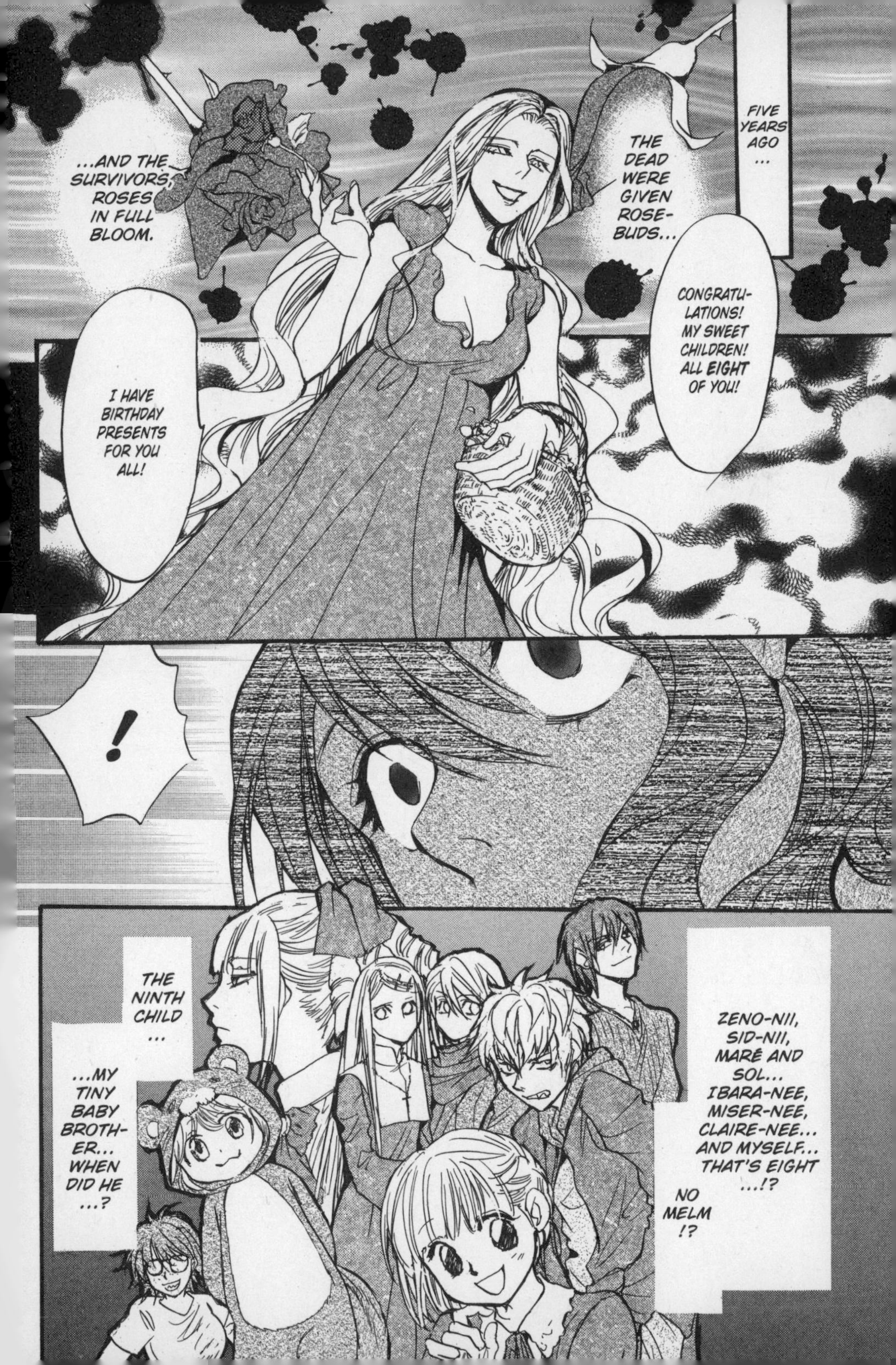
FIVE YEARS AGO...
THE DEAD WERE GIVEN ROSE-BUDS...
...AND THE SURVIVORS, ROSES IN FULL BLOOM.
CONGRATULATIONS! MY SWEET CHILDREN! ALL EIGHT OF YOU!
I HAVE BIRTHDAY PRESENTS FOR YOU ALL!
!
ZENO-NII, SID-NII, MARÉ AND SOL... IBARA-NEE, MISER-NEE, CLAIRE-NEE... AND MYSELF... THAT'S EIGHT ...!?
NO MELM !?
THE NINTH CHILD ...
...MY TINY BABY BROTHER... WHEN DID HE ...?

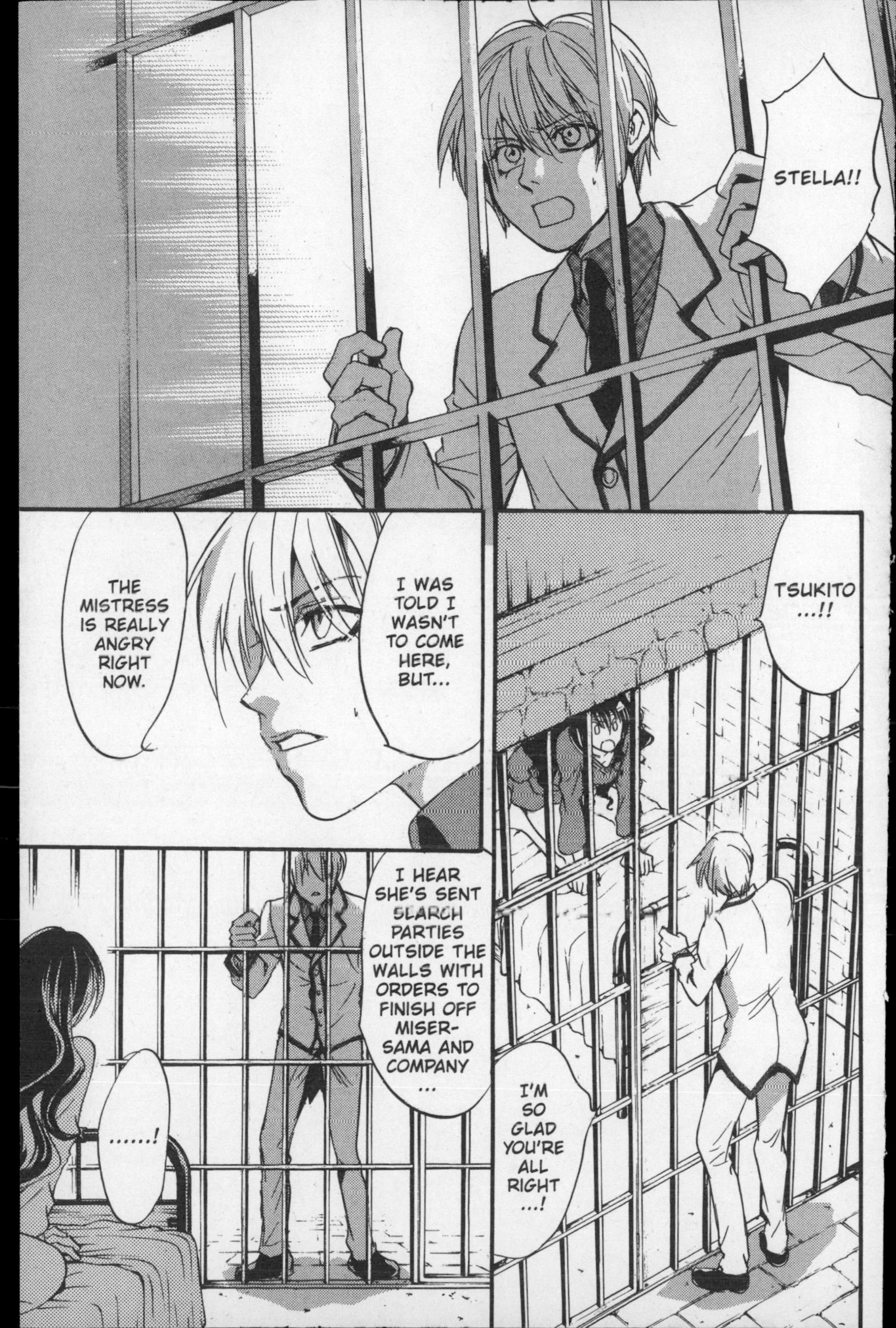
STELLA!!
TSUKITO ...!!
I'M SO GLAD YOU'RE ALL RIGHT ...!
I WAS TOLD I WASN'T TO COME HERE, BUT...
THE MISTRESS IS REALLY ANGRY RIGHT NOW.
I HEAR SHE'S SENT SEARCH PARTIES OUTSIDE THE WALLS WITH ORDERS TO FINISH OFF MISER-SAMA AND COMPANY ...
......!

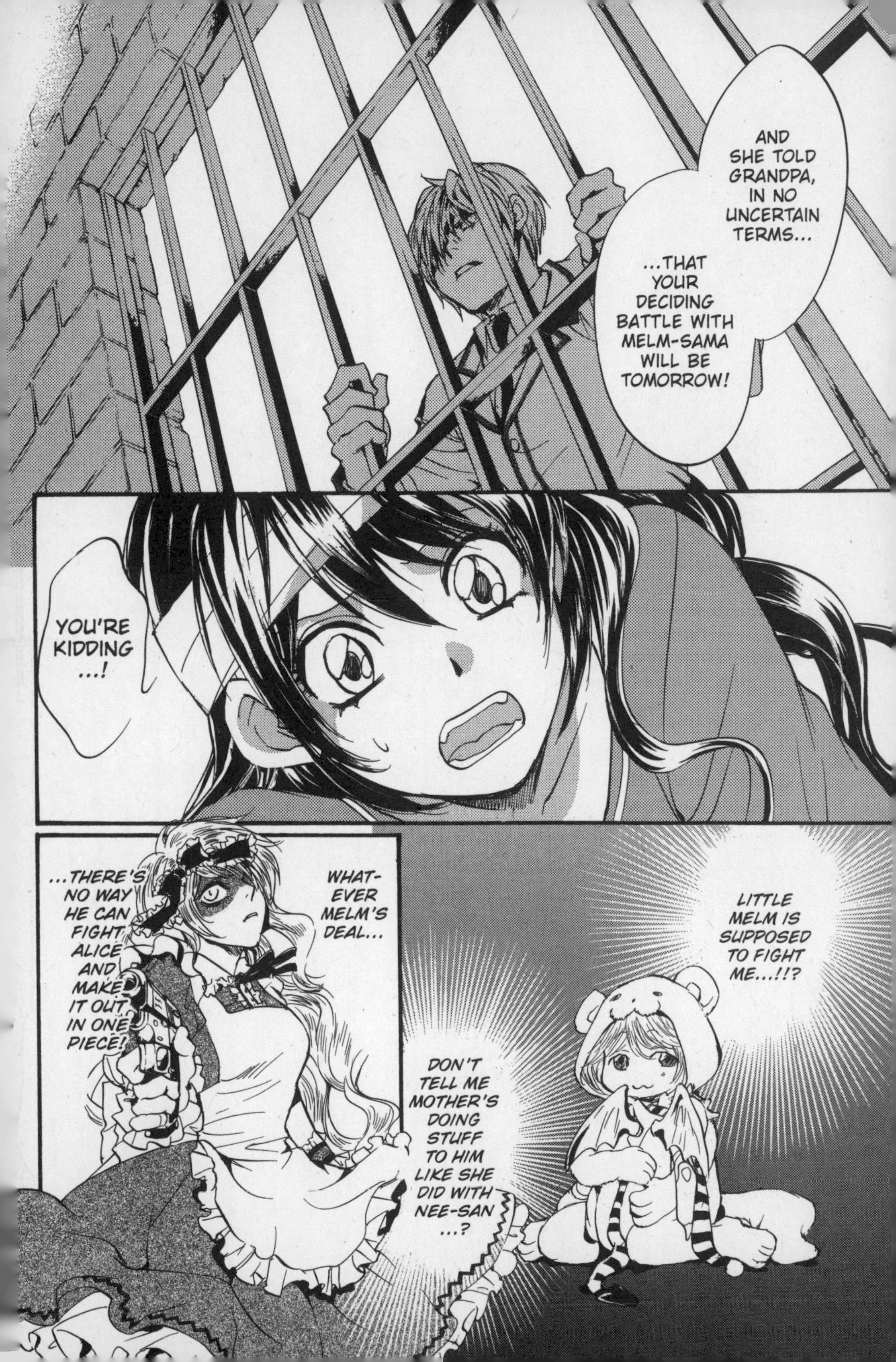
AND SHE TOLD GRANDPA, IN NO UNCERTAIN TERMS...
...THAT YOUR DECIDING BATTLE WITH MELM-SAMA WILL BE TOMORROW!
YOU'RE KIDDING ...!
LITTLE MELM IS SUPPOSED TO FIGHT ME...!!?
DON'T TELL ME MOTHER'S DOING STUFF TO HIM LIKE SHE DID WITH NEE-SAN ...?
WHAT-EVER MELM'S DEAL...
...THERE'S NO WAY HE CAN FIGHT ALICE AND MAKE IT OUT IN ONE PIECE!

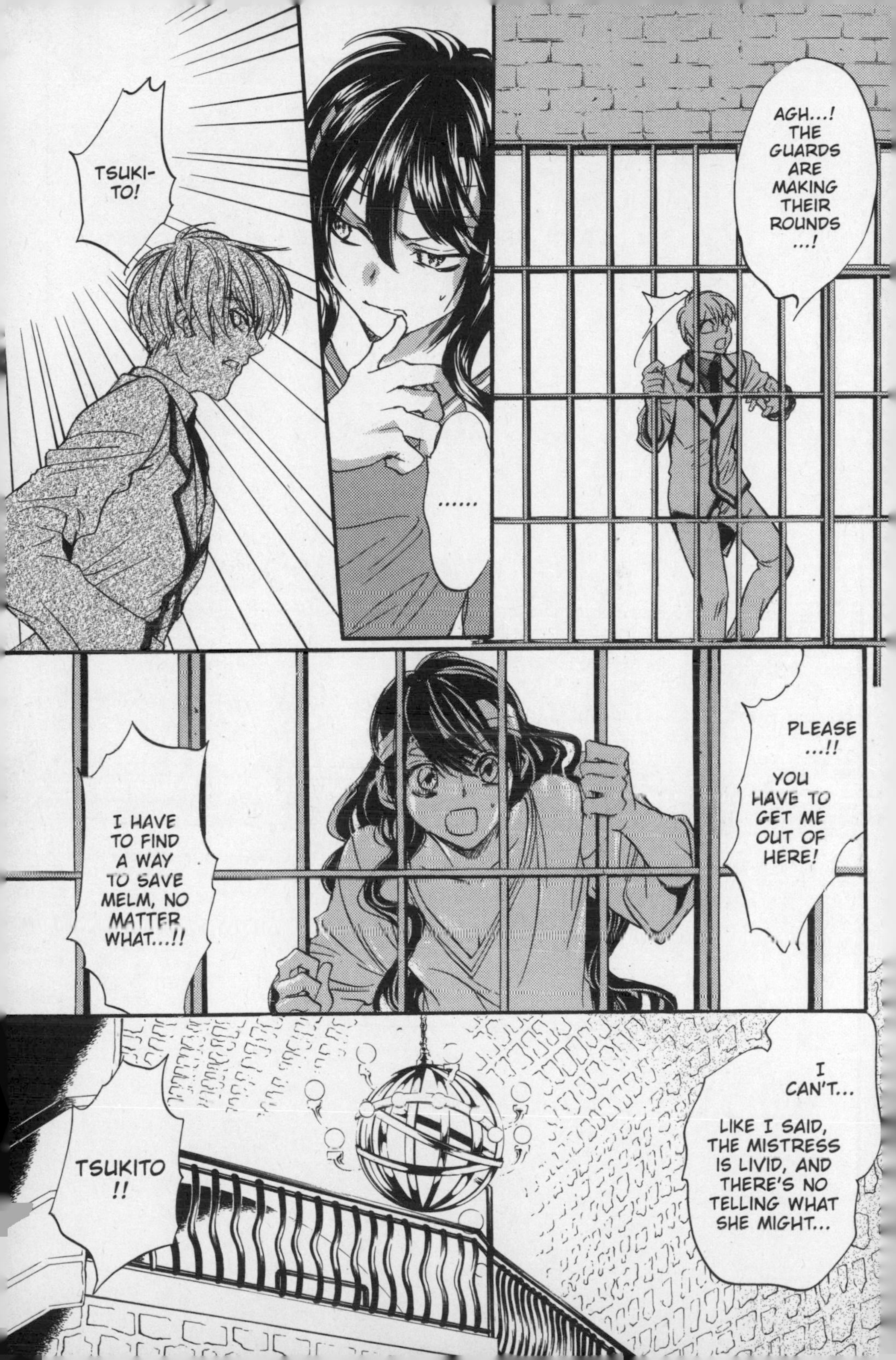
AGH...! THE GUARDS ARE MAKING THEIR ROUNDS ...!
......
TSUKI-TO!
PLEASE ...!!
YOU HAVE TO GET ME OUT OF HERE!
I HAVE TO FIND A WAY TO SAVE MELM, NO MATTER WHAT...!!
I CAN'T...
LIKE I SAID, THE MISTRESS IS LIVID, AND THERE'S NO TELLING WHAT SHE MIGHT...
TSUKITO !!

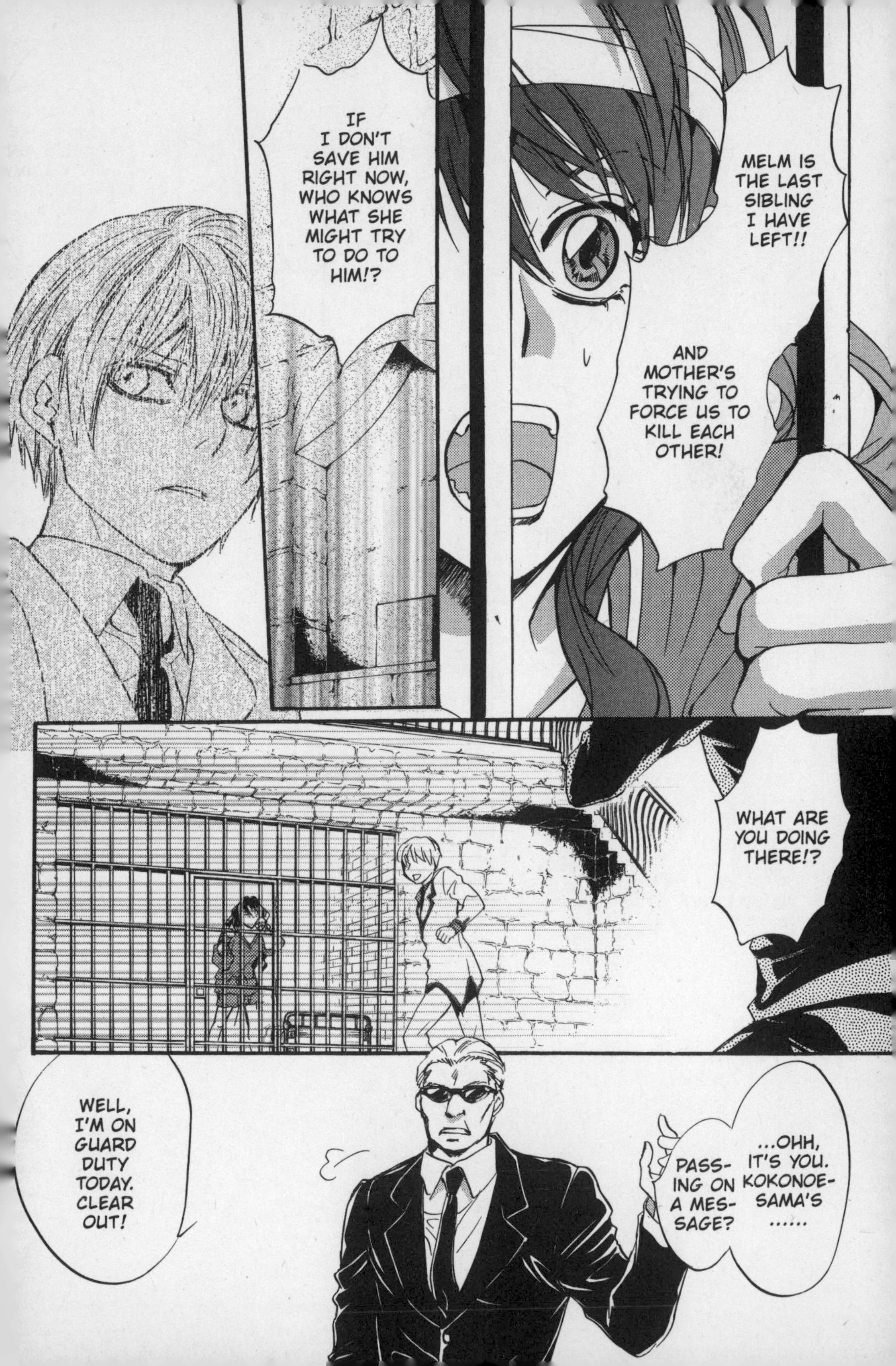
MELM IS THE LAST SIBLING I HAVE LEFT!!
AND MOTHER'S TRYING TO FORCE US TO KILL EACH OTHER!
IF I DON'T SAVE HIM RIGHT NOW, WHO KNOWS WHAT SHE MIGHT TRY TO DO TO HIM!?
WHAT ARE YOU DOING THERE!?
...OHH, IT'S YOU. KOKONOE-SAMA'S ......
PASS-ING ON A MES-SAGE?
WELL, I'M ON GUARD DUTY TODAY. CLEAR OUT!

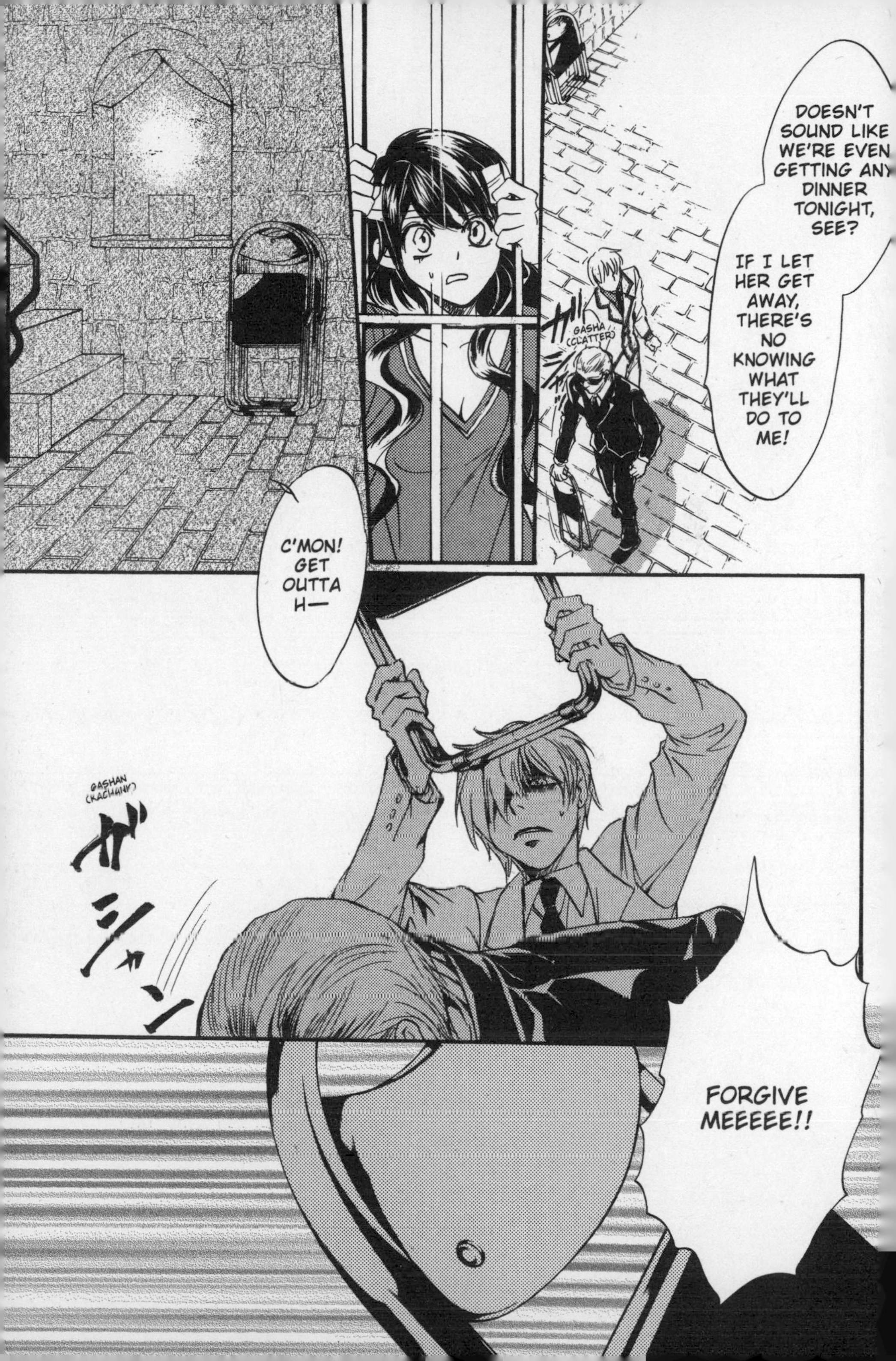
DOESN'T SOUND LIKE WE'RE EVEN GETTING ANY DINNER TONIGHT, SEE?
IF I LET HER GET AWAY, THERE'S NO KNOWING WHAT THEY'LL DO TO ME!
GASHA (CLATTER)
C'MON! GET OUTTA H—
GASHAN (KACHUNK)
ガシャン
FORGIVE MEEEEE!!

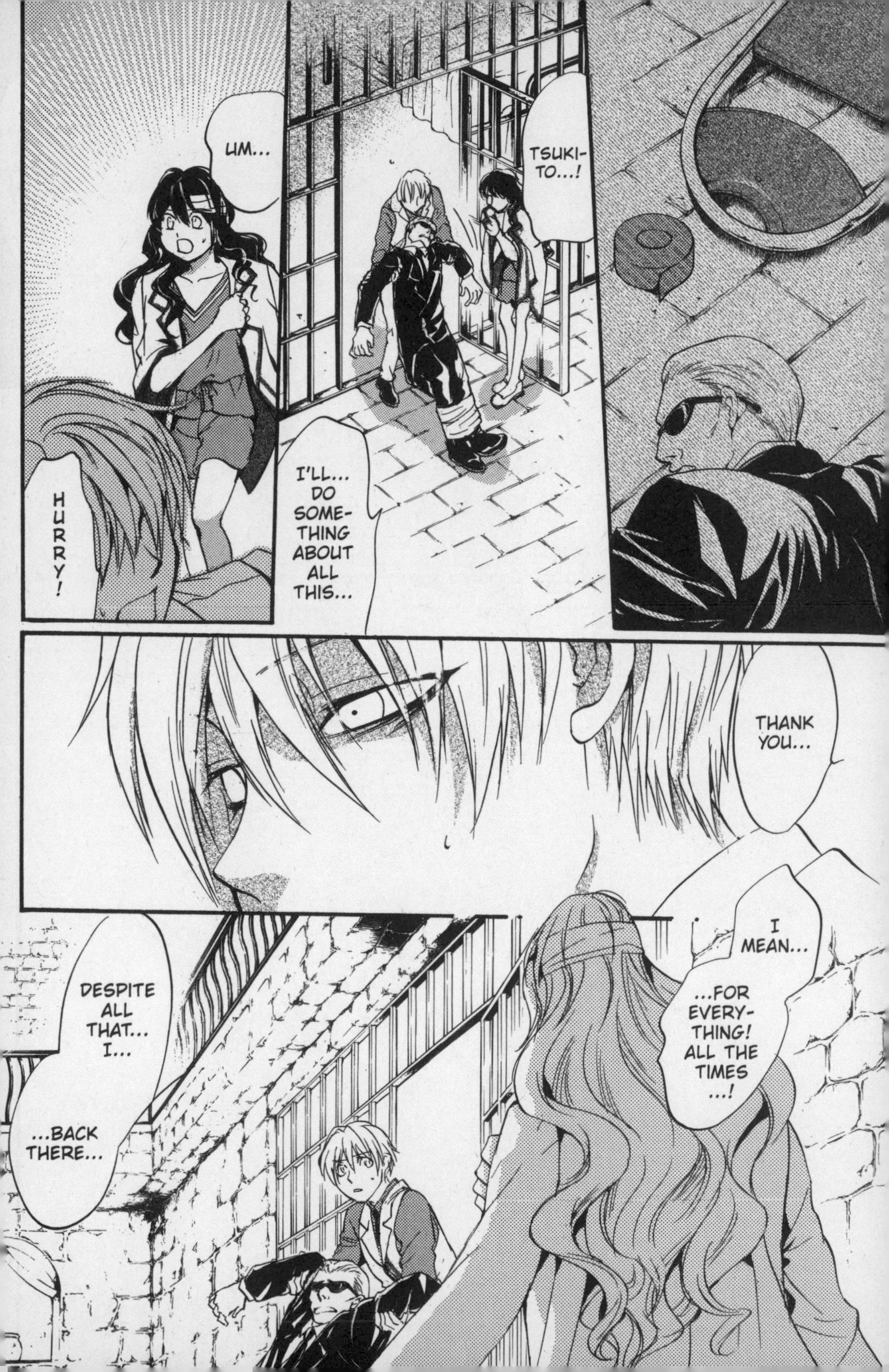
TSUKI-TO...!
I'LL... DO SOMETHING ABOUT ALL THIS...
UM...
HURRY!
THANK YOU...
I MEAN...
...FOR EVERYTHING! ALL THE TIMES ...!
DESPITE ALL THAT... I...
...BACK THERE...

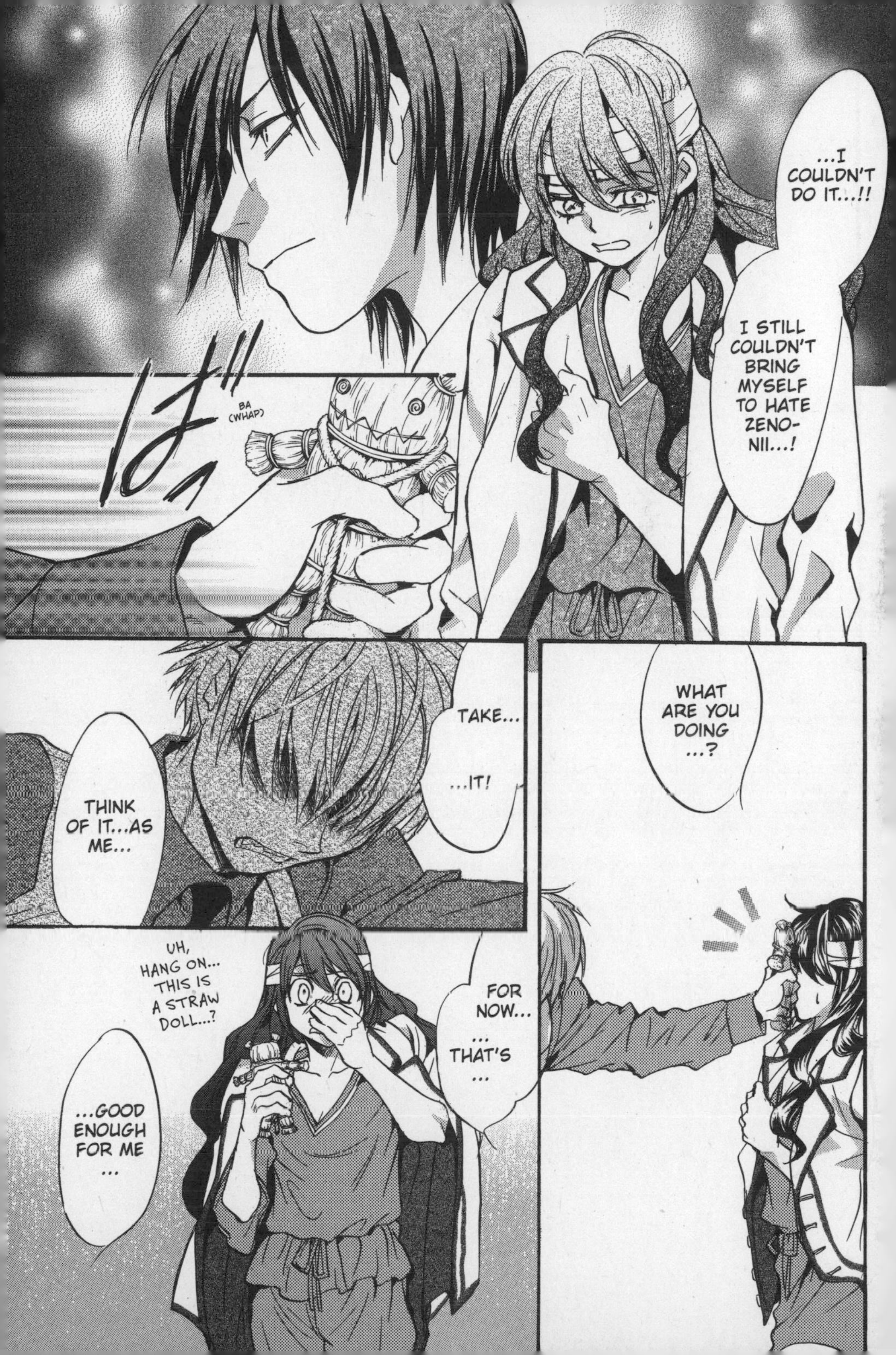
...I COULDN'T DO IT...!!
I STILL COULDN'T BRING MYSELF TO HATE ZENO-NII...!
BA (WHAP)
WHAT ARE YOU DOING ...?
TAKE...
...IT!
THINK OF IT...AS ME...
FOR NOW... ... THAT'S ...
...GOOD ENOUGH FOR ME ...
UH, HANG ON... THIS IS A STRAW DOLL...?

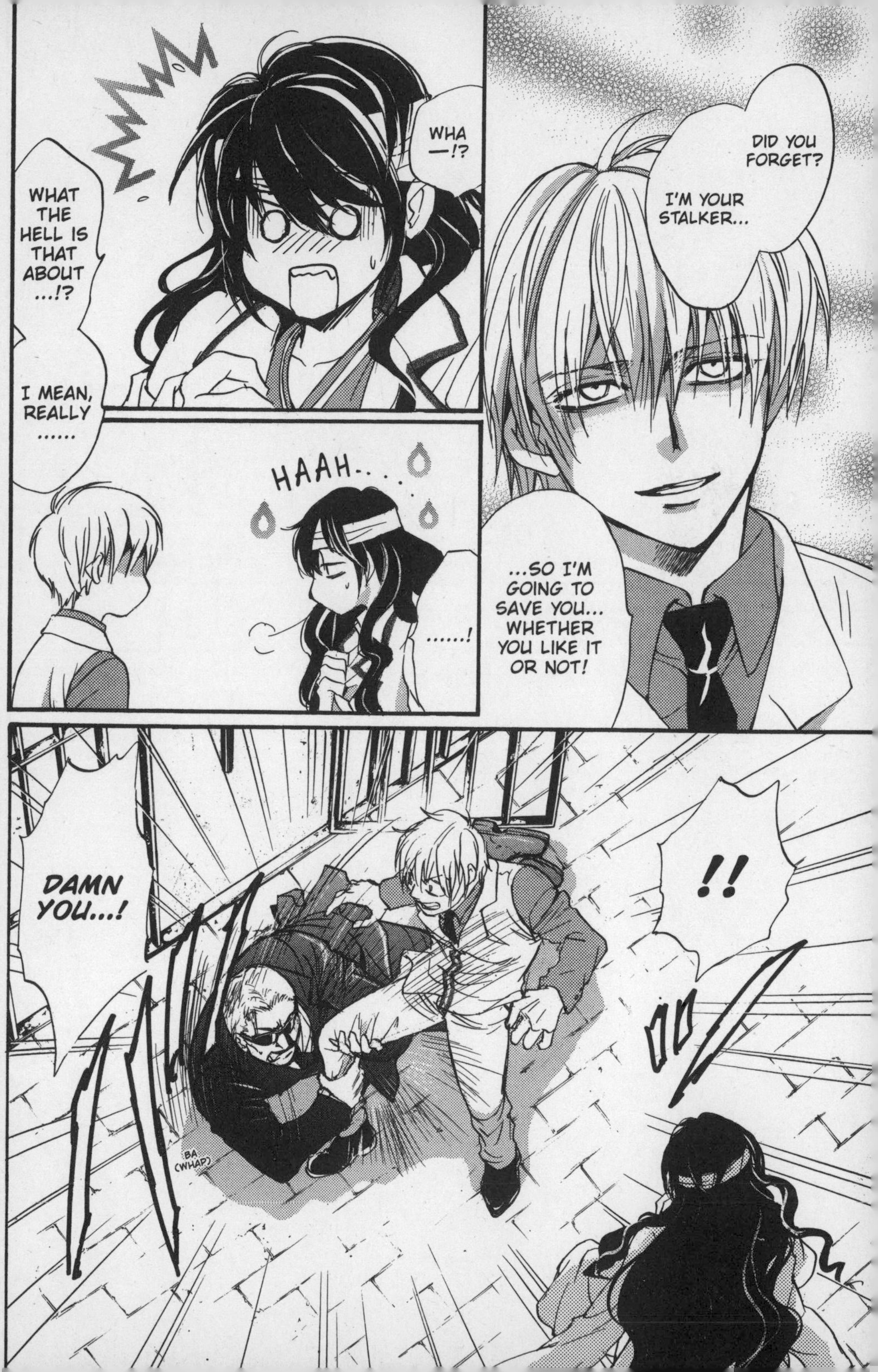
DID YOU FORGET?
I'M YOUR STALKER...
...SO I'M GOING TO SAVE YOU... WHETHER YOU LIKE IT OR NOT!
WHA—!?
WHAT THE HELL IS THAT ABOUT ...!?
I MEAN, REALLY ......
HAAH......
......!
!!
DAMN YOU...!
BA (WHAP)

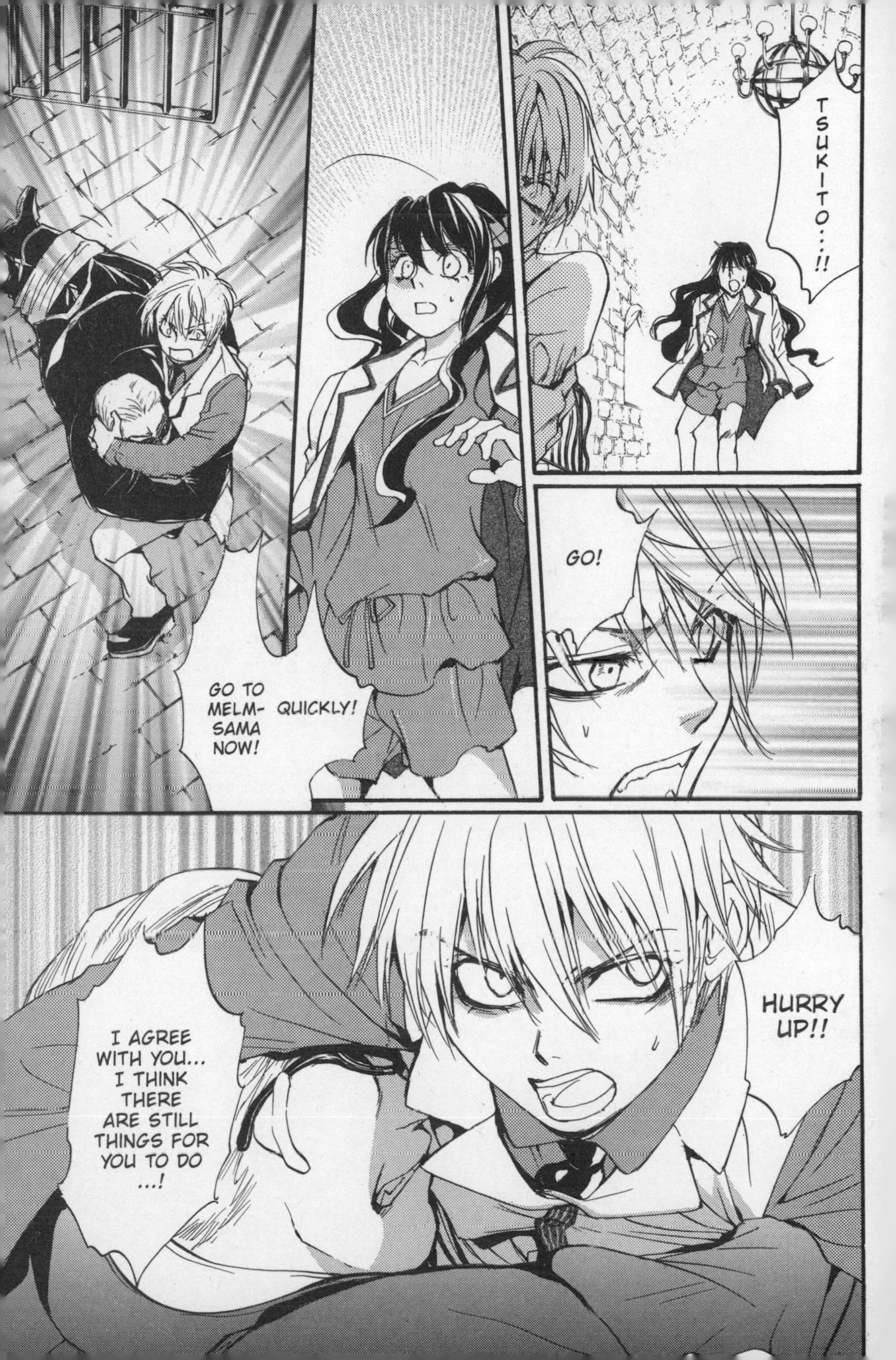
TSUKITO...!!
GO!
QUICKLY!
GO TO MELM-SAMA NOW!
HURRY UP!!
I AGREE WITH YOU... I THINK THERE ARE STILL THINGS FOR YOU TO DO ...!

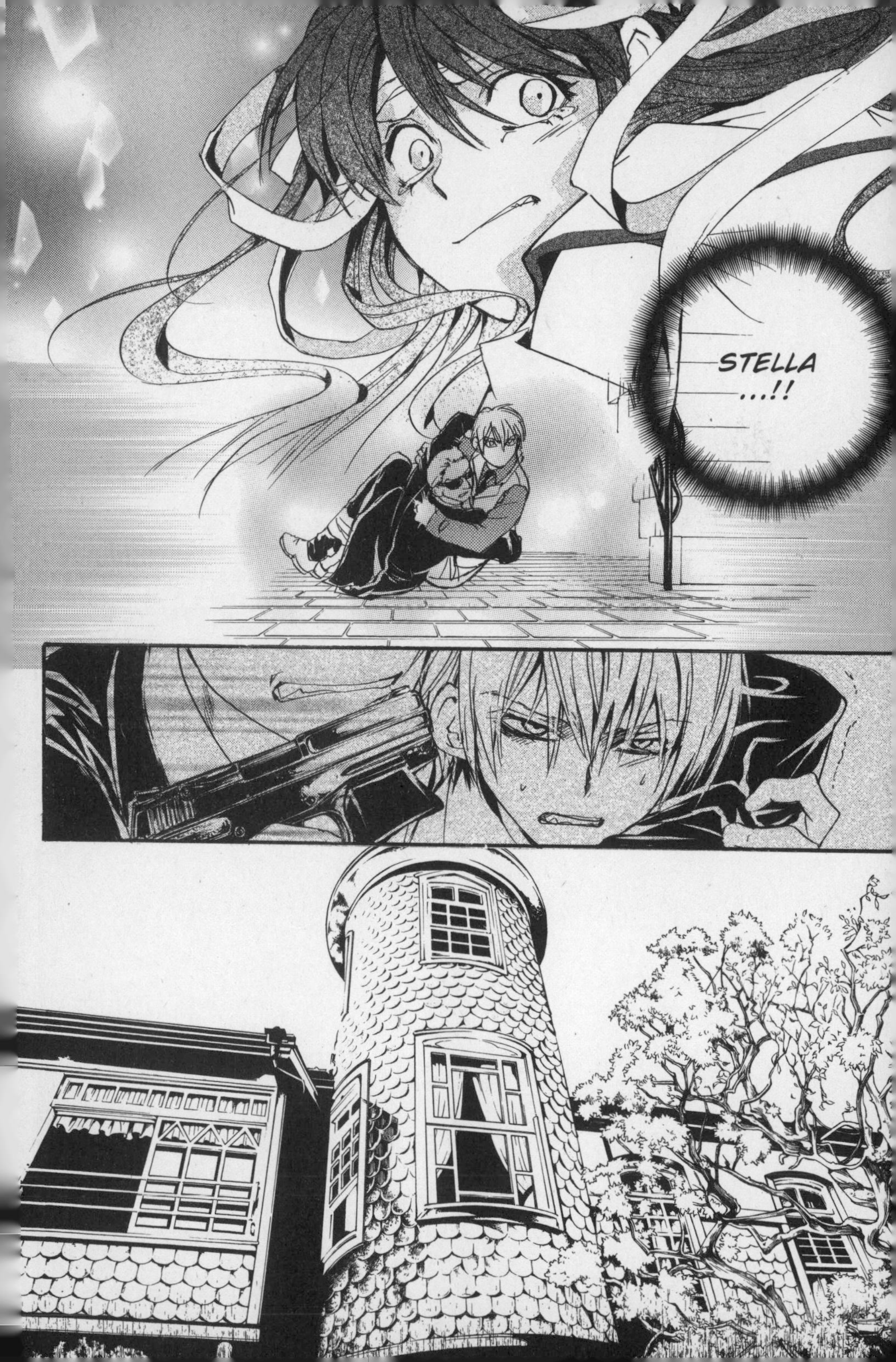
STELLA ...!!

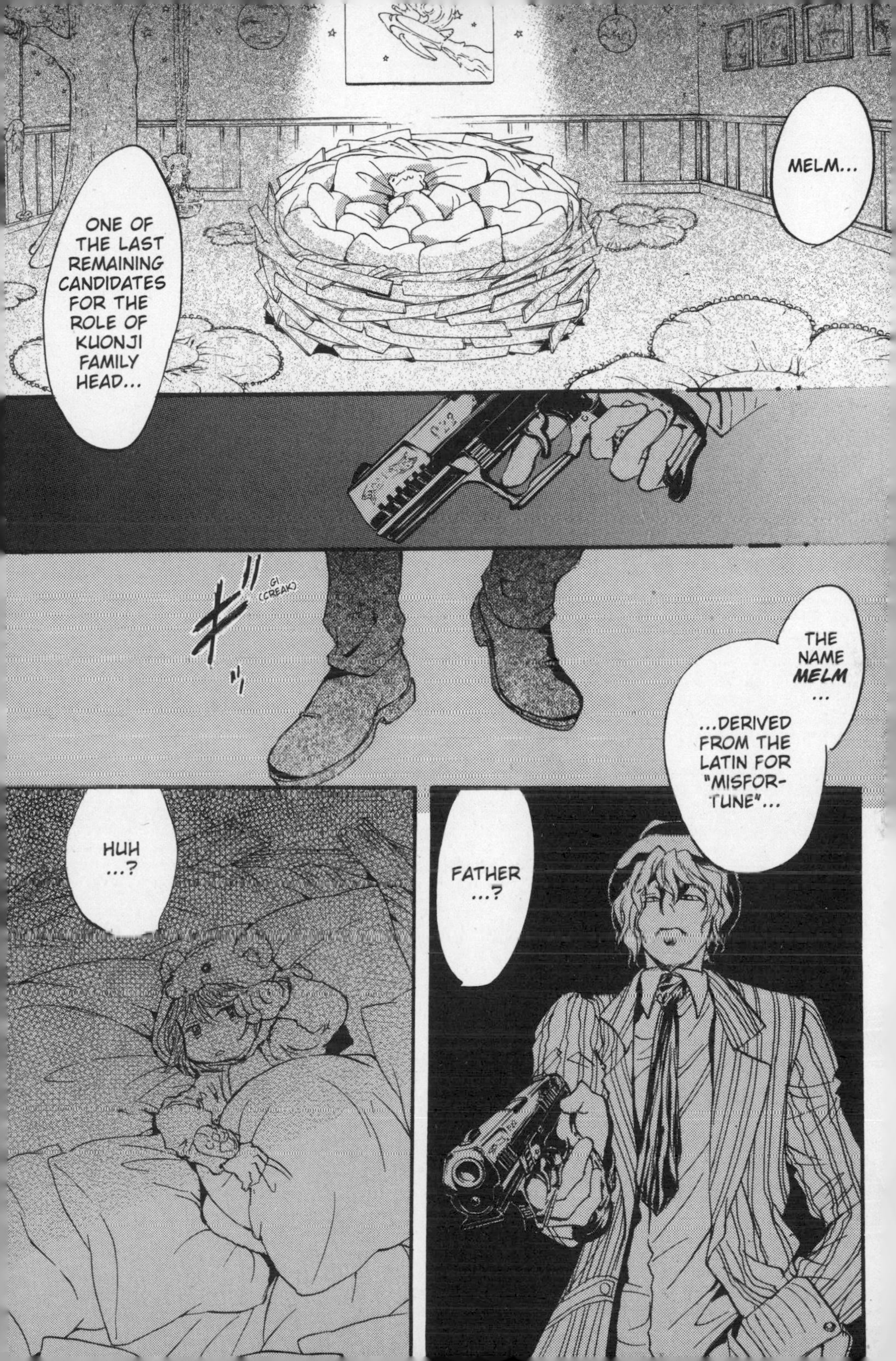
MELM...
ONE OF THE LAST REMAINING CANDIDATES FOR THE ROLE OF KUONJI FAMILY HEAD...
THE NAME MELM...
...DERIVED FROM THE LATIN FOR "MISFORTUNE"...
GI (CREAK)
FATHER...?
HUH...?

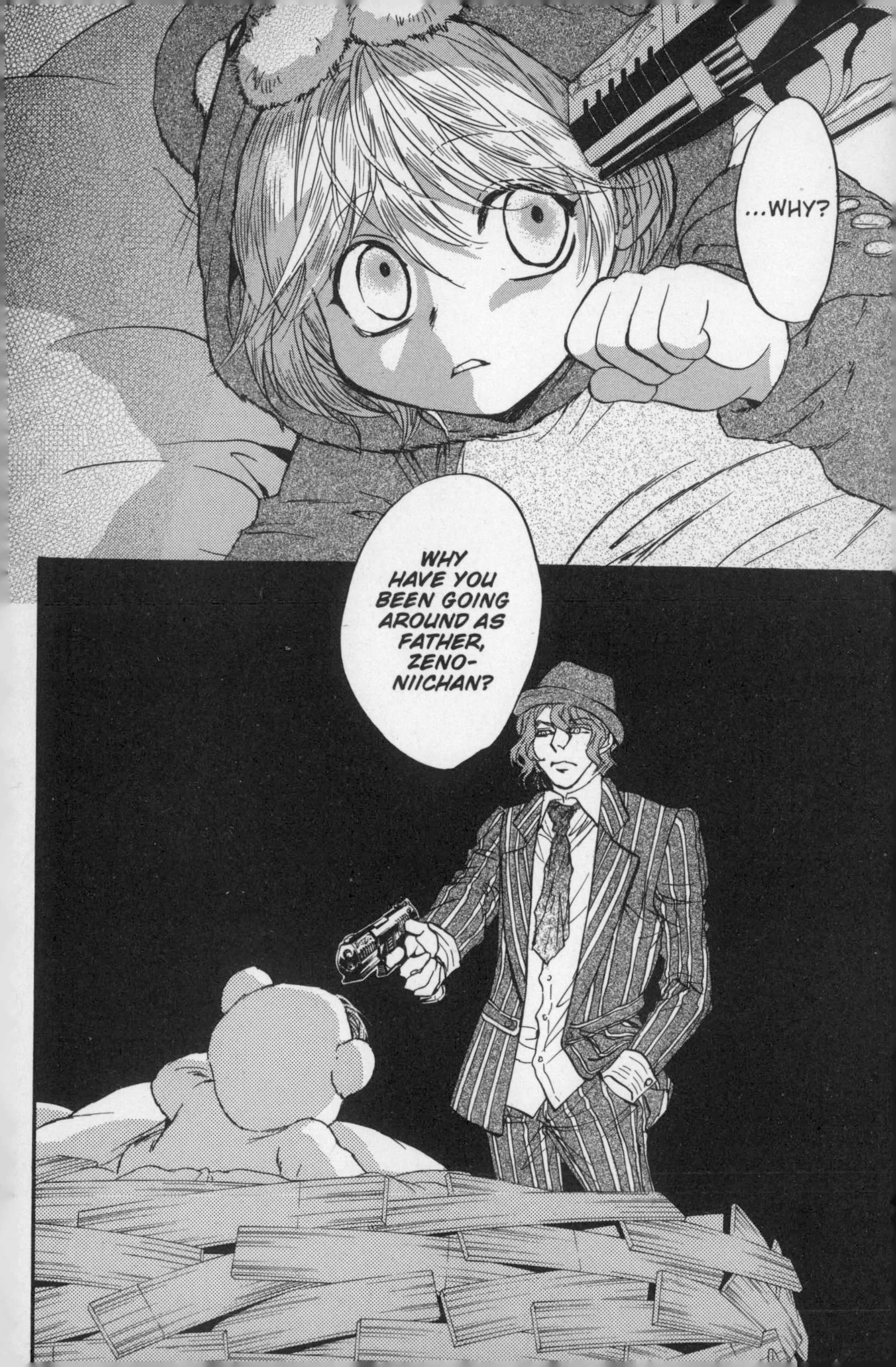
...WHY?
WHY HAVE YOU BEEN GOING AROUND AS FATHER, ZENO-NIICHAN?

Alice
in
MURDERLAND

Alice in Murderland

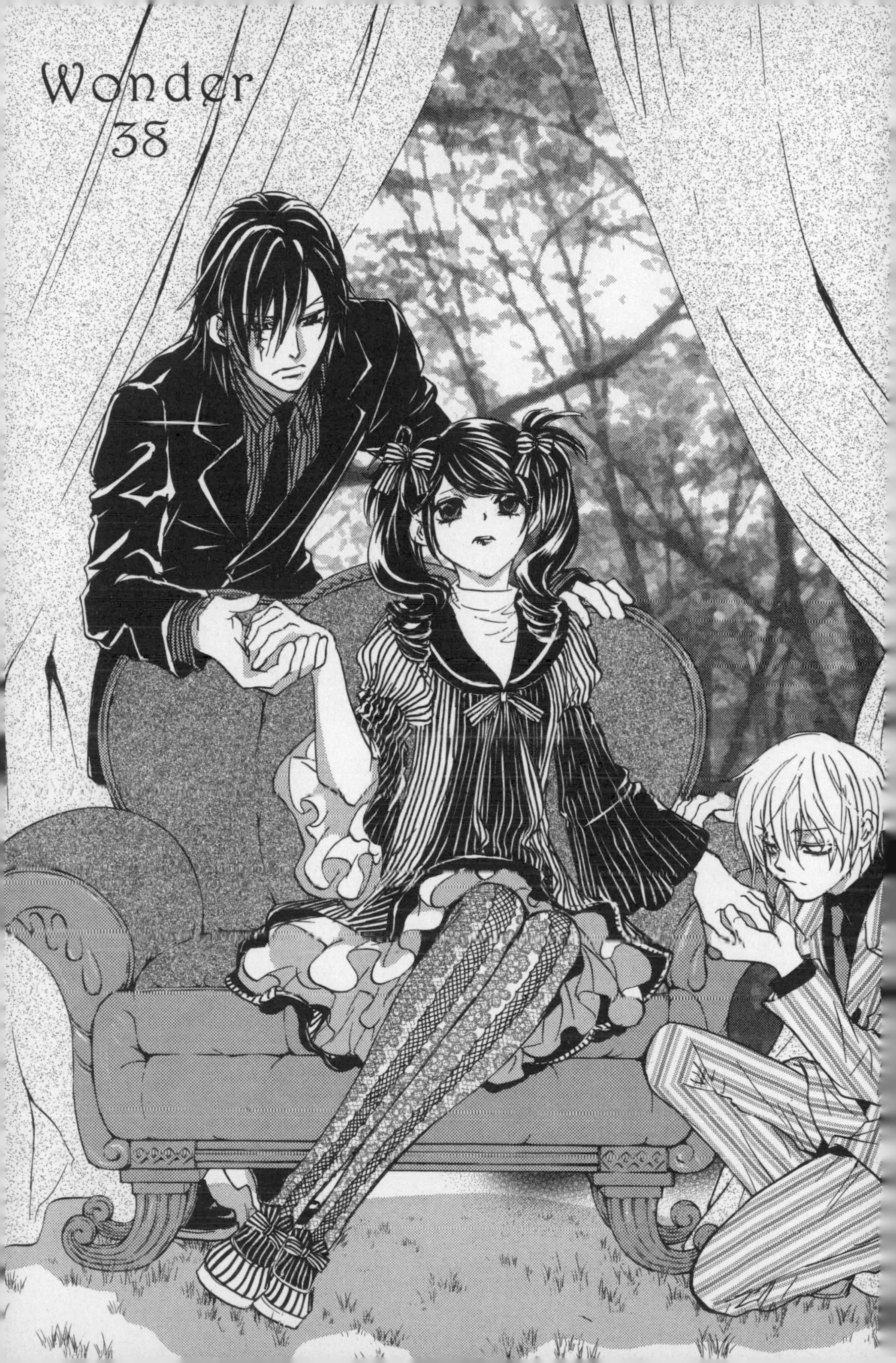
Wonder
38

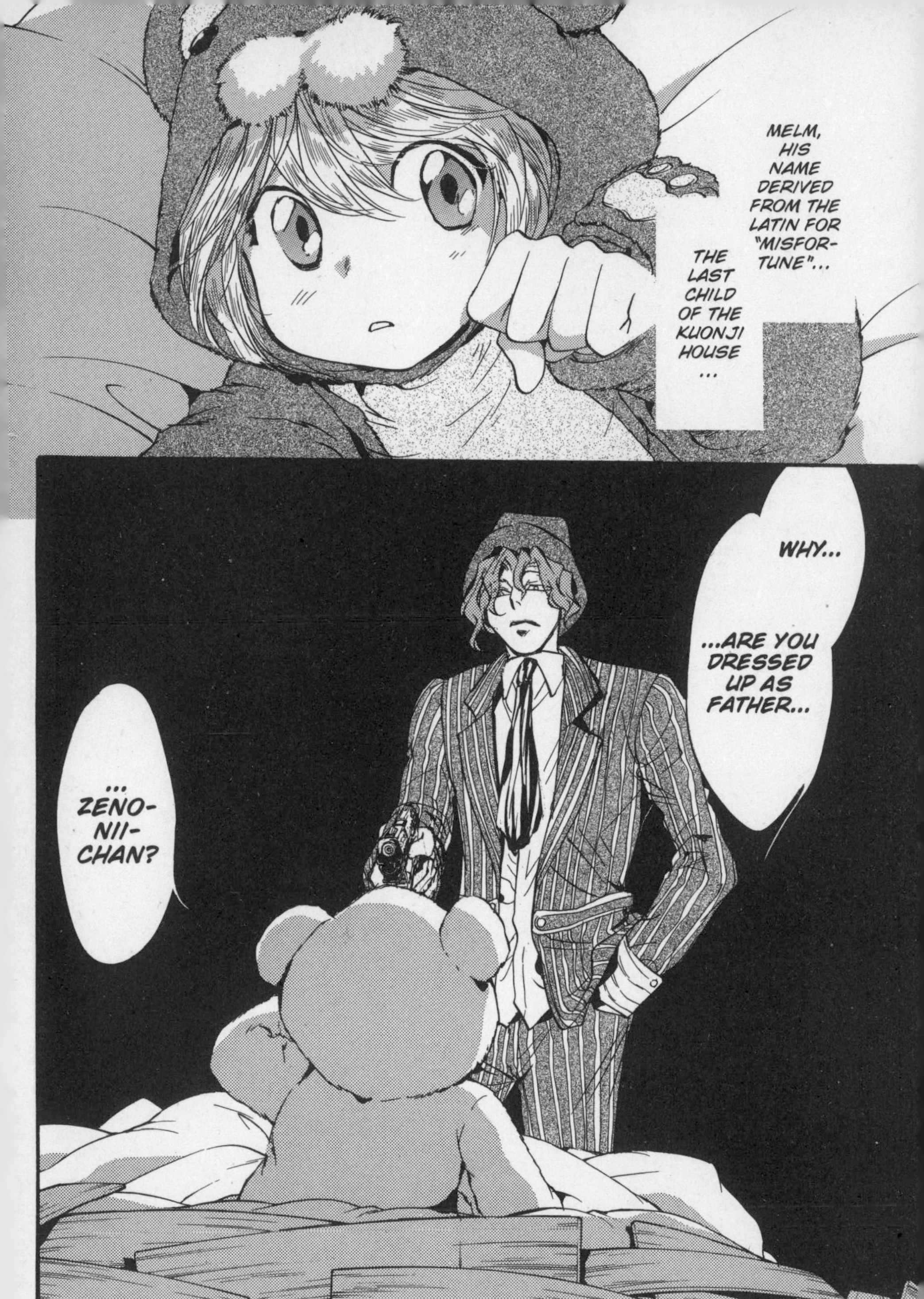
MELM, HIS NAME DERIVED FROM THE LATIN FOR "MISFOR-TUNE"...
THE LAST CHILD OF THE KUONJI HOUSE ...
WHY...
...ARE YOU DRESSED UP AS FATHER...
... ZENO-NII-CHAN?

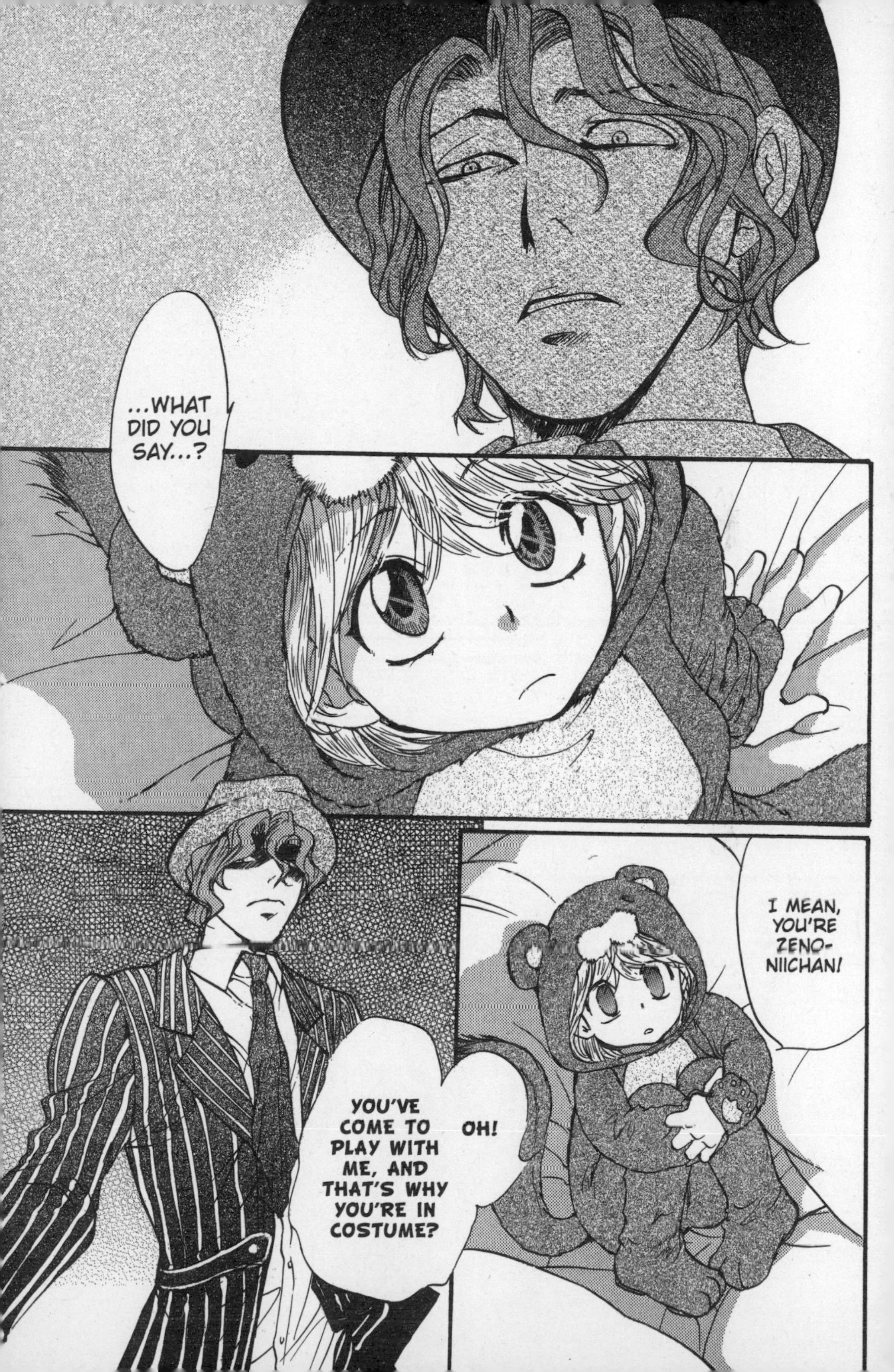
...WHAT DID YOU SAY...?
I MEAN, YOU'RE ZENO-NIICHAN!
OH!
YOU'VE COME TO PLAY WITH ME, AND THAT'S WHY YOU'RE IN COSTUME?

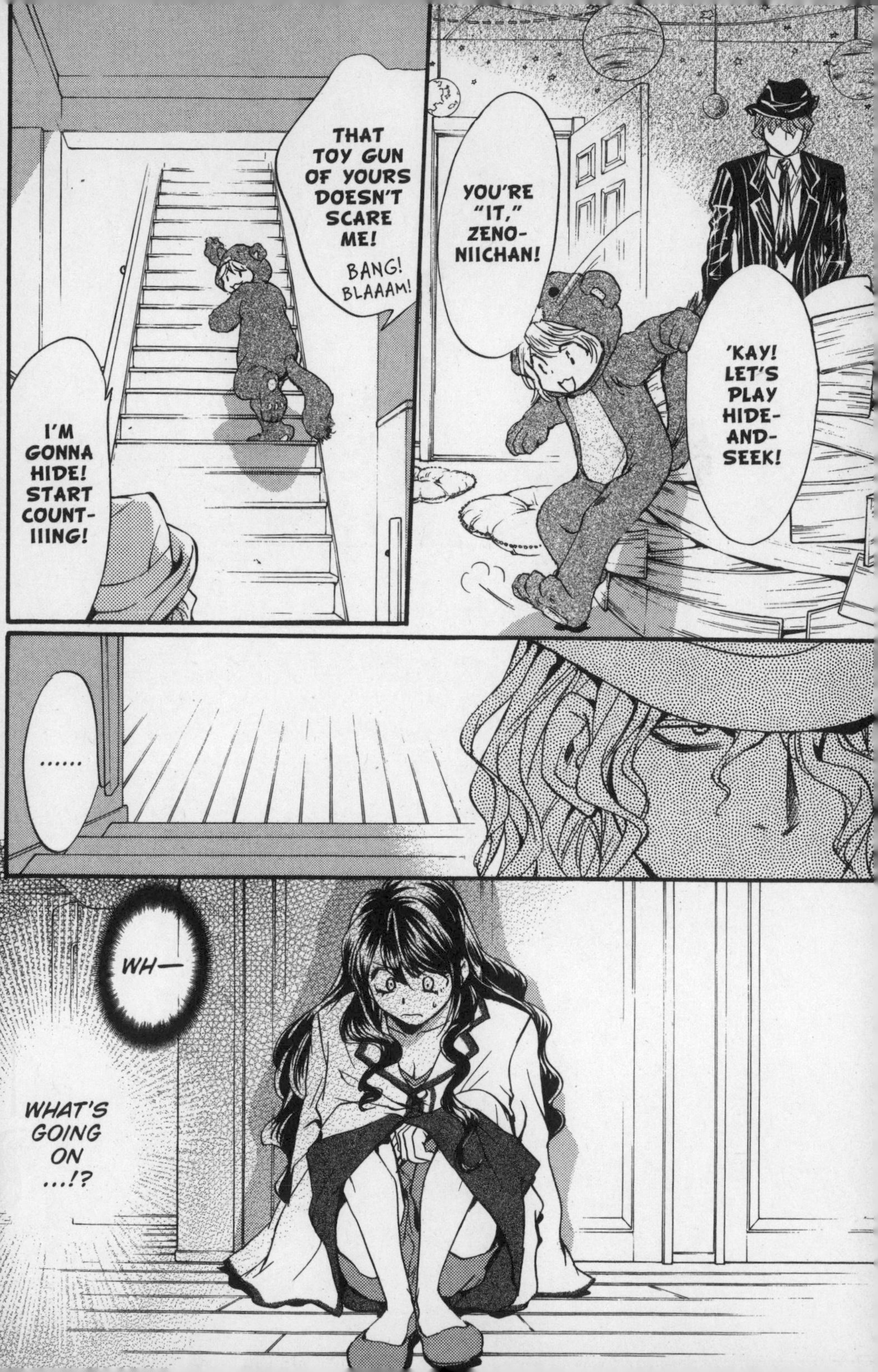
'KAY! LET'S PLAY HIDE-AND-SEEK!
YOU'RE "IT," ZENO-NIICHAN!
THAT TOY GUN OF YOURS DOESN'T SCARE ME!
BANG! BLAAAM!
I'M GONNA HIDE! START COUNT-IIING!
......
WH—
WHAT'S GOING ON ...!?

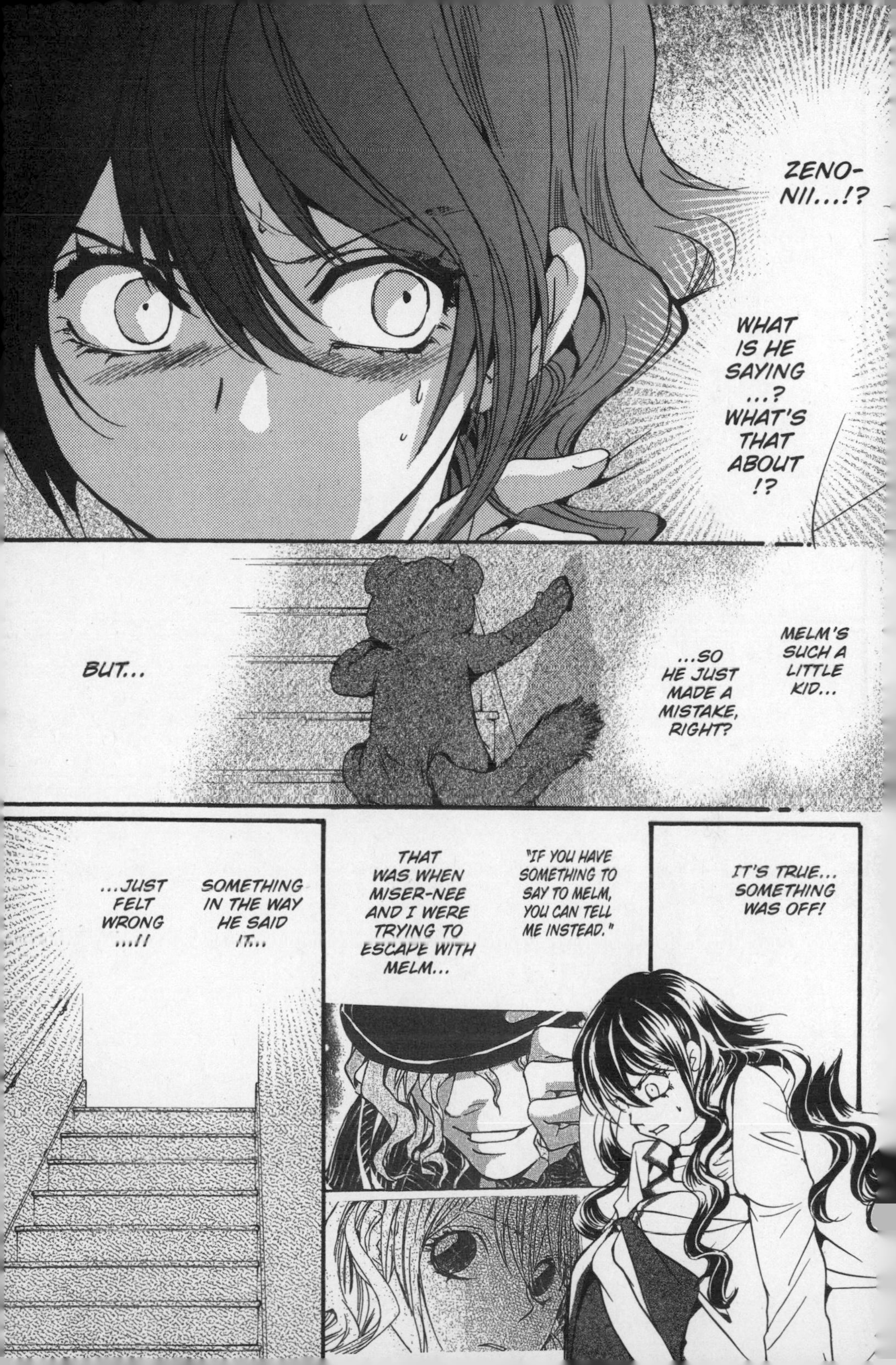
ZENO-NII...!?
WHAT IS HE SAYING...? WHAT'S THAT ABOUT!?
MELM'S SUCH A LITTLE KID...
...SO HE JUST MADE A MISTAKE, RIGHT?
BUT...
IT'S TRUE... SOMETHING WAS OFF!
"IF YOU HAVE SOMETHING TO SAY TO MELM, YOU CAN TELL ME INSTEAD."
THAT WAS WHEN MISER-NEE AND I WERE TRYING TO ESCAPE WITH MELM...
SOMETHING IN THE WAY HE SAID IT...
...JUST FELT WRONG...!!

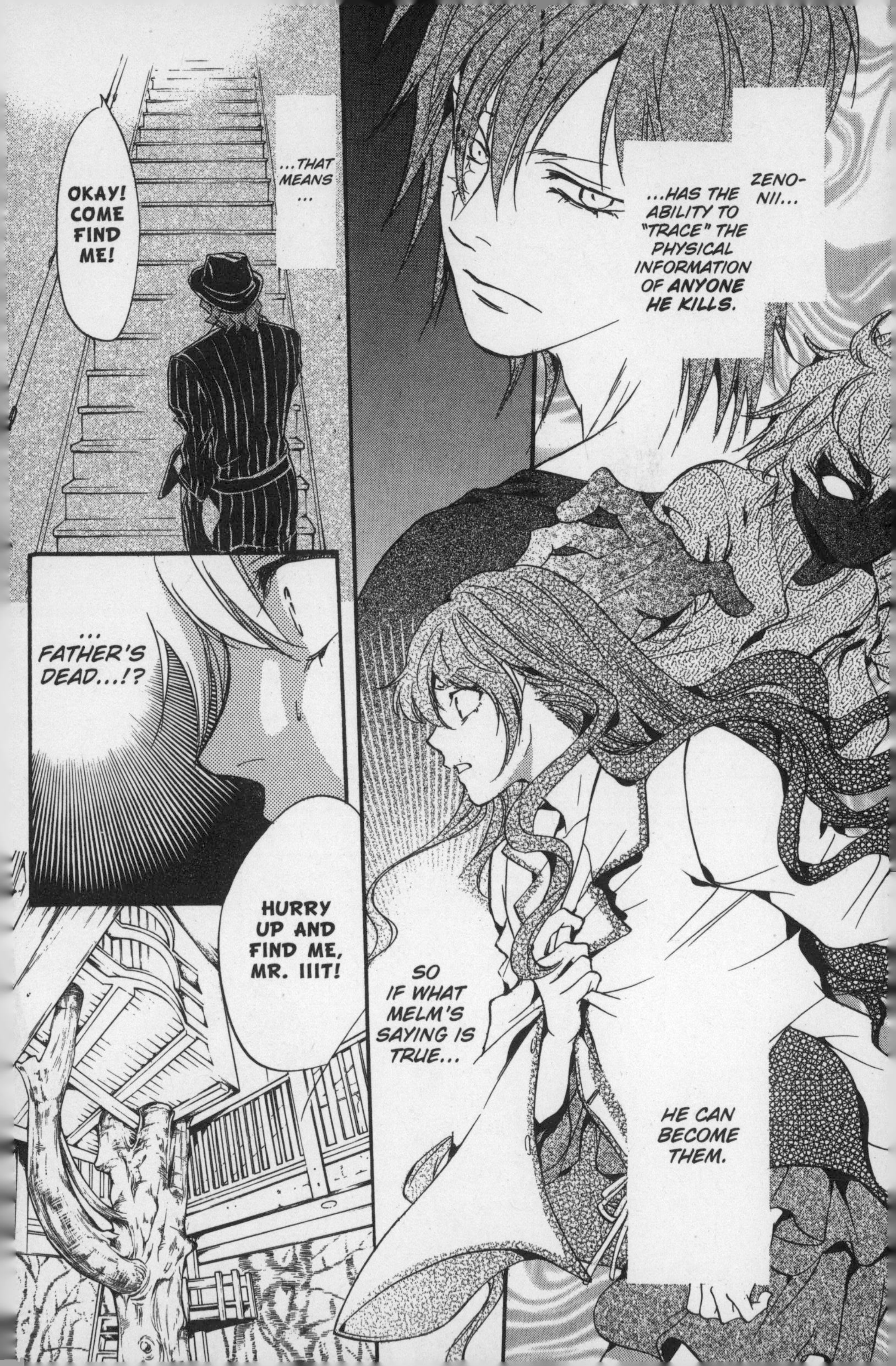
ZENO-NII...
...HAS THE ABILITY TO "TRACE" THE PHYSICAL INFORMATION OF ANYONE HE KILLS.
SO IF WHAT MELM'S SAYING IS TRUE...
HE CAN BECOME THEM.
...THAT MEANS...
OKAY! COME FIND ME!
...FATHER'S DEAD...!?
HURRY UP AND FIND ME, MR. IIIT!

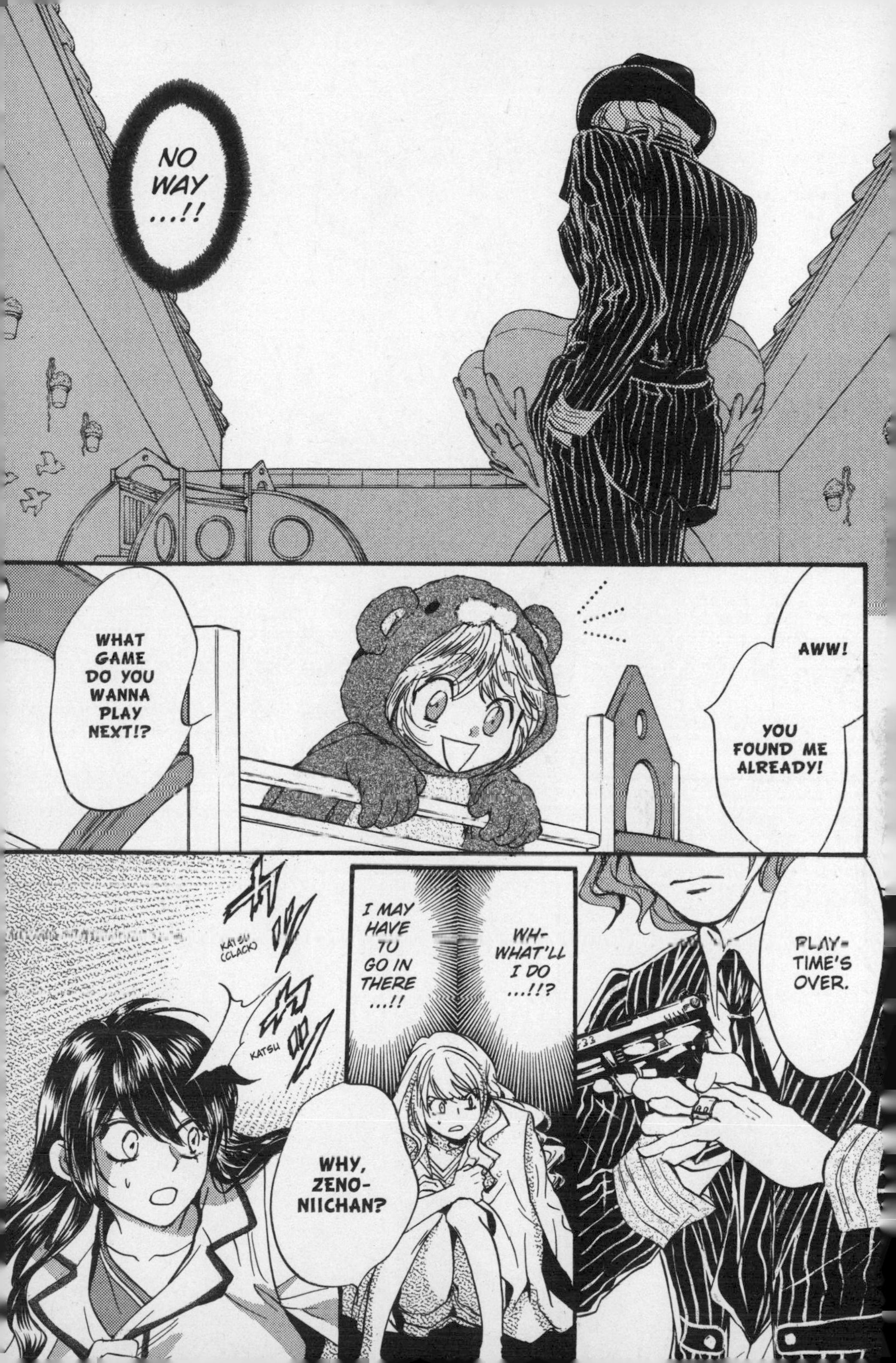
NO WAY ...!!
AWW!
YOU FOUND ME ALREADY!
WHAT GAME DO YOU WANNA PLAY NEXT!?
PLAY-TIME'S OVER.
WH-WHAT'LL I DO ...!!?
I MAY HAVE TO GO IN THERE ...!!
WHY, ZENO-NIICHAN?
KATSU (CLACK)
KATSU

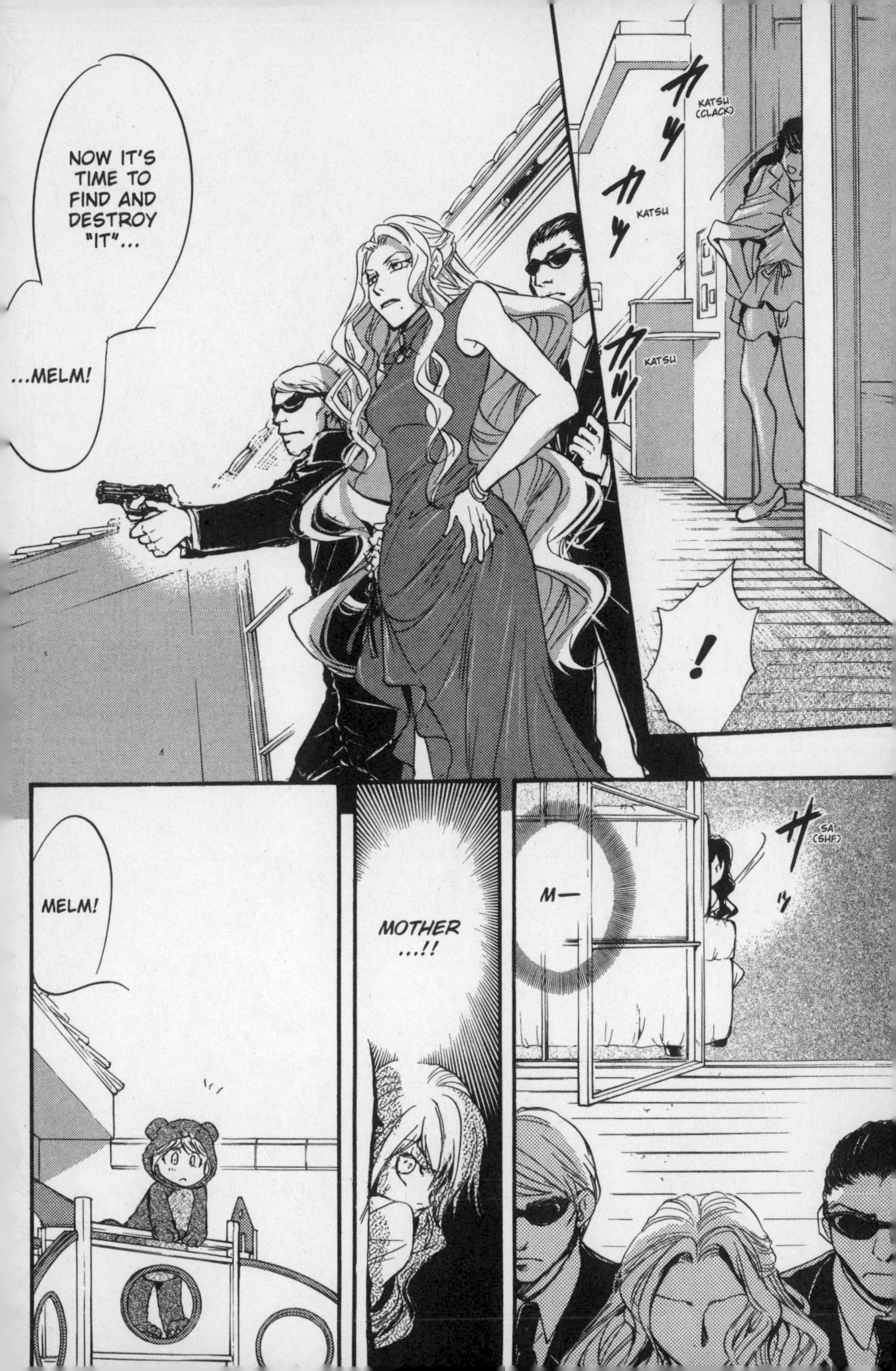
KATSU (CLACK)
KATSU
KATSU
!
NOW IT'S TIME TO FIND AND DESTROY "IT"...
...MELM!
SA (SHF)
M—
MOTHER ...!!
MELM!

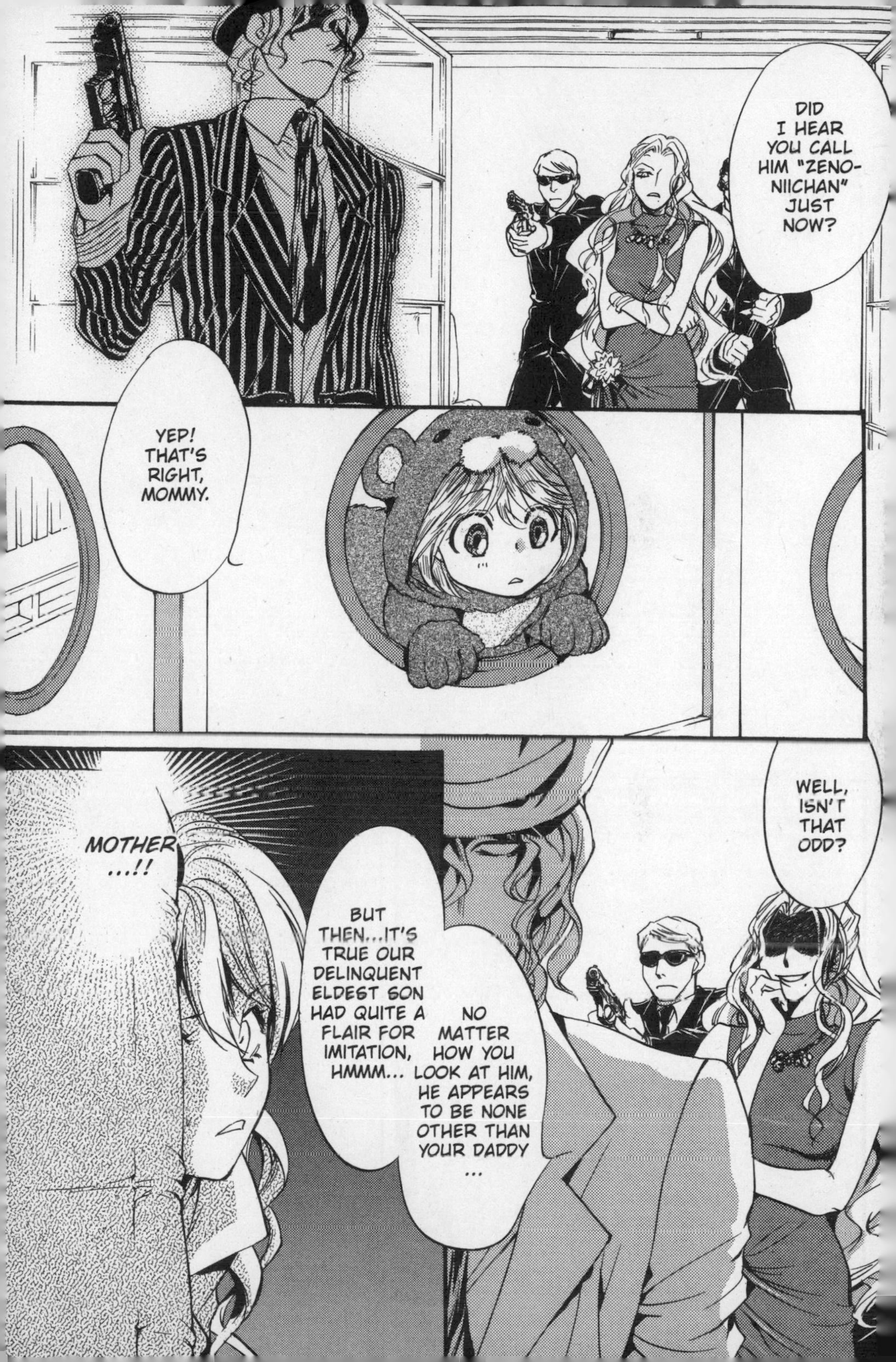
DID I HEAR YOU CALL HIM "ZENO-NIICHAN" JUST NOW?
YEP! THAT'S RIGHT, MOMMY.
WELL, ISN'T THAT ODD?
NO MATTER HOW YOU LOOK AT HIM, HE APPEARS TO BE NONE OTHER THAN YOUR DADDY ...
BUT THEN...IT'S TRUE OUR DELINQUENT ELDEST SON HAD QUITE A FLAIR FOR IMITATION, HMMM...
MOTHER ...!!

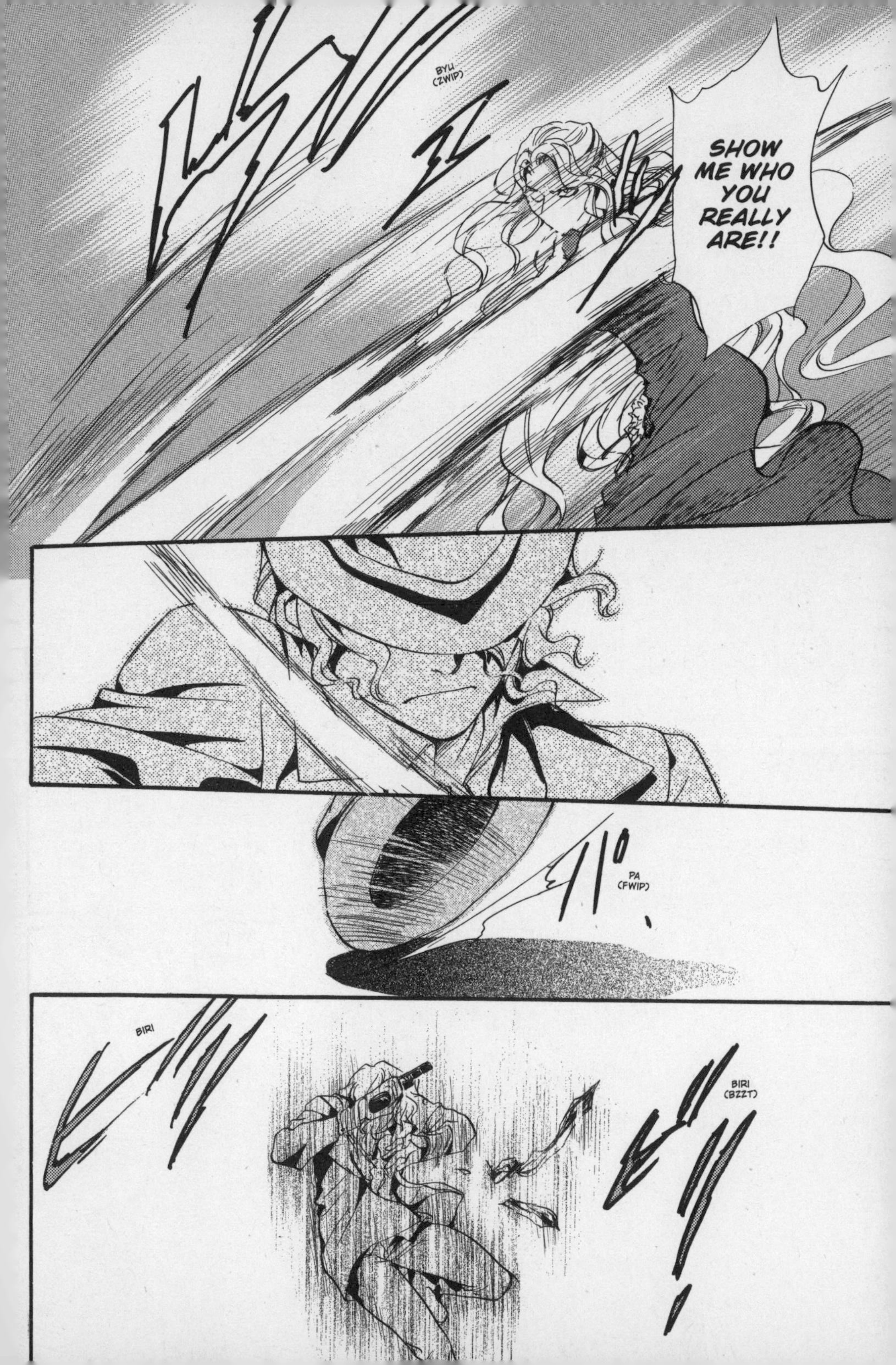
SHOW ME WHO YOU REALLY ARE!!
BYU (ZWIP)
PA (FWIP)
BIRI (BZZT)
BIRI

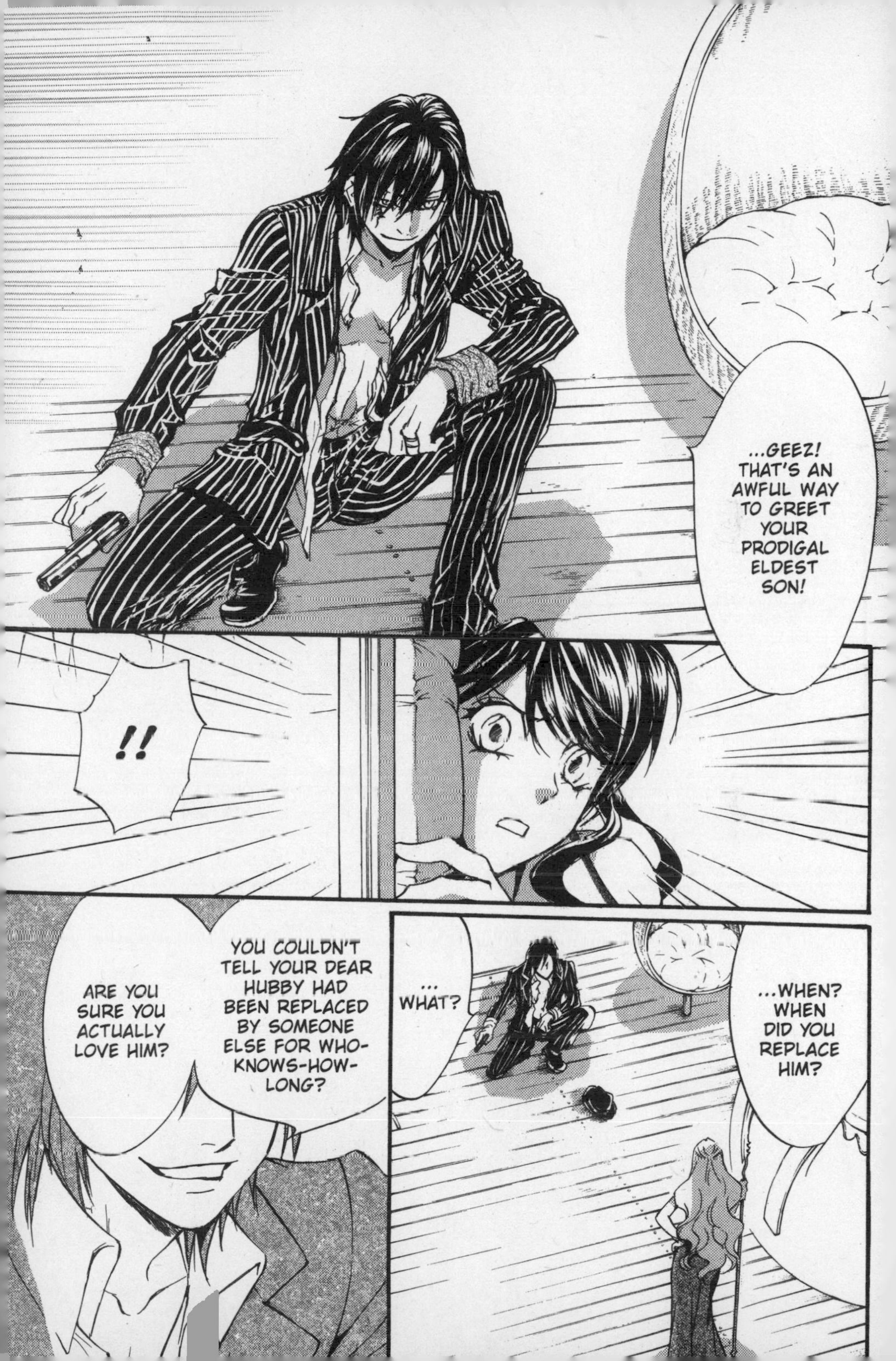
...GEEZ! THAT'S AN AWFUL WAY TO GREET YOUR PRODIGAL ELDEST SON!
!!
...WHEN? WHEN DID YOU REPLACE HIM?
... WHAT?
YOU COULDN'T TELL YOUR DEAR HUBBY HAD BEEN REPLACED BY SOMEONE ELSE FOR WHO-KNOWS-HOW-LONG?
ARE YOU SURE YOU ACTUALLY LOVE HIM?

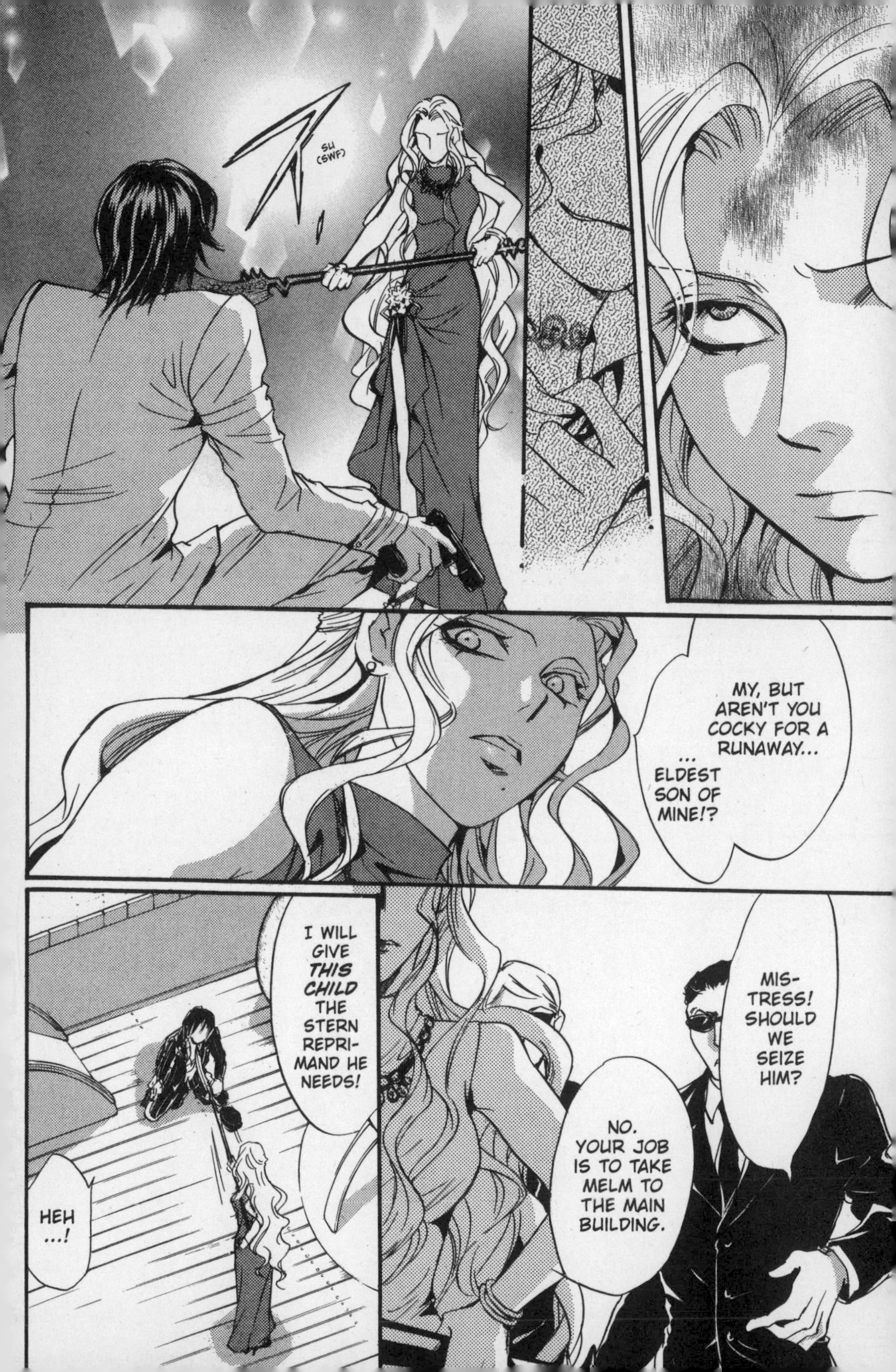
SU (SWF)
MY, BUT AREN'T YOU COCKY FOR A RUNAWAY...
... ELDEST SON OF MINE!?
MIS-TRESS! SHOULD WE SEIZE HIM?
NO. YOUR JOB IS TO TAKE MELM TO THE MAIN BUILDING.
I WILL GIVE *THIS CHILD* THE STERN REPRI-MAND HE NEEDS!
HEH ...!

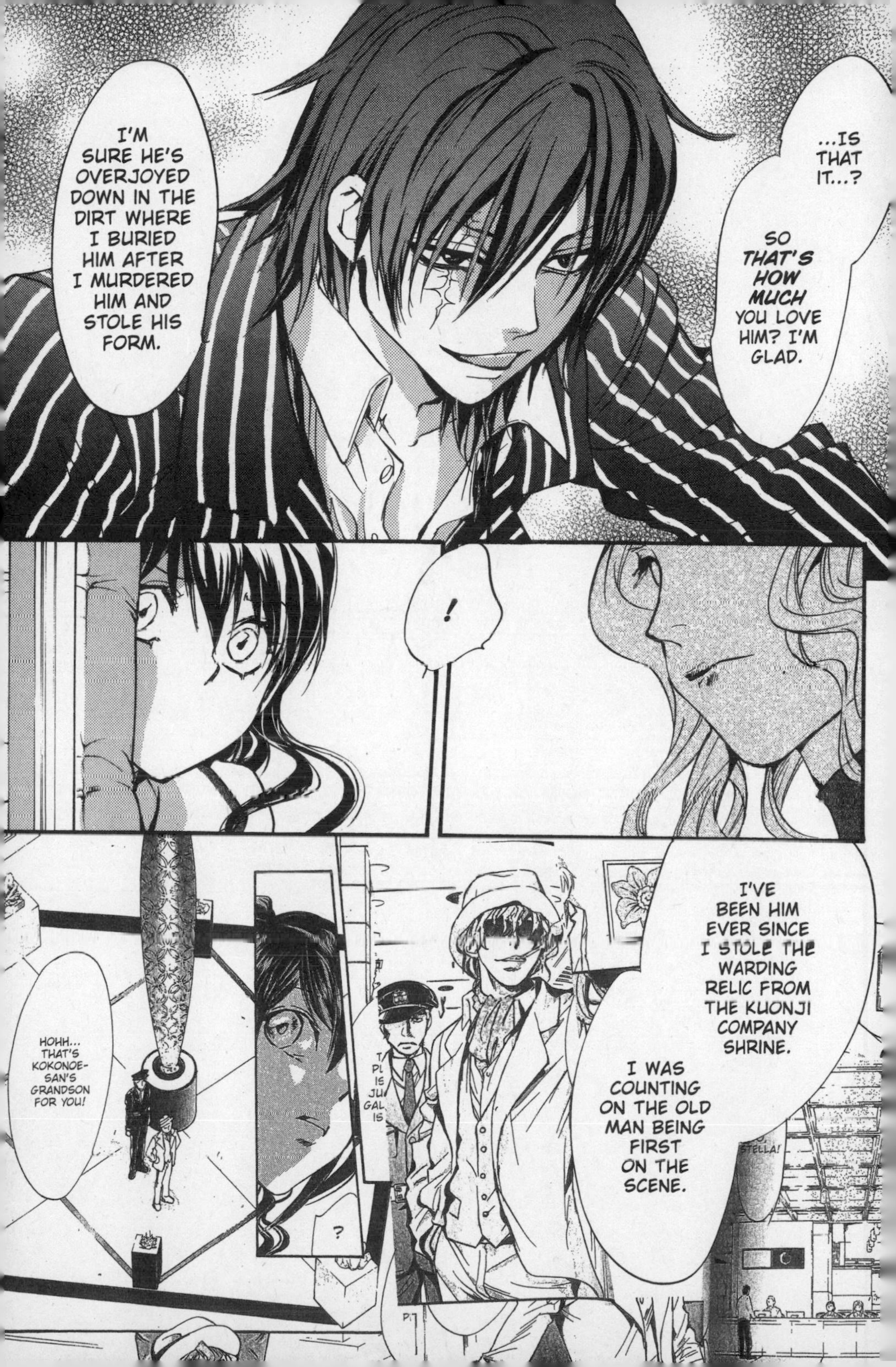
...IS THAT IT...?
SO *THAT'S HOW MUCH* YOU LOVE HIM? I'M GLAD.
I'M SURE HE'S OVERJOYED DOWN IN THE DIRT WHERE I BURIED HIM AFTER I MURDERED HIM AND STOLE HIS FORM.
!
I'VE BEEN HIM EVER SINCE I STOLE THE WARDING RELIC FROM THE KUONJI COMPANY SHRINE.
I WAS COUNTING ON THE OLD MAN BEING FIRST ON THE SCENE.
?
HOHH... THAT'S KOKONOE-SAN'S GRANDSON FOR YOU!

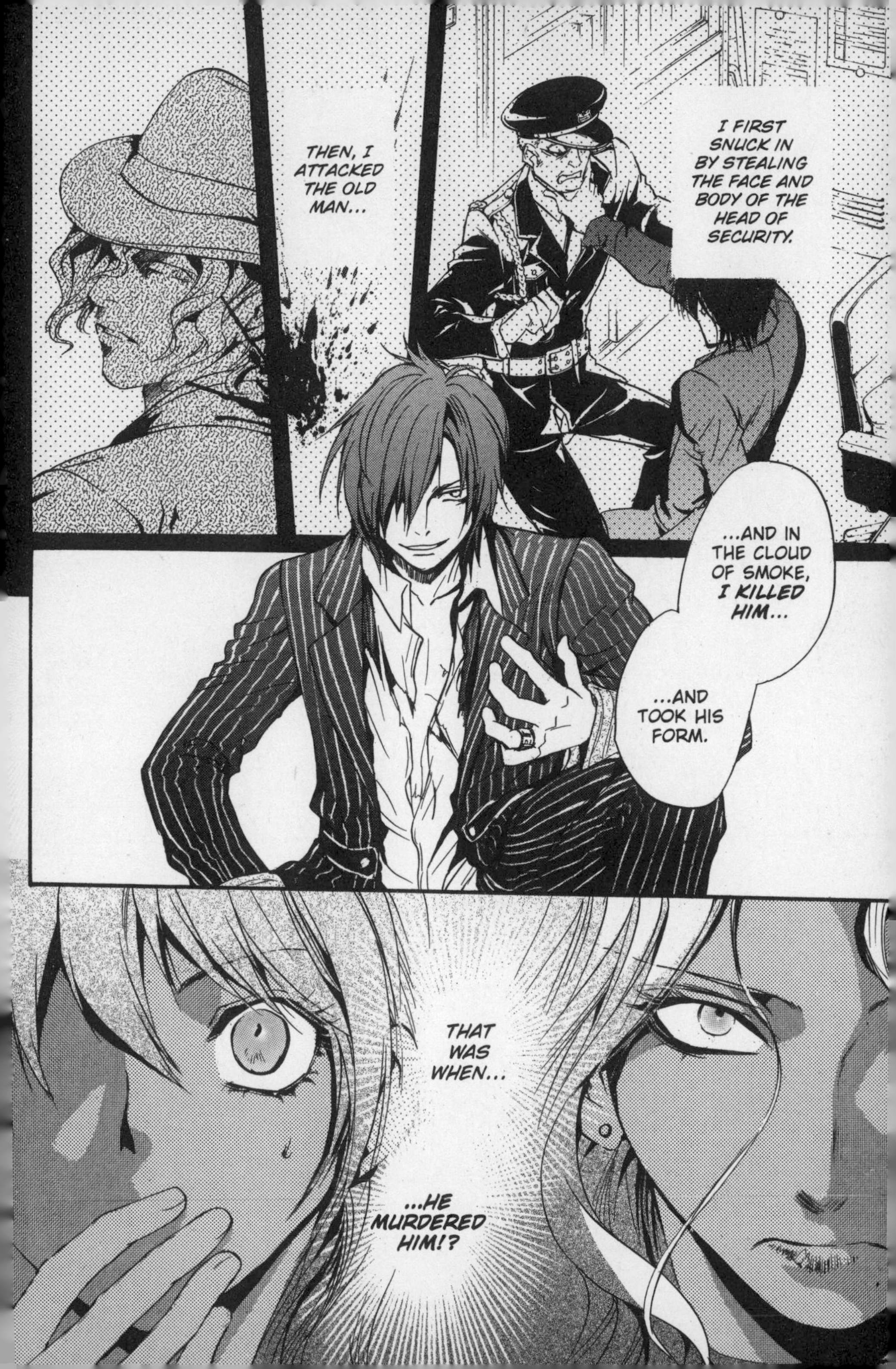
I FIRST SNUCK IN BY STEALING THE FACE AND BODY OF THE HEAD OF SECURITY.
THEN, I ATTACKED THE OLD MAN...
...AND IN THE CLOUD OF SMOKE, I KILLED HIM...
...AND TOOK HIS FORM.
THAT WAS WHEN...
...HE MURDERED HIM!?

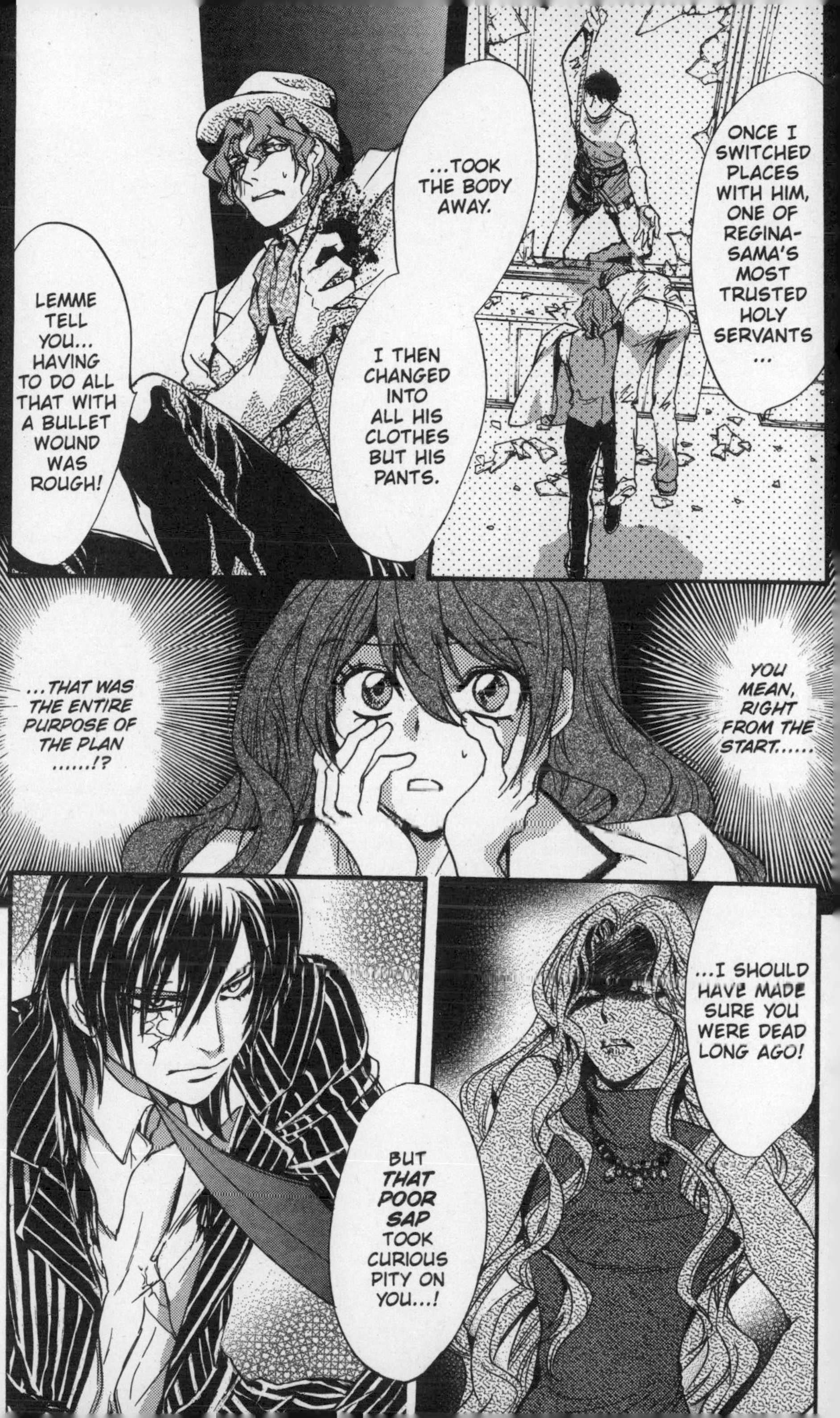
ONCE I SWITCHED PLACES WITH HIM, ONE OF REGINA-SAMA'S MOST TRUSTED HOLY SERVANTS...
...TOOK THE BODY AWAY.
I THEN CHANGED INTO ALL HIS CLOTHES BUT HIS PANTS.
LEMME TELL YOU... HAVING TO DO ALL THAT WITH A BULLET WOUND WAS ROUGH!
YOU MEAN, RIGHT FROM THE START......
...THAT WAS THE ENTIRE PURPOSE OF THE PLAN......!?
...I SHOULD HAVE MADE SURE YOU WERE DEAD LONG AGO!
BUT THAT POOR SAP TOOK CURIOUS PITY ON YOU...!

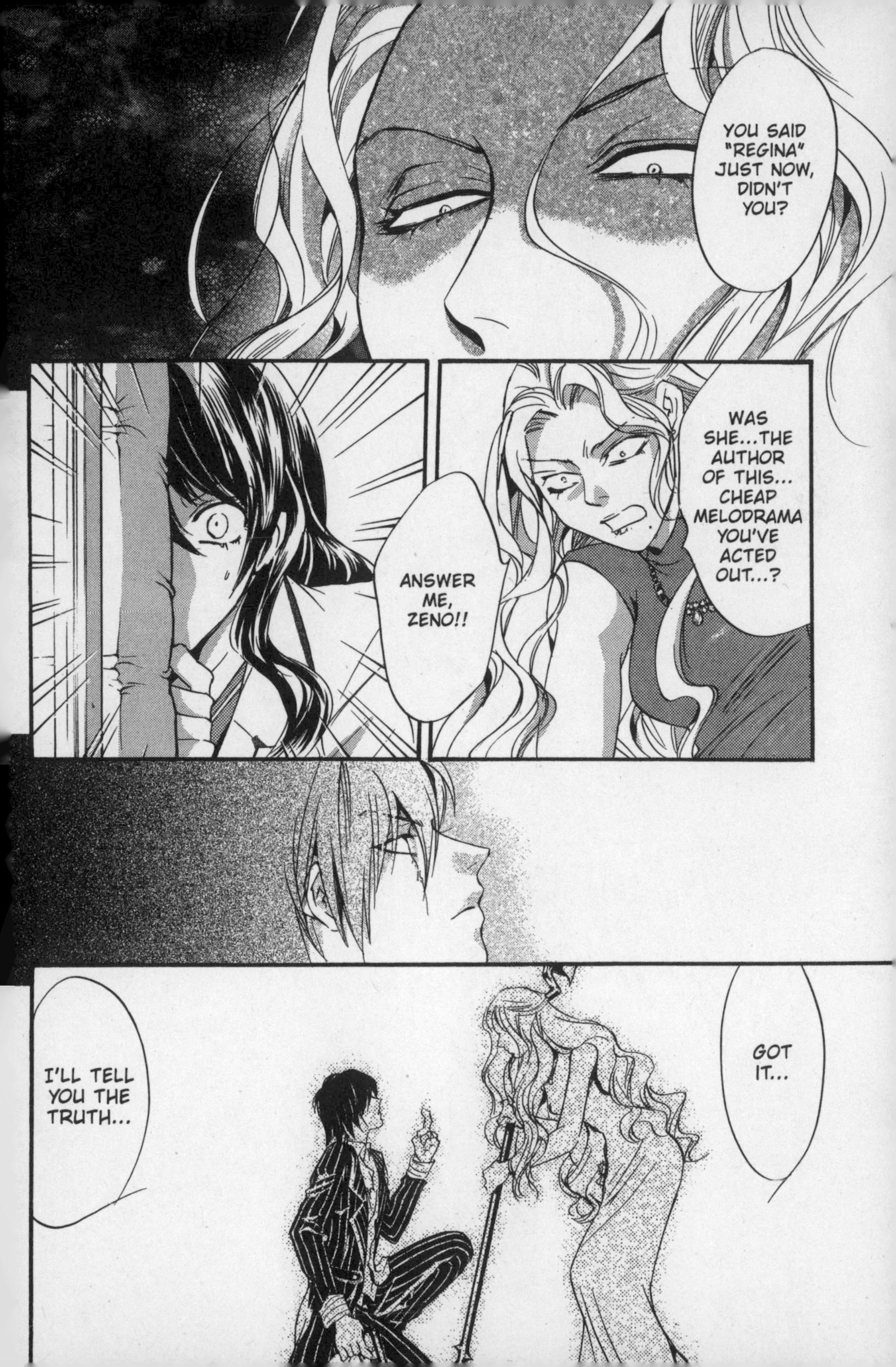
YOU SAID "REGINA" JUST NOW, DIDN'T YOU?
WAS SHE...THE AUTHOR OF THIS... CHEAP MELODRAMA YOU'VE ACTED OUT...?
ANSWER ME, ZENO!!
GOT IT...
I'LL TELL YOU THE TRUTH...

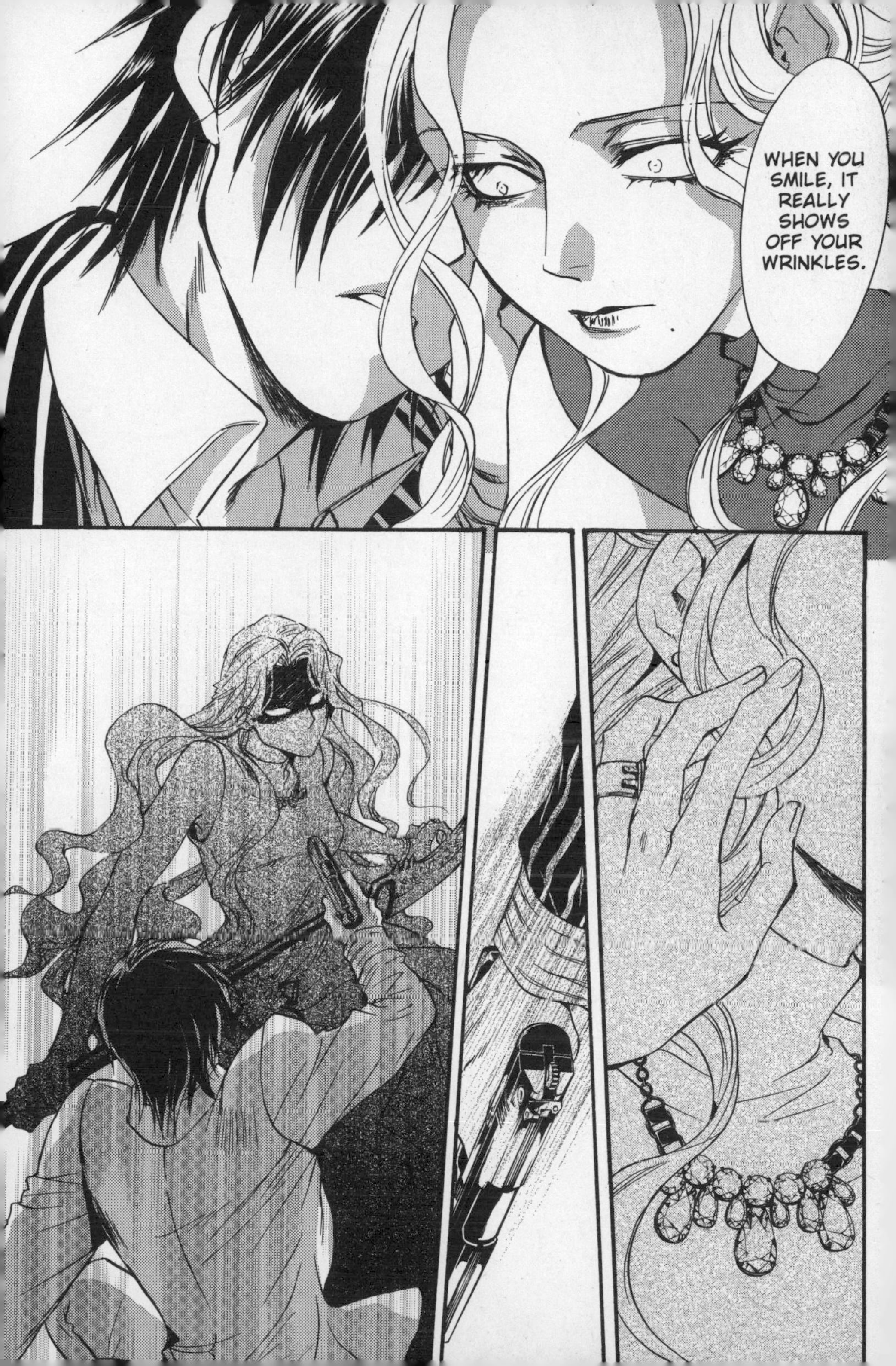
WHEN YOU SMILE, IT REALLY SHOWS OFF YOUR WRINKLES.

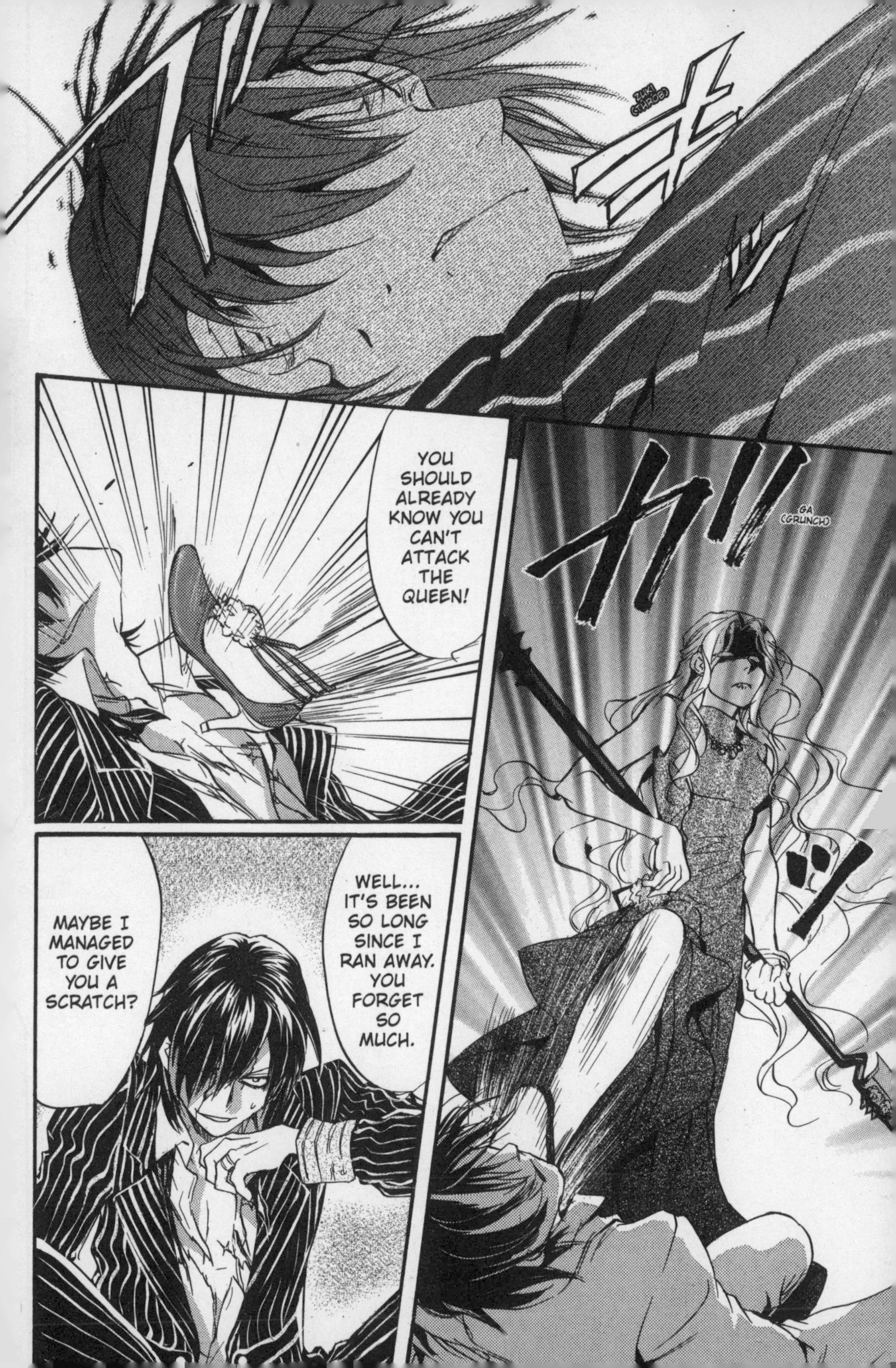
ZUKI (THROB)
GA (GRUNCH)
YOU SHOULD ALREADY KNOW YOU CAN'T ATTACK THE QUEEN!
WELL... IT'S BEEN SO LONG SINCE I RAN AWAY. YOU FORGET SO MUCH.
MAYBE I MANAGED TO GIVE YOU A SCRATCH?

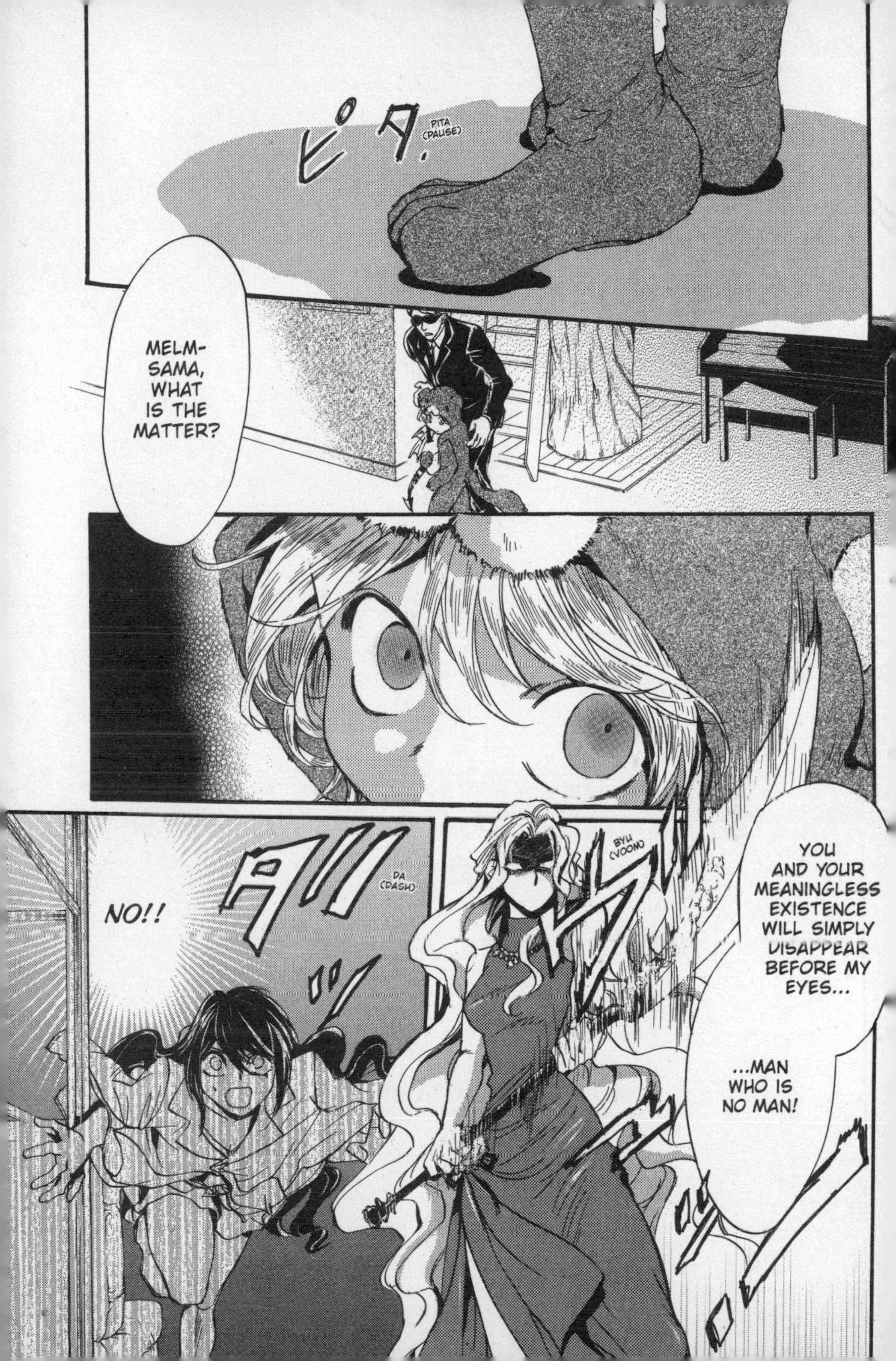
ピタ
PITA (PAUSE)
MELM-SAMA, WHAT IS THE MATTER?
BYU (VOOM)
YOU AND YOUR MEANINGLESS EXISTENCE WILL SIMPLY DISAPPEAR BEFORE MY EYES...
...MAN WHO IS NO MAN!
DA (DASH)
NO!!

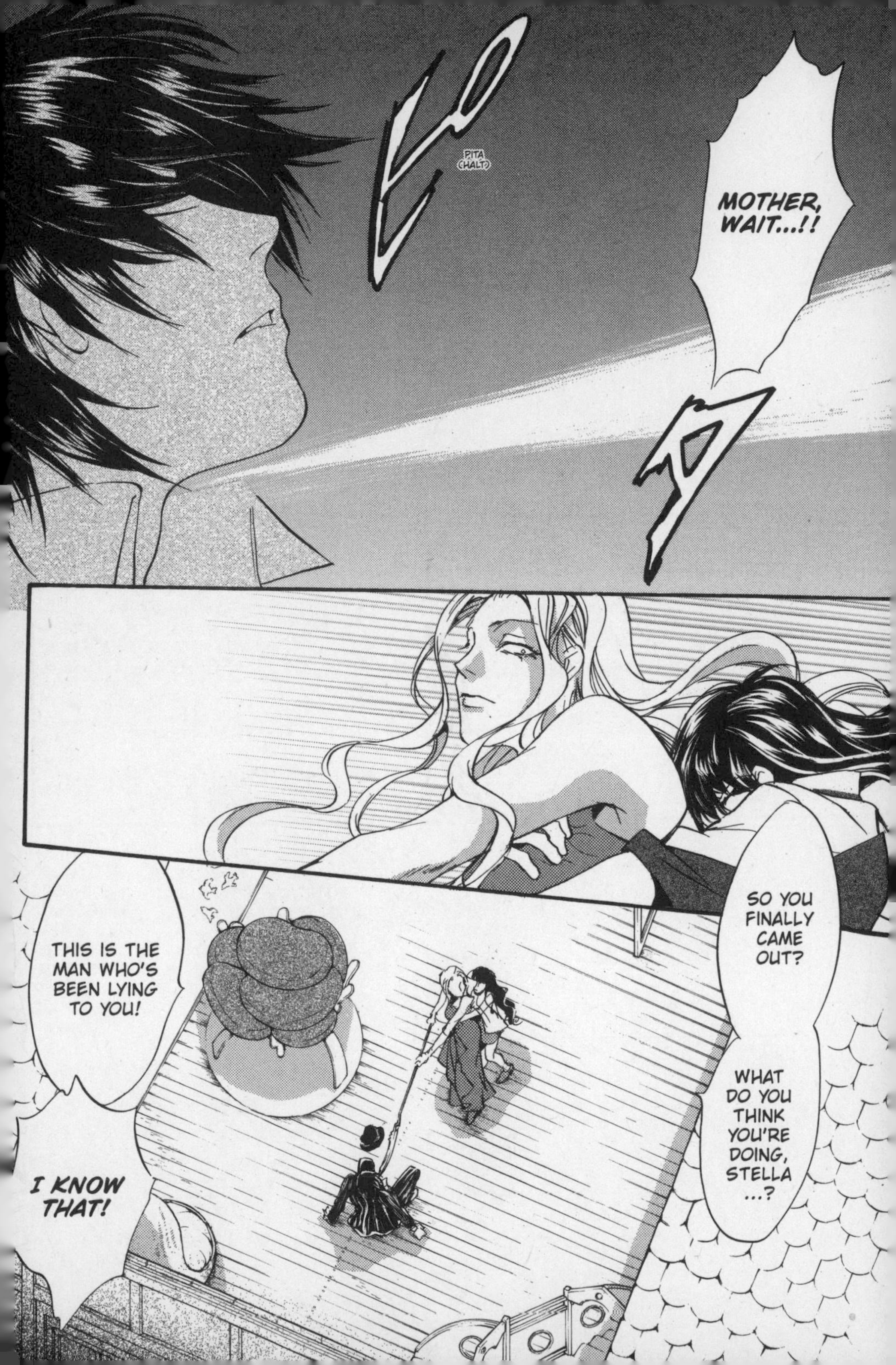
MOTHER, WAIT...!!
PITA (HALT)
SO YOU FINALLY CAME OUT?
WHAT DO YOU THINK YOU'RE DOING, STELLA ...?
THIS IS THE MAN WHO'S BEEN LYING TO YOU!
I KNOW THAT!

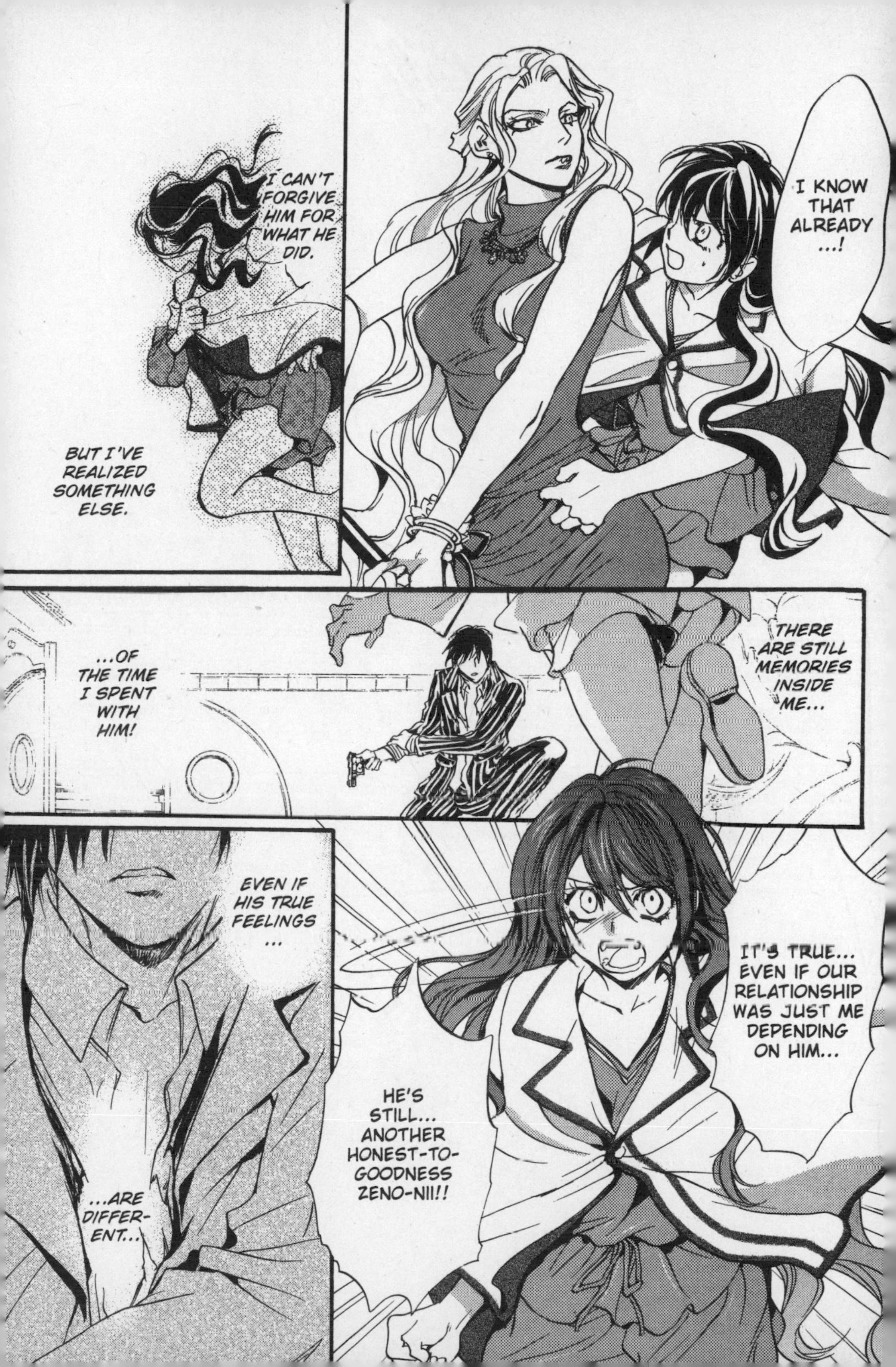
I KNOW THAT ALREADY ...!
I CAN'T FORGIVE HIM FOR WHAT HE DID.
BUT I'VE REALIZED SOMETHING ELSE.
THERE ARE STILL MEMORIES INSIDE ME...
...OF THE TIME I SPENT WITH HIM!
IT'S TRUE... EVEN IF OUR RELATIONSHIP WAS JUST ME DEPENDING ON HIM...
HE'S STILL... ANOTHER HONEST-TO-GOODNESS ZENO-NII!!
EVEN IF HIS TRUE FEELINGS ...
...ARE DIFFER-ENT...

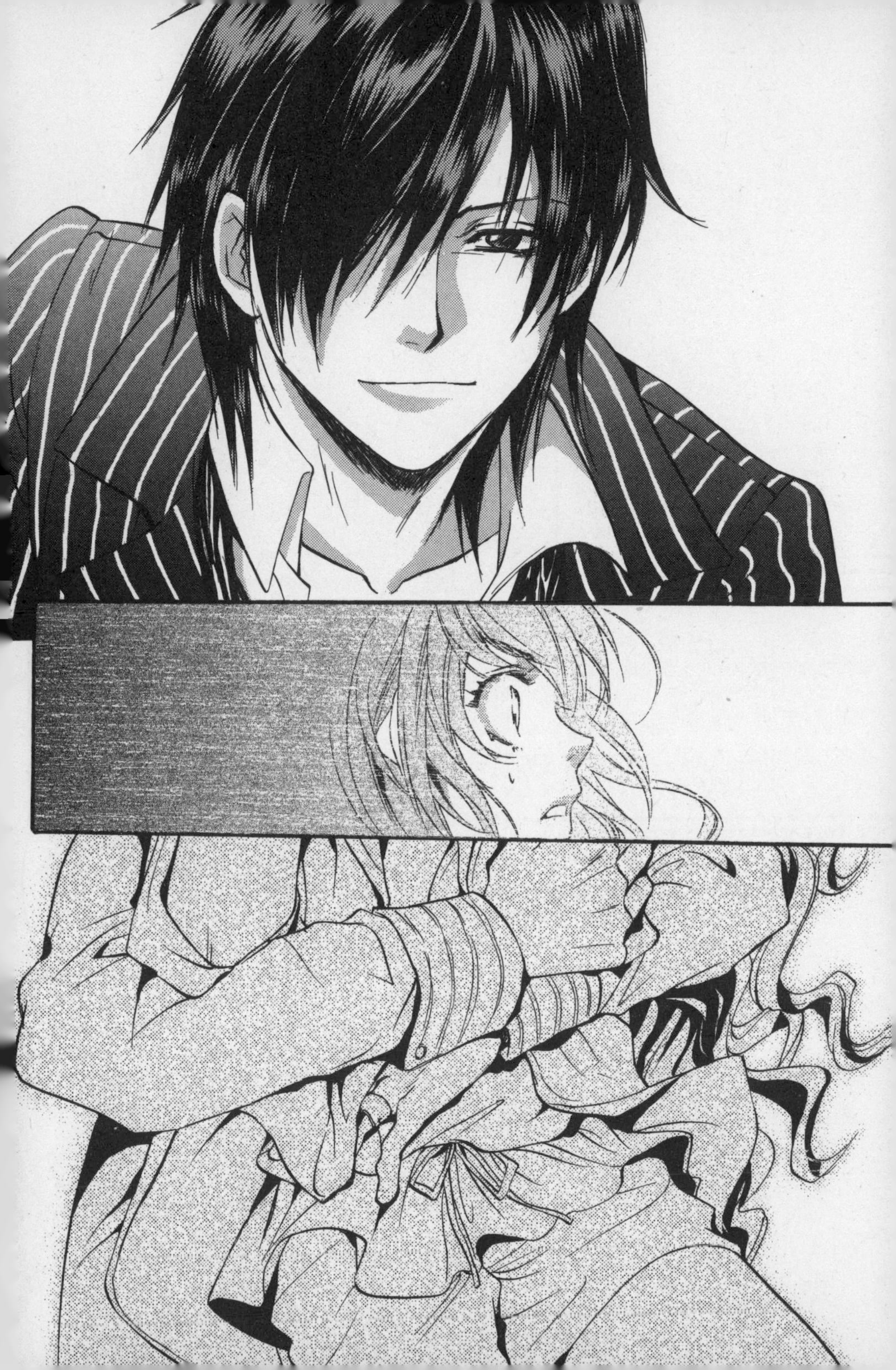

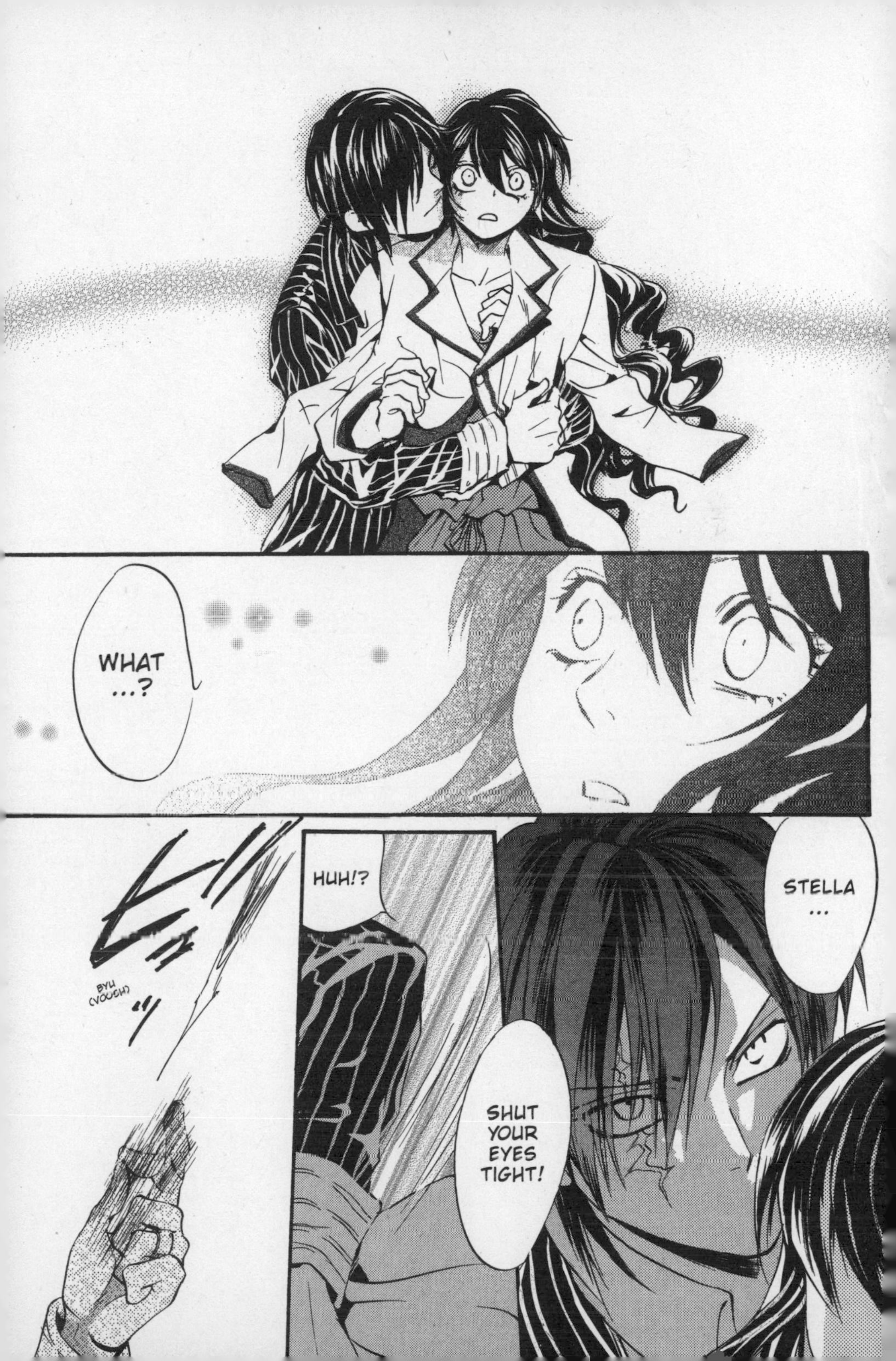
WHAT ...?
STELLA ...
SHUT YOUR EYES TIGHT!
HUH!?
BYU (VOOSH)

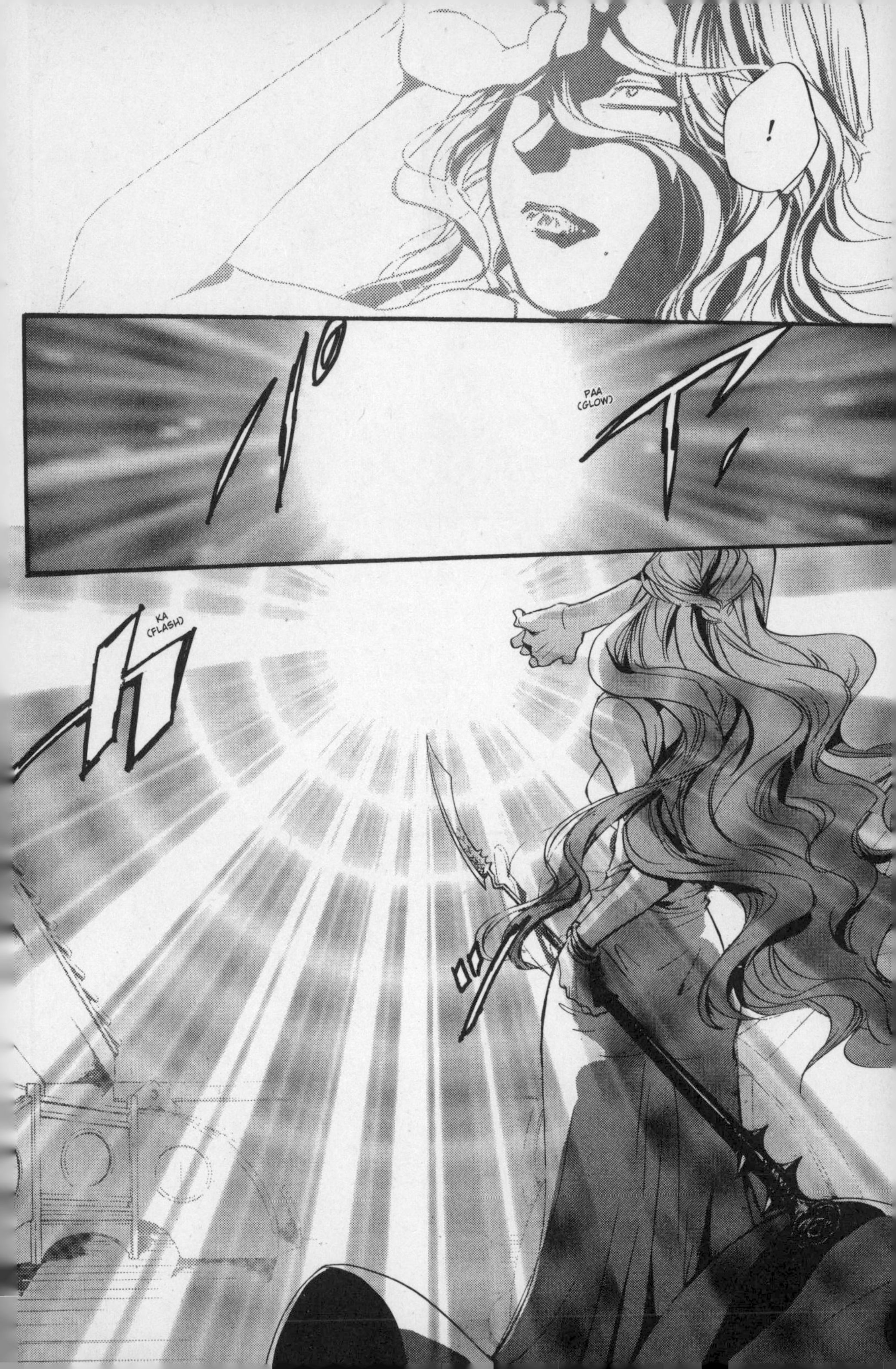
!
PAA (GLOW)
KA (FLASH)

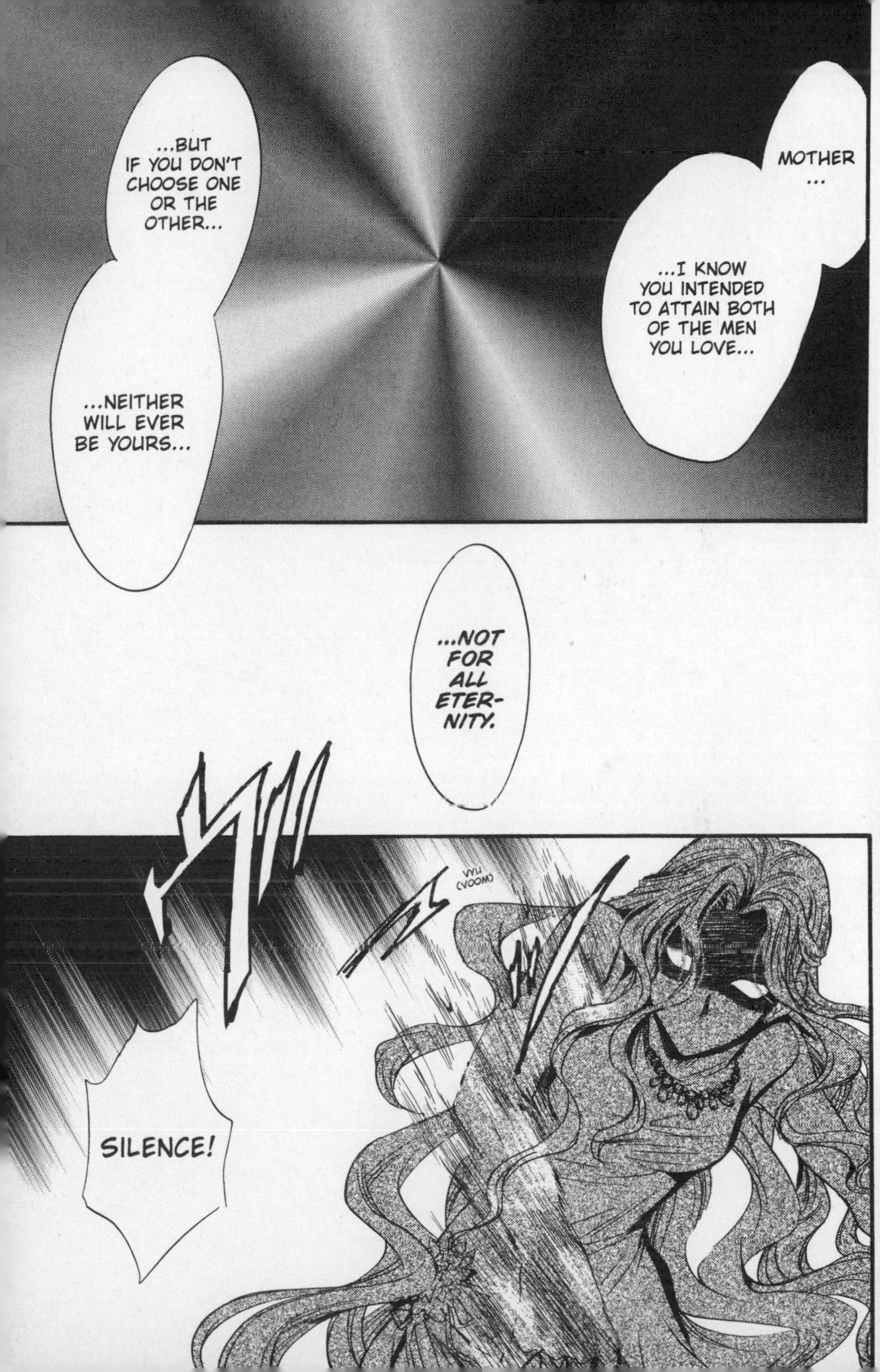
MOTHER ...
...I KNOW YOU INTENDED TO ATTAIN BOTH OF THE MEN YOU LOVE...
...BUT IF YOU DON'T CHOOSE ONE OR THE OTHER...
...NEITHER WILL EVER BE YOURS...
...NOT FOR ALL ETER-NITY.
VYU (VOOM)
SILENCE!

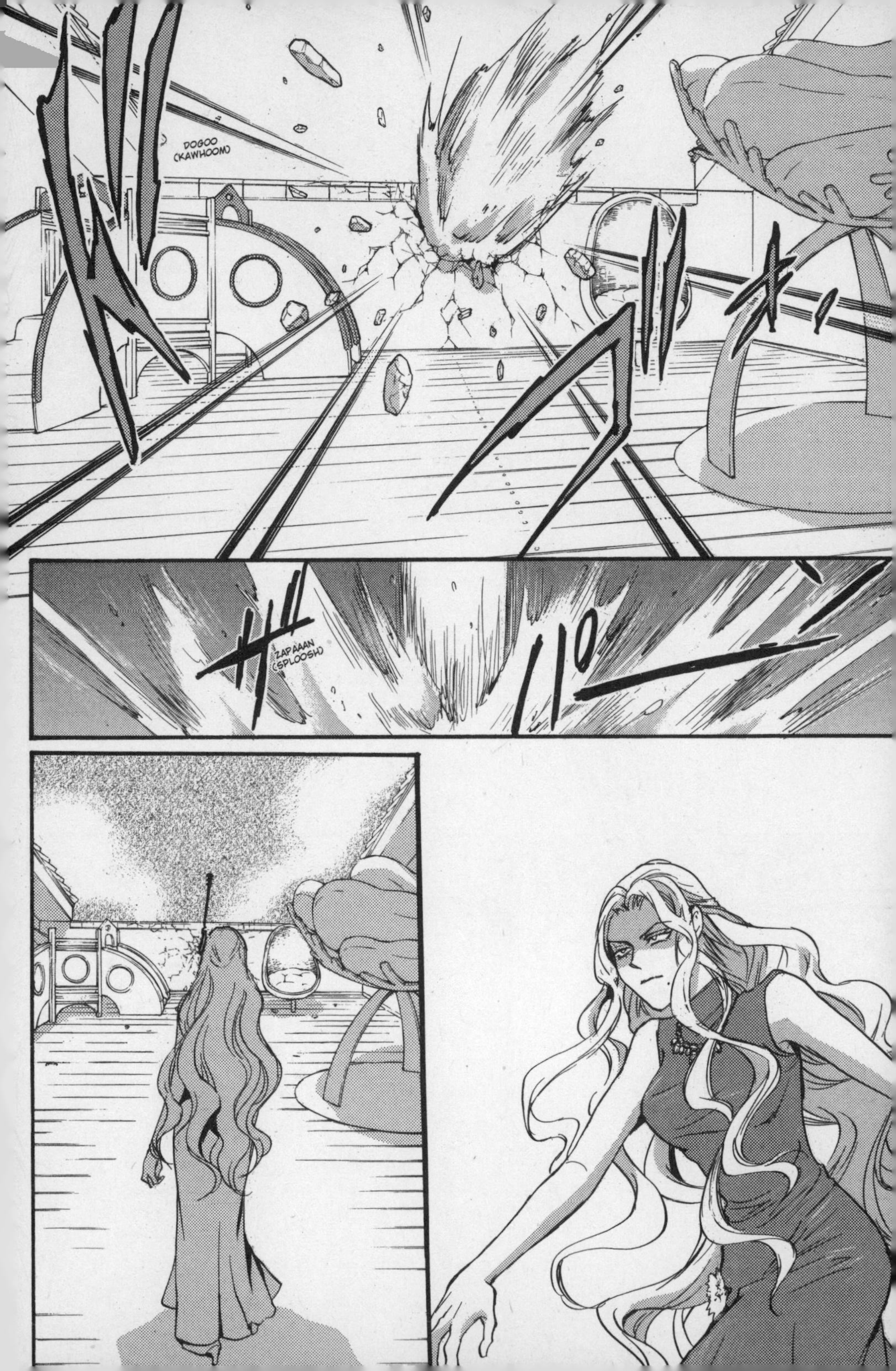
DOGOO
(KAWHOOM)
ZAPAAAN
(SPLOOSH)

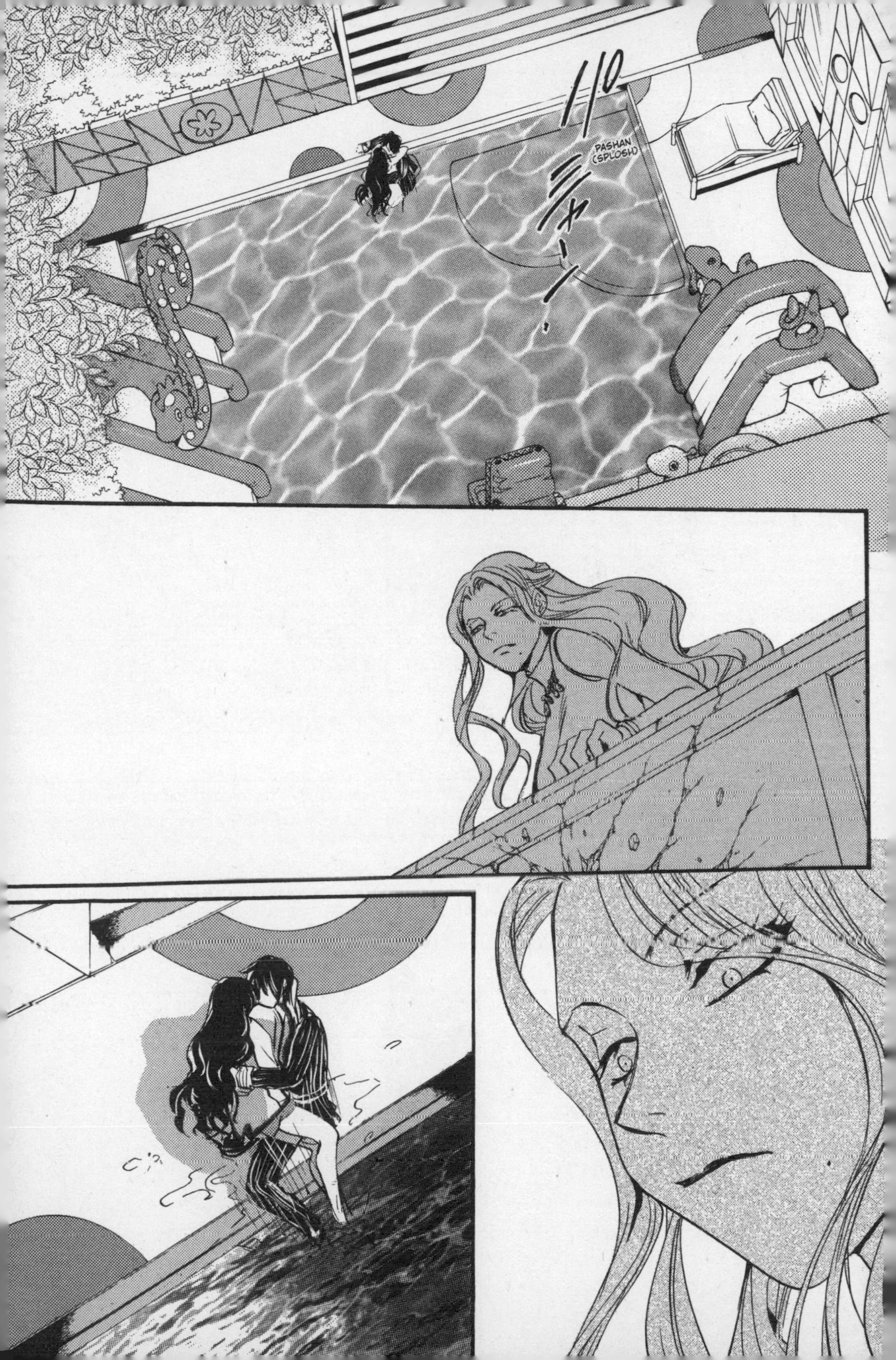
PASHAN (SPLOSH)

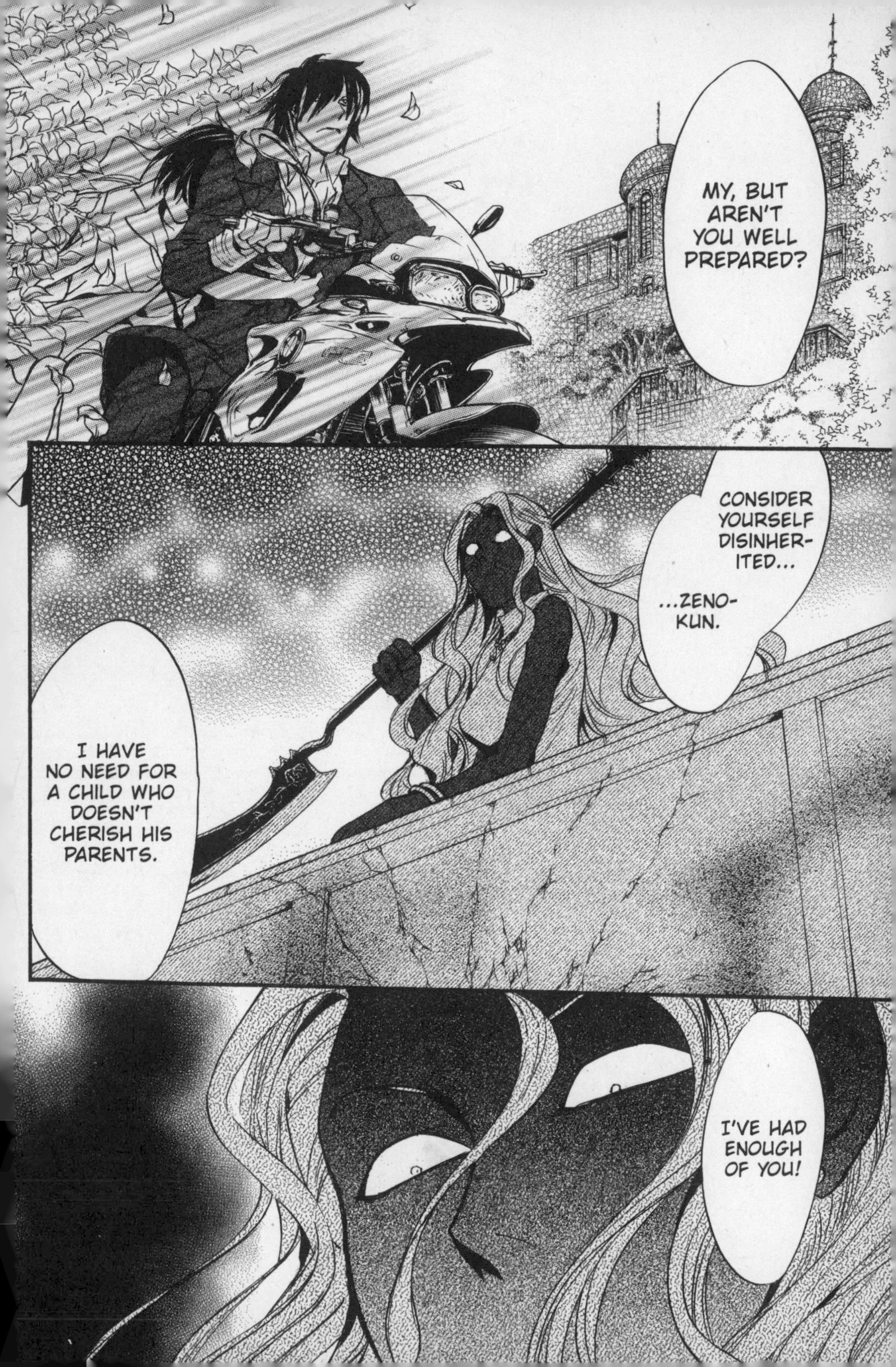
MY, BUT AREN'T YOU WELL PREPARED?
CONSIDER YOURSELF DISINHER-ITED...
...ZENO-KUN.
I HAVE NO NEED FOR A CHILD WHO DOESN'T CHERISH HIS PARENTS.
I'VE HAD ENOUGH OF YOU!

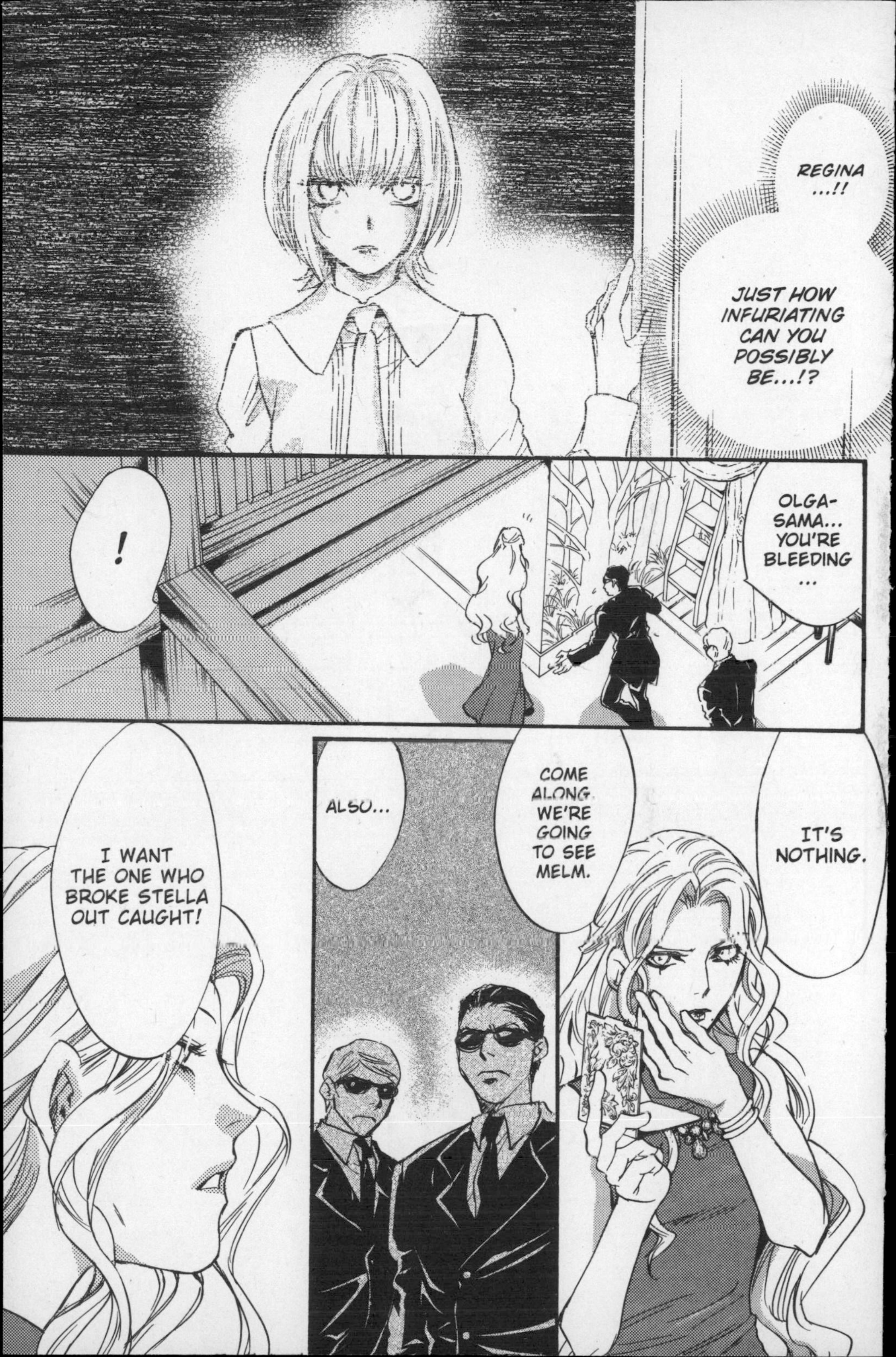
REGINA ...!!
JUST HOW INFURIATING CAN YOU POSSIBLY BE...!?
OLGA-SAMA... YOU'RE BLEEDING ...
!
IT'S NOTHING.
COME ALONG. WE'RE GOING TO SEE MELM.
ALSO...
I WANT THE ONE WHO BROKE STELLA OUT CAUGHT!

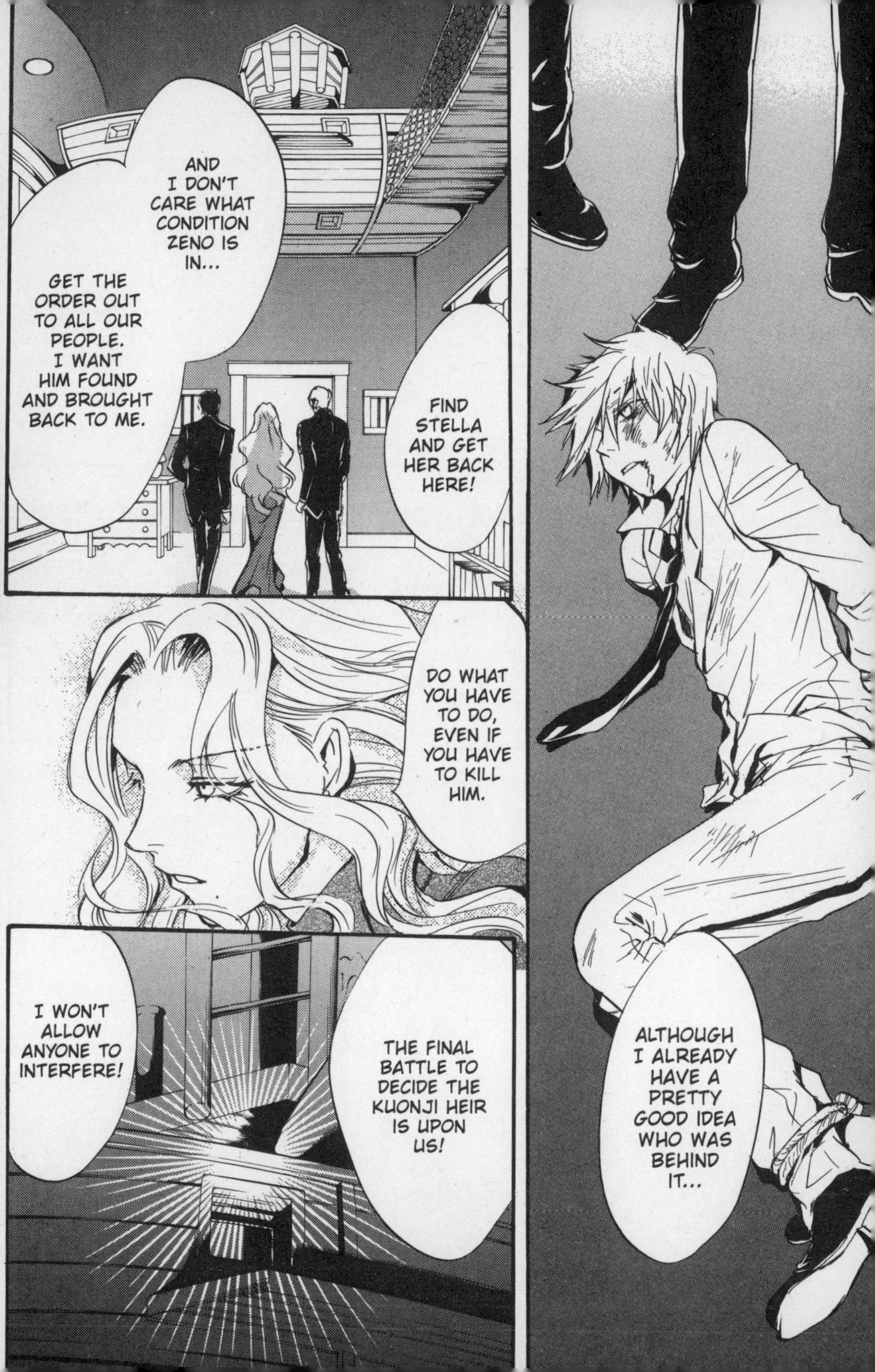
ALTHOUGH I ALREADY HAVE A PRETTY GOOD IDEA WHO WAS BEHIND IT...
FIND STELLA AND GET HER BACK HERE!
AND I DON'T CARE WHAT CONDITION ZENO IS IN...
GET THE ORDER OUT TO ALL OUR PEOPLE. I WANT HIM FOUND AND BROUGHT BACK TO ME.
DO WHAT YOU HAVE TO DO, EVEN IF YOU HAVE TO KILL HIM.
THE FINAL BATTLE TO DECIDE THE KUONJI HEIR IS UPON US!
I WON'T ALLOW ANYONE TO INTERFERE!

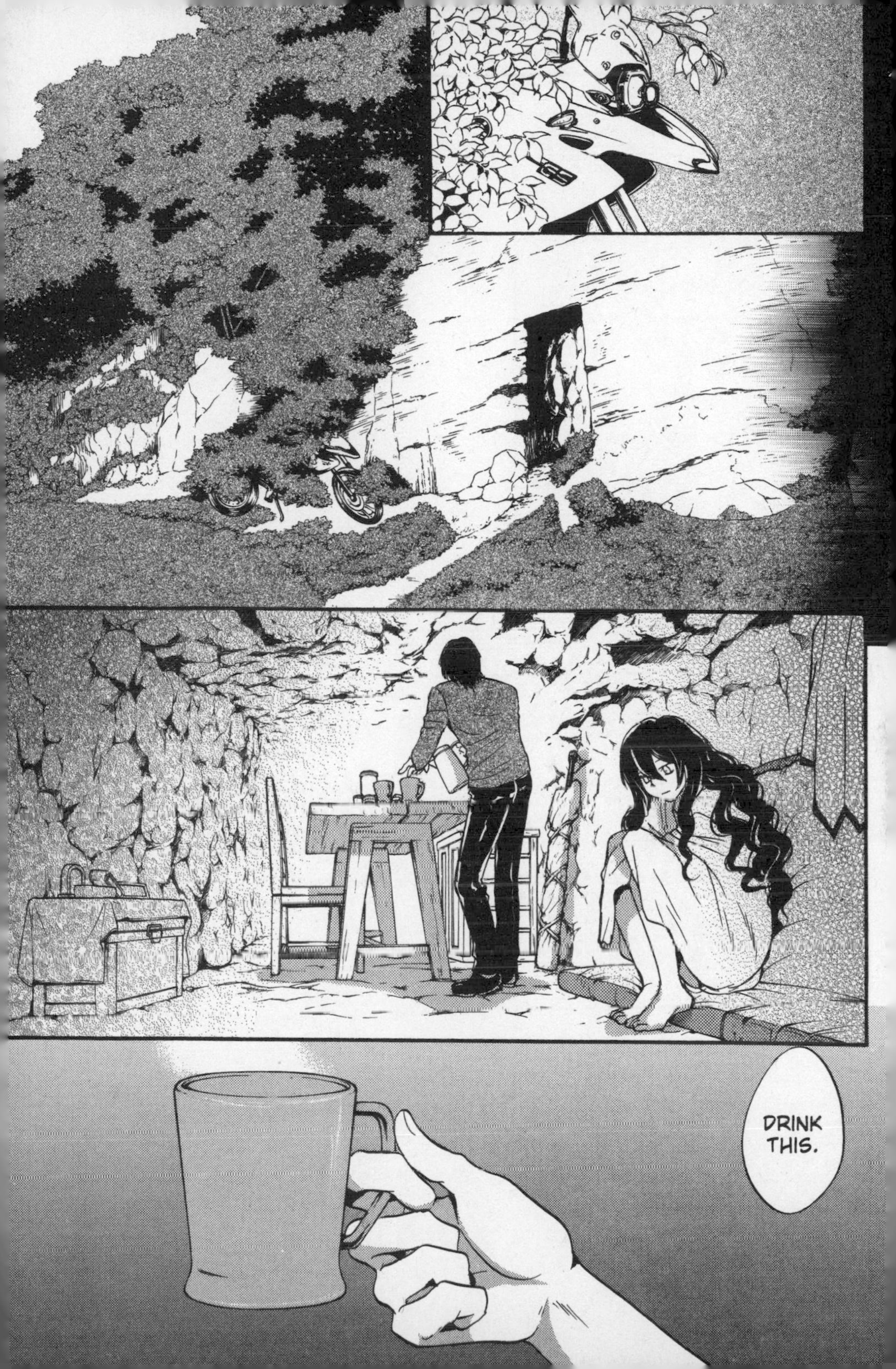
DRINK THIS.

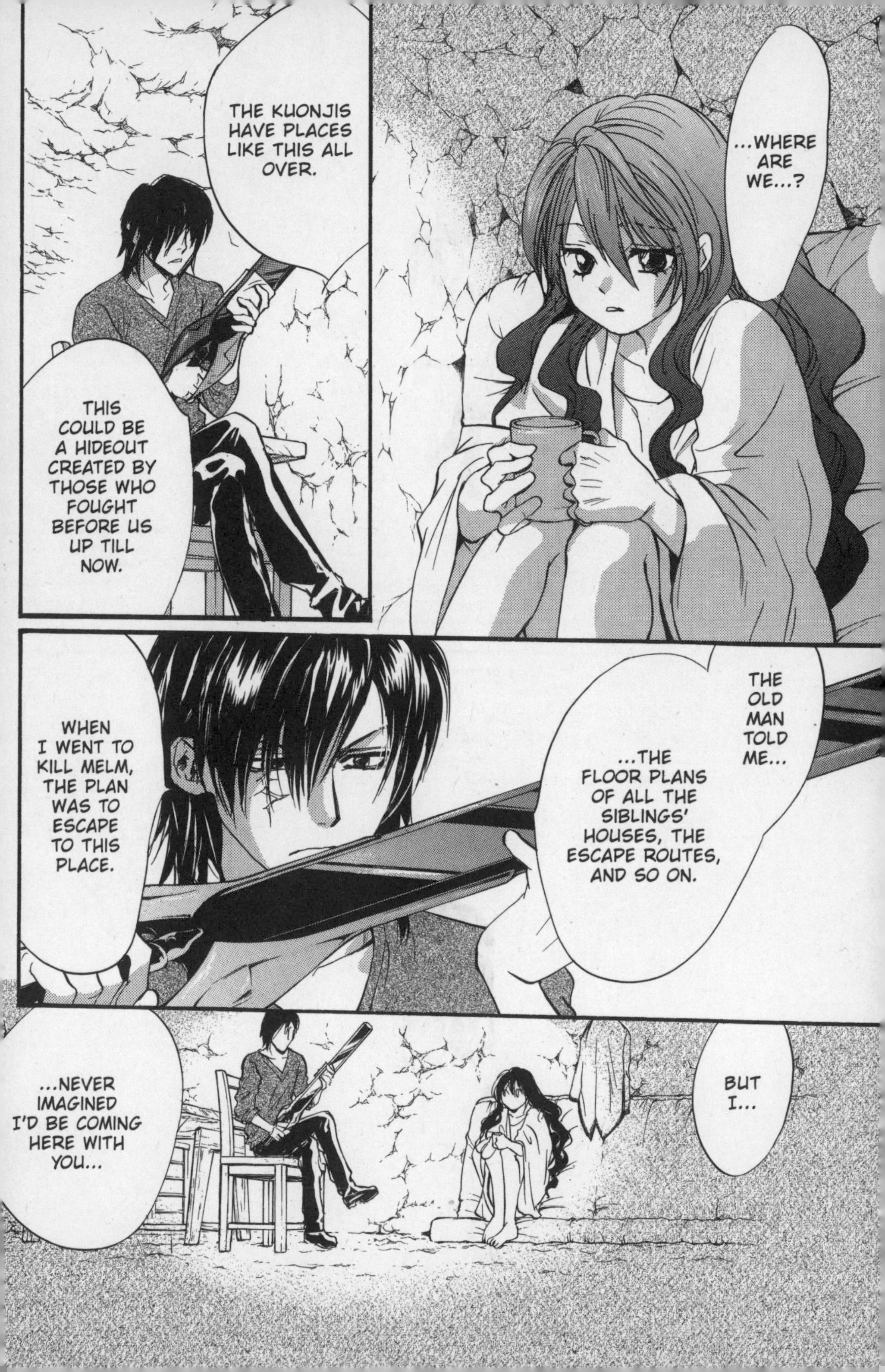
...WHERE ARE WE...?
THE KUONJIS HAVE PLACES LIKE THIS ALL OVER.
THIS COULD BE A HIDEOUT CREATED BY THOSE WHO FOUGHT BEFORE US UP TILL NOW.
THE OLD MAN TOLD ME...
...THE FLOOR PLANS OF ALL THE SIBLINGS' HOUSES, THE ESCAPE ROUTES, AND SO ON.
WHEN I WENT TO KILL MELM, THE PLAN WAS TO ESCAPE TO THIS PLACE.
BUT I...
...NEVER IMAGINED I'D BE COMING HERE WITH YOU...

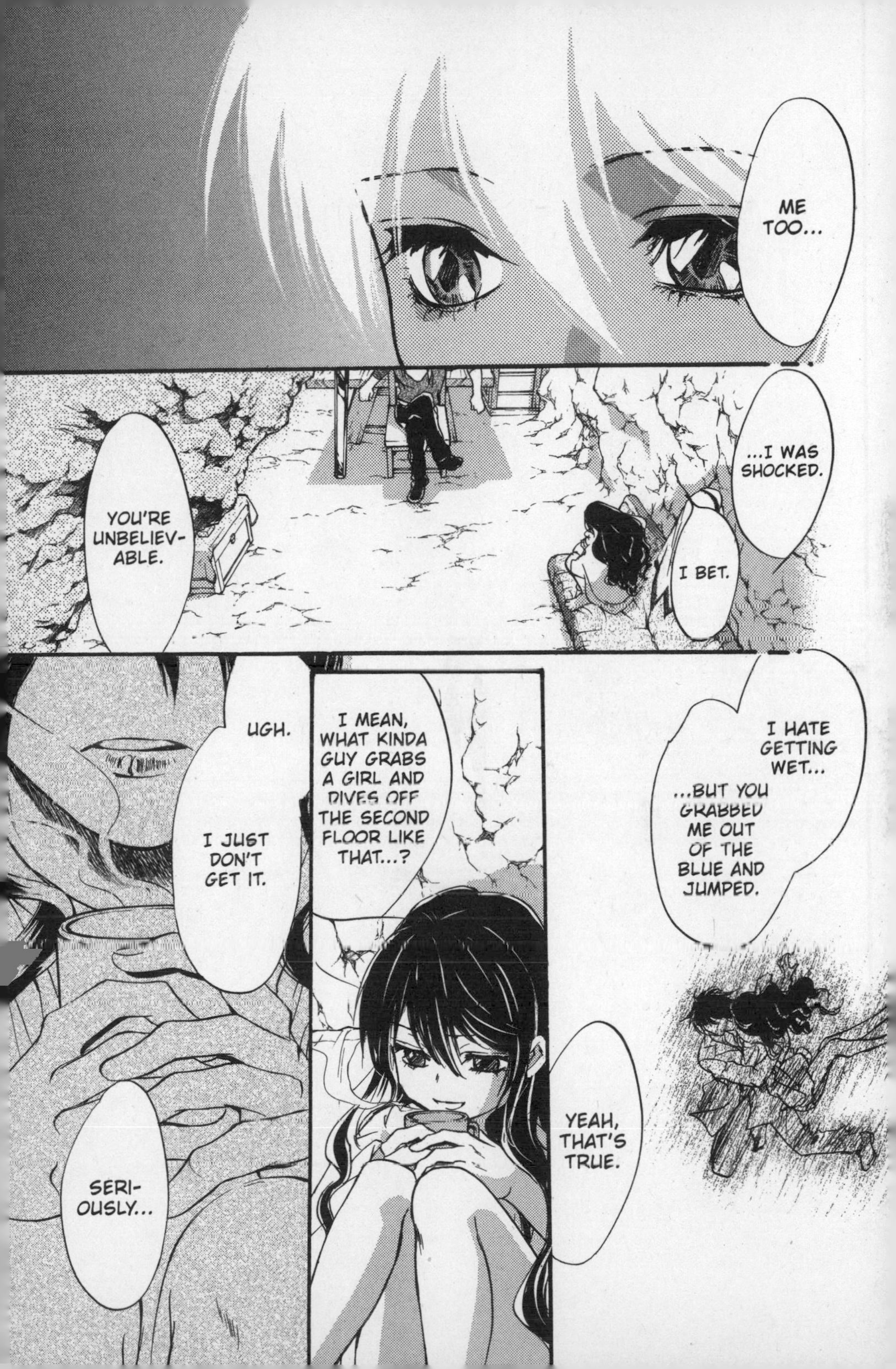
ME TOO...
...I WAS SHOCKED.
I BET.
YOU'RE UNBELIEVABLE.
I HATE GETTING WET...
...BUT YOU GRABBED ME OUT OF THE BLUE AND JUMPED.
I MEAN, WHAT KINDA GUY GRABS A GIRL AND DIVES OFF THE SECOND FLOOR LIKE THAT...?
YEAH, THAT'S TRUE.
UGH.
I JUST DON'T GET IT.
SERIOUSLY...

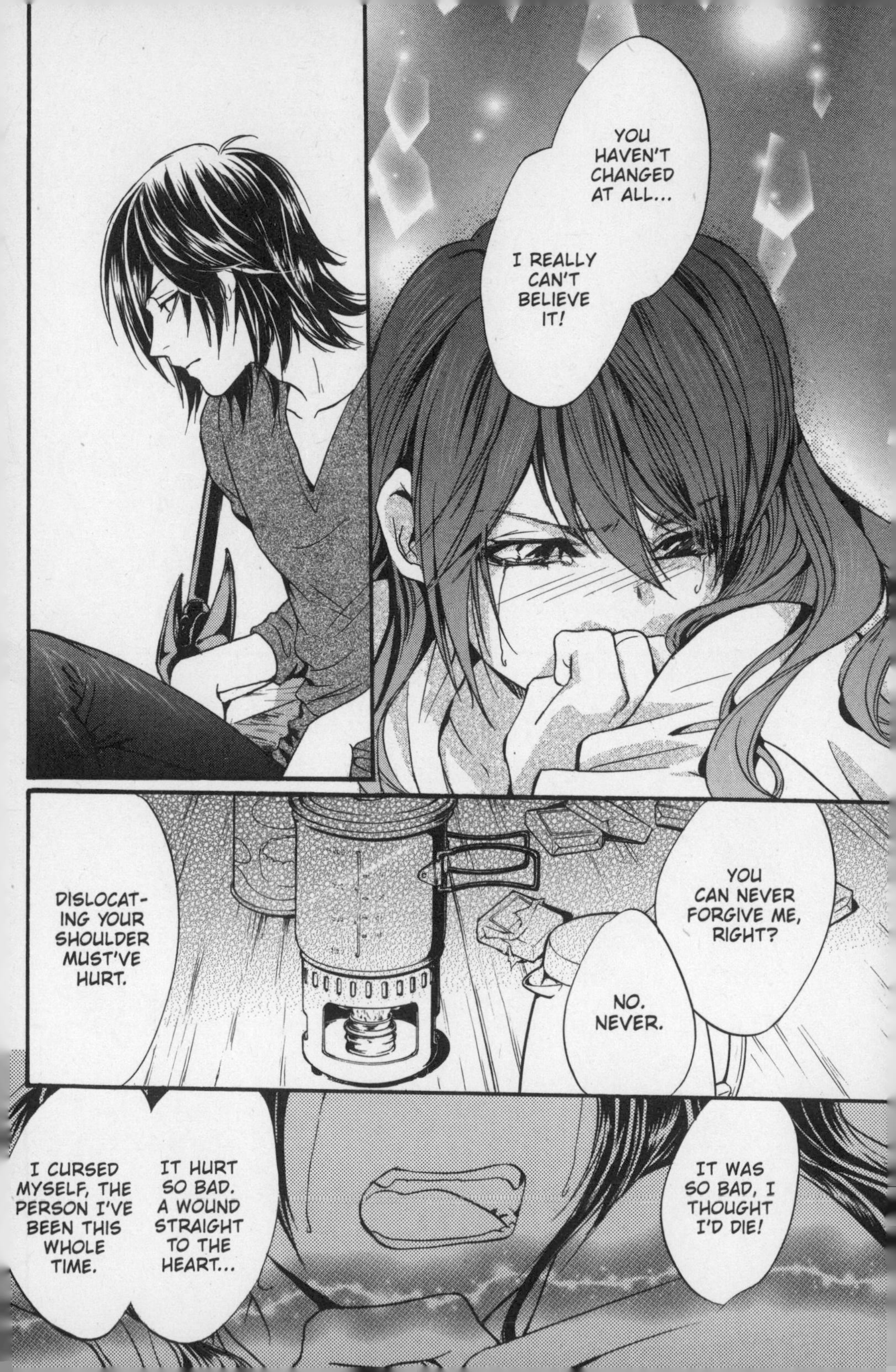
YOU HAVEN'T CHANGED AT ALL...
I REALLY CAN'T BELIEVE IT!
YOU CAN NEVER FORGIVE ME, RIGHT?
NO. NEVER.
DISLOCATING YOUR SHOULDER MUST'VE HURT.
IT WAS SO BAD, I THOUGHT I'D DIE!
IT HURT SO BAD. A WOUND STRAIGHT TO THE HEART...
I CURSED MYSELF, THE PERSON I'VE BEEN THIS WHOLE TIME.

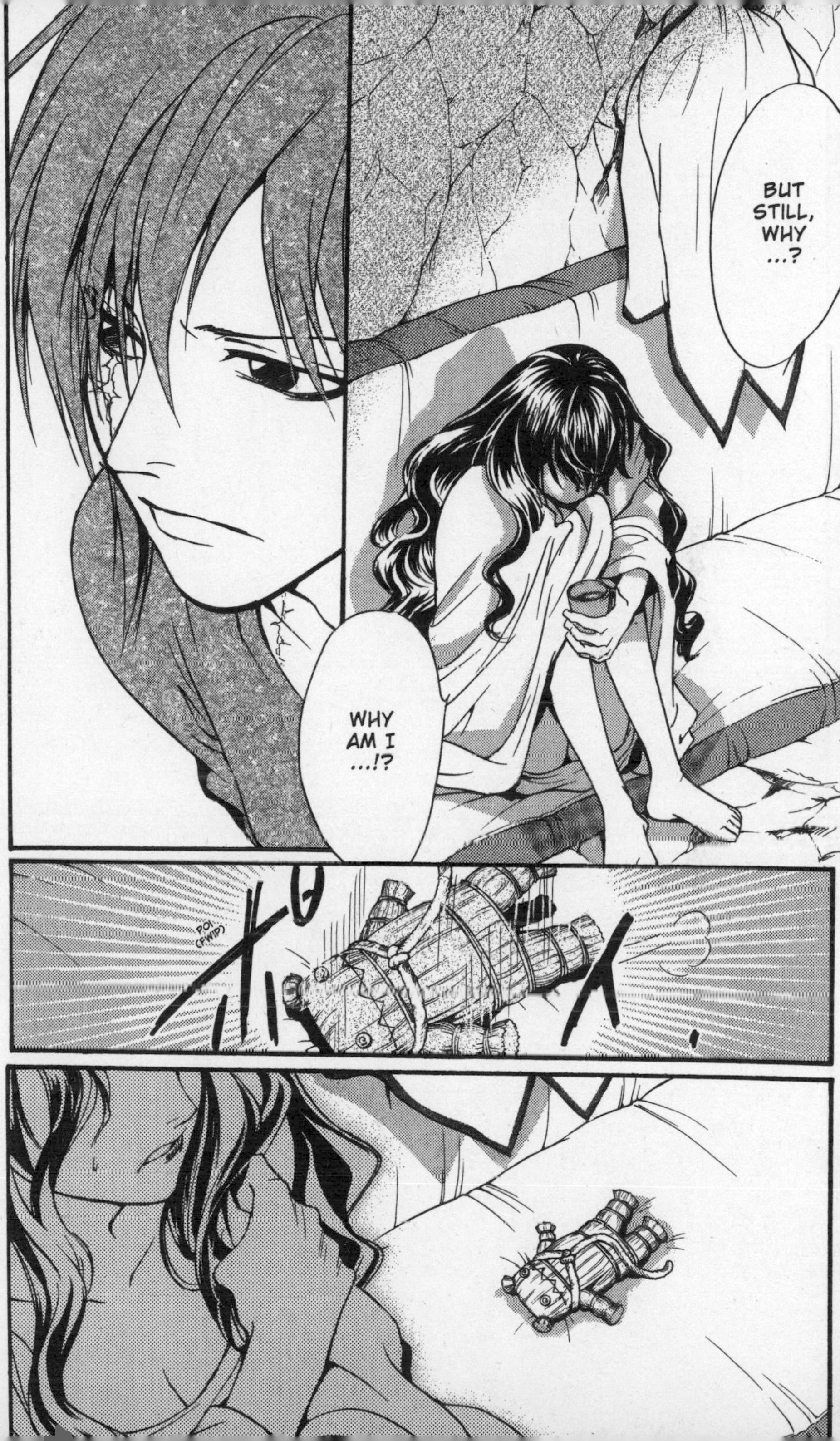
BUT STILL, WHY ...?
WHY AM I ...!?
POI (FWIP)

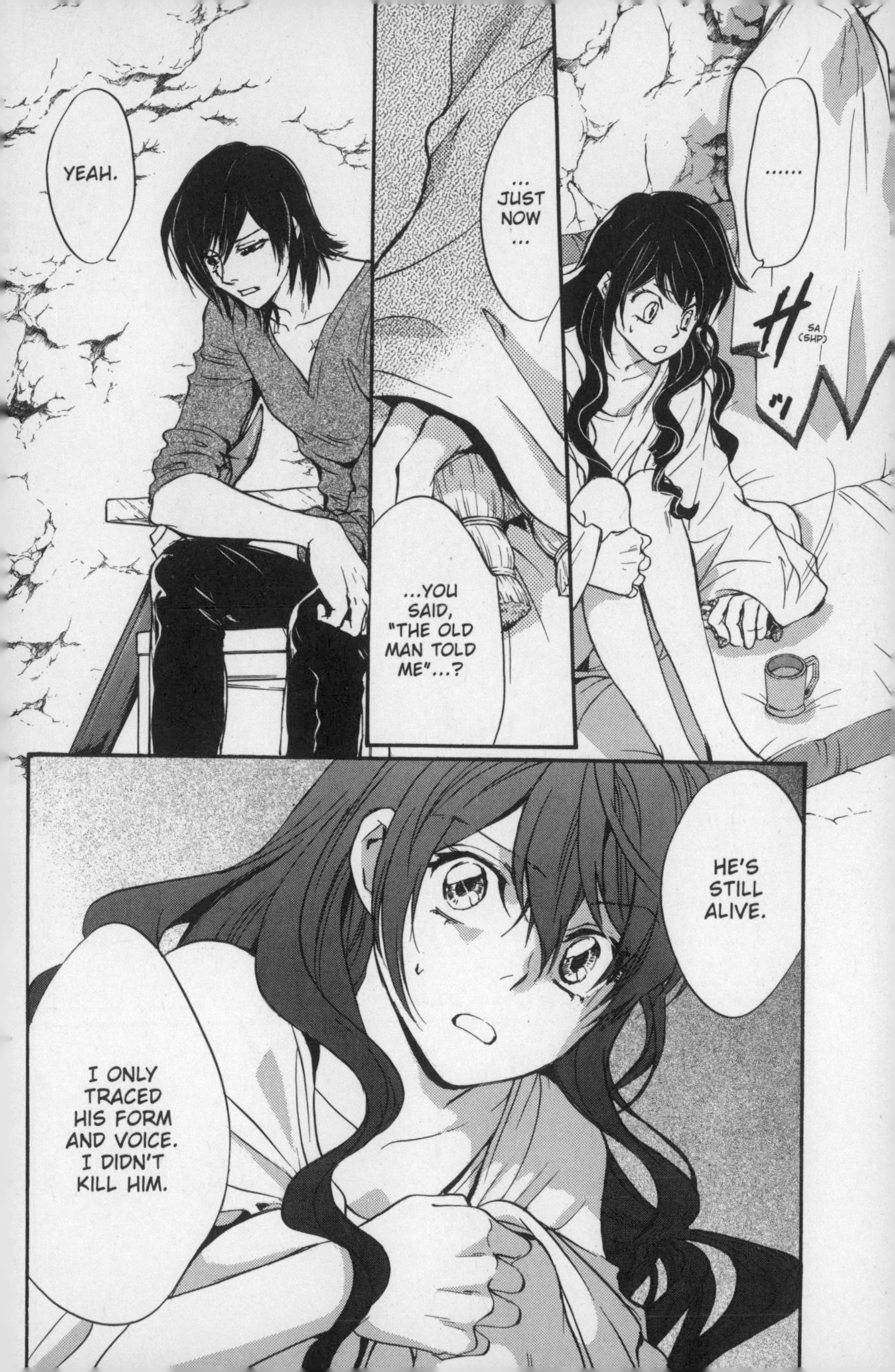
......
SA (SHP)
... JUST NOW ...
...YOU SAID, "THE OLD MAN TOLD ME"...?
YEAH.
HE'S STILL ALIVE.
I ONLY TRACED HIS FORM AND VOICE. I DIDN'T KILL HIM.

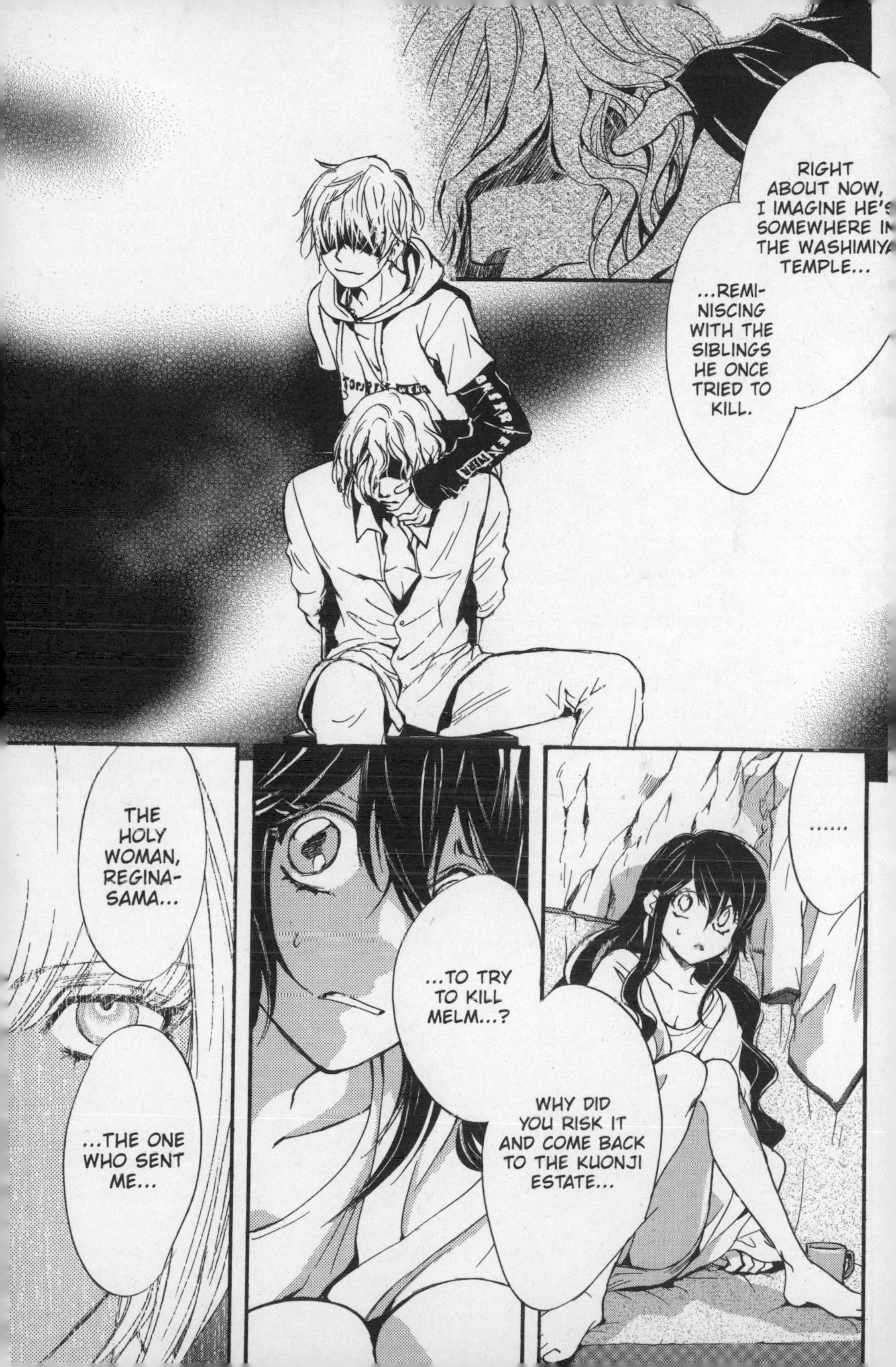
RIGHT ABOUT NOW, I IMAGINE HE'S SOMEWHERE IN THE WASHIMIYA TEMPLE...
...REMINISCING WITH THE SIBLINGS HE ONCE TRIED TO KILL.
......
WHY DID YOU RISK IT AND COME BACK TO THE KUONJI ESTATE...
...TO TRY TO KILL MELM...?
THE HOLY WOMAN, REGINA-SAMA...
...THE ONE WHO SENT ME...

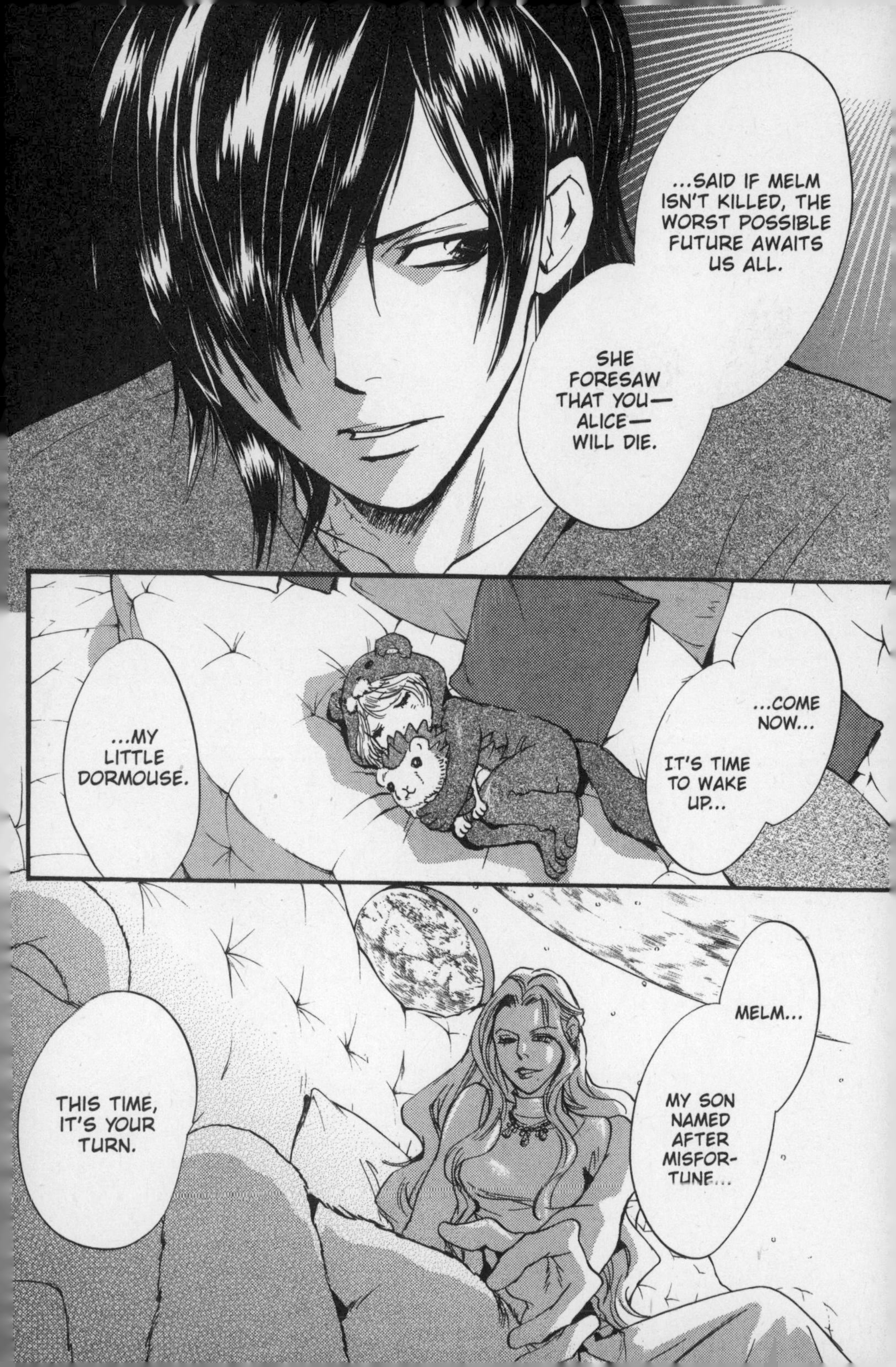
...SAID IF MELM ISN'T KILLED, THE WORST POSSIBLE FUTURE AWAITS US ALL.
SHE FORESAW THAT YOU—ALICE—WILL DIE.
...COME NOW...
IT'S TIME TO WAKE UP...
...MY LITTLE DORMOUSE.
MELM...
MY SON NAMED AFTER MISFOR-TUNE...
THIS TIME, IT'S YOUR TURN.

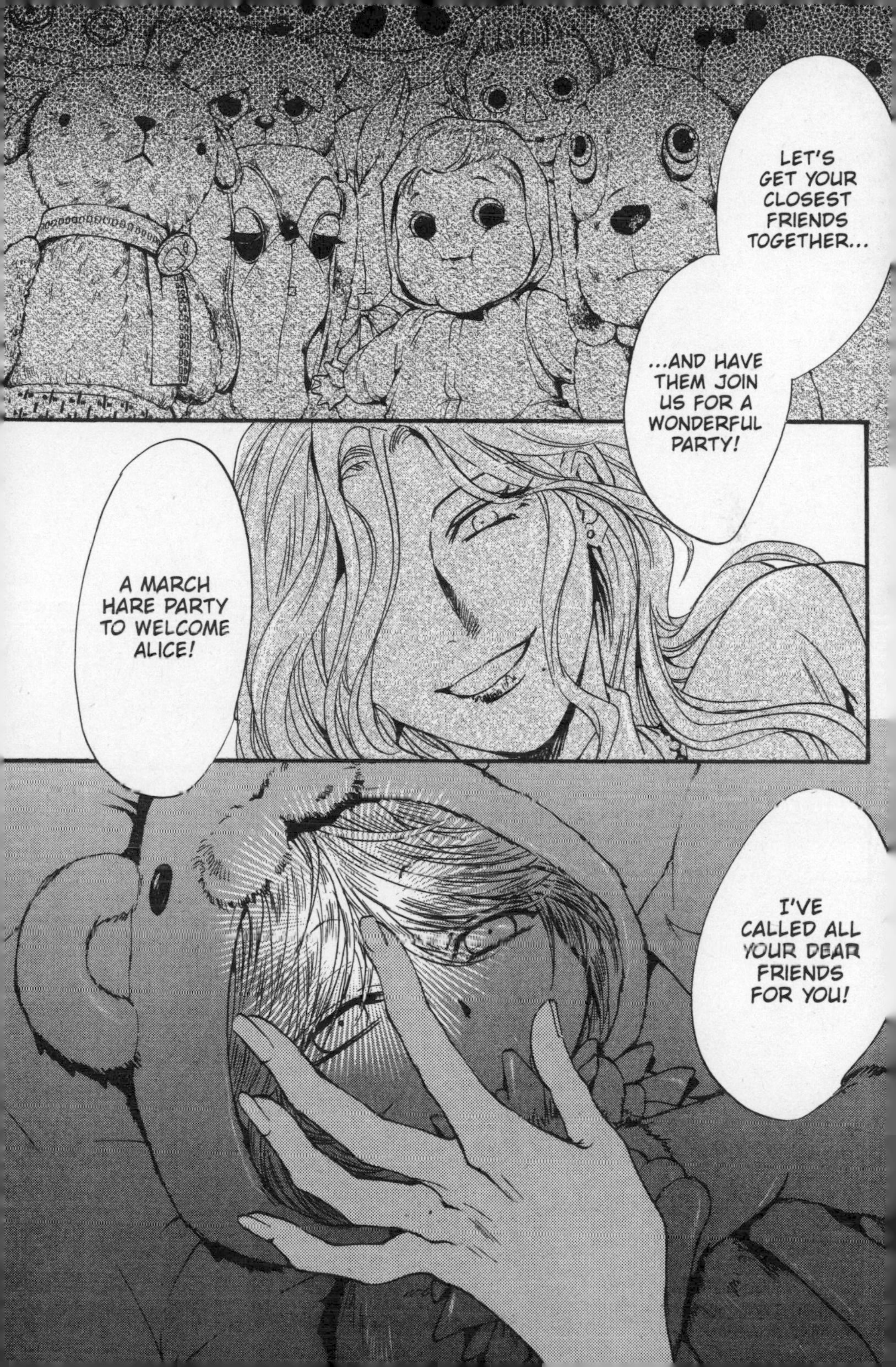
LET'S GET YOUR CLOSEST FRIENDS TOGETHER...
...AND HAVE THEM JOIN US FOR A WONDERFUL PARTY!
A MARCH HARE PARTY TO WELCOME ALICE!
I'VE CALLED ALL YOUR DEAR FRIENDS FOR YOU!

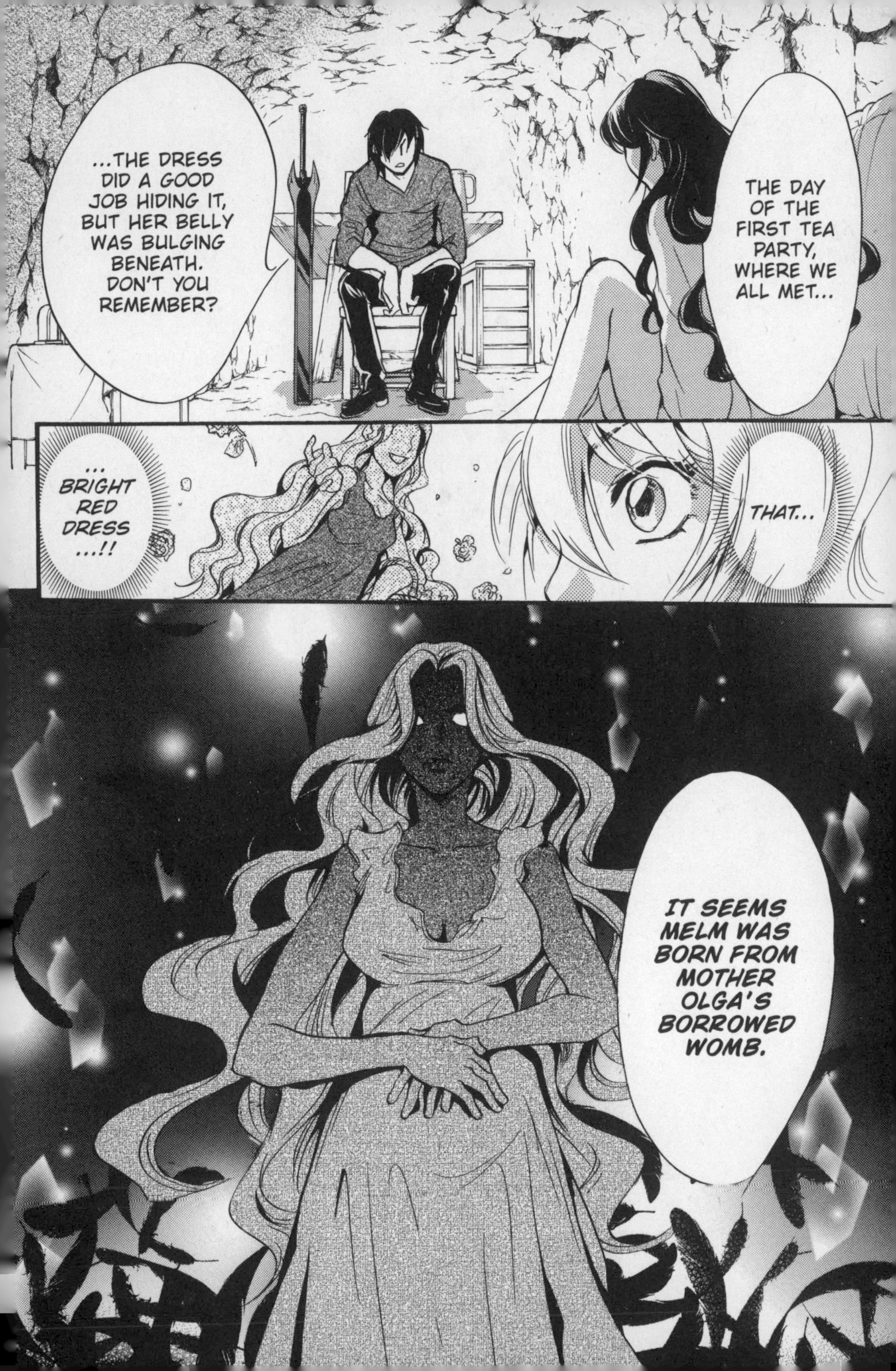
THE DAY OF THE FIRST TEA PARTY, WHERE WE ALL MET...
...THE DRESS DID A GOOD JOB HIDING IT, BUT HER BELLY WAS BULGING BENEATH. DON'T YOU REMEMBER?
THAT...
...BRIGHT RED DRESS...!!
IT SEEMS MELM WAS BORN FROM MOTHER OLGA'S BORROWED WOMB.

Alice
in
MURDERLAND

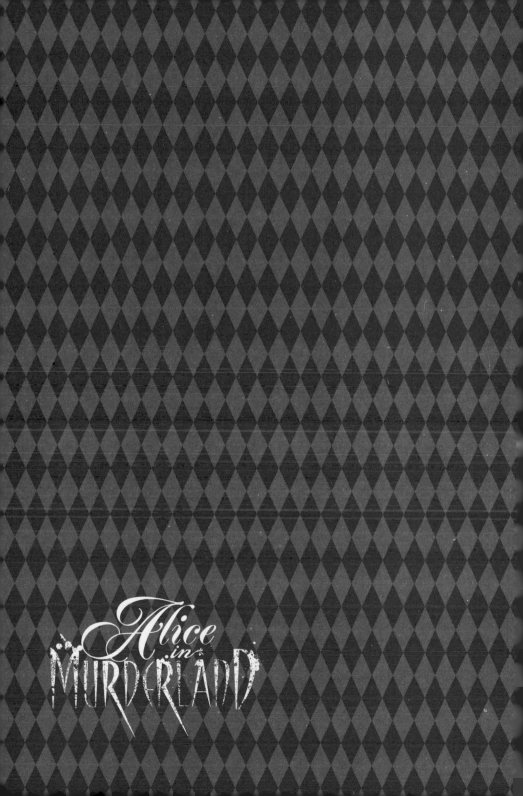

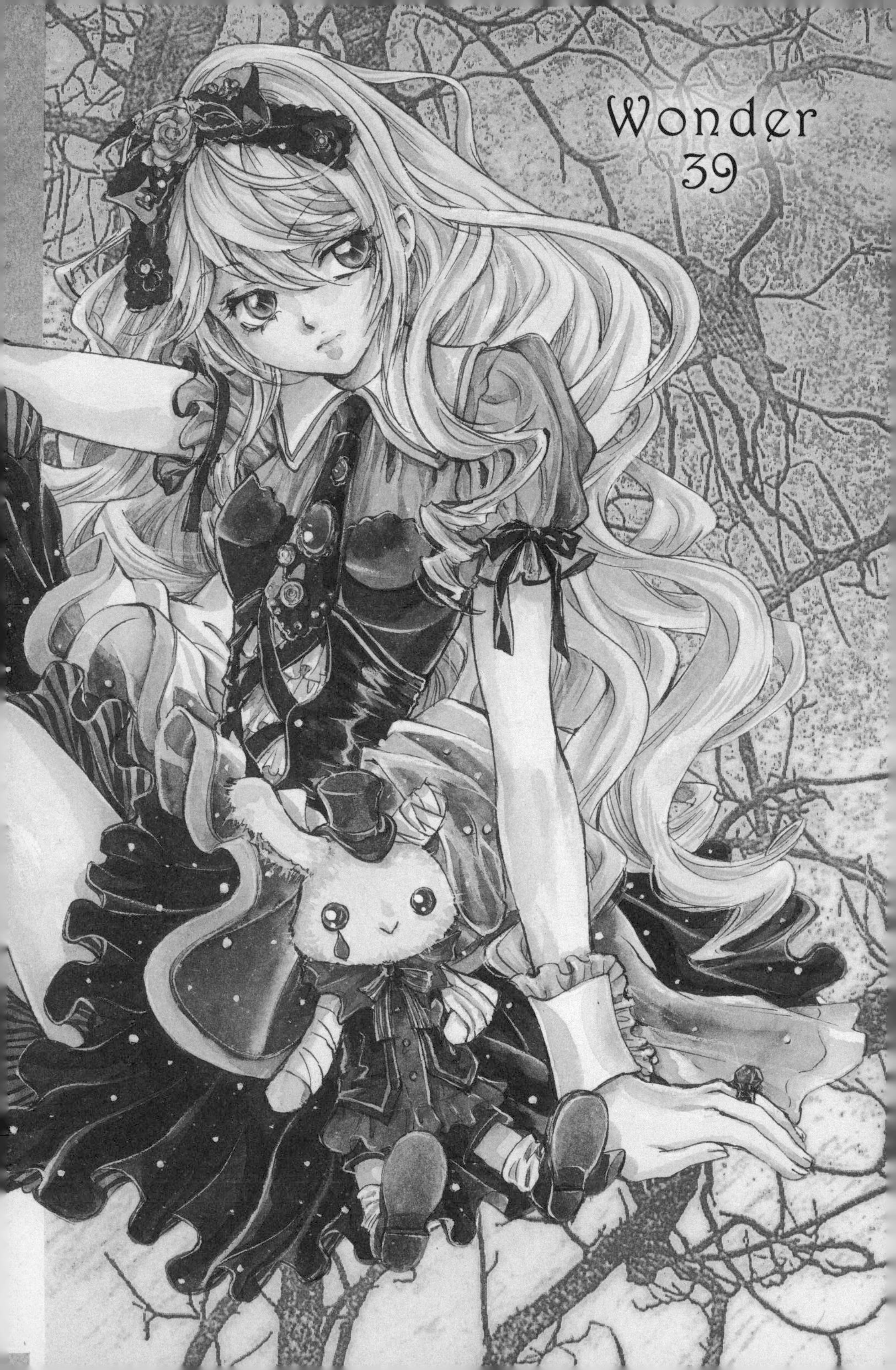
Wonder
39

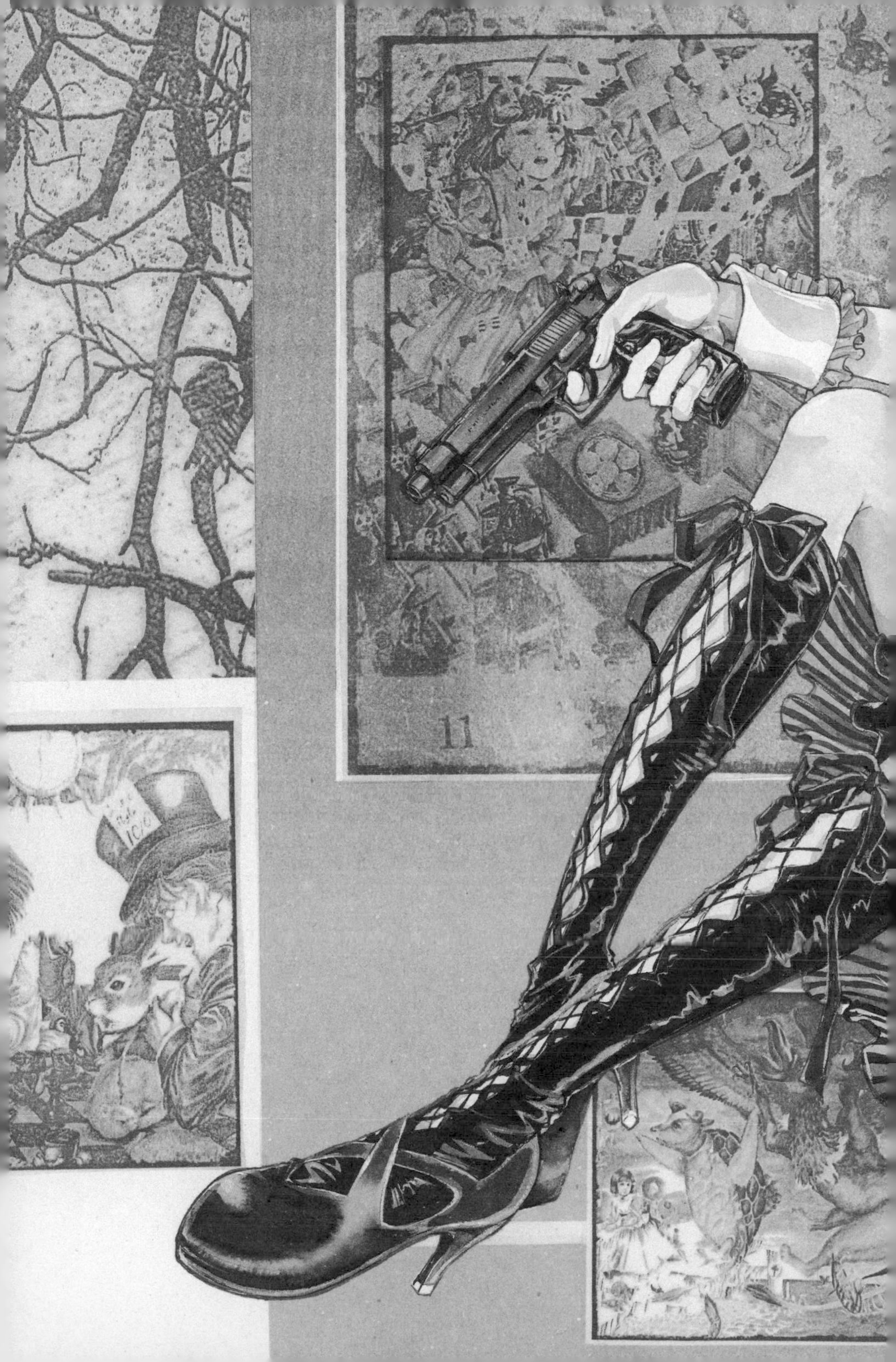
11

Alice in MURDERLAND

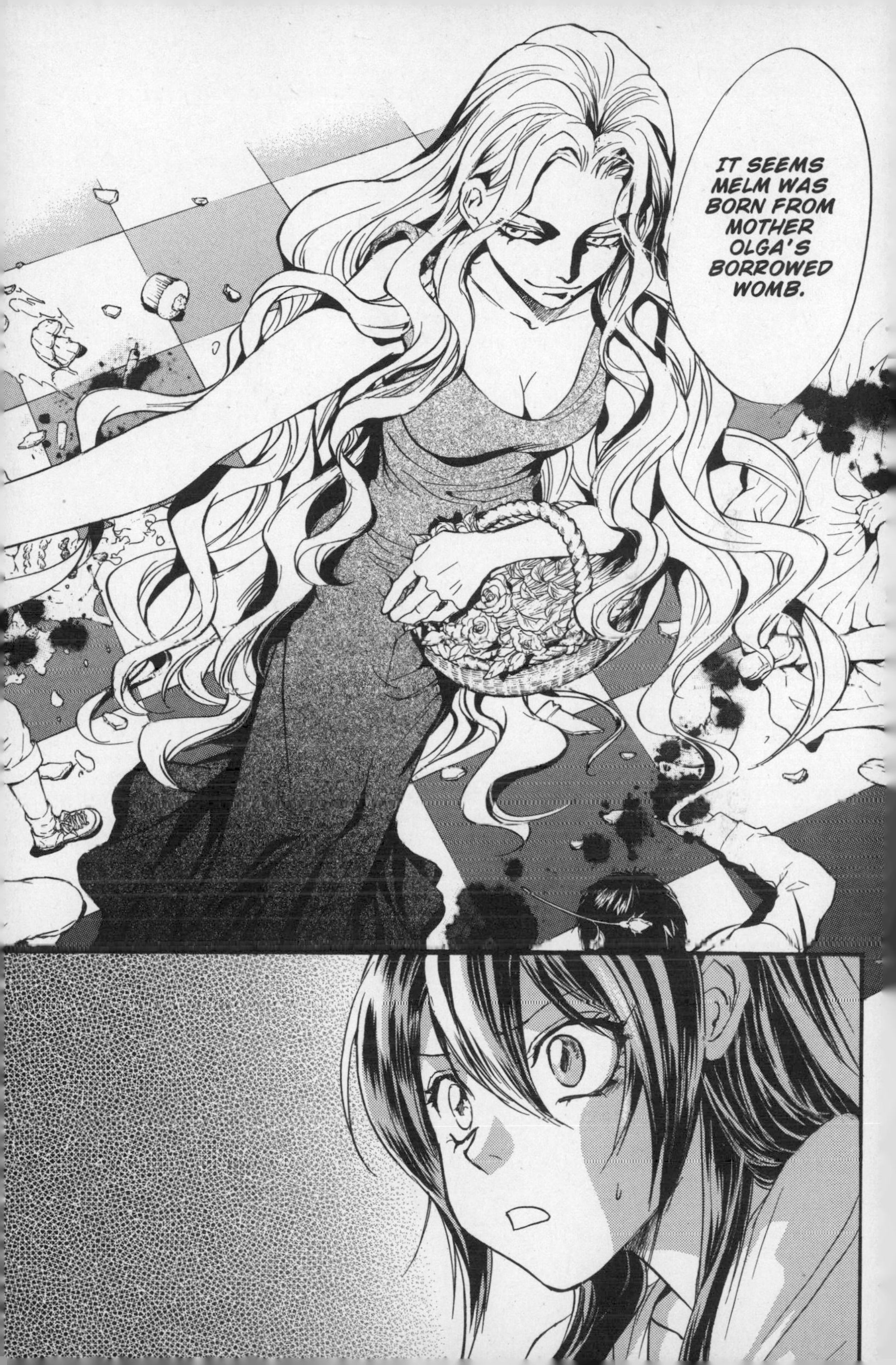
IT SEEMS MELM WAS BORN FROM MOTHER OLGA'S BORROWED WOMB.

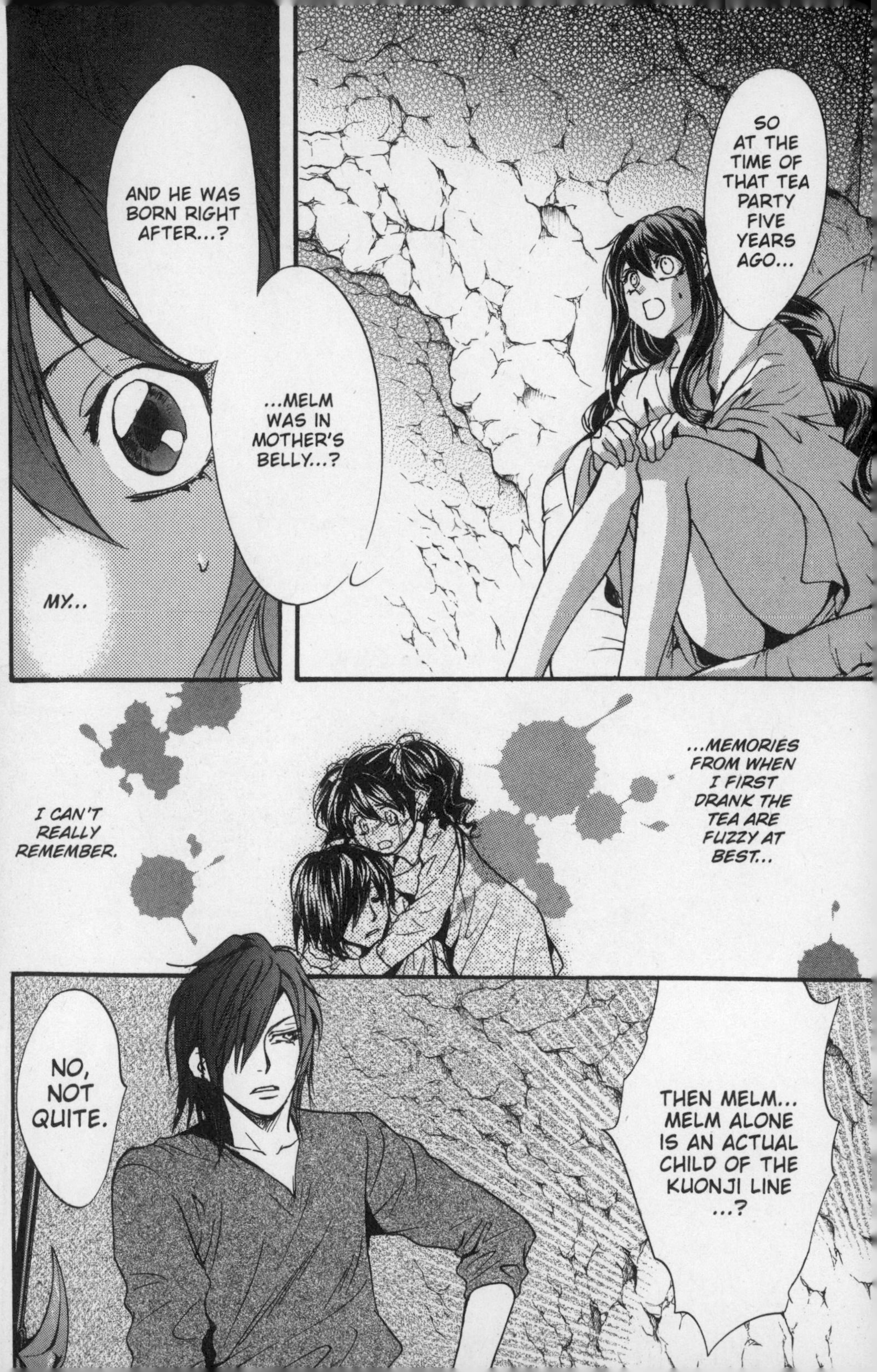
SO AT THE TIME OF THAT TEA PARTY FIVE YEARS AGO...
...MELM WAS IN MOTHER'S BELLY...?
AND HE WAS BORN RIGHT AFTER...?
MY...
...MEMORIES FROM WHEN I FIRST DRANK THE TEA ARE FUZZY AT BEST...
I CAN'T REALLY REMEMBER.
THEN MELM... MELM ALONE IS AN ACTUAL CHILD OF THE KUONJI LINE ...?
NO, NOT QUITE.

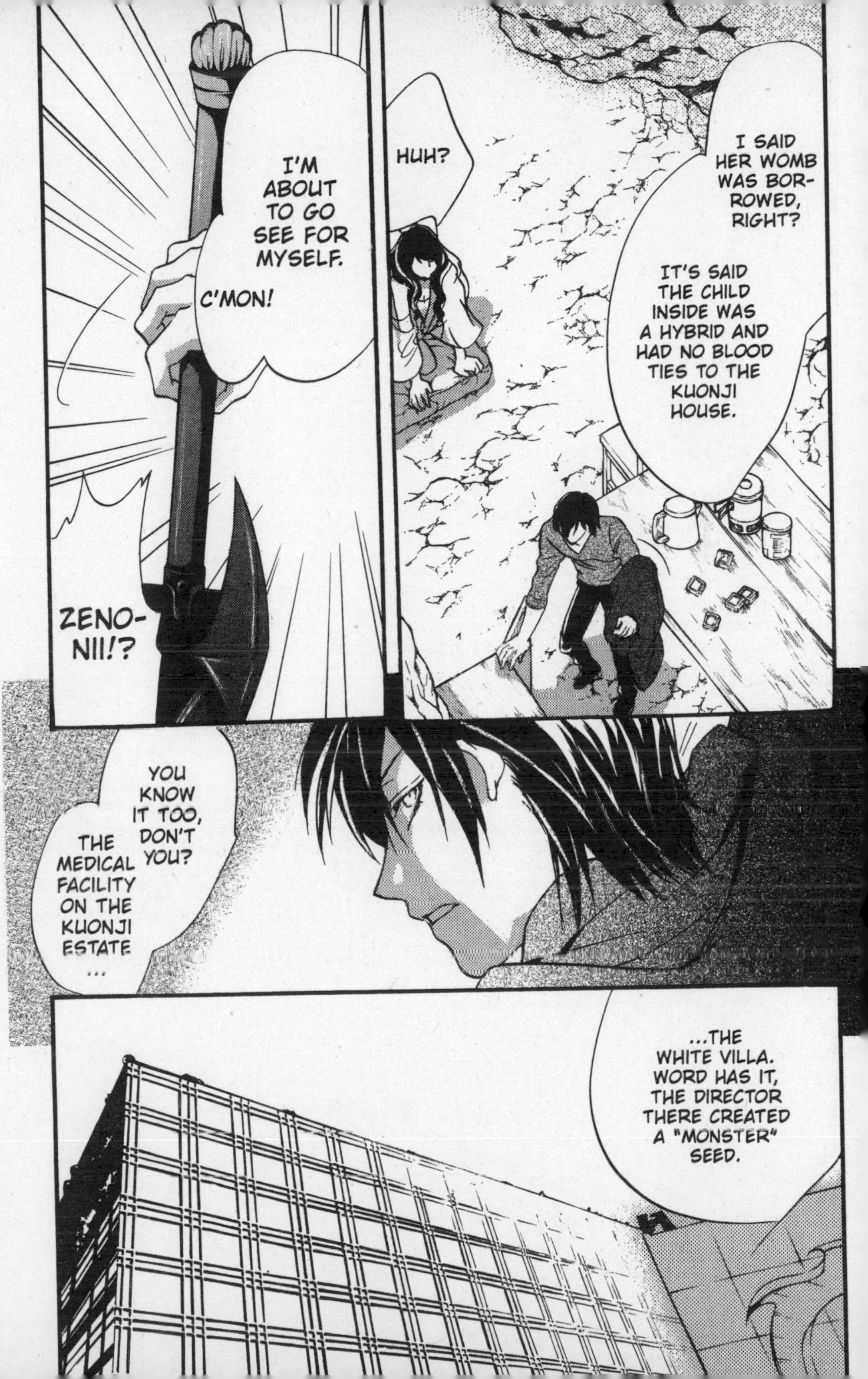
I SAID HER WOMB WAS BOR-ROWED, RIGHT?
IT'S SAID THE CHILD INSIDE WAS A HYBRID AND HAD NO BLOOD TIES TO THE KUONJI HOUSE.
HUH?
I'M ABOUT TO GO SEE FOR MYSELF.
C'MON!
ZENO-NII!?
YOU KNOW IT TOO, DON'T YOU?
THE MEDICAL FACILITY ON THE KUONJI ESTATE ...
...THE WHITE VILLA. WORD HAS IT, THE DIRECTOR THERE CREATED A "MONSTER" SEED.

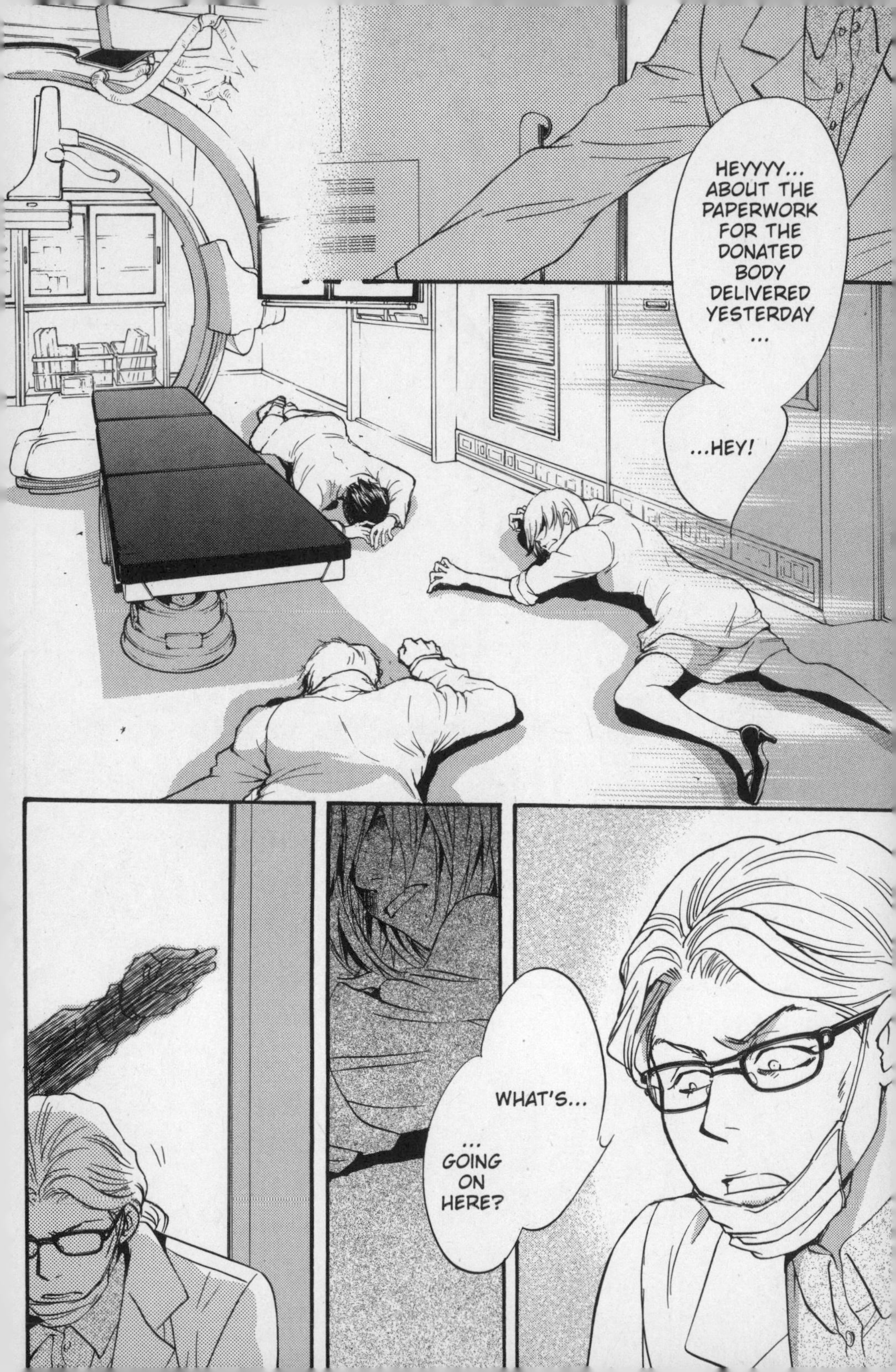

HEYYYY... ABOUT THE PAPERWORK FOR THE DONATED BODY DELIVERED YESTERDAY ...
...HEY!
WHAT'S...
... GOING ON HERE?

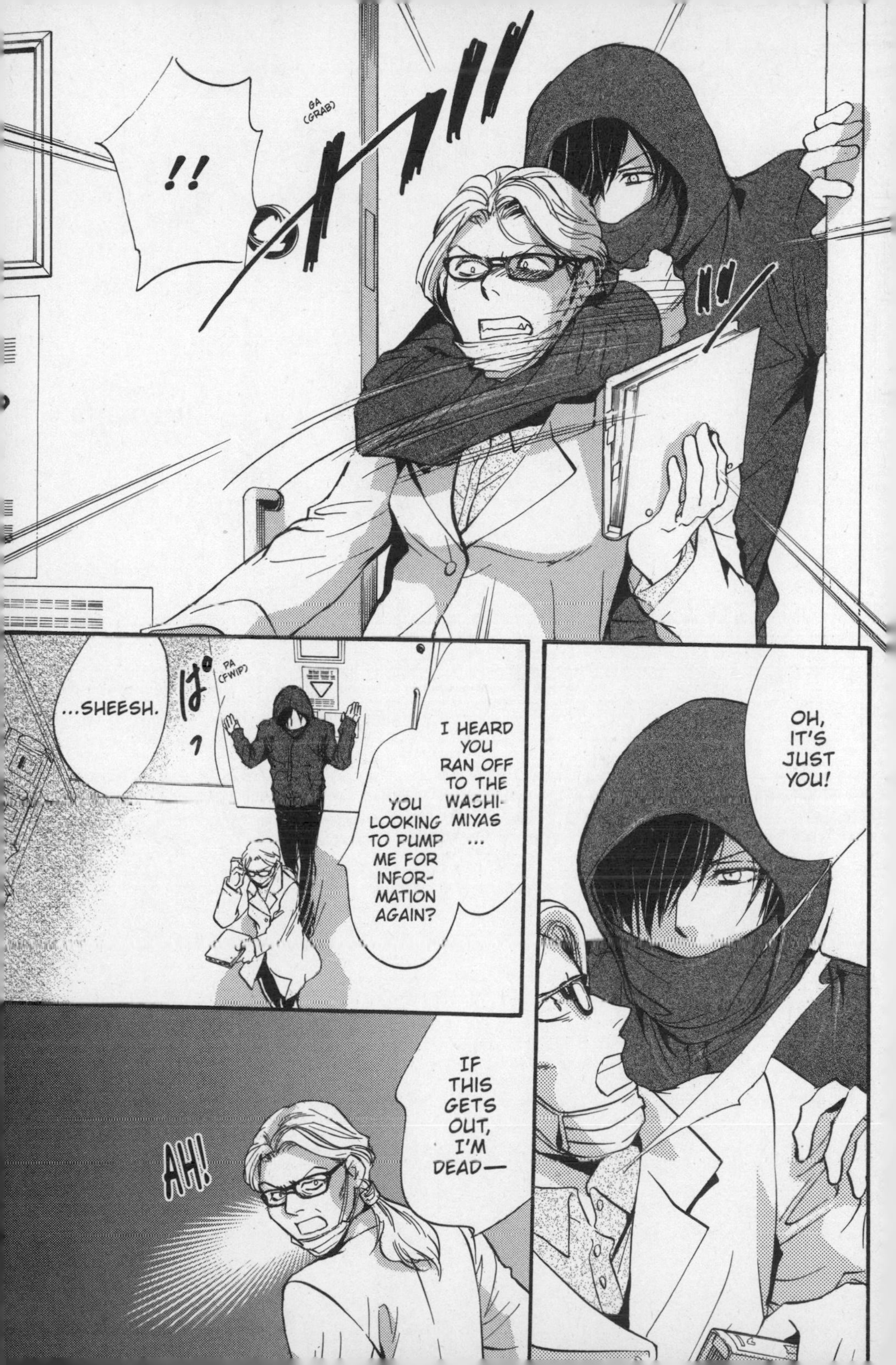
GA (GRAB)
!!
OH, IT'S JUST YOU!
I HEARD YOU RAN OFF TO THE WASHIMIYAS...
YOU LOOKING TO PUMP ME FOR INFORMATION AGAIN?
PA (FWIP)
...SHEESH.
IF THIS GETS OUT, I'M DEAD—
AH!

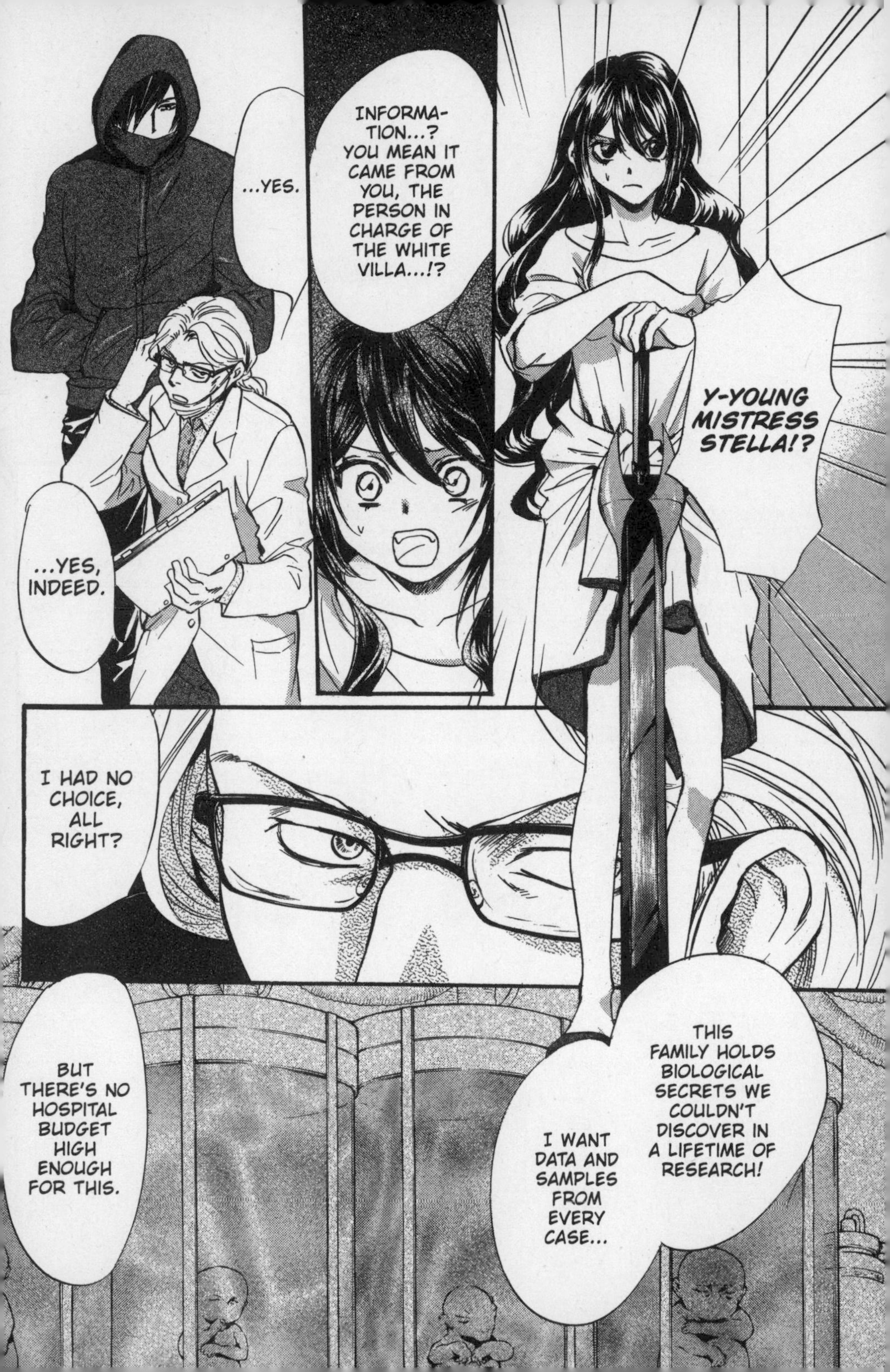
Y-YOUNG MISTRESS STELLA!?
INFORMATION...? YOU MEAN IT CAME FROM YOU, THE PERSON IN CHARGE OF THE WHITE VILLA...!?
...YES.
...YES, INDEED.
I HAD NO CHOICE, ALL RIGHT?
THIS FAMILY HOLDS BIOLOGICAL SECRETS WE COULDN'T DISCOVER IN A LIFETIME OF RESEARCH!
I WANT DATA AND SAMPLES FROM EVERY CASE...
BUT THERE'S NO HOSPITAL BUDGET HIGH ENOUGH FOR THIS.

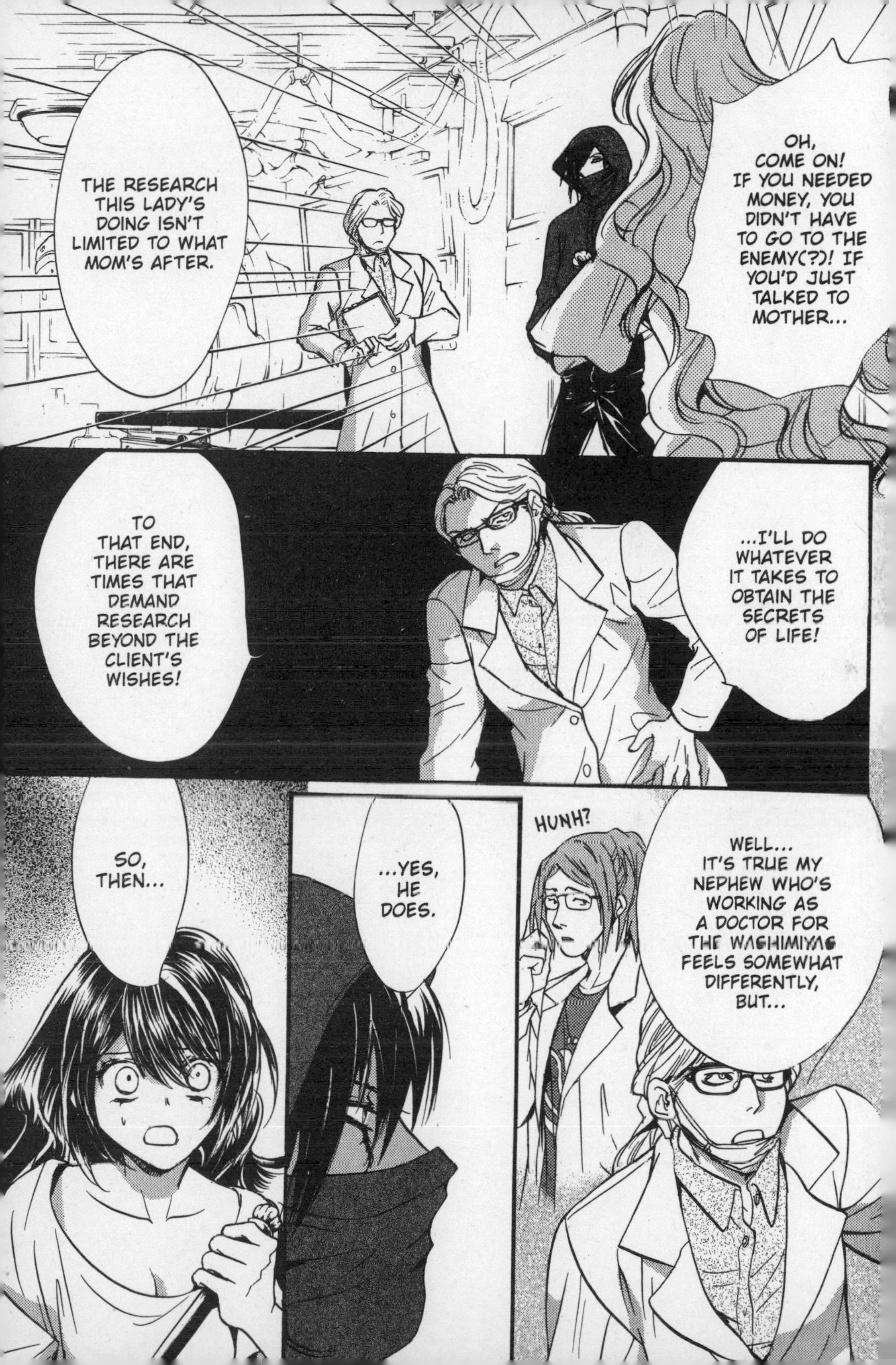
OH, COME ON! IF YOU NEEDED MONEY, YOU DIDN'T HAVE TO GO TO THE ENEMY(?)! IF YOU'D JUST TALKED TO MOTHER...
THE RESEARCH THIS LADY'S DOING ISN'T LIMITED TO WHAT MOM'S AFTER.
...I'LL DO WHATEVER IT TAKES TO OBTAIN THE SECRETS OF LIFE!
TO THAT END, THERE ARE TIMES THAT DEMAND RESEARCH BEYOND THE CLIENT'S WISHES!
HUNH?
WELL... IT'S TRUE MY NEPHEW WHO'S WORKING AS A DOCTOR FOR THE WASHIMIYAS FEELS SOMEWHAT DIFFERENTLY, BUT...
...YES, HE DOES.
SO, THEN...

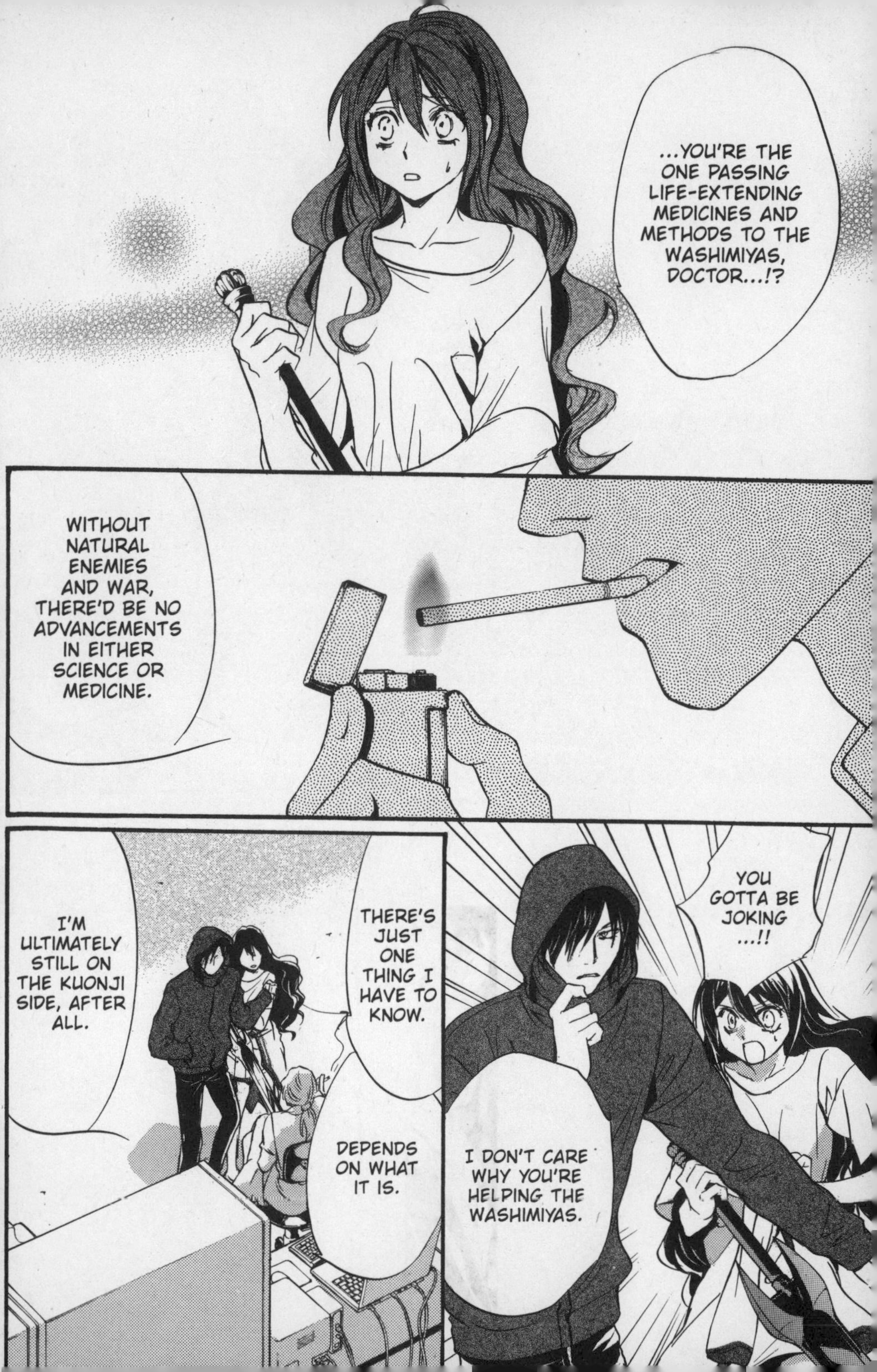
...YOU'RE THE ONE PASSING LIFE-EXTENDING MEDICINES AND METHODS TO THE WASHIMIYAS, DOCTOR...!?
WITHOUT NATURAL ENEMIES AND WAR, THERE'D BE NO ADVANCEMENTS IN EITHER SCIENCE OR MEDICINE.
YOU GOTTA BE JOKING...!!
I DON'T CARE WHY YOU'RE HELPING THE WASHIMIYAS.
THERE'S JUST ONE THING I HAVE TO KNOW.
DEPENDS ON WHAT IT IS.
I'M ULTIMATELY STILL ON THE KUONJI SIDE, AFTER ALL.

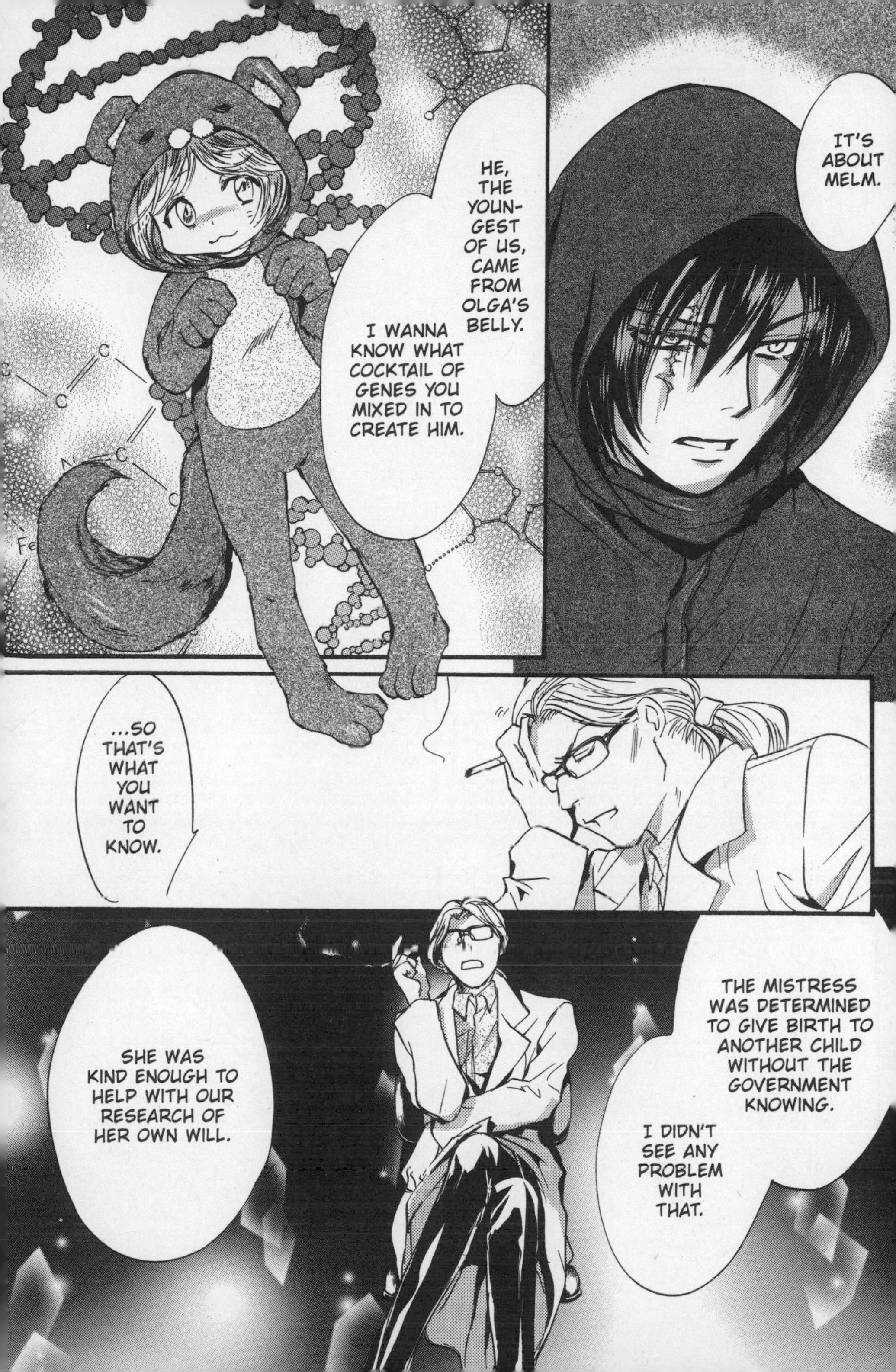
IT'S ABOUT MELM.
HE, THE YOUNGEST OF US, CAME FROM OLGA'S BELLY.
I WANNA KNOW WHAT COCKTAIL OF GENES YOU MIXED IN TO CREATE HIM.
...SO THAT'S WHAT YOU WANT TO KNOW.
THE MISTRESS WAS DETERMINED TO GIVE BIRTH TO ANOTHER CHILD WITHOUT THE GOVERNMENT KNOWING.
I DIDN'T SEE ANY PROBLEM WITH THAT.
SHE WAS KIND ENOUGH TO HELP WITH OUR RESEARCH OF HER OWN WILL.

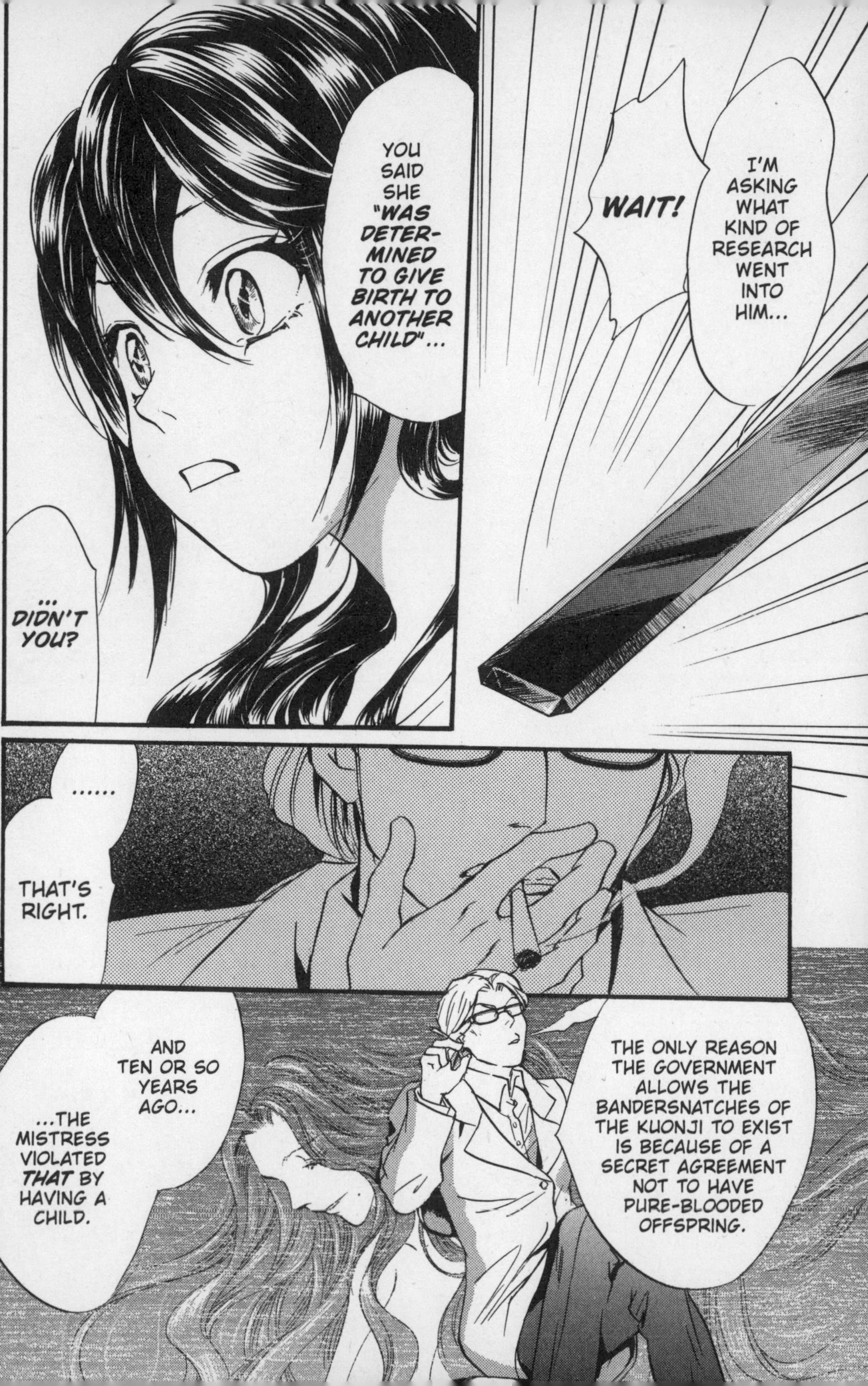
I'M ASKING WHAT KIND OF RESEARCH WENT INTO HIM...
WAIT!
YOU SAID SHE "WAS DETERMINED TO GIVE BIRTH TO ANOTHER CHILD"...
...DIDN'T YOU?
......
THAT'S RIGHT.
THE ONLY REASON THE GOVERNMENT ALLOWS THE BANDERSNATCHES OF THE KUONJI TO EXIST IS BECAUSE OF A SECRET AGREEMENT NOT TO HAVE PURE-BLOODED OFFSPRING.
AND TEN OR SO YEARS AGO...
...THE MISTRESS VIOLATED THAT BY HAVING A CHILD.

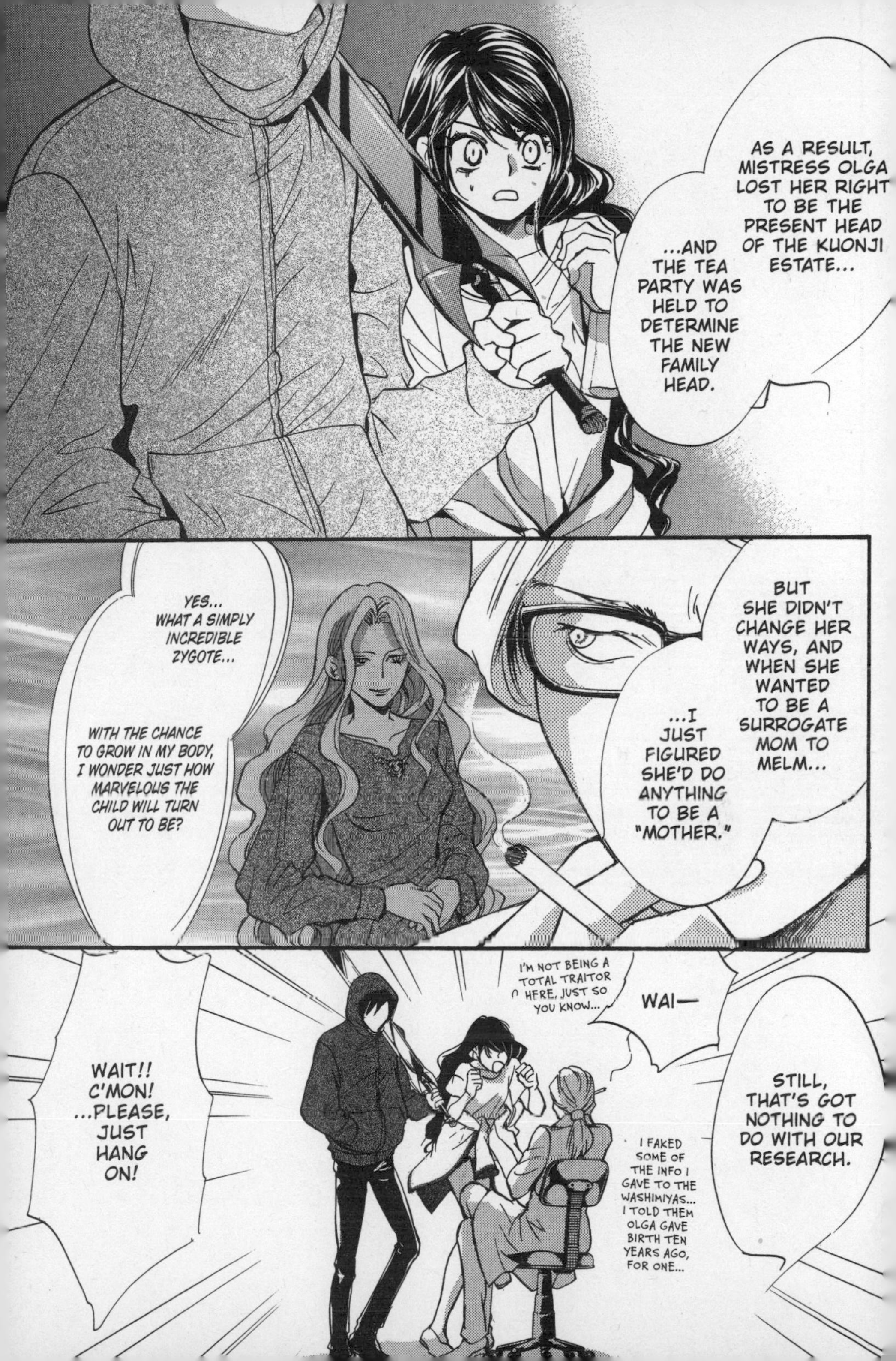
AS A RESULT, MISTRESS OLGA LOST HER RIGHT TO BE THE PRESENT HEAD OF THE KUONJI ESTATE...
...AND THE TEA PARTY WAS HELD TO DETERMINE THE NEW FAMILY HEAD.
BUT SHE DIDN'T CHANGE HER WAYS, AND WHEN SHE WANTED TO BE A SURROGATE MOM TO MELM...
...I JUST FIGURED SHE'D DO ANYTHING TO BE A "MOTHER."
YES... WHAT A SIMPLY INCREDIBLE ZYGOTE...
WITH THE CHANCE TO GROW IN MY BODY, I WONDER JUST HOW MARVELOUS THE CHILD WILL TURN OUT TO BE?
STILL, THAT'S GOT NOTHING TO DO WITH OUR RESEARCH.
WAI—
I'M NOT BEING A TOTAL TRAITOR HERE, JUST SO YOU KNOW...
I FAKED SOME OF THE INFO I GAVE TO THE WASHIMIYAS... I TOLD THEM OLGA GAVE BIRTH TEN YEARS AGO, FOR ONE...
WAIT!! C'MON! ...PLEASE, JUST HANG ON!

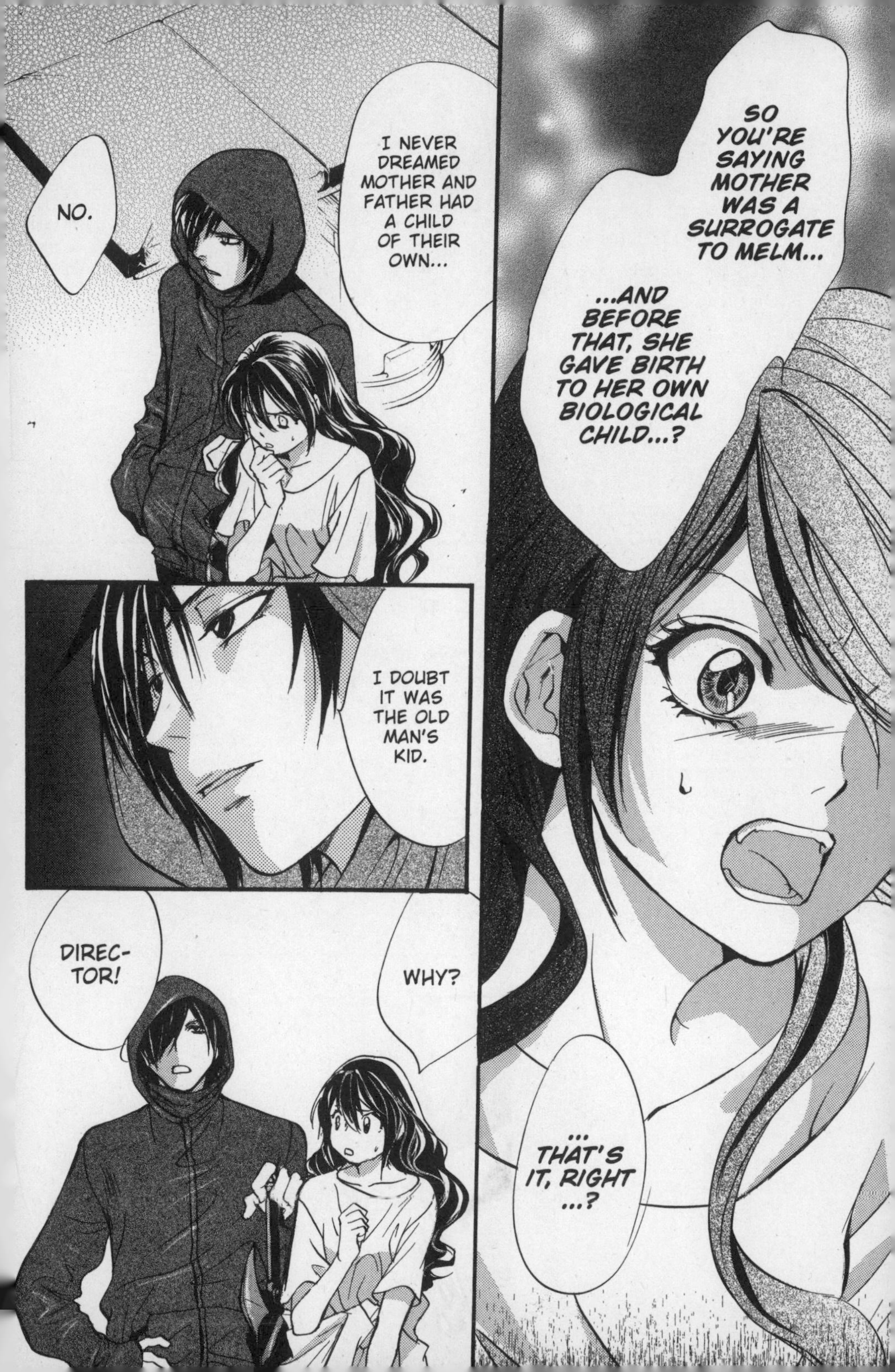
SO YOU'RE SAYING MOTHER WAS A SURROGATE TO MELM...
...AND BEFORE THAT, SHE GAVE BIRTH TO HER OWN BIOLOGICAL CHILD...?
...THAT'S IT, RIGHT...?
I NEVER DREAMED MOTHER AND FATHER HAD A CHILD OF THEIR OWN...
NO.
I DOUBT IT WAS THE OLD MAN'S KID.
WHY?
DIRECTOR!

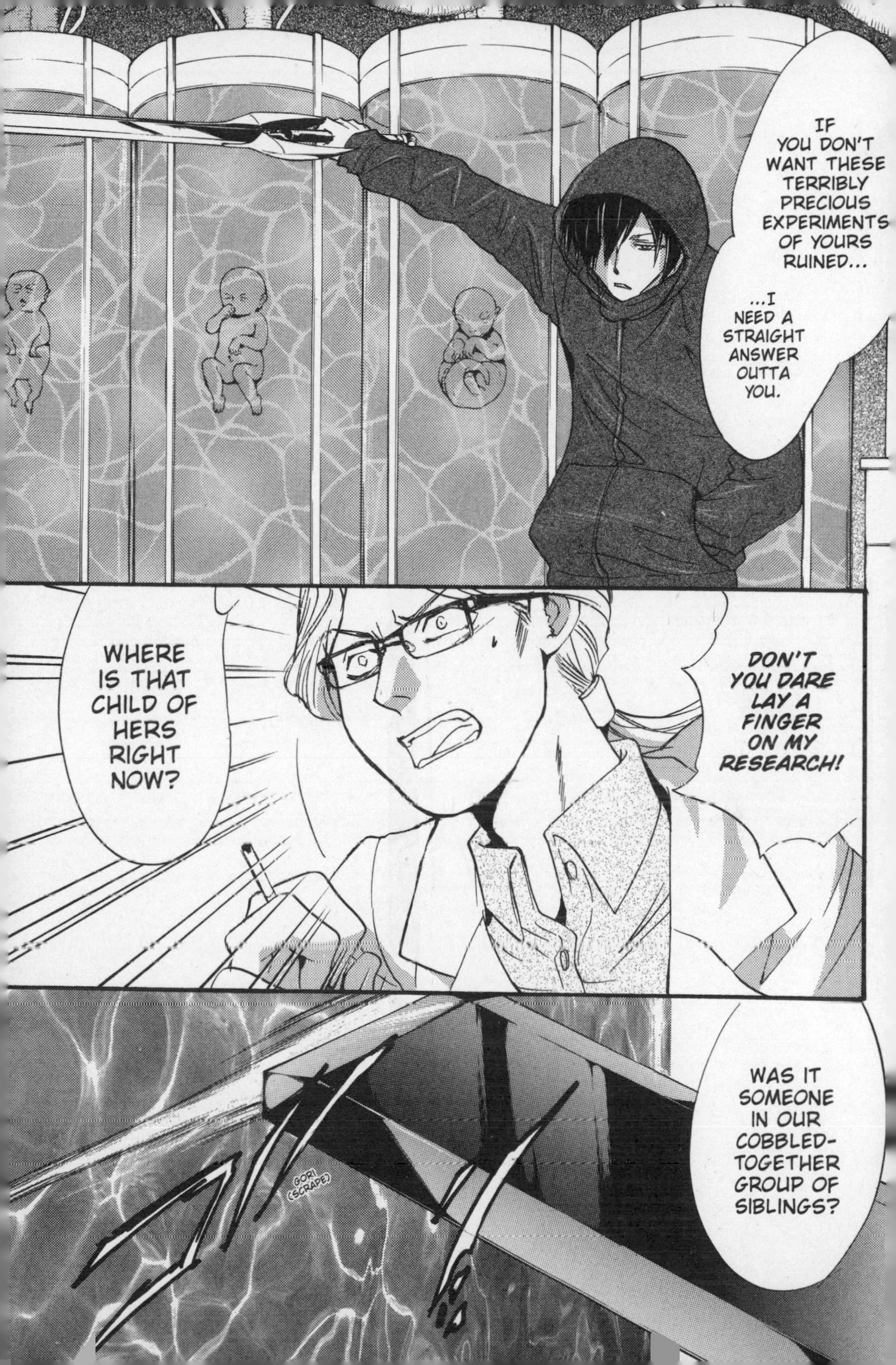
IF YOU DON'T WANT THESE TERRIBLY PRECIOUS EXPERIMENTS OF YOURS RUINED...
...I NEED A STRAIGHT ANSWER OUTTA YOU.
DON'T YOU DARE LAY A FINGER ON MY RESEARCH!
WHERE IS THAT CHILD OF HERS RIGHT NOW?
WAS IT SOMEONE IN OUR COBBLED-TOGETHER GROUP OF SIBLINGS?
GORI (SCRAPE)

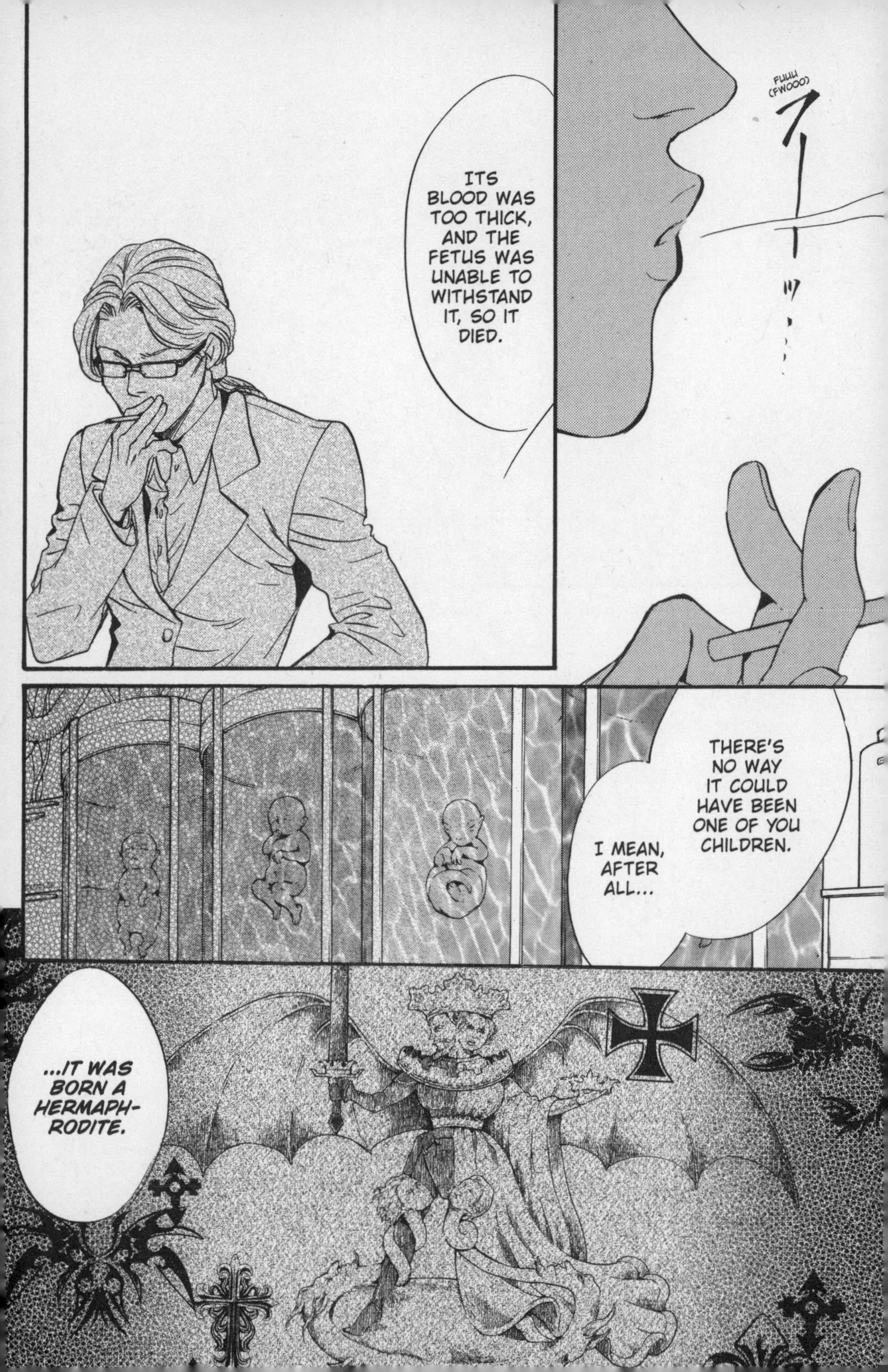
FUUU (FWOOO)
ITS BLOOD WAS TOO THICK, AND THE FETUS WAS UNABLE TO WITHSTAND IT, SO IT DIED.
THERE'S NO WAY IT COULD HAVE BEEN ONE OF YOU CHILDREN.
I MEAN, AFTER ALL...
...IT WAS BORN A HERMAPH-RODITE.

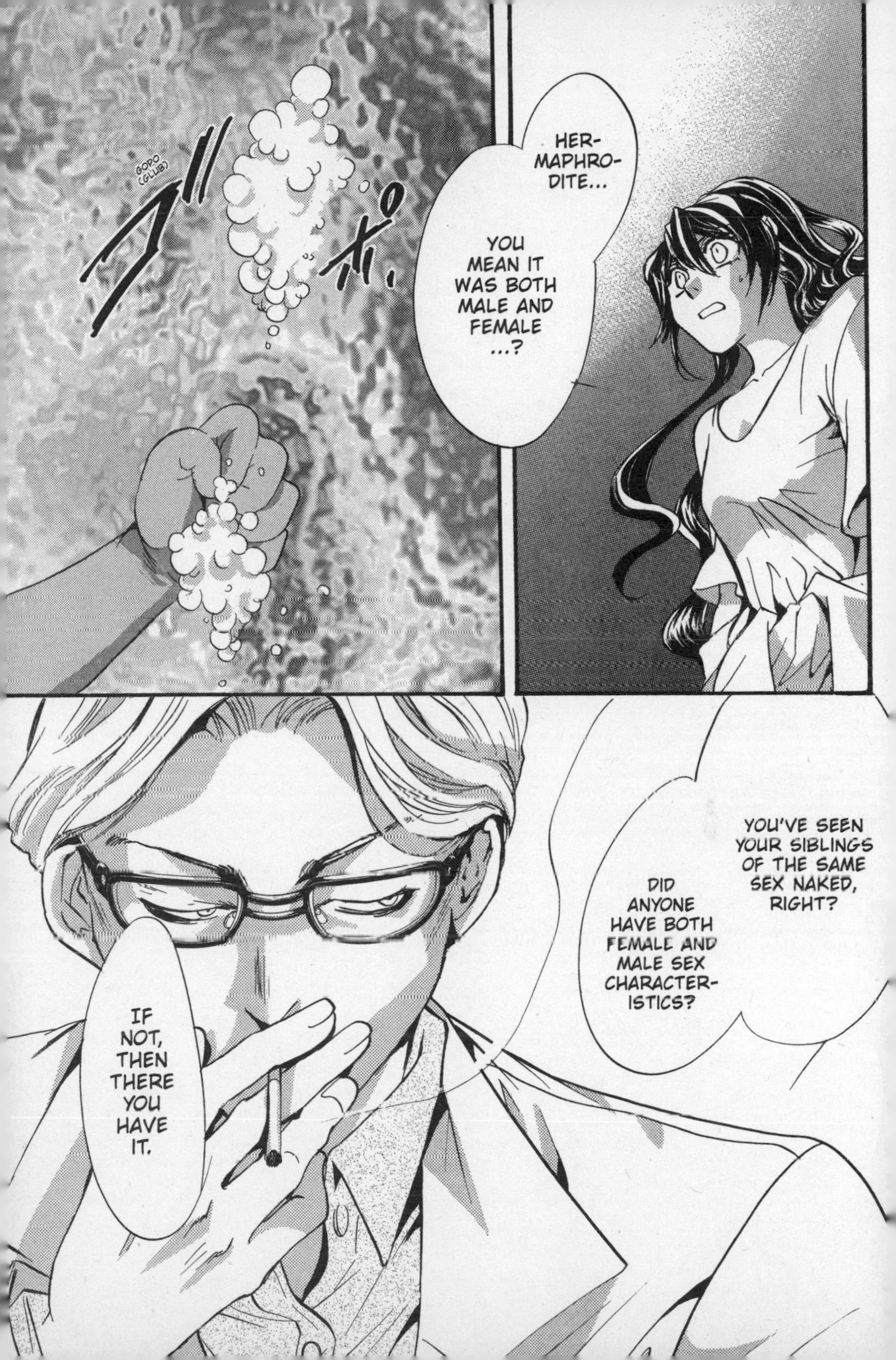
HER-MAPHRO-DITE...
YOU MEAN IT WAS BOTH MALE AND FEMALE ...?
GOPO (GLUB)
YOU'VE SEEN YOUR SIBLINGS OF THE SAME SEX NAKED, RIGHT?
DID ANYONE HAVE BOTH FEMALE AND MALE SEX CHARACTER-ISTICS?
IF NOT, THEN THERE YOU HAVE IT.

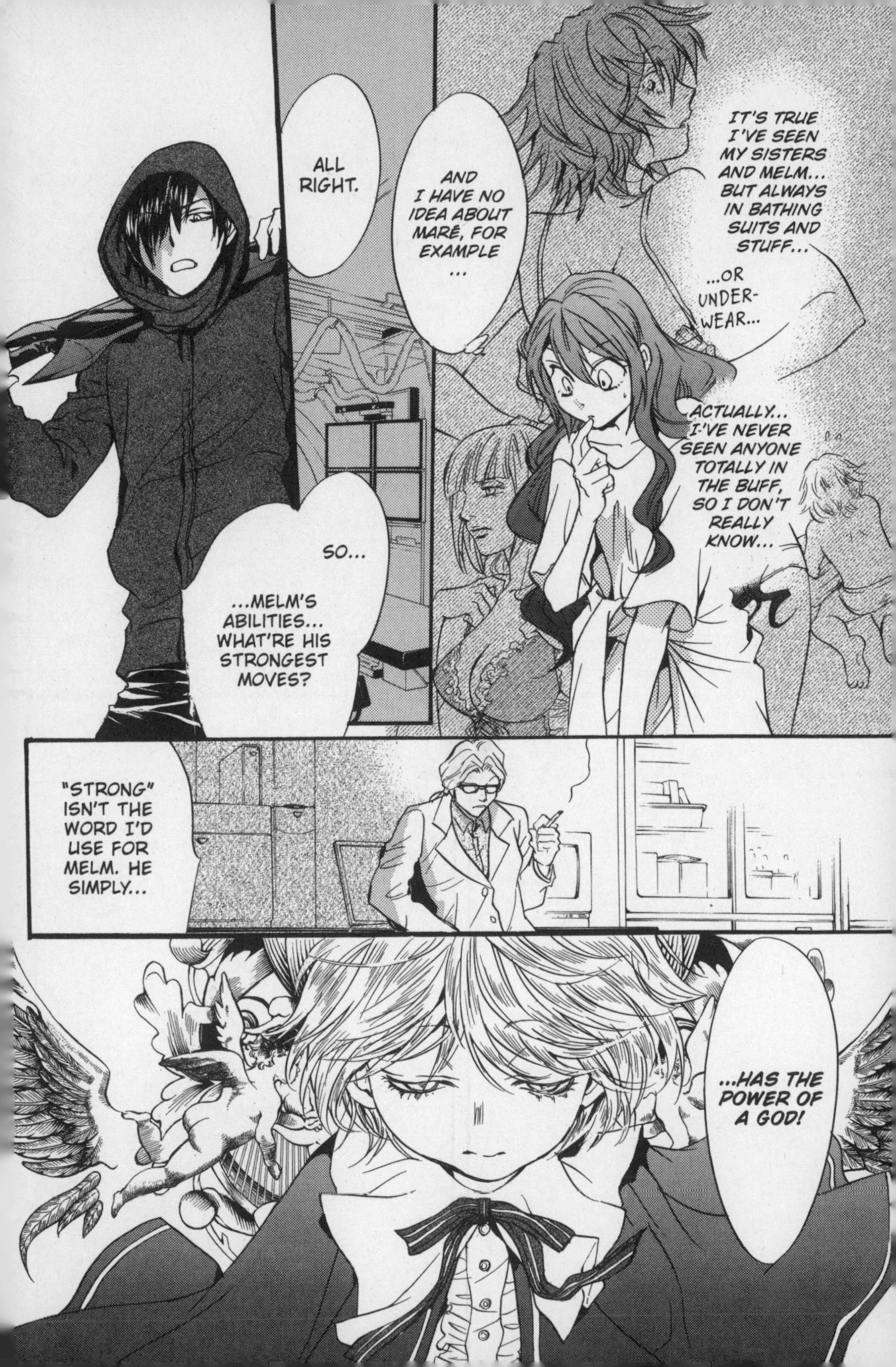
IT'S TRUE I'VE SEEN MY SISTERS AND MELM... BUT ALWAYS IN BATHING SUITS AND STUFF...
...OR UNDER-WEAR...
ACTUALLY... I'VE NEVER SEEN ANYONE TOTALLY IN THE BUFF, SO I DON'T REALLY KNOW...
AND I HAVE NO IDEA ABOUT MARÉ, FOR EXAMPLE ...
ALL RIGHT.
SO...
...MELM'S ABILITIES... WHAT'RE HIS STRONGEST MOVES?
"STRONG" ISN'T THE WORD I'D USE FOR MELM. HE SIMPLY...
...HAS THE POWER OF A GOD!

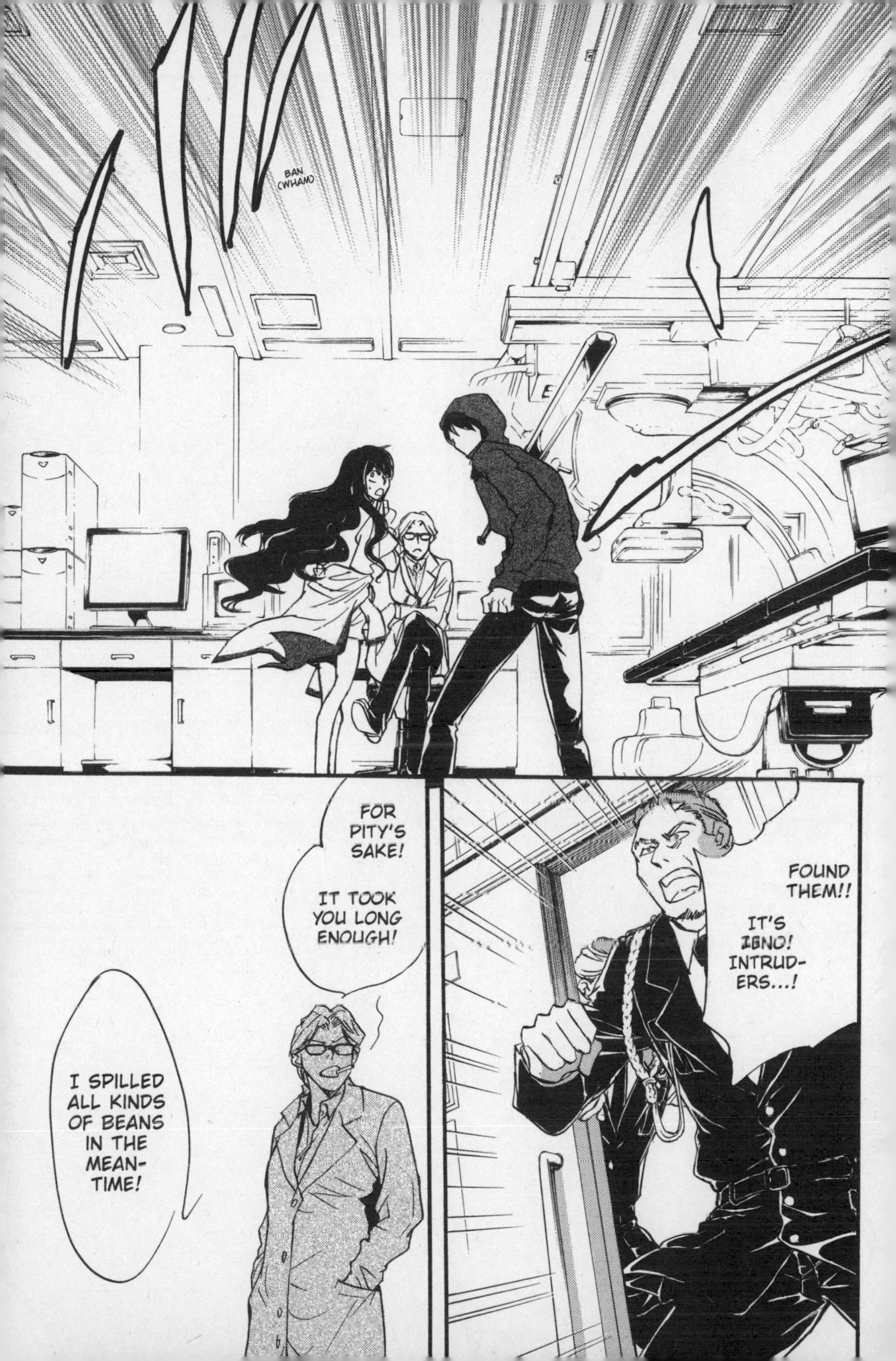
BAN (WHAM)
FOUND THEM!!
IT'S IGNO! INTRUDERS...!
FOR PITY'S SAKE!
IT TOOK YOU LONG ENOUGH!
I SPILLED ALL KINDS OF BEANS IN THE MEANTIME!

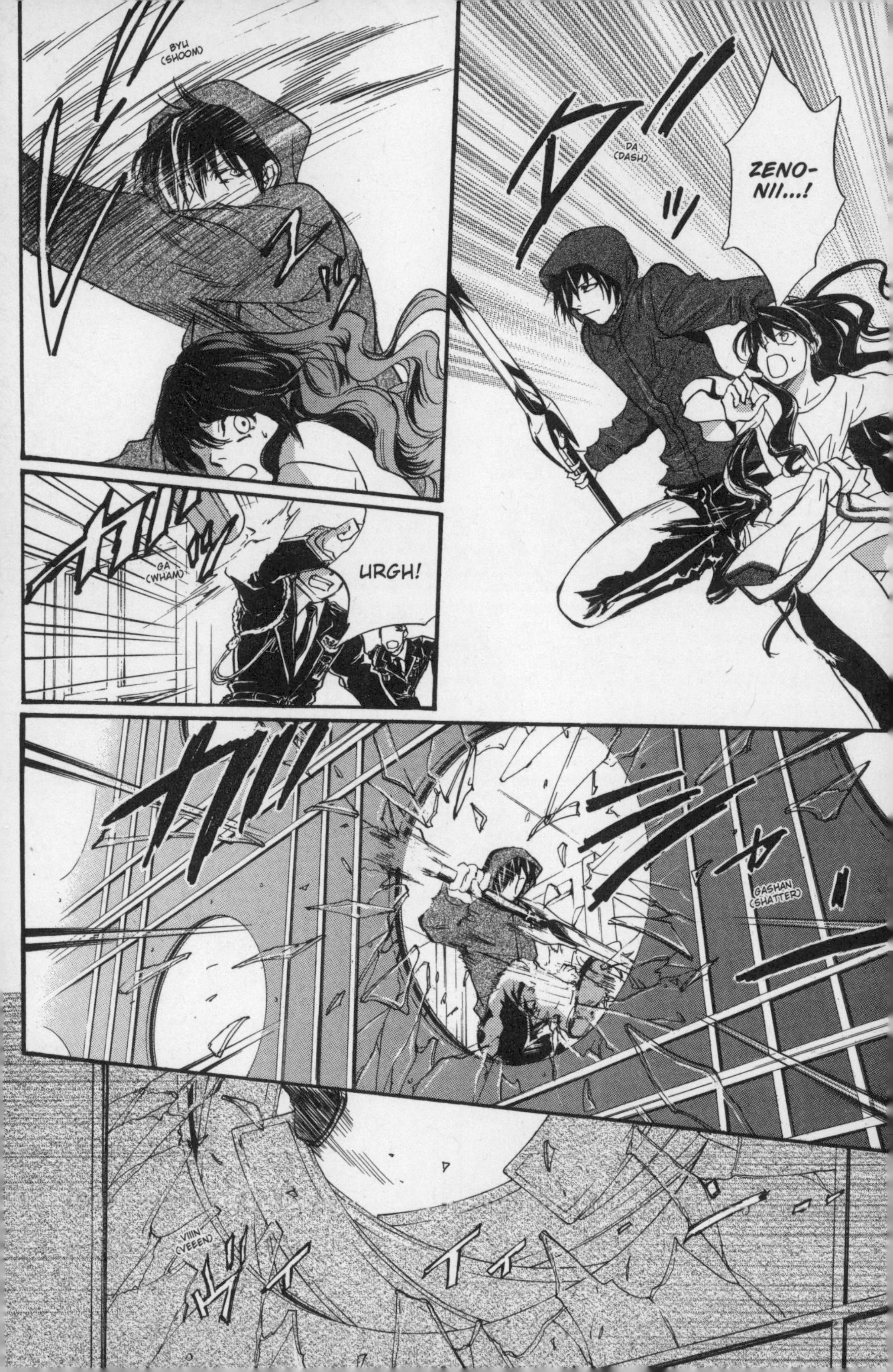
DA
(DASH)
ZENO-NII...!
BYU
(SHOOM)
GA
(WHAM)
URGH!
GASHAN
(SHATTER)
VIIN
(VEEEN)

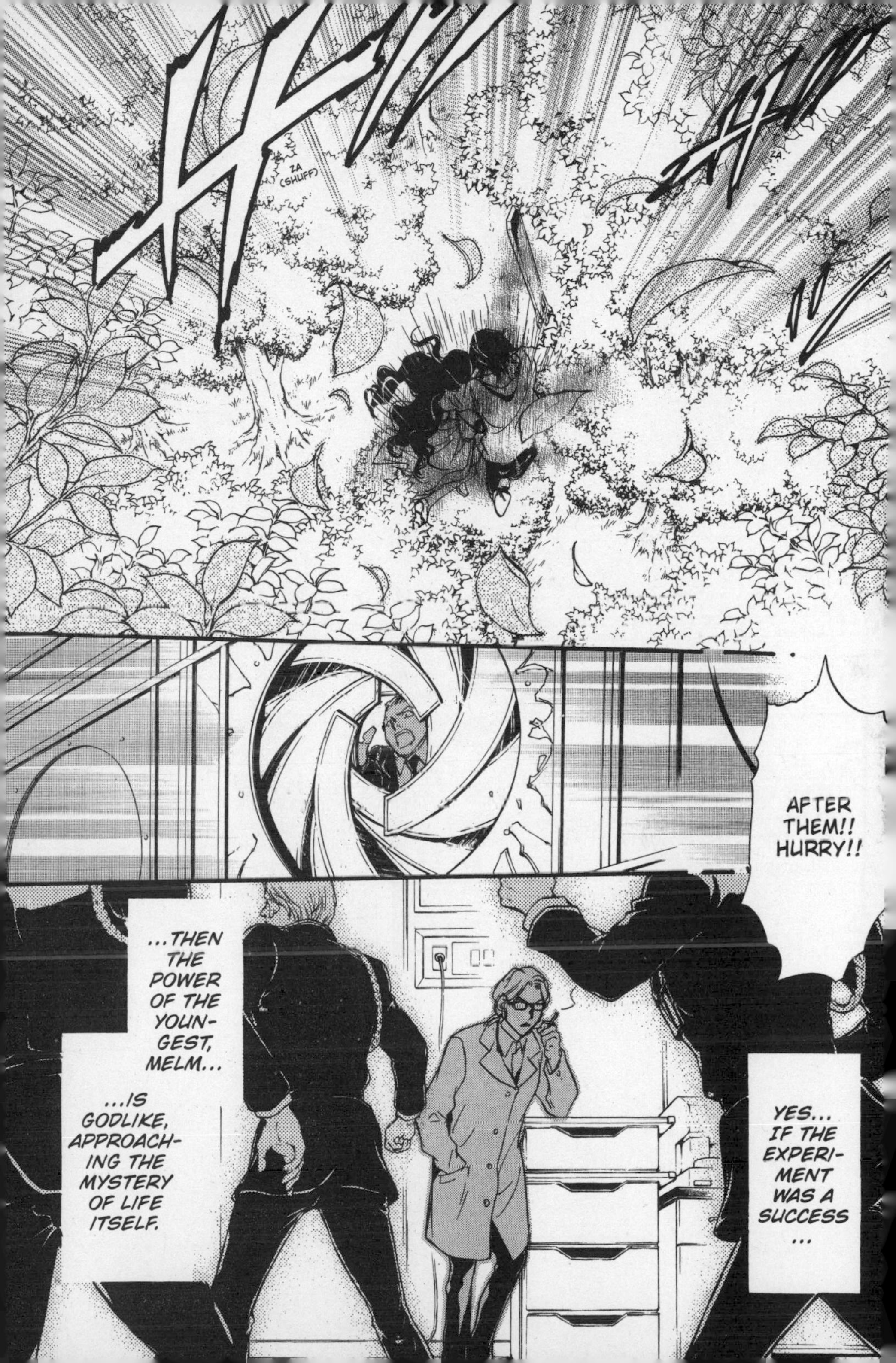
ZA
ZA (SHUFF)
AFTER THEM!! HURRY!!
YES... IF THE EXPERIMENT WAS A SUCCESS...
...THEN THE POWER OF THE YOUNGEST, MELM...
...IS GODLIKE, APPROACHING THE MYSTERY OF LIFE ITSELF.

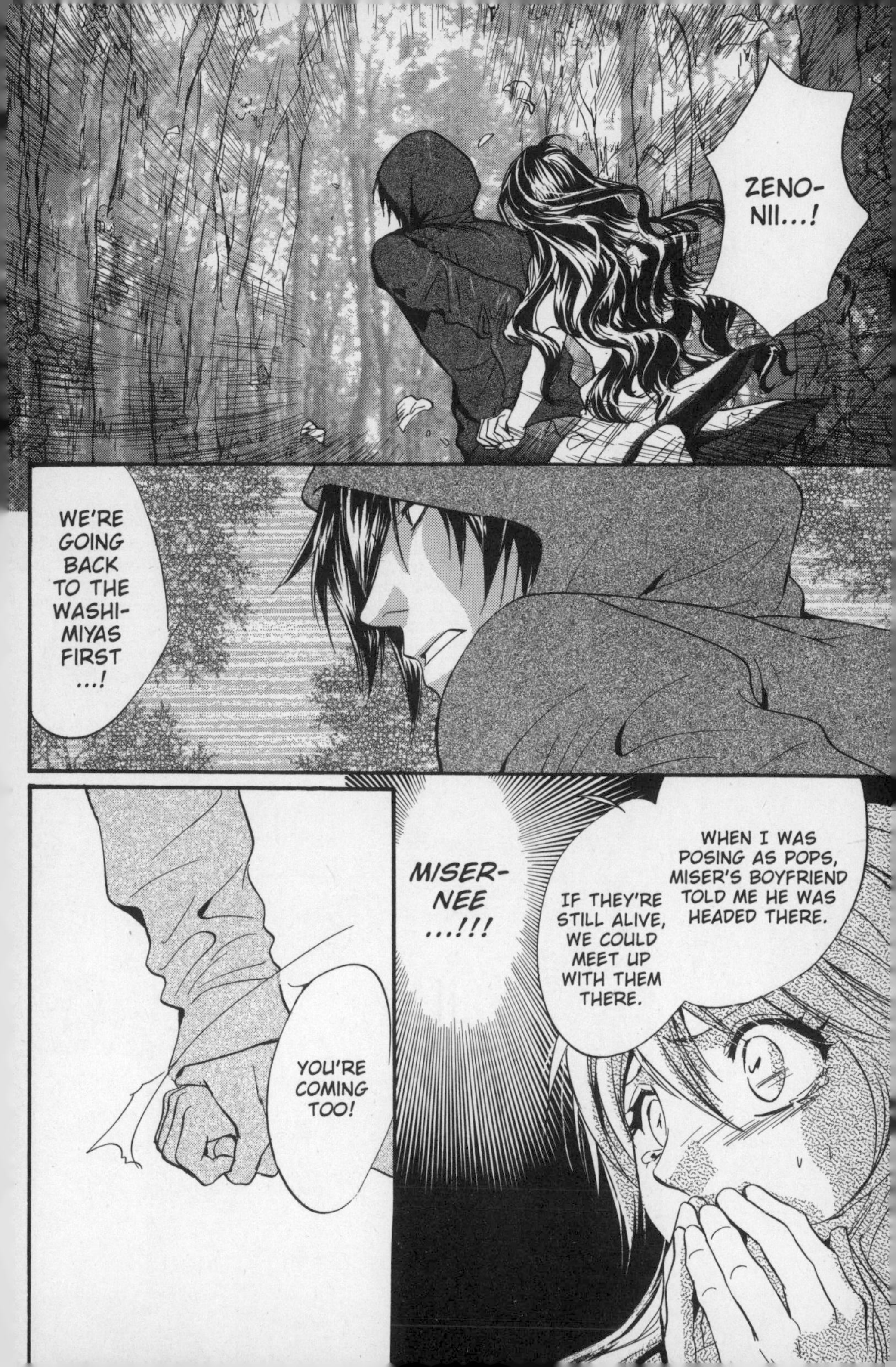
ZENO-NII...!
WE'RE GOING BACK TO THE WASHI-MIYAS FIRST ...!
WHEN I WAS POSING AS POPS, MISER'S BOYFRIEND TOLD ME HE WAS HEADED THERE.
IF THEY'RE STILL ALIVE, WE COULD MEET UP WITH THEM THERE.
MISER-NEE ...!!!
YOU'RE COMING TOO!

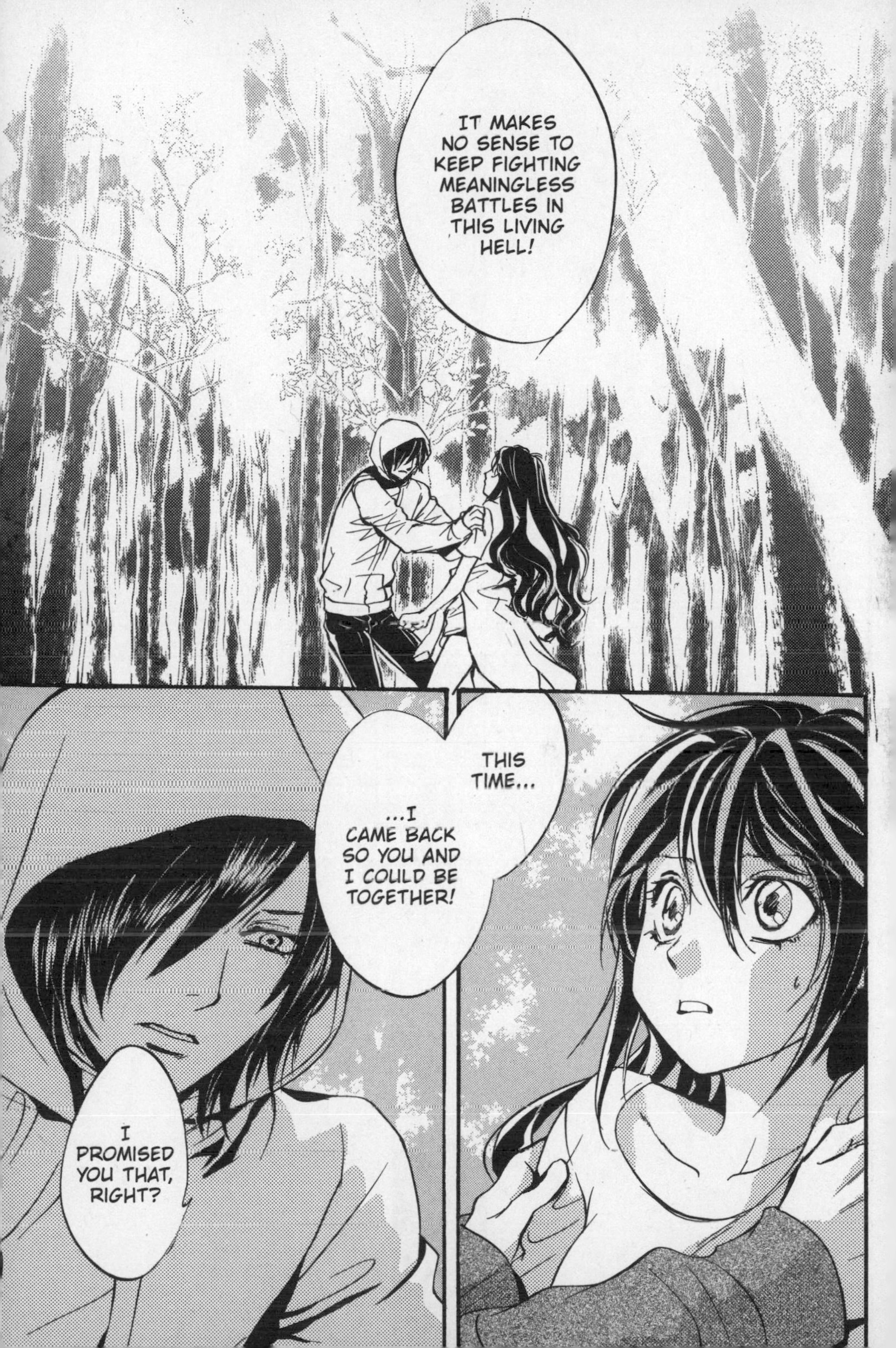
IT MAKES NO SENSE TO KEEP FIGHTING MEANINGLESS BATTLES IN THIS LIVING HELL!
THIS TIME...
...I CAME BACK SO YOU AND I COULD BE TOGETHER!
I PROMISED YOU THAT, RIGHT?

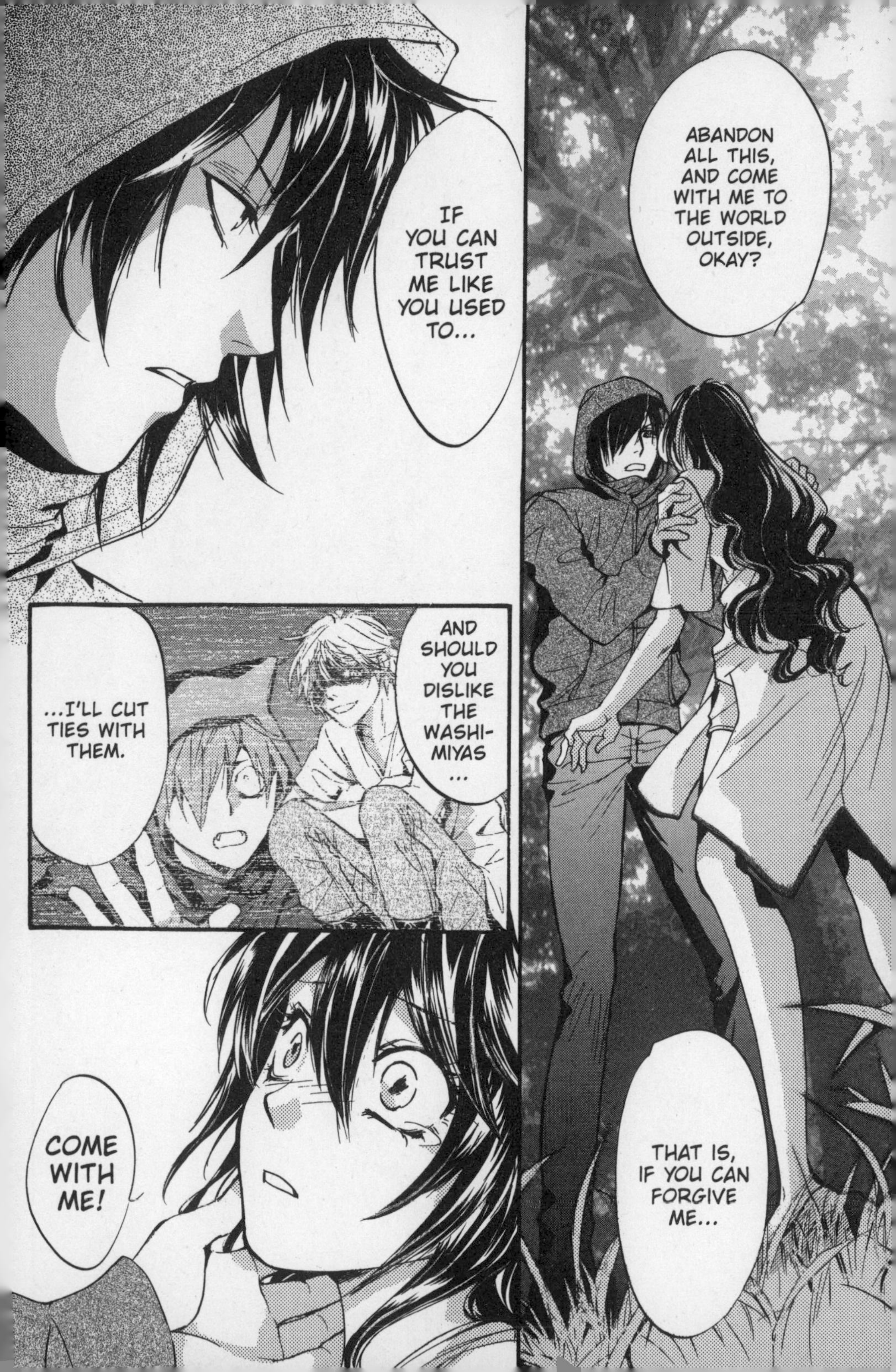
ABANDON ALL THIS, AND COME WITH ME TO THE WORLD OUTSIDE, OKAY?
THAT IS, IF YOU CAN FORGIVE ME...
IF YOU CAN TRUST ME LIKE YOU USED TO...
AND SHOULD YOU DISLIKE THE WASHI-MIYAS...
...I'LL CUT TIES WITH THEM.
COME WITH ME!

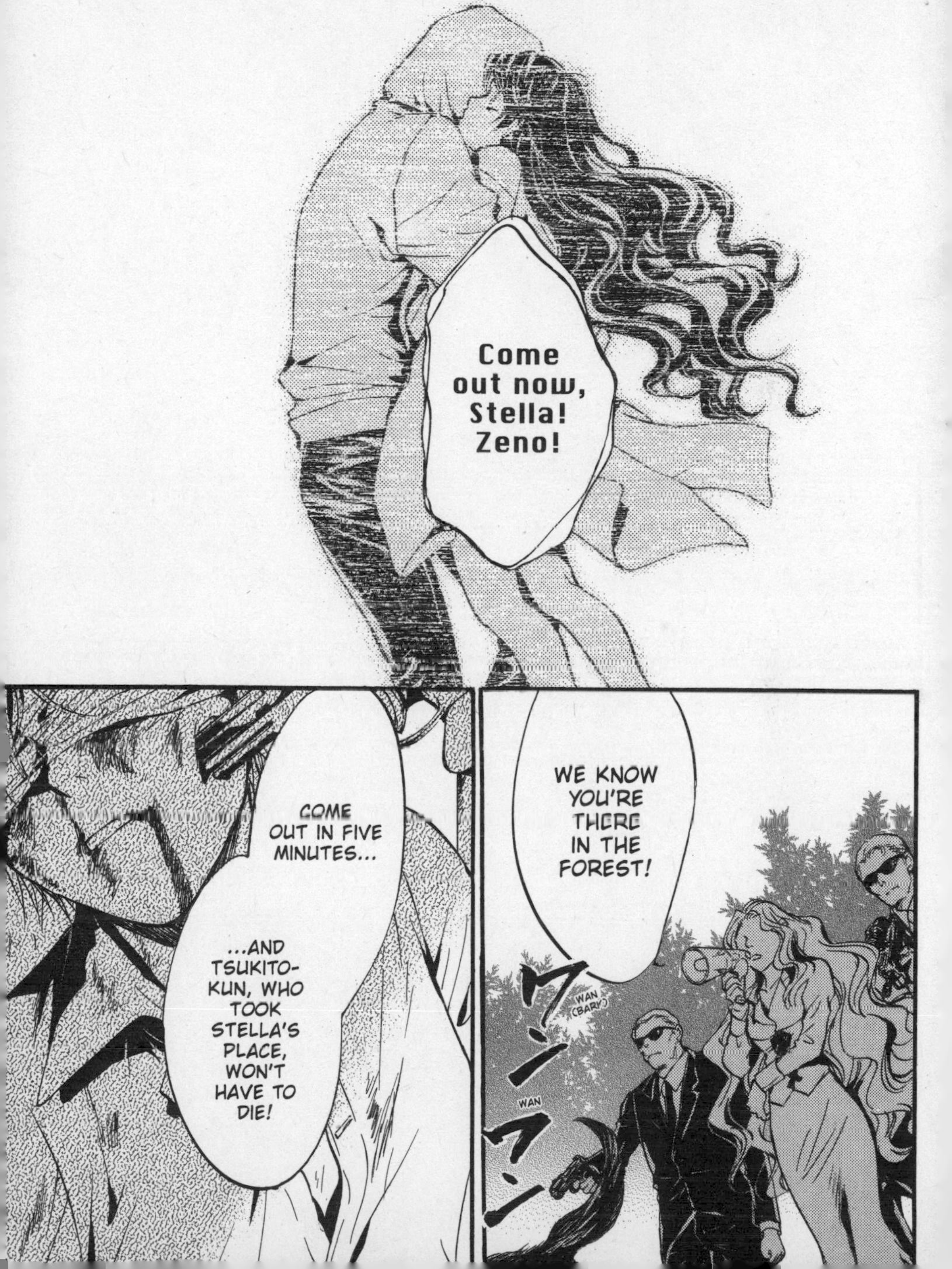
Come out now, Stella! Zeno!
WE KNOW YOU'RE THERE IN THE FOREST!
WAN (BARK)
WAN
COME OUT IN FIVE MINUTES...
...AND TSUKITO-KUN, WHO TOOK STELLA'S PLACE, WON'T HAVE TO DIE!

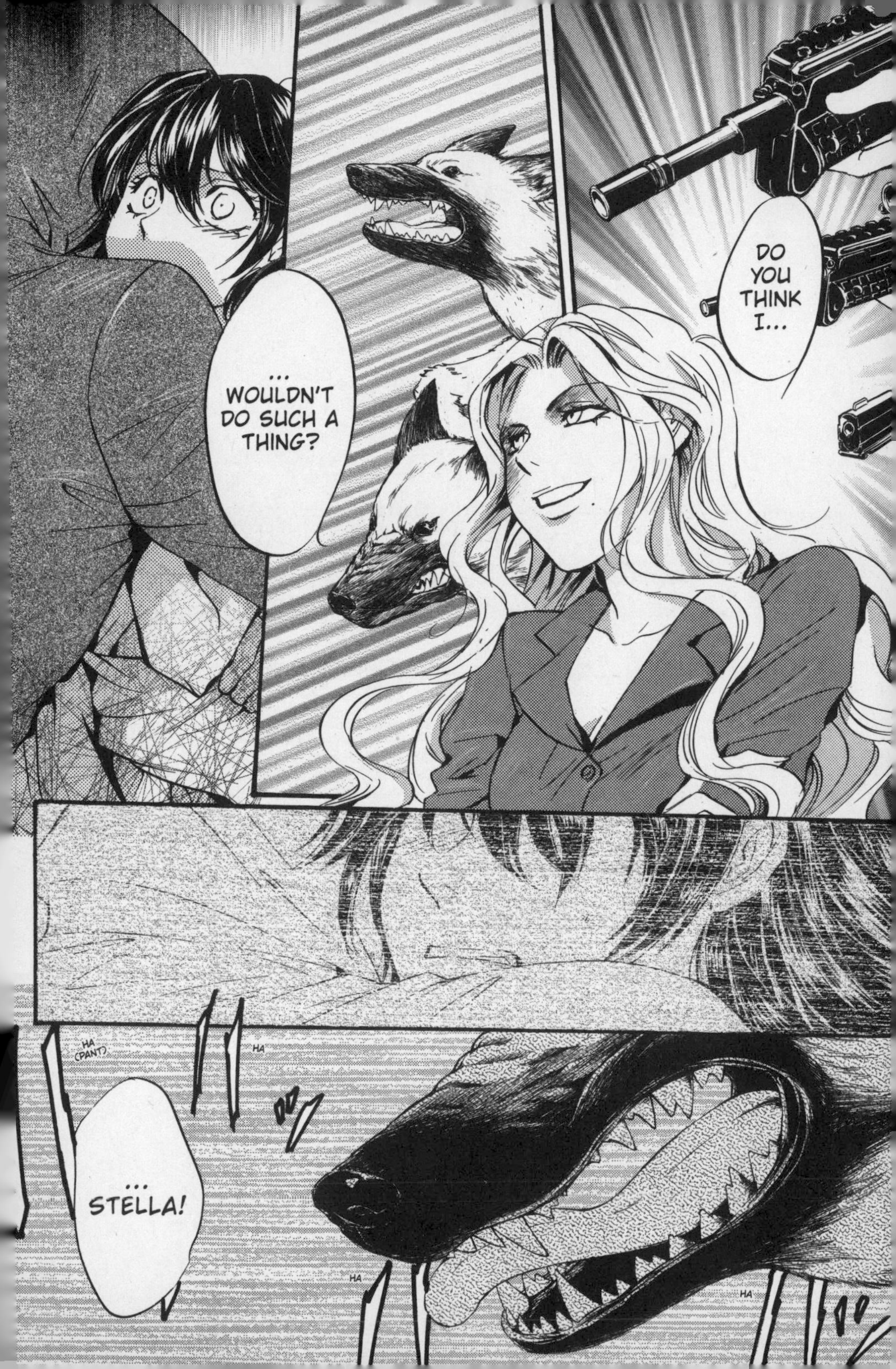
DO YOU THINK I...
...WOULDN'T DO SUCH A THING?
HA
HA (PANT)
...STELLA!
HA
HA

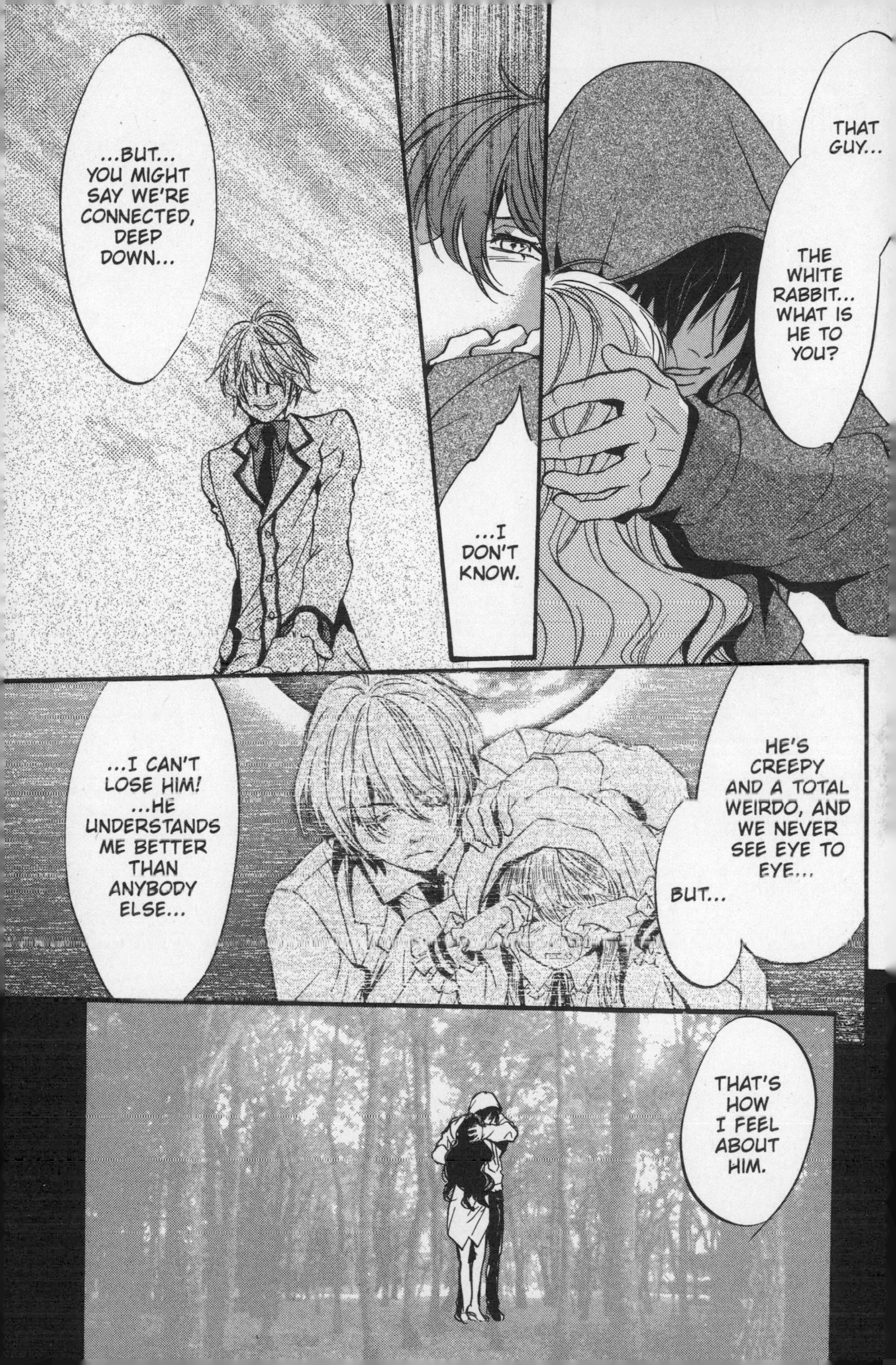
THAT GUY...
THE WHITE RABBIT... WHAT IS HE TO YOU?
...I DON'T KNOW.
...BUT... YOU MIGHT SAY WE'RE CONNECTED, DEEP DOWN...
HE'S CREEPY AND A TOTAL WEIRDO, AND WE NEVER SEE EYE TO EYE...
BUT...
...I CAN'T LOSE HIM! ...HE UNDERSTANDS ME BETTER THAN ANYBODY ELSE...
THAT'S HOW I FEEL ABOUT HIM.

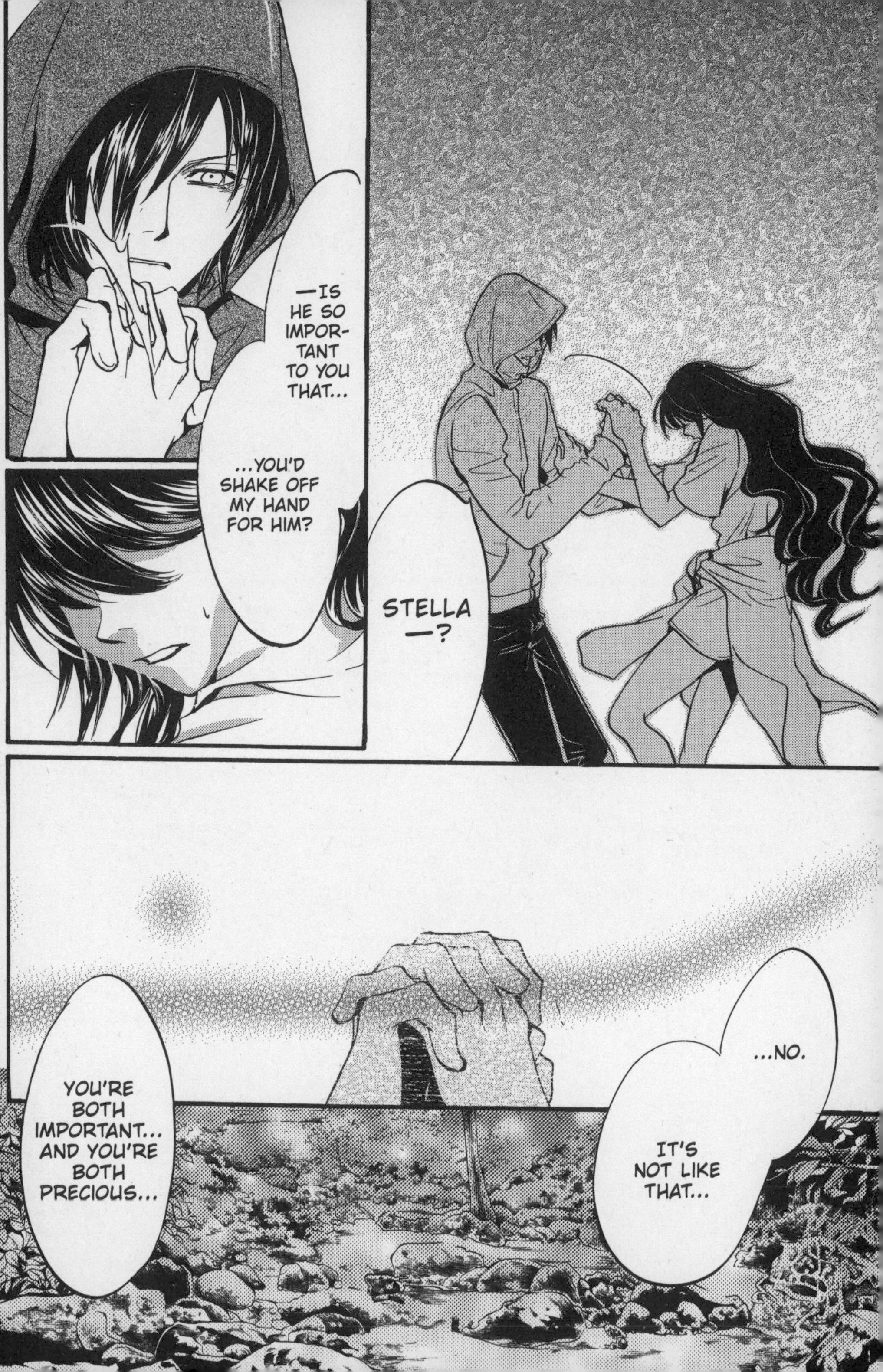
STELLA—?
—IS HE SO IMPORTANT TO YOU THAT...
...YOU'D SHAKE OFF MY HAND FOR HIM?
...NO.
IT'S NOT LIKE THAT...
YOU'RE BOTH IMPORTANT... AND YOU'RE BOTH PRECIOUS...

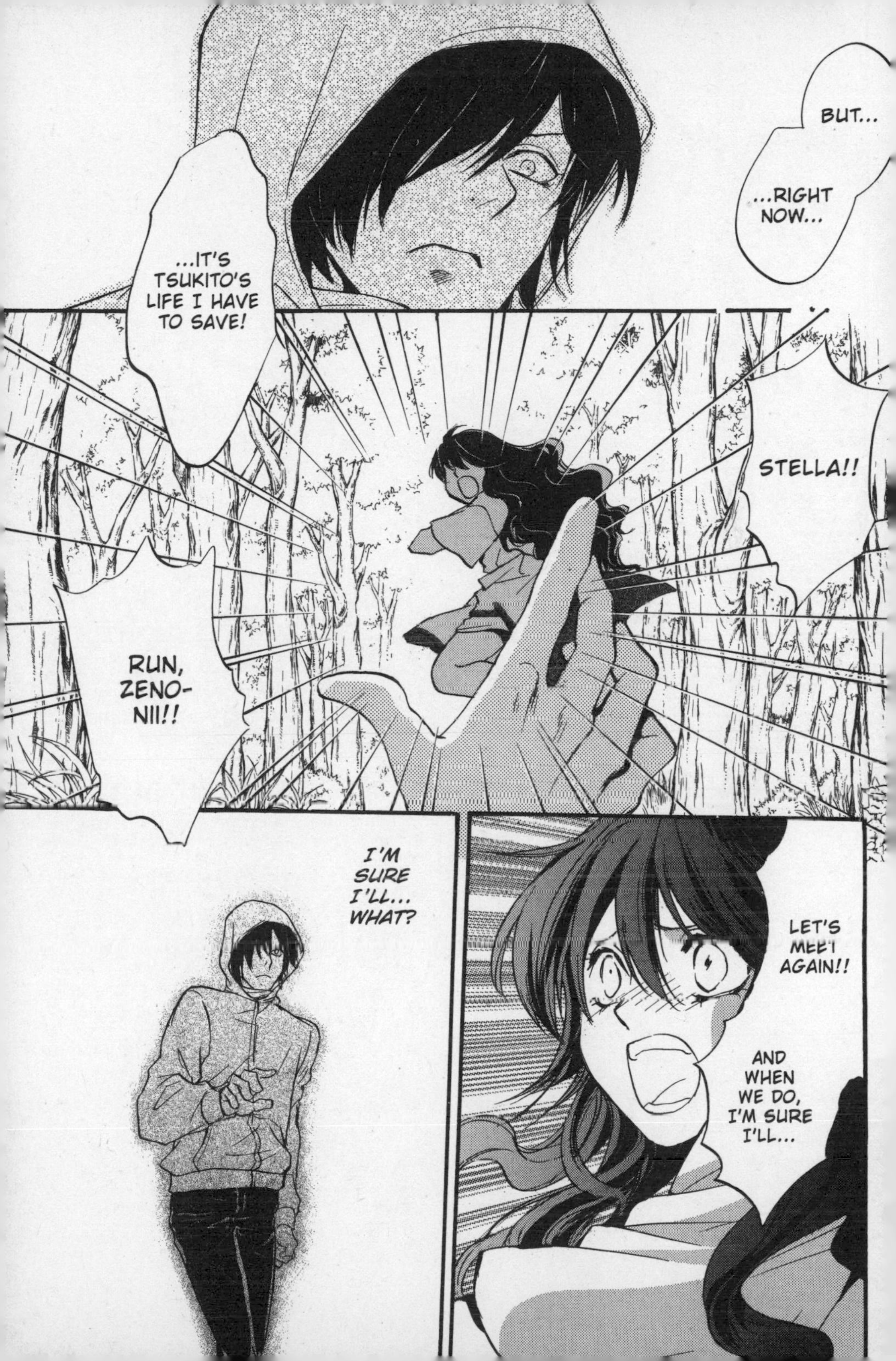
BUT...
...RIGHT NOW...
...IT'S TSUKITO'S LIFE I HAVE TO SAVE!
STELLA!!
RUN, ZENO-NII!!
LET'S MEET AGAIN!!
AND WHEN WE DO, I'M SURE I'LL...
I'M SURE I'LL... WHAT?

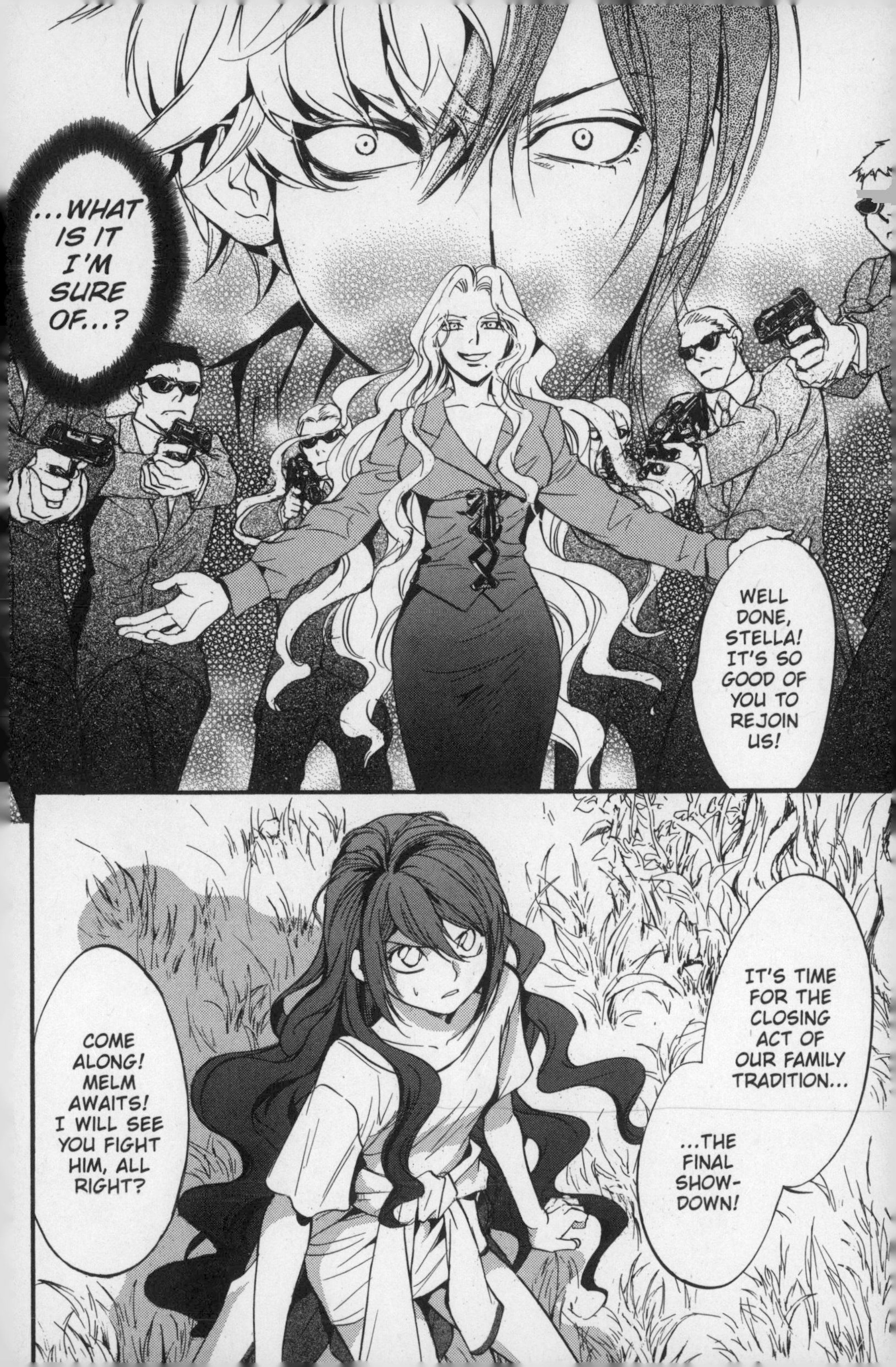
...WHAT IS IT I'M SURE OF...?
WELL DONE, STELLA! IT'S SO GOOD OF YOU TO REJOIN US!
IT'S TIME FOR THE CLOSING ACT OF OUR FAMILY TRADITION...
...THE FINAL SHOW-DOWN!
COME ALONG! MELM AWAITS! I WILL SEE YOU FIGHT HIM, ALL RIGHT?

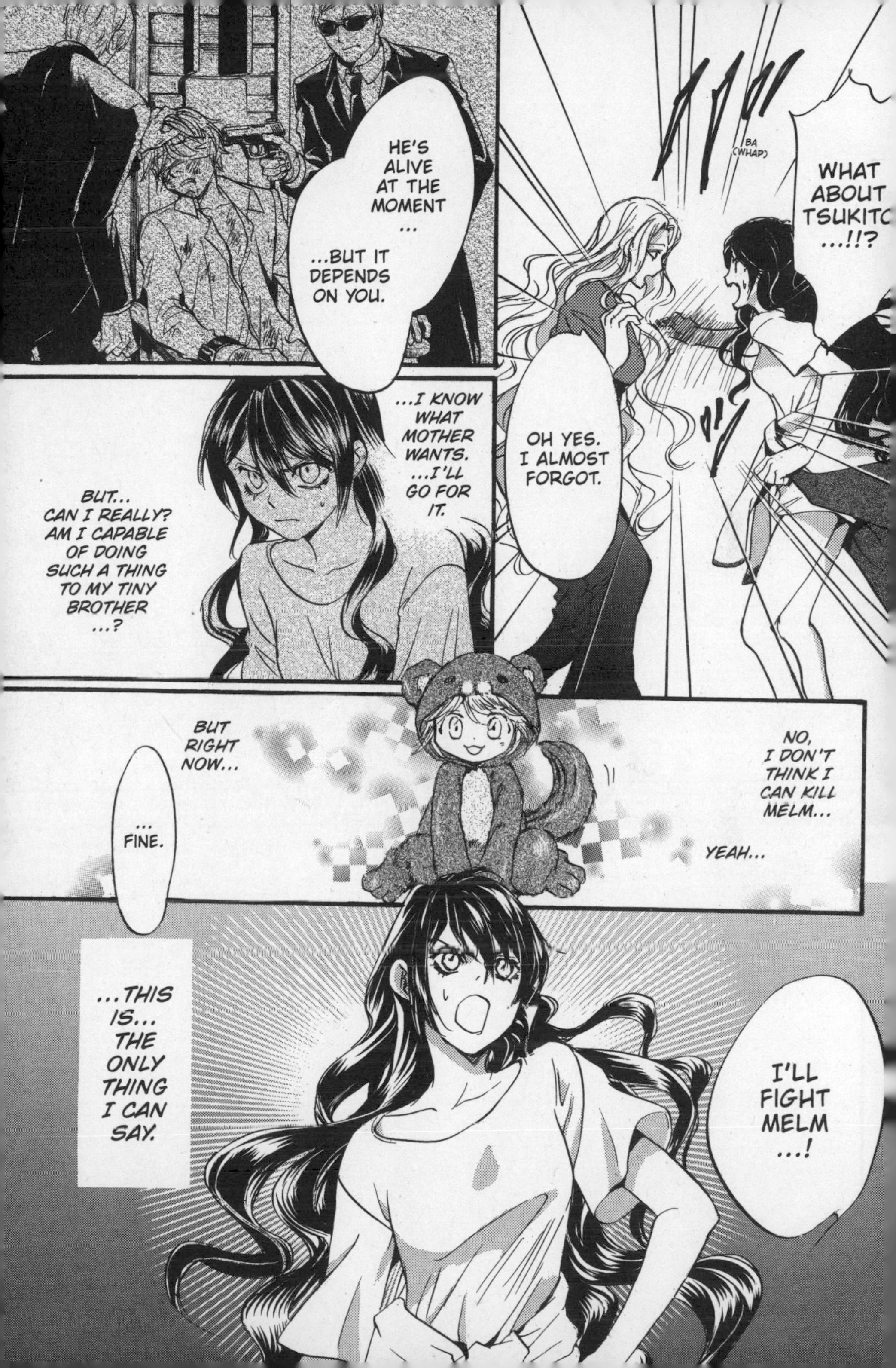
WHAT ABOUT TSUKITO ...!!?
BA (WHAP)
OH YES. I ALMOST FORGOT.
HE'S ALIVE AT THE MOMENT ...
...BUT IT DEPENDS ON YOU.
...I KNOW WHAT MOTHER WANTS. ...I'LL GO FOR IT.
BUT... CAN I REALLY? AM I CAPABLE OF DOING SUCH A THING TO MY TINY BROTHER ...?
NO, I DON'T THINK I CAN KILL MELM...
YEAH...
BUT RIGHT NOW...
... FINE.
I'LL FIGHT MELM ...!
...THIS IS... THE ONLY THING I CAN SAY.

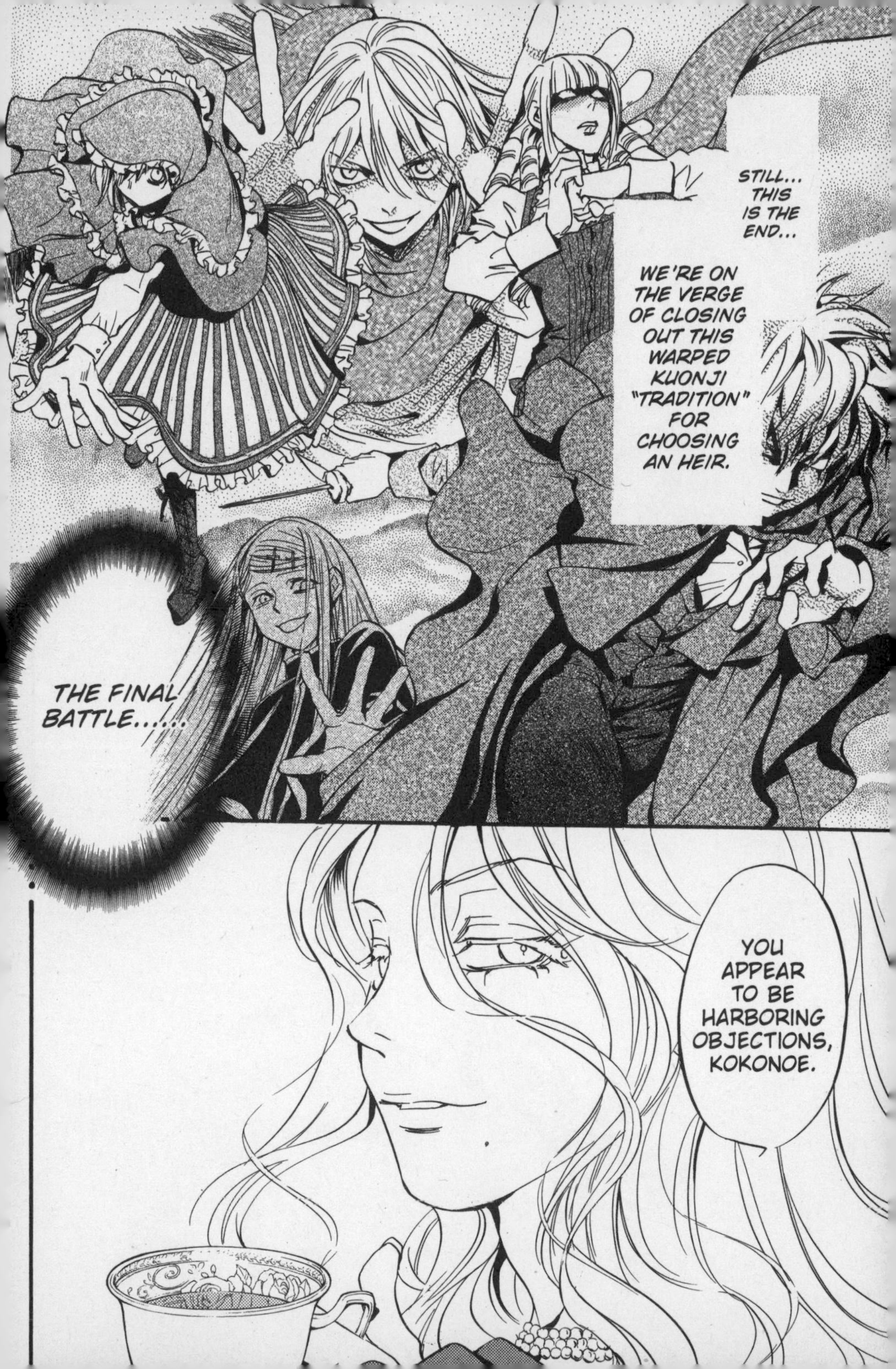
STILL... THIS IS THE END...
WE'RE ON THE VERGE OF CLOSING OUT THIS WARPED KUONJI "TRADITION" FOR CHOOSING AN HEIR.
THE FINAL BATTLE......
YOU APPEAR TO BE HARBORING OBJECTIONS, KOKONOE.

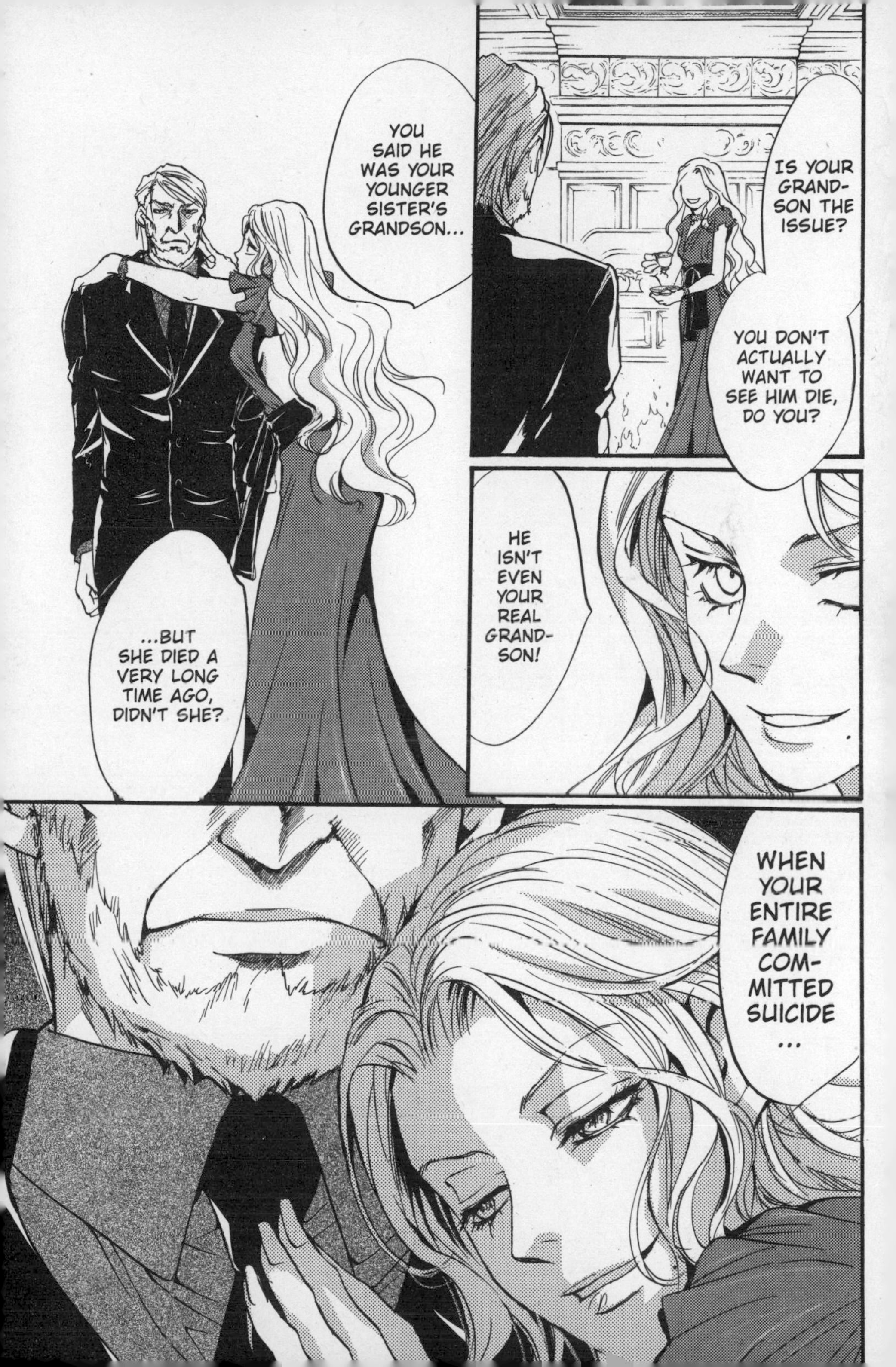
IS YOUR GRANDSON THE ISSUE?
YOU DON'T ACTUALLY WANT TO SEE HIM DIE, DO YOU?
HE ISN'T EVEN YOUR REAL GRANDSON!
YOU SAID HE WAS YOUR YOUNGER SISTER'S GRANDSON...
...BUT SHE DIED A VERY LONG TIME AGO, DIDN'T SHE?
WHEN YOUR ENTIRE FAMILY COMMITTED SUICIDE...

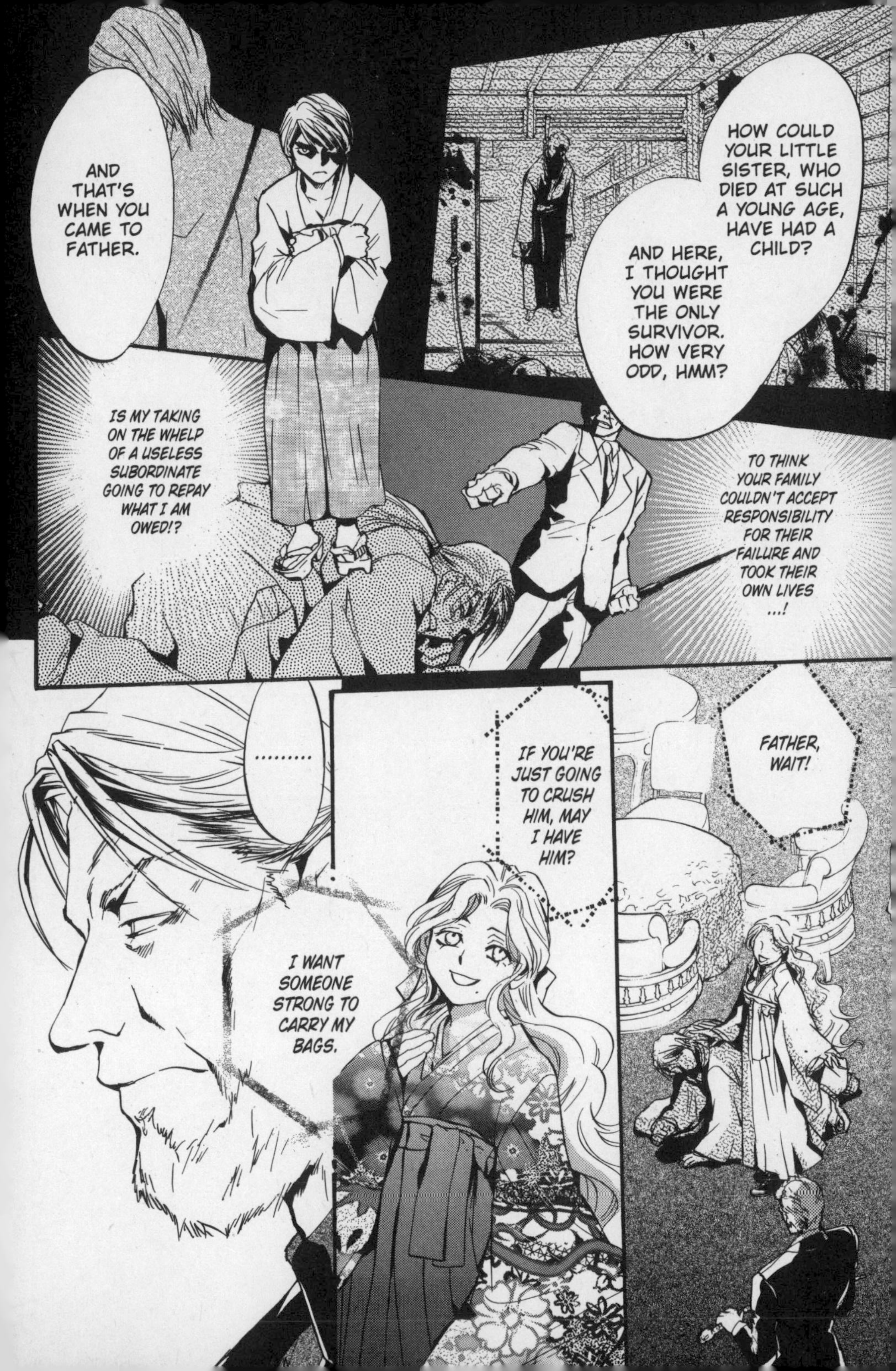
HOW COULD YOUR LITTLE SISTER, WHO DIED AT SUCH A YOUNG AGE, HAVE HAD A CHILD?
AND HERE, I THOUGHT YOU WERE THE ONLY SURVIVOR. HOW VERY ODD, HMM?
TO THINK YOUR FAMILY COULDN'T ACCEPT RESPONSIBILITY FOR THEIR FAILURE AND TOOK THEIR OWN LIVES ...!
IS MY TAKING ON THE WHELP OF A USELESS SUBORDINATE GOING TO REPAY WHAT I AM OWED!?
AND THAT'S WHEN YOU CAME TO FATHER.
FATHER, WAIT!
IF YOU'RE JUST GOING TO CRUSH HIM, MAY I HAVE HIM?
I WANT SOMEONE STRONG TO CARRY MY BAGS.
....

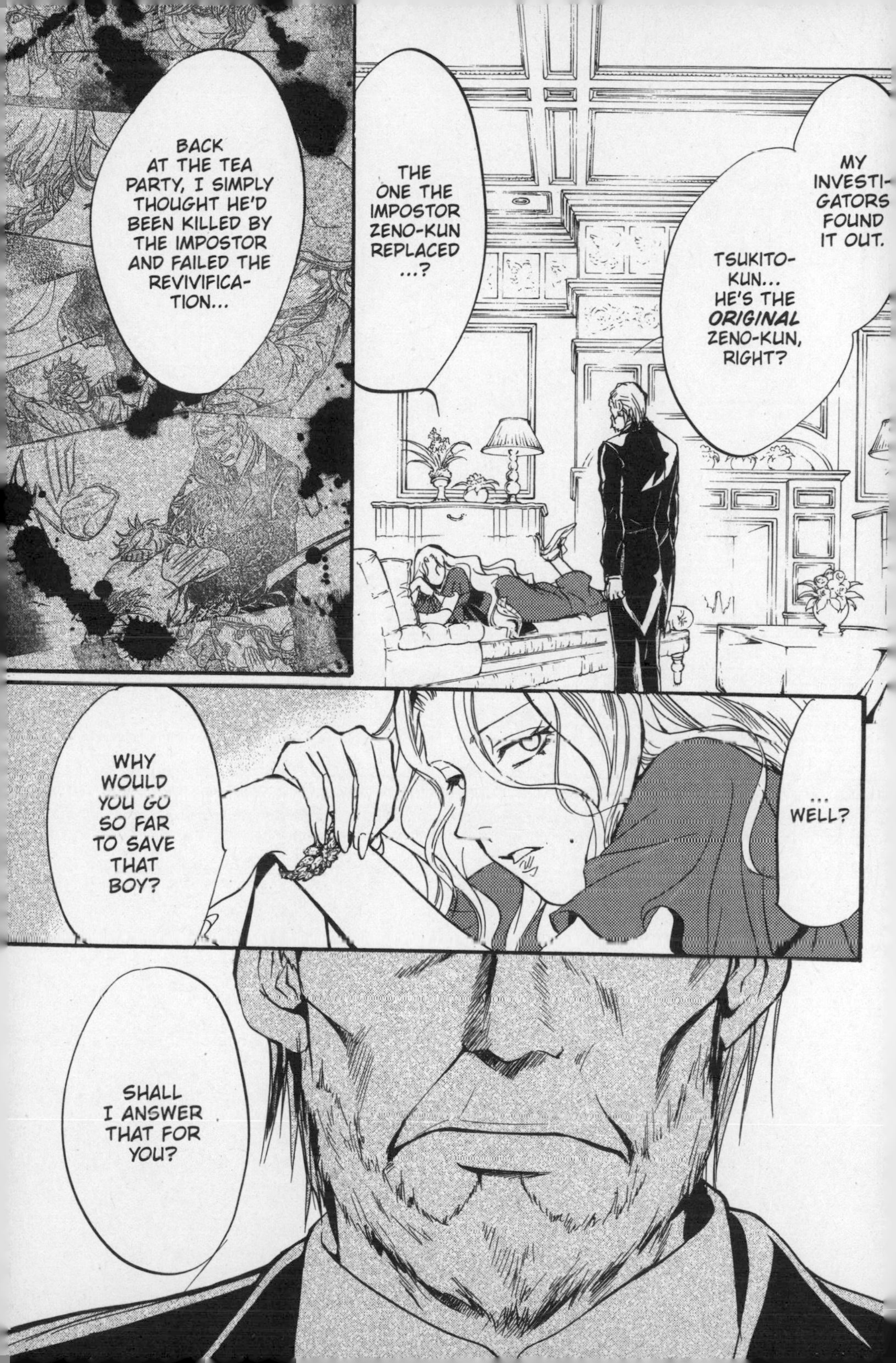
MY INVESTIGATORS FOUND IT OUT.
TSUKITO-KUN... HE'S THE ***ORIGINAL*** ZENO-KUN, RIGHT?
THE ONE THE IMPOSTOR ZENO-KUN REPLACED ...?
BACK AT THE TEA PARTY, I SIMPLY THOUGHT HE'D BEEN KILLED BY THE IMPOSTOR AND FAILED THE REVIVIFICATION...
...WELL?
WHY WOULD YOU GO SO FAR TO SAVE THAT BOY?
SHALL I ANSWER THAT FOR YOU?

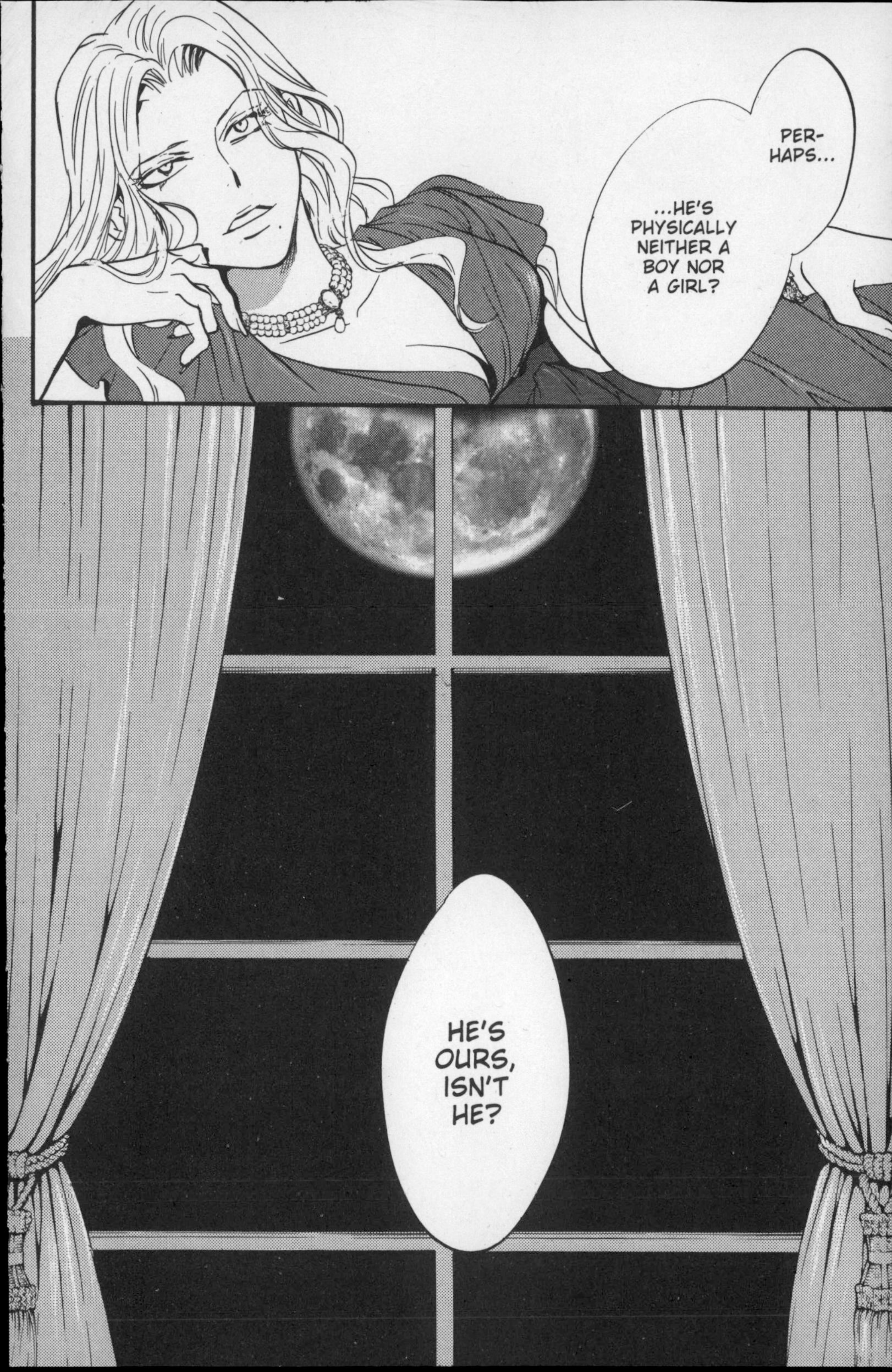
PER-HAPS...
...HE'S PHYSICALLY NEITHER A BOY NOR A GIRL?
HE'S OURS, ISN'T HE?

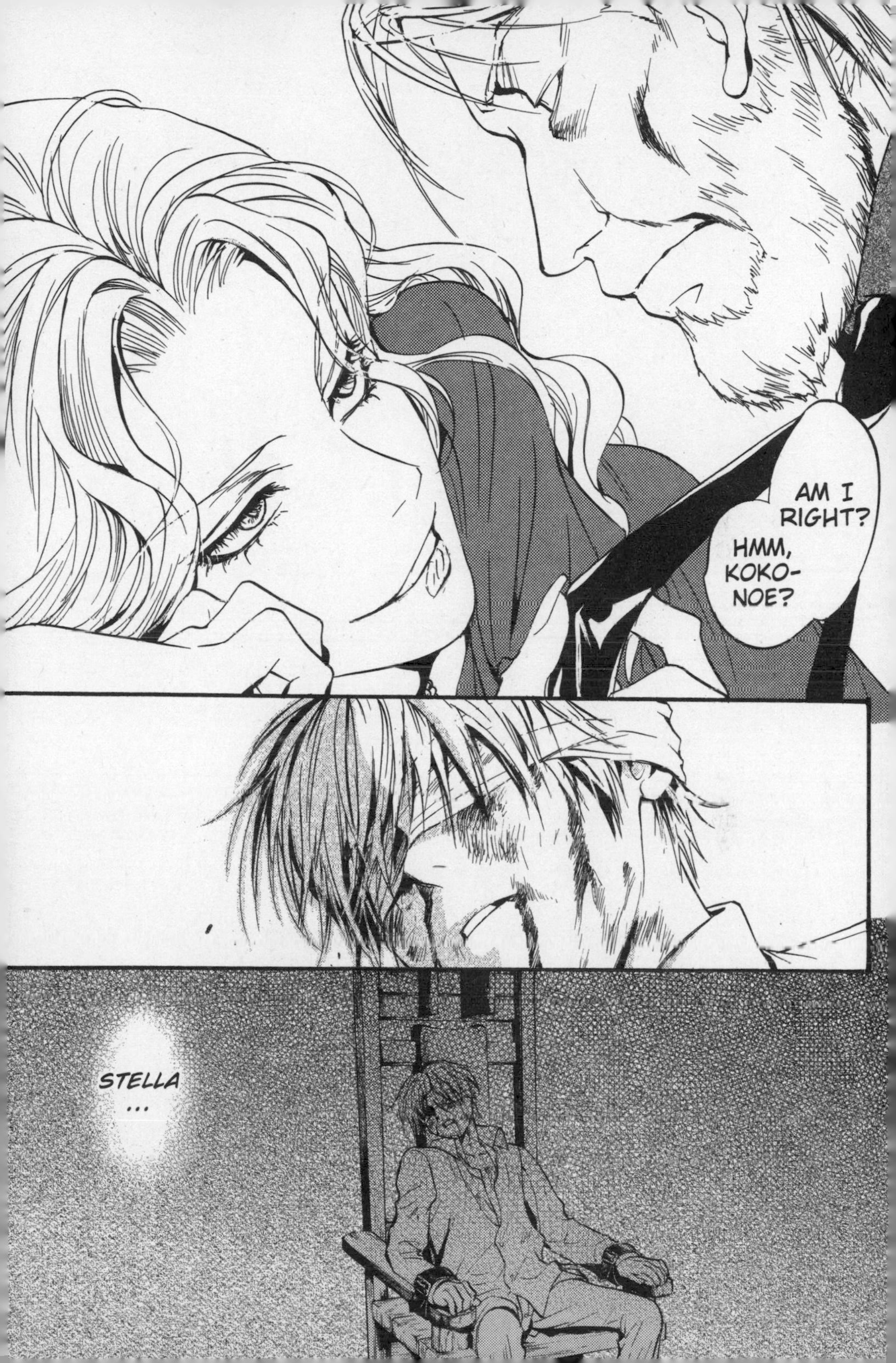
AM I RIGHT?
HMM, KOKO-NOE?
STELLA ...

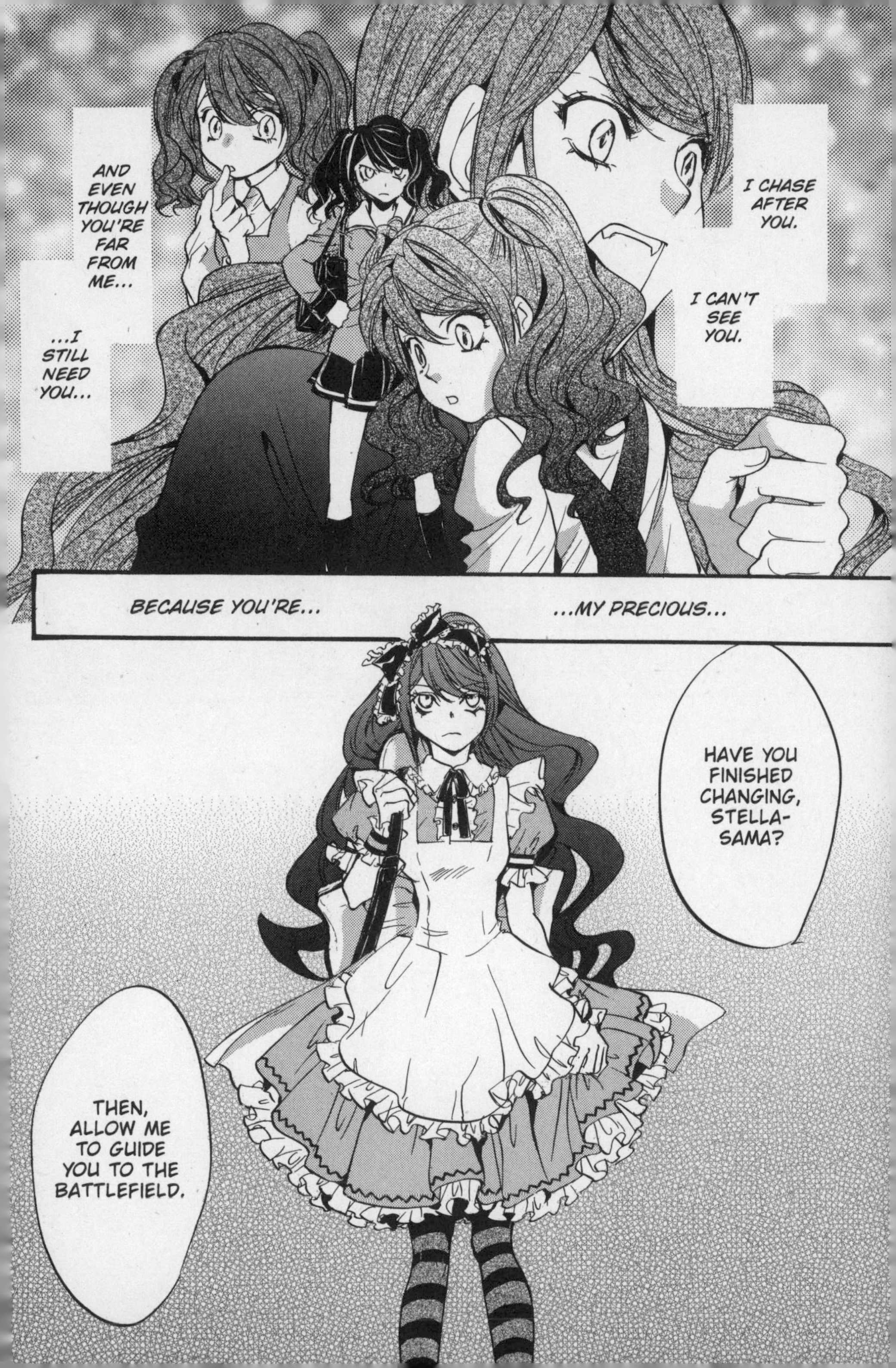

I CHASE AFTER YOU.
I CAN'T SEE YOU.
AND EVEN THOUGH YOU'RE FAR FROM ME...
...I STILL NEED YOU...
BECAUSE YOU'RE... ...MY PRECIOUS...
HAVE YOU FINISHED CHANGING, STELLA-SAMA?
THEN, ALLOW ME TO GUIDE YOU TO THE BATTLEFIELD.

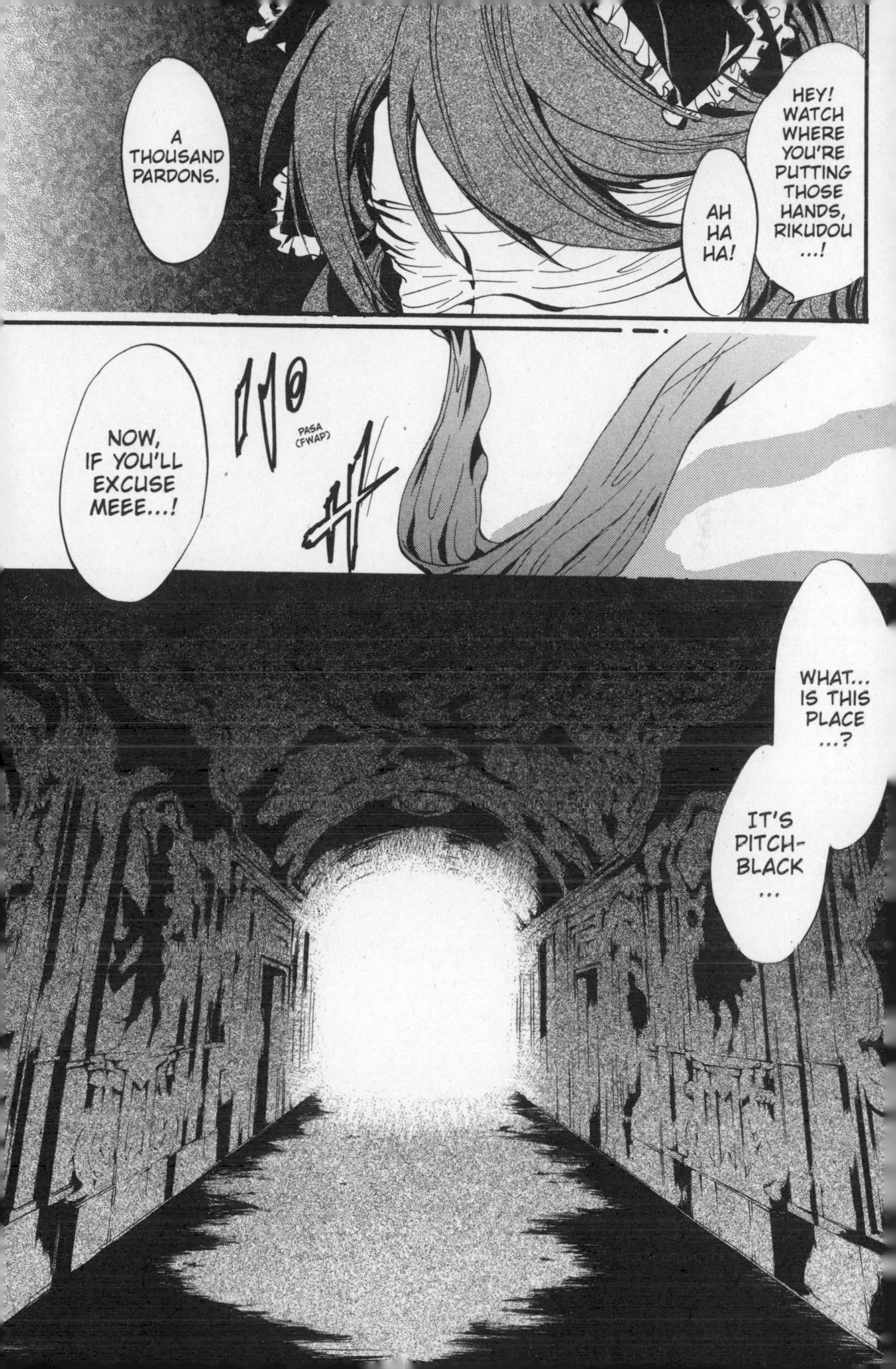
HEY! WATCH WHERE YOU'RE PUTTING THOSE HANDS, RIKUDOU...!
AH HA HA!
A THOUSAND PARDONS.
PASA (FWAP)
NOW, IF YOU'LL EXCUSE MEEE...!
WHAT... IS THIS PLACE...?
IT'S PITCH-BLACK...

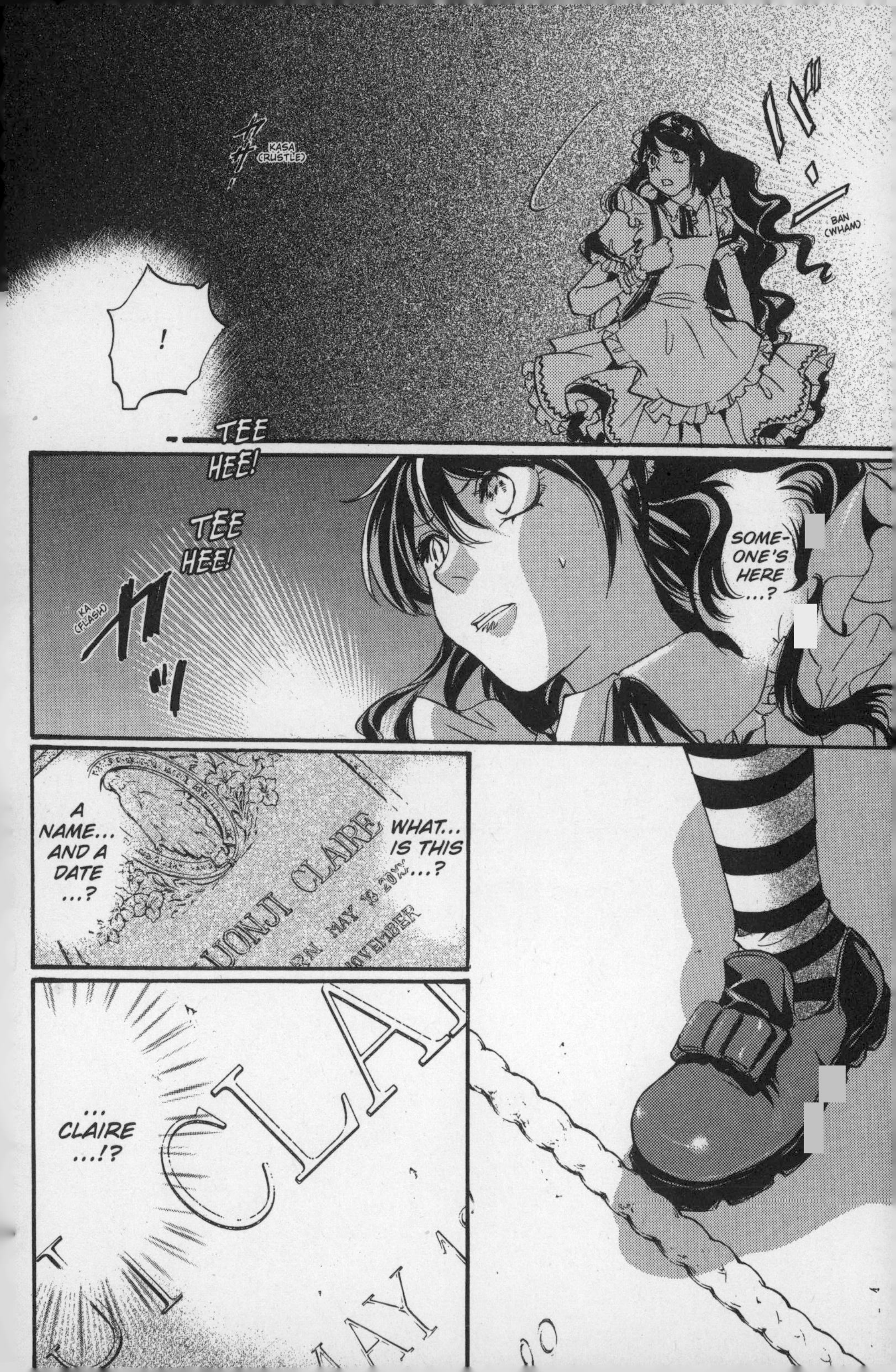
BAN (WHAM)
KASA (RUSTLE)
!
TEE HEE!
SOME-ONE'S HERE ...?
TEE HEE!
KA (FLASH)
WHAT... IS THIS ...?
A NAME... AND A DATE ...?
UONJI CLAIRE
NOVEMBER
... CLAIRE ...!?

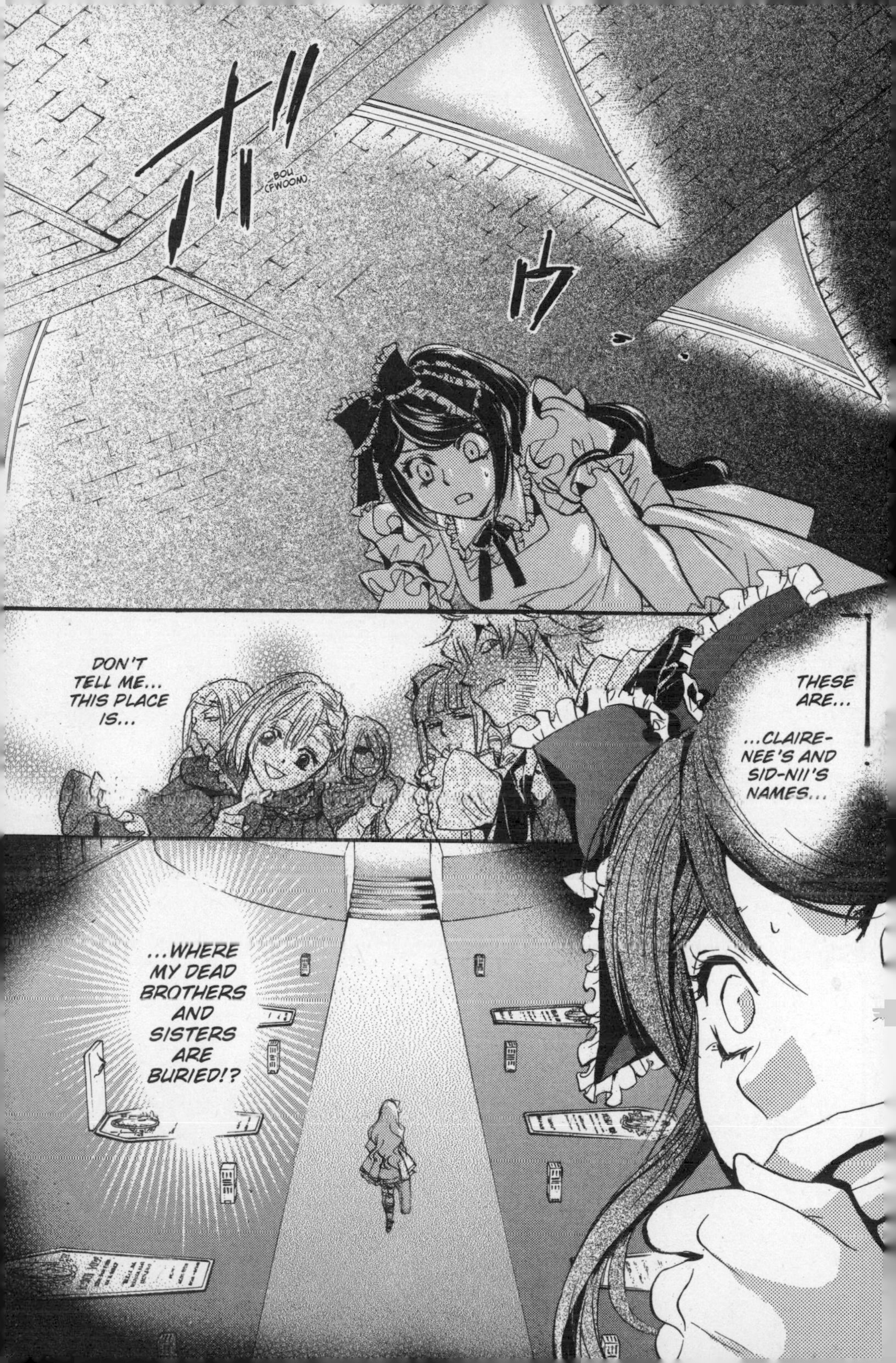
BOU (FWOOM)
THESE ARE...
...CLAIRE-NEE'S AND SID-NII'S NAMES...
DON'T TELL ME... THIS PLACE IS...
...WHERE MY DEAD BROTHERS AND SISTERS ARE BURIED!?

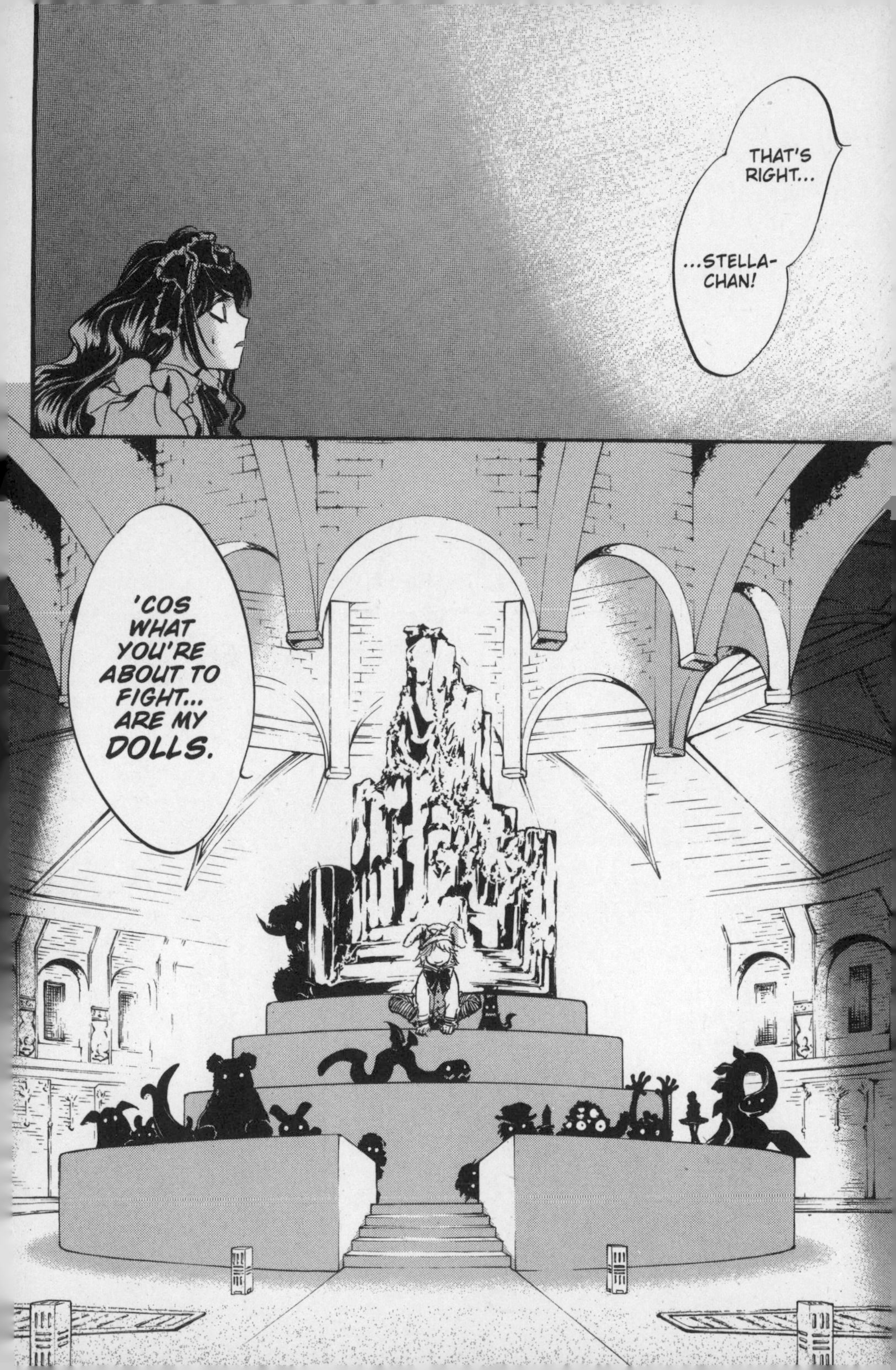
THAT'S RIGHT...
...STELLA-CHAN!
'COS WHAT YOU'RE ABOUT TO FIGHT... ARE MY DOLLS.

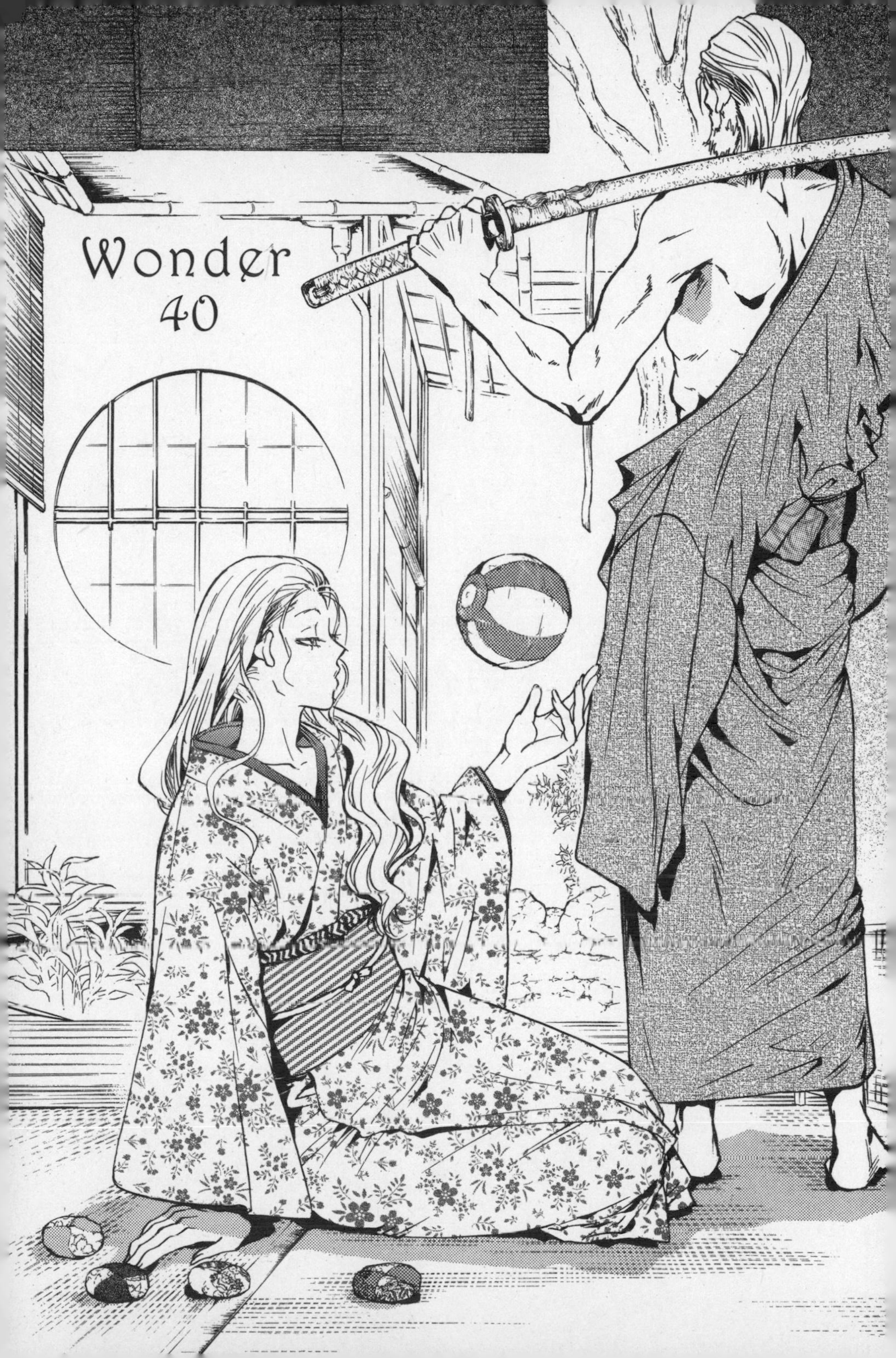
Wonder
40

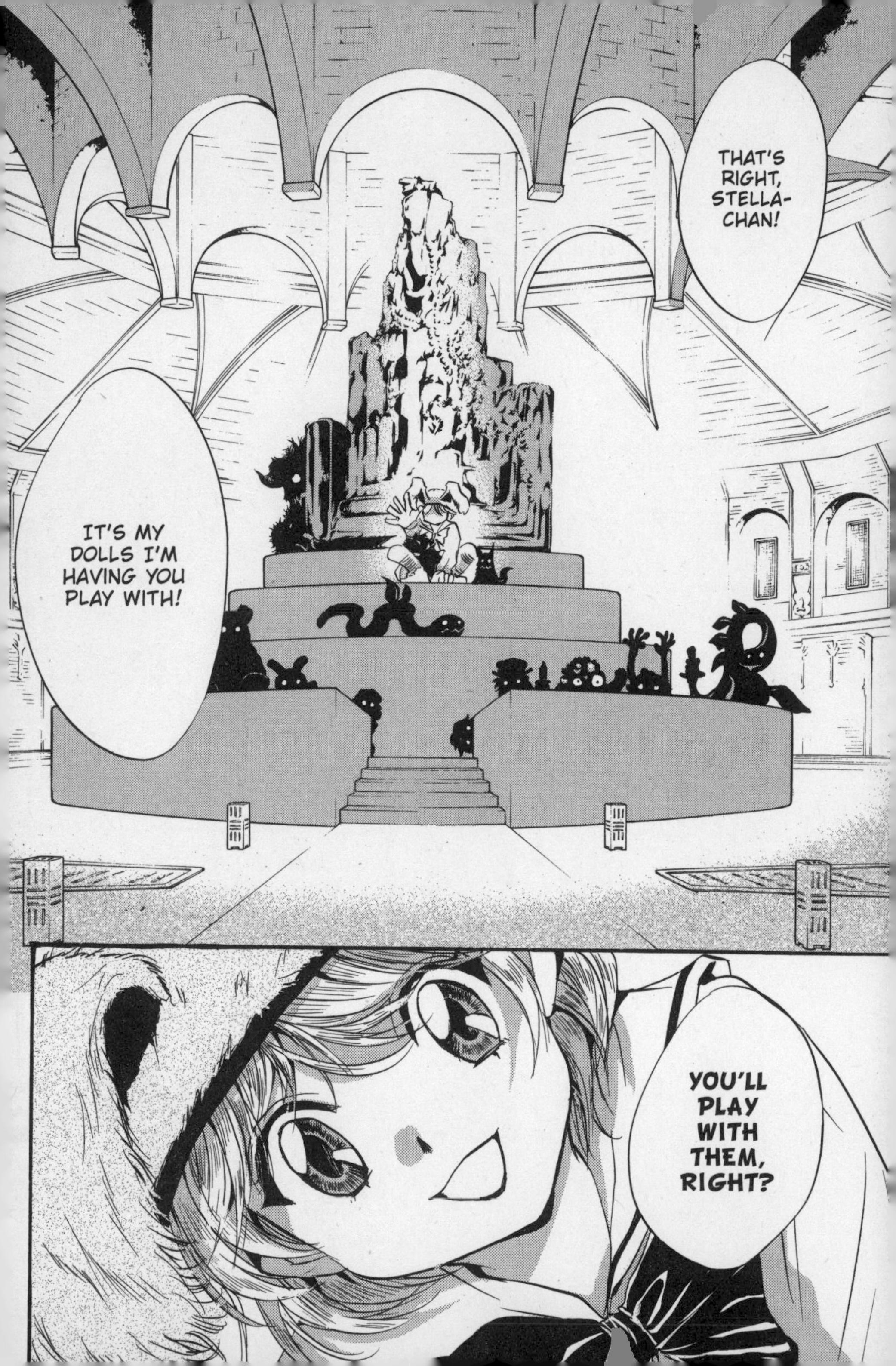
THAT'S RIGHT, STELLA-CHAN!
IT'S MY DOLLS I'M HAVING YOU PLAY WITH!
YOU'LL PLAY WITH THEM, RIGHT?

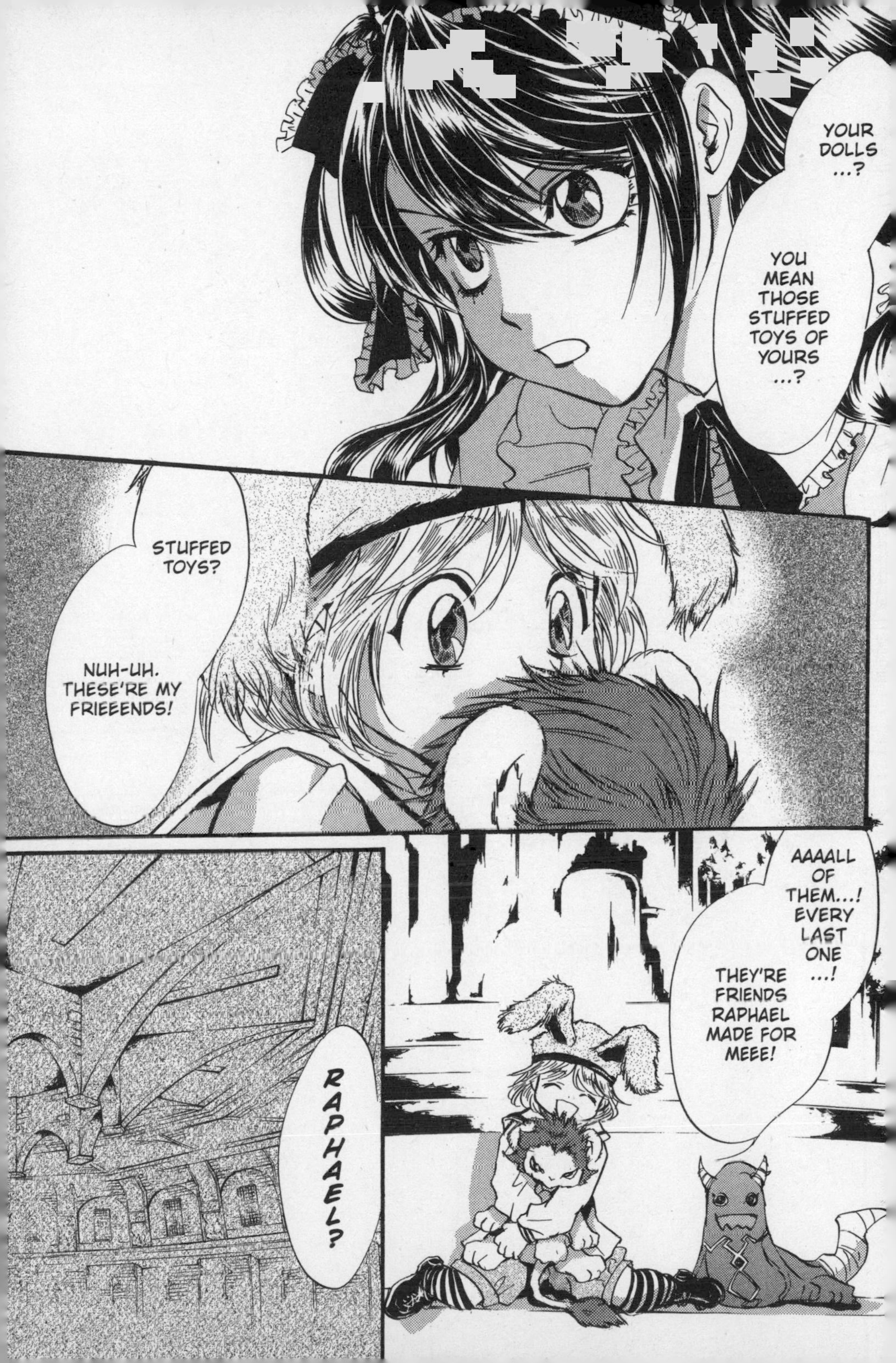
YOUR DOLLS ...?
YOU MEAN THOSE STUFFED TOYS OF YOURS ...?
STUFFED TOYS?
NUH-UH. THESE'RE MY FRIEEENDS!
AAAALL OF THEM...! EVERY LAST ONE ...!
THEY'RE FRIENDS RAPHAEL MADE FOR MEEE!
RAPHAEL?

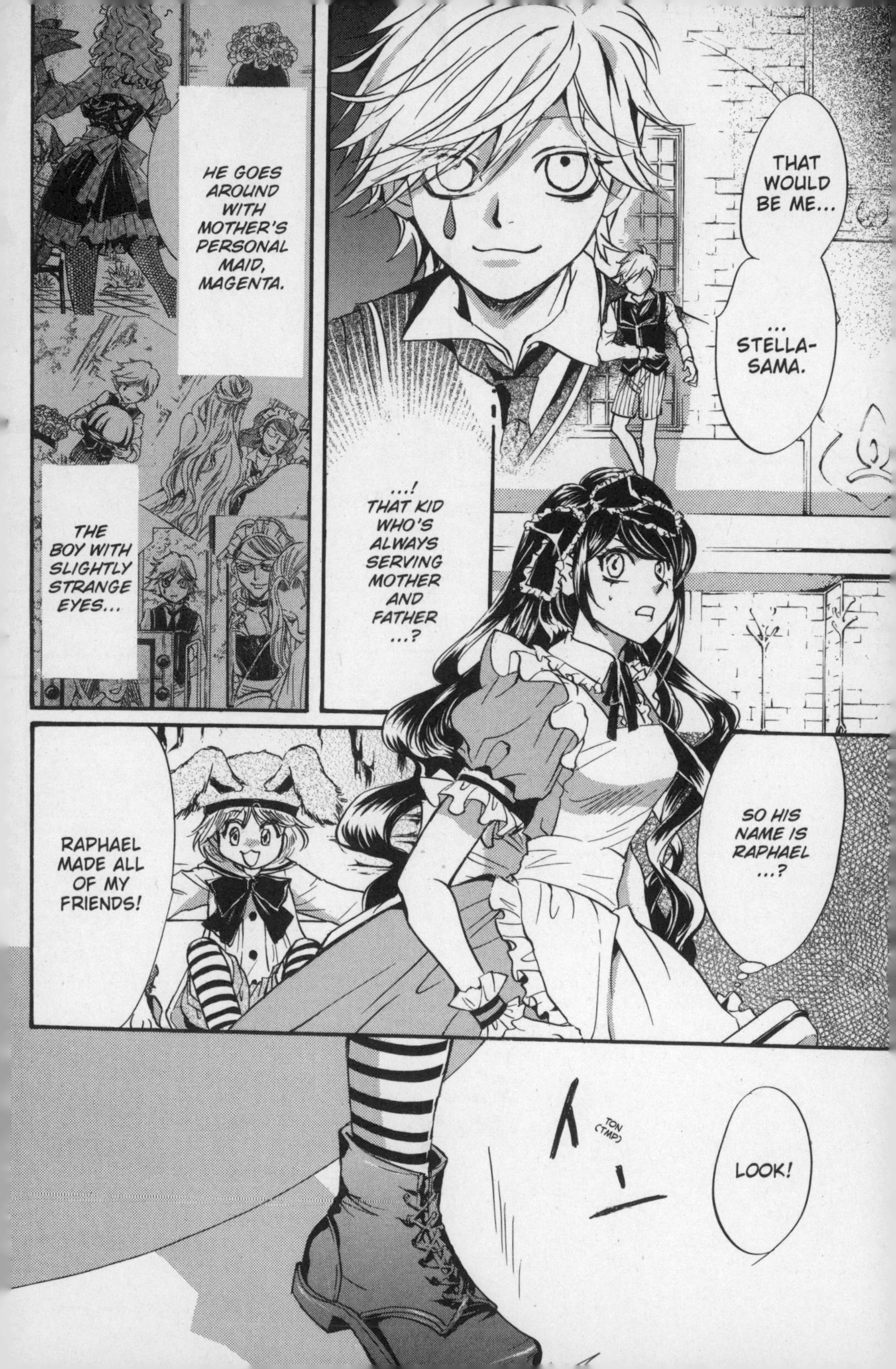
THAT WOULD BE ME...
...STELLA-SAMA.
...! THAT KID WHO'S ALWAYS SERVING MOTHER AND FATHER ...?
HE GOES AROUND WITH MOTHER'S PERSONAL MAID, MAGENTA.
THE BOY WITH SLIGHTLY STRANGE EYES...
SO HIS NAME IS RAPHAEL ...?
RAPHAEL MADE ALL OF MY FRIENDS!
LOOK!
TON (TMP)

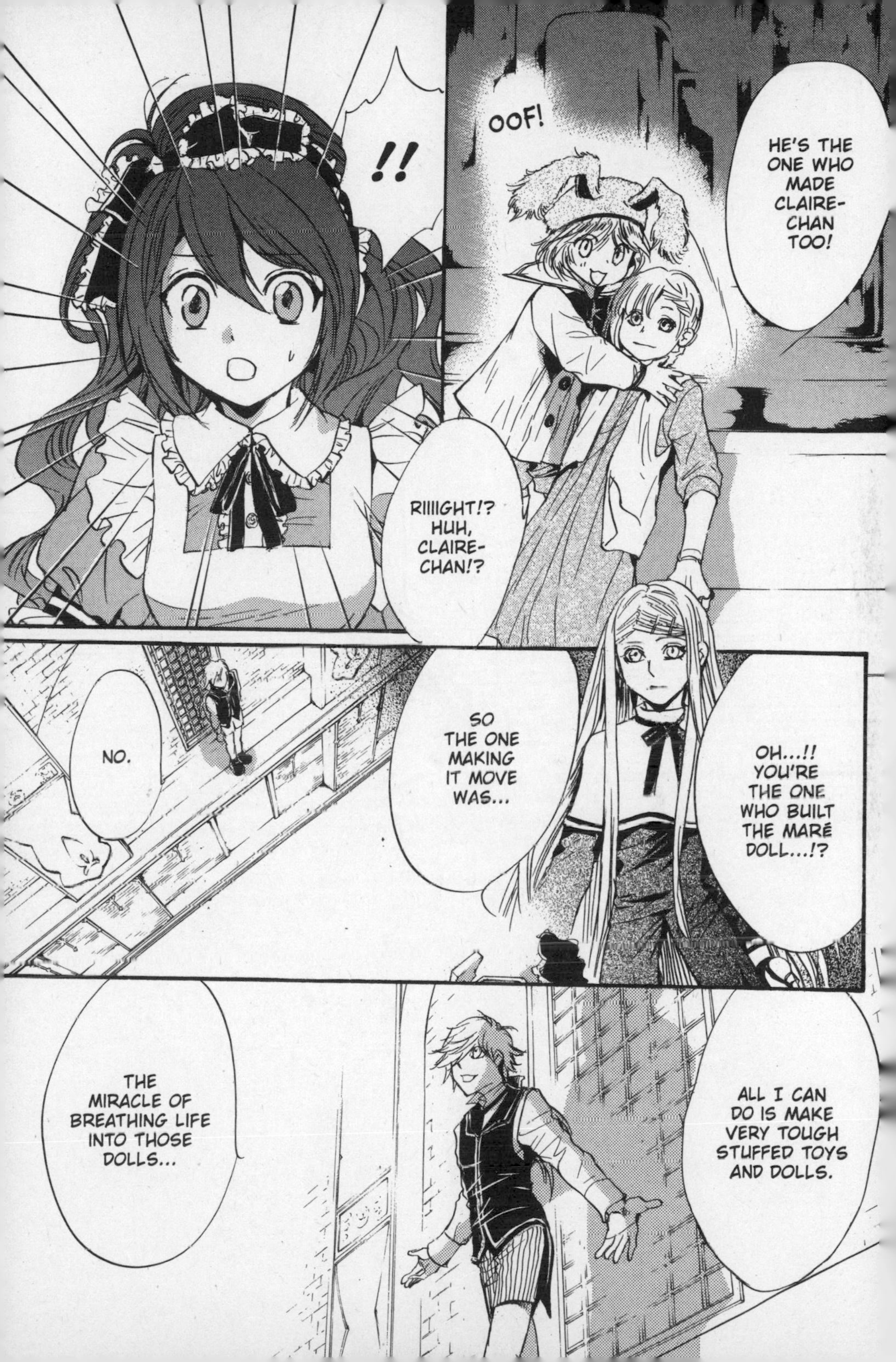
HE'S THE ONE WHO MADE CLAIRE-CHAN TOO!
OOF!
RIIIIGHT!? HUH, CLAIRE-CHAN!?
!!
OH...!! YOU'RE THE ONE WHO BUILT THE MARÉ DOLL...!?
SO THE ONE MAKING IT MOVE WAS...
NO.
ALL I CAN DO IS MAKE VERY TOUGH STUFFED TOYS AND DOLLS.
THE MIRACLE OF BREATHING LIFE INTO THOSE DOLLS...

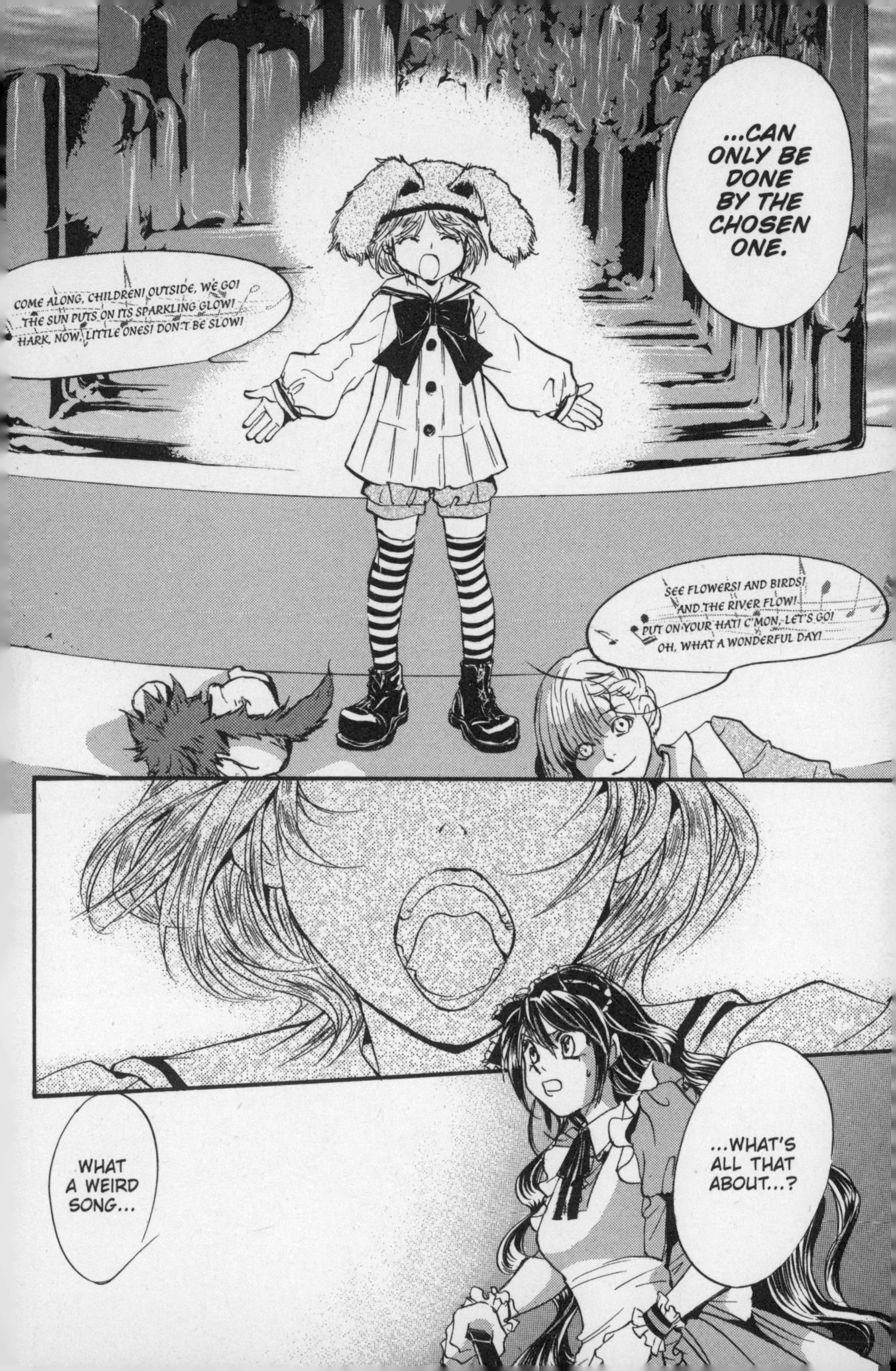
...CAN ONLY BE DONE BY THE CHOSEN ONE.
COME ALONG, CHILDREN! OUTSIDE, WE GO! THE SUN PUTS ON ITS SPARKLING GLOW! HARK, NOW, LITTLE ONES! DON'T BE SLOW!
SEE FLOWERS! AND BIRDS! AND THE RIVER FLOW! PUT ON YOUR HAT! C'MON, LET'S GO! OH, WHAT A WONDERFUL DAY!
...WHAT'S ALL THAT ABOUT...?
WHAT A WEIRD SONG...

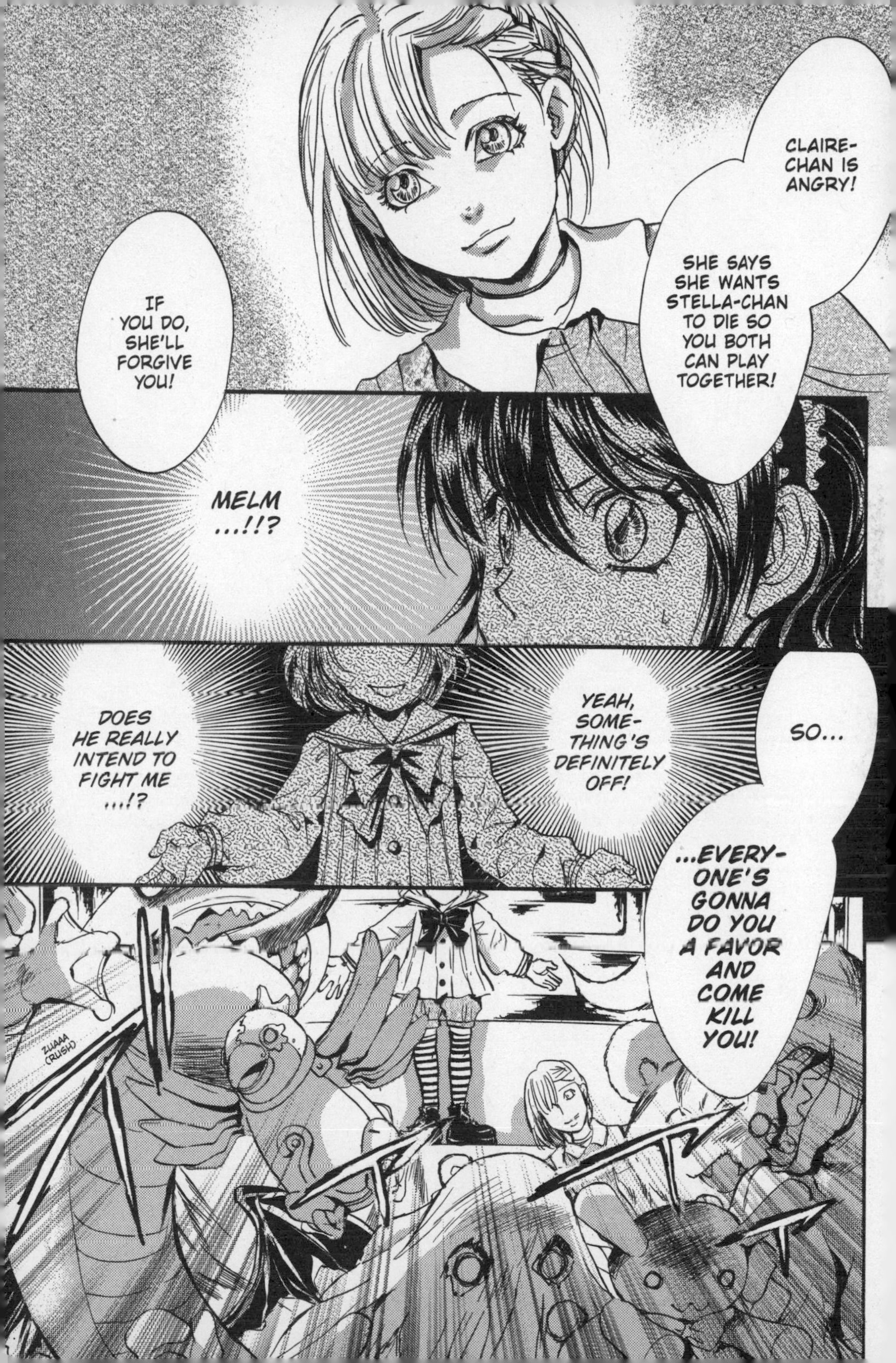
CLAIRE-CHAN IS ANGRY!
SHE SAYS SHE WANTS STELLA-CHAN TO DIE SO YOU BOTH CAN PLAY TOGETHER!
IF YOU DO, SHE'LL FORGIVE YOU!
MELM ...!!?
SO...
YEAH, SOME-THING'S DEFINITELY OFF!
DOES HE REALLY INTEND TO FIGHT ME ...!?
...EVERY-ONE'S GONNA DO YOU A FAVOR AND COME KILL YOU!
ZUAAA (RUSH)

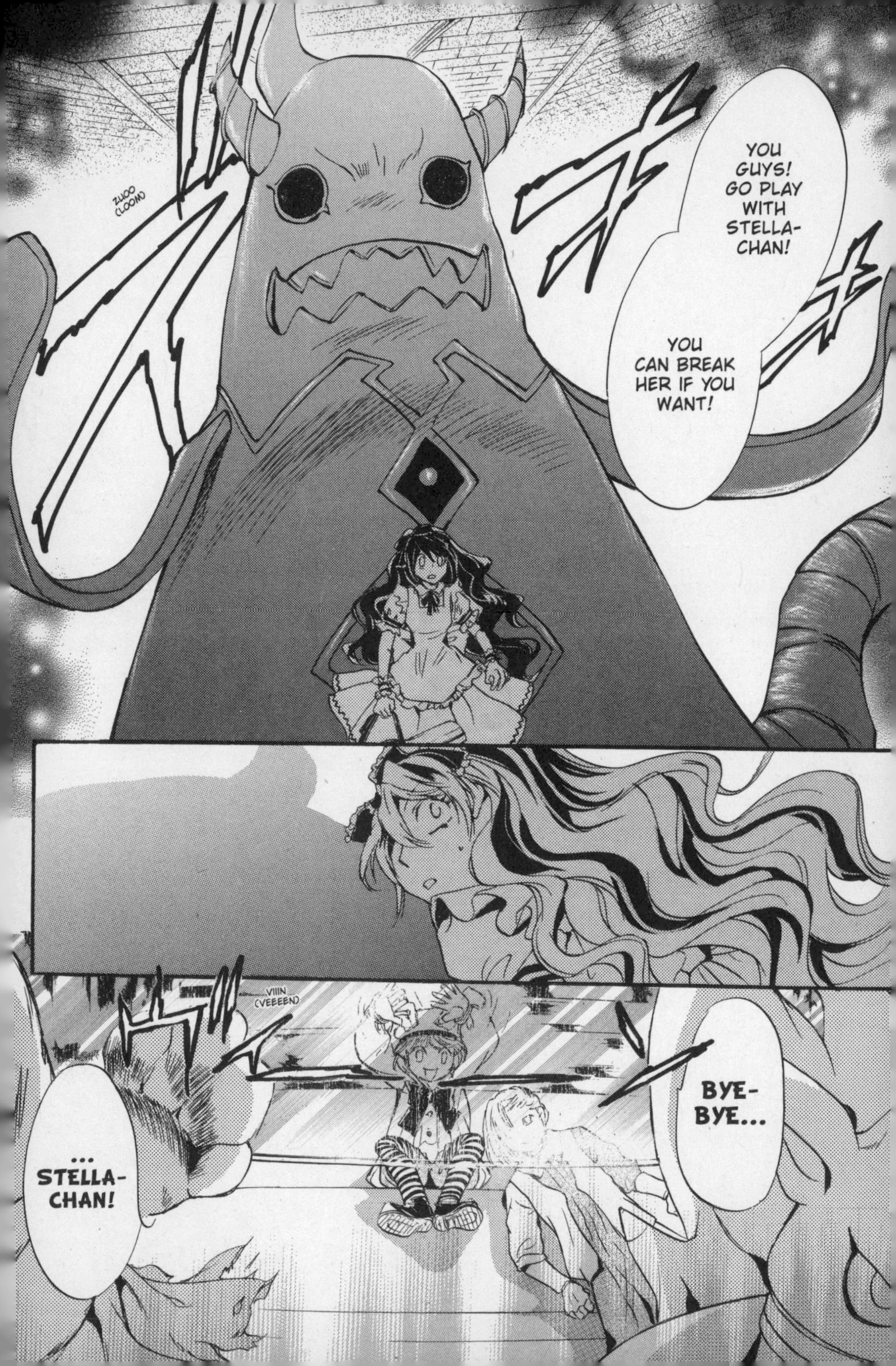
YOU GUYS! GO PLAY WITH STELLA-CHAN!
YOU CAN BREAK HER IF YOU WANT!
ZUOO (LOOM)
VIIIN (VEEEEN)
BYE-BYE...
...STELLA-CHAN!

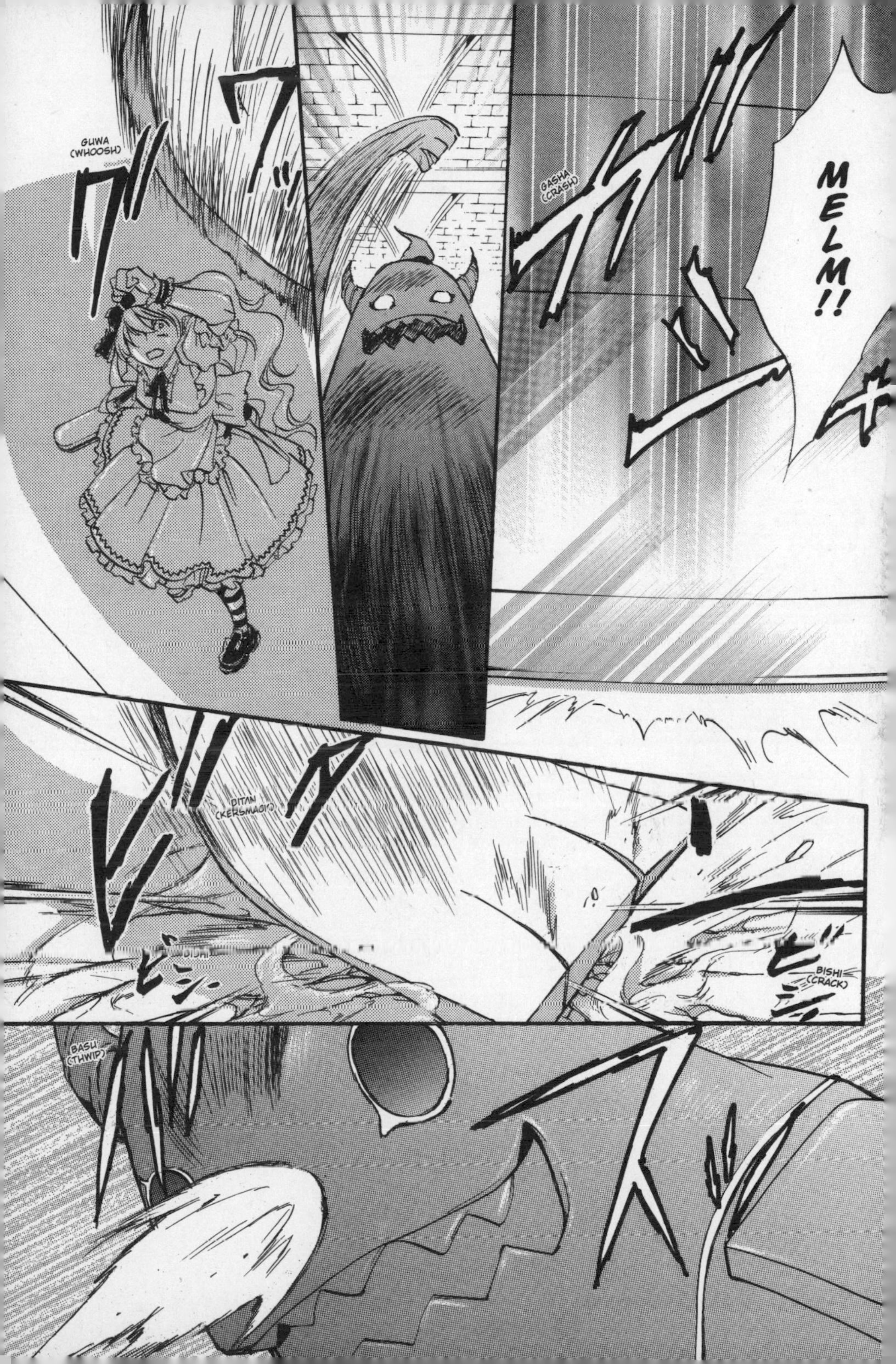
MELM!!
GASHA (CRASH)
GUWA (WHOOSH)
BISHI (CRACK)
DITAN (KERSMACK)
BISHI
BASU (THWIP)

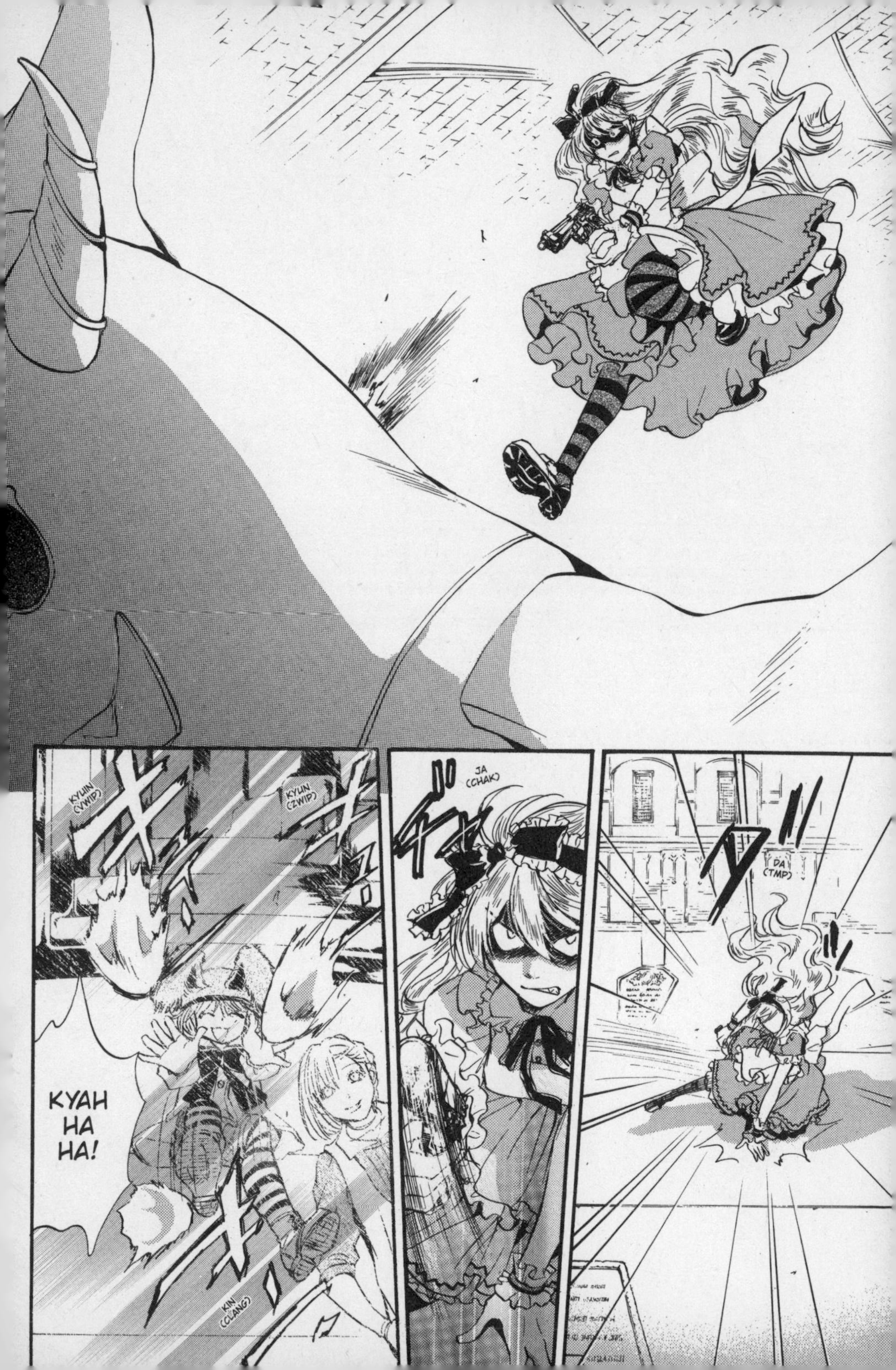
DA (TMP)
JA (CHAK)
KYUN (ZWIP)
KYUIN (VWIP)
KYAH HA HA!
KIN (CLANG)

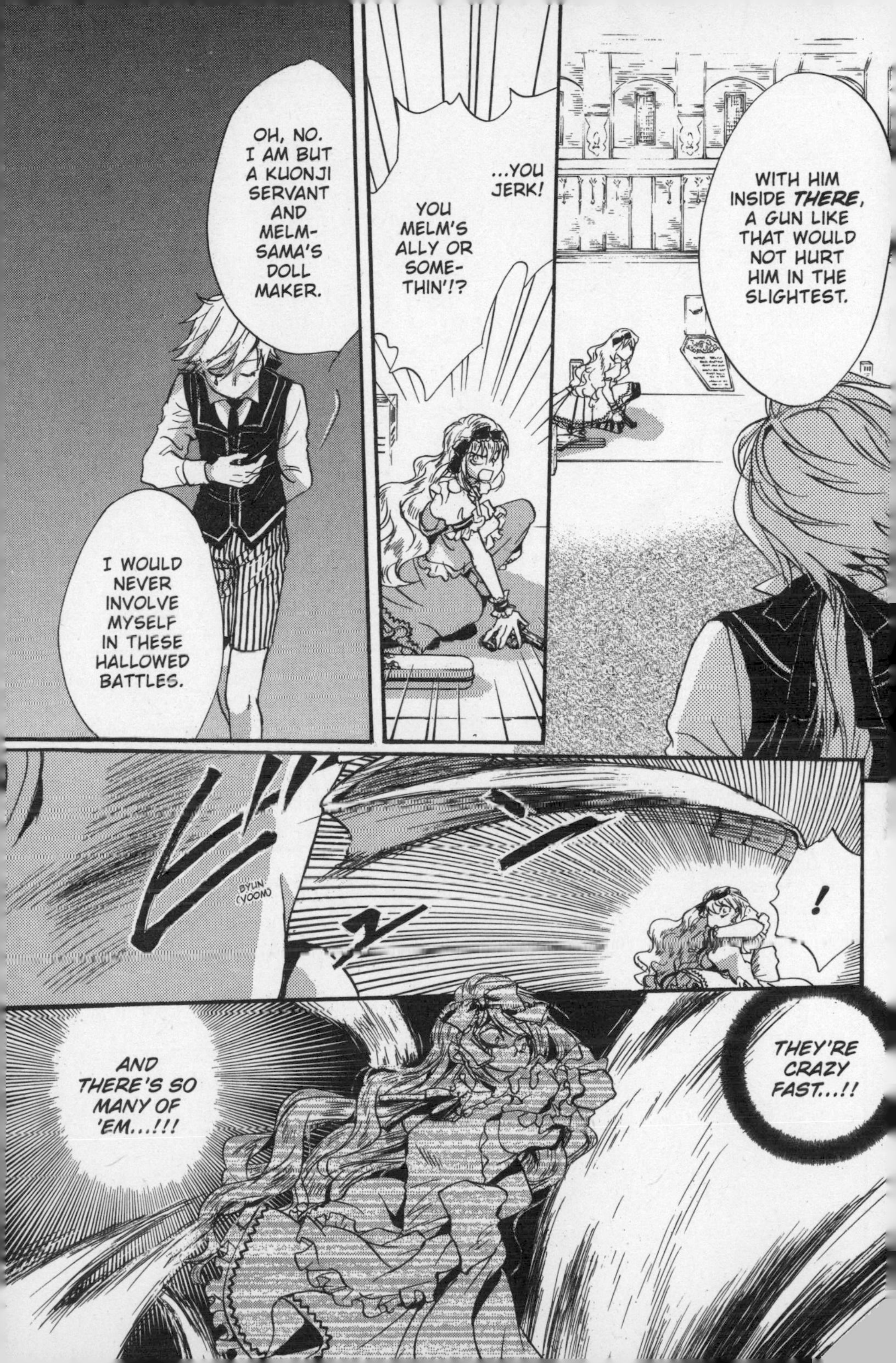

WITH HIM INSIDE *THERE*, A GUN LIKE THAT WOULD NOT HURT HIM IN THE SLIGHTEST.
...YOU JERK!
YOU MELM'S ALLY OR SOME-THIN'!?
OH, NO. I AM BUT A KUONJI SERVANT AND MELM-SAMA'S DOLL MAKER.
I WOULD NEVER INVOLVE MYSELF IN THESE HALLOWED BATTLES.
!
BYUN (YOOM)
THEY'RE CRAZY FAST...!!
AND THERE'S SO MANY OF 'EM...!!!

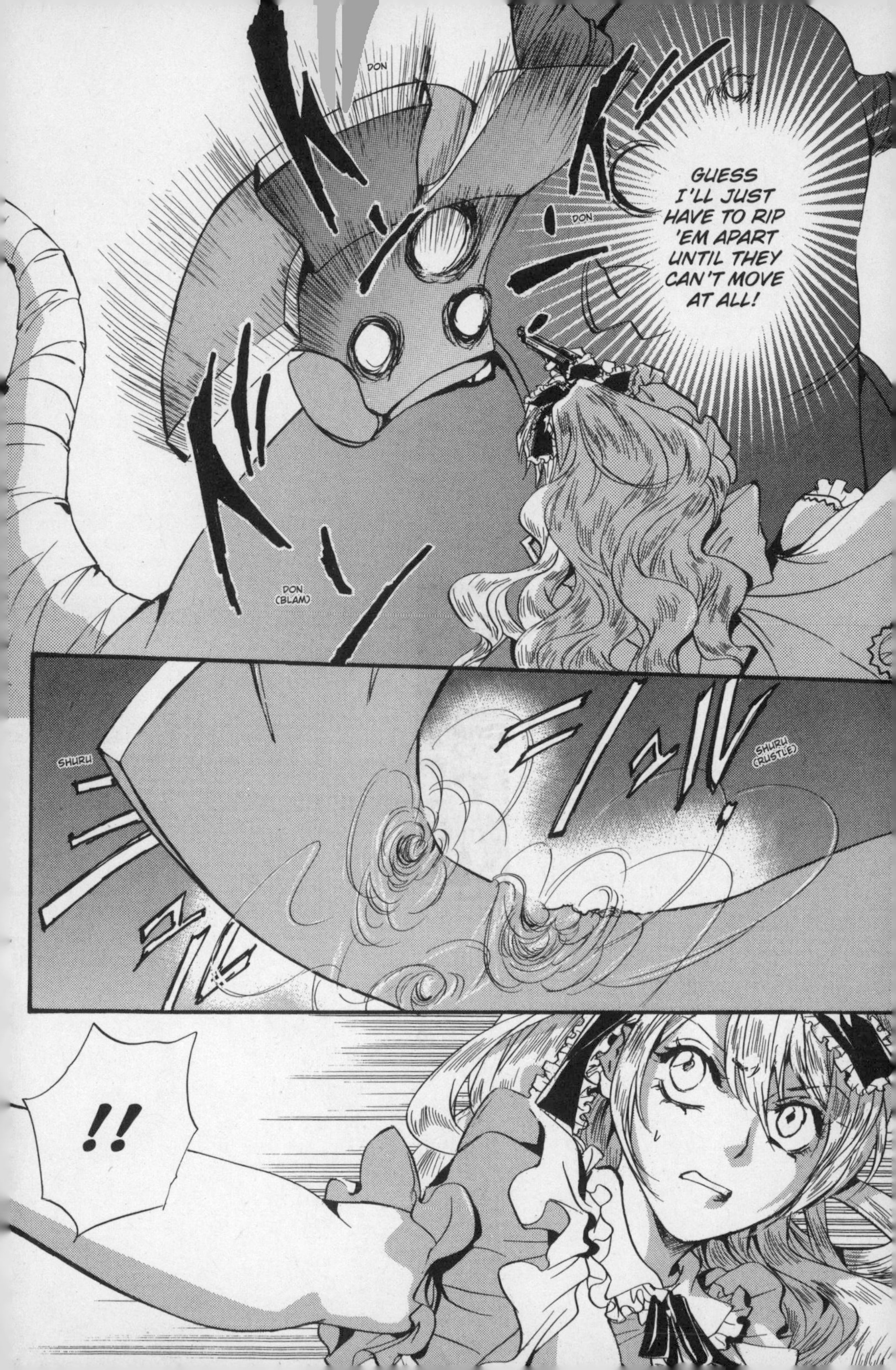
DON
GUESS I'LL JUST HAVE TO RIP 'EM APART UNTIL THEY CAN'T MOVE AT ALL!
DON
DON (BLAM)
SHURU (RUSTLE)
SHURU
!!

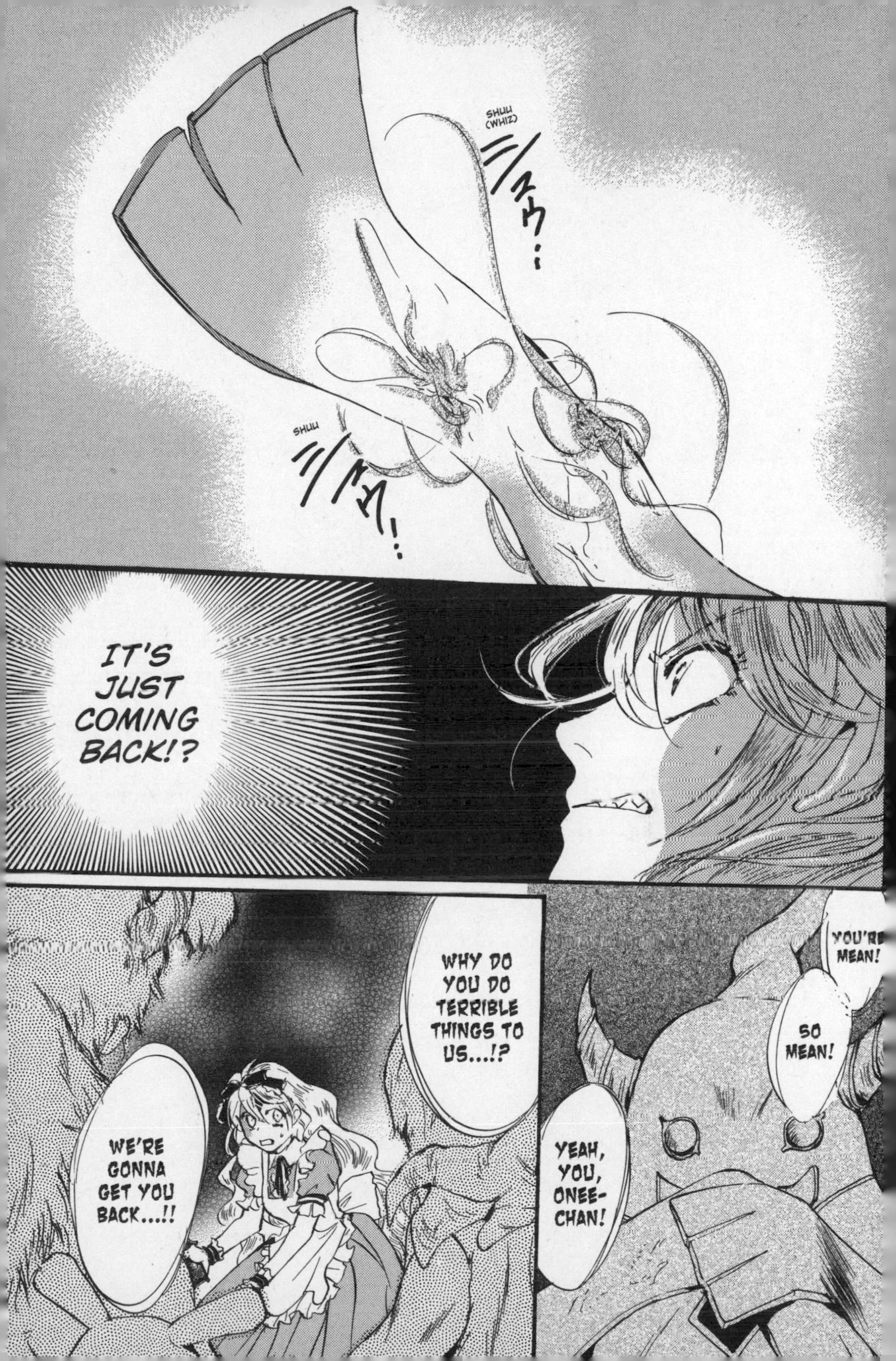
SHUU (WHIZ)
SHUU
IT'S JUST COMING BACK!?
YOU'RE MEAN!
SO MEAN!
YEAH, YOU, ONEE-CHAN!
WHY DO YOU DO TERRIBLE THINGS TO US...!?
WE'RE GONNA GET YOU BACK...!!

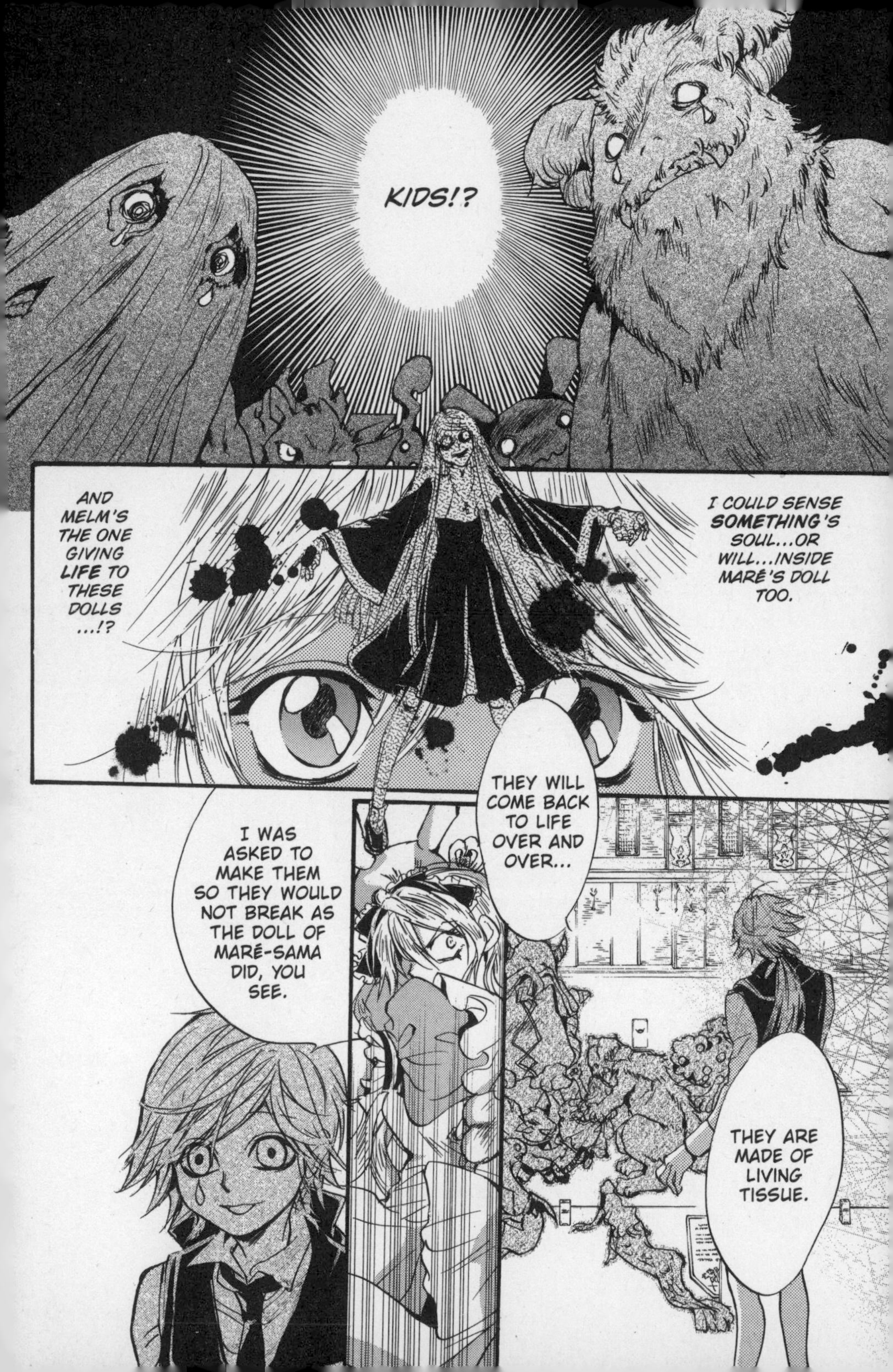
KIDS!?
I COULD SENSE SOMETHING'S SOUL...OR WILL...INSIDE MARÉ'S DOLL TOO.
AND MELM'S THE ONE GIVING LIFE TO THESE DOLLS ...!?
THEY WILL COME BACK TO LIFE OVER AND OVER...
THEY ARE MADE OF LIVING TISSUE.
I WAS ASKED TO MAKE THEM SO THEY WOULD NOT BREAK AS THE DOLL OF MARÉ-SAMA DID, YOU SEE.

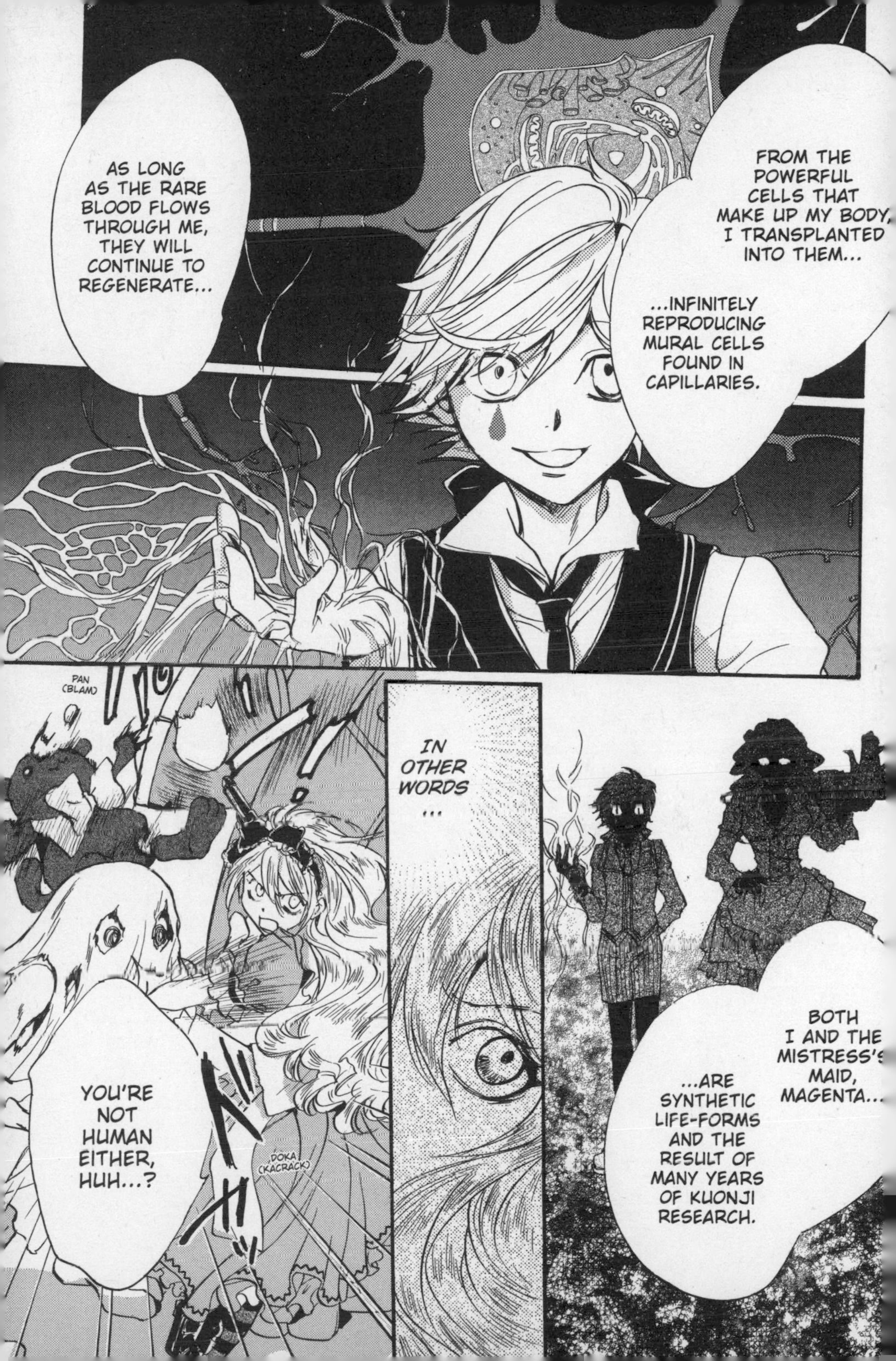
FROM THE POWERFUL CELLS THAT MAKE UP MY BODY, I TRANSPLANTED INTO THEM...
...INFINITELY REPRODUCING MURAL CELLS FOUND IN CAPILLARIES.
AS LONG AS THE RARE BLOOD FLOWS THROUGH ME, THEY WILL CONTINUE TO REGENERATE...
BOTH I AND THE MISTRESS'S MAID, MAGENTA...
...ARE SYNTHETIC LIFE-FORMS AND THE RESULT OF MANY YEARS OF KUONJI RESEARCH.
IN OTHER WORDS ...
PAN (BLAM)
YOU'RE NOT HUMAN EITHER, HUH...?
DOKA (KACRACK)

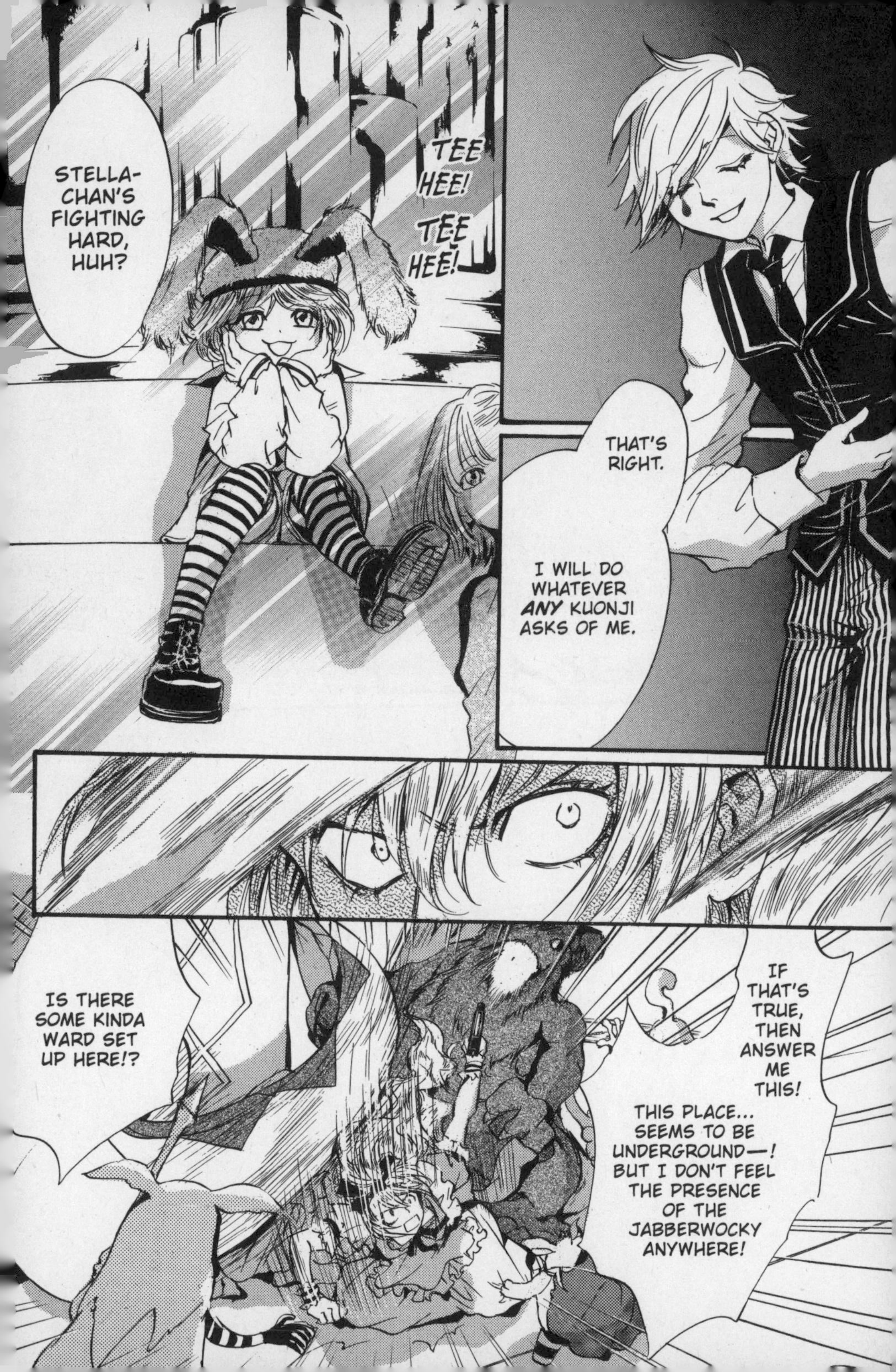
THAT'S RIGHT.
I WILL DO WHATEVER *ANY* KUONJI ASKS OF ME.
STELLA-CHAN'S FIGHTING HARD, HUH?
TEE HEE!
TEE HEE!
IF THAT'S TRUE, THEN ANSWER ME THIS!
THIS PLACE... SEEMS TO BE UNDERGROUND—! BUT I DON'T FEEL THE PRESENCE OF THE JABBERWOCKY ANYWHERE!
IS THERE SOME KINDA WARD SET UP HERE!?

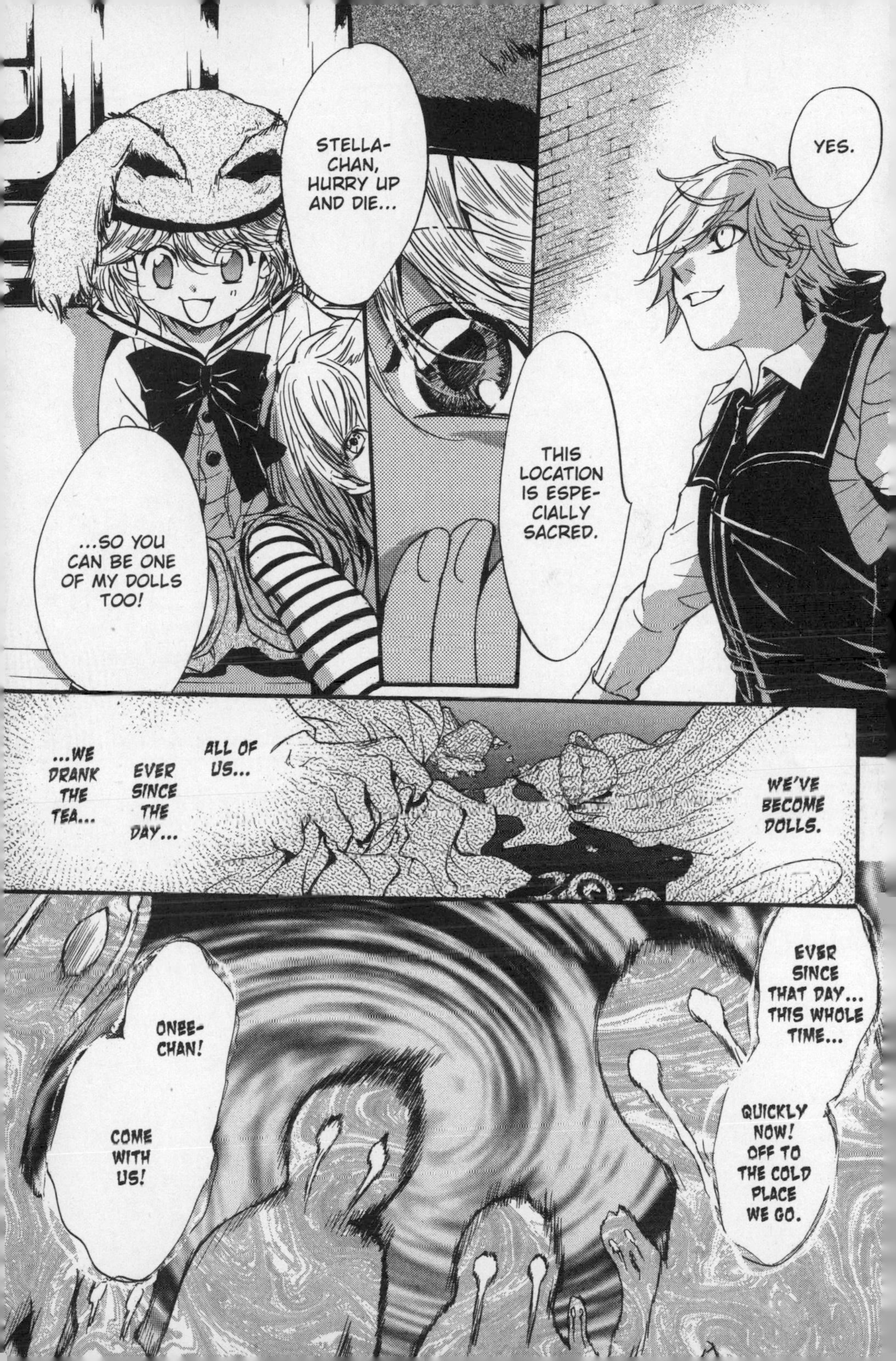
YES.
THIS LOCATION IS ESPECIALLY SACRED.
STELLA-CHAN, HURRY UP AND DIE...
...SO YOU CAN BE ONE OF MY DOLLS TOO!
WE'VE BECOME DOLLS.
ALL OF US...
EVER SINCE THE DAY...
...WE DRANK THE TEA...
EVER SINCE THAT DAY... THIS WHOLE TIME...
QUICKLY NOW! OFF TO THE COLD PLACE WE GO.
ONEE-CHAN!
COME WITH US!

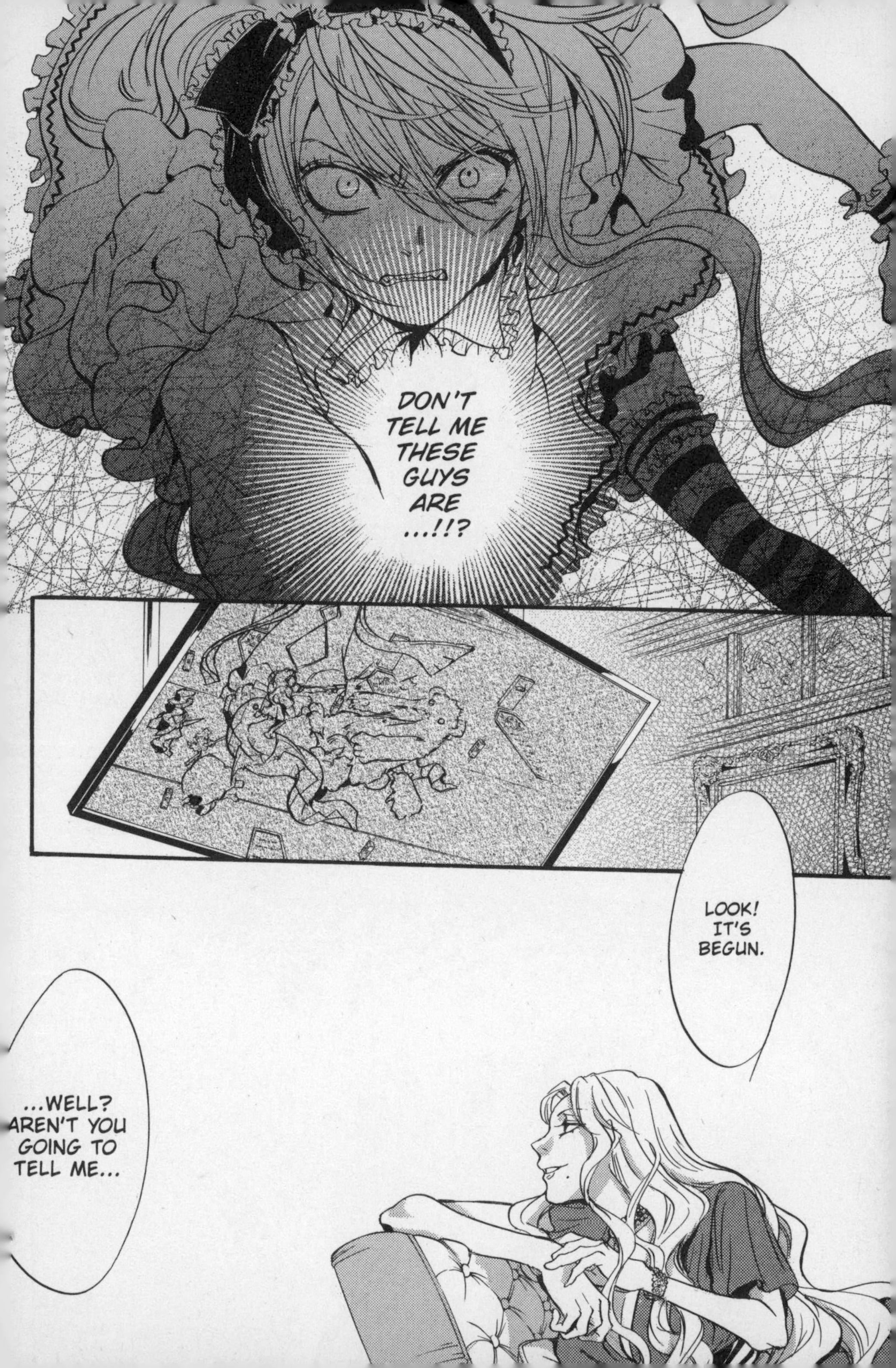
DON'T TELL ME THESE GUYS ARE ...!!?
LOOK! IT'S BEGUN.
...WELL? AREN'T YOU GOING TO TELL ME...

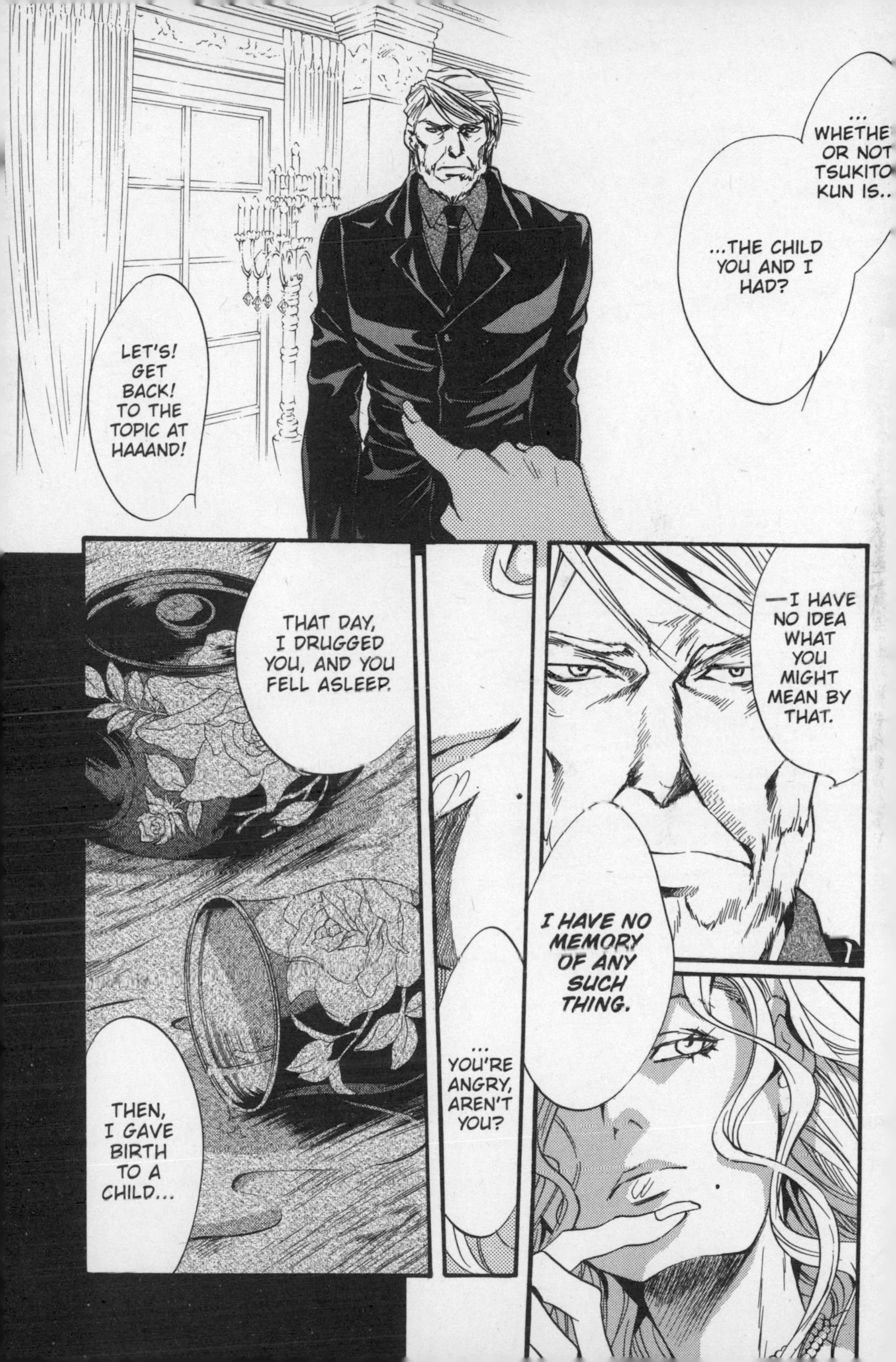

... WHETHE OR NOT TSUKITO KUN IS..
...THE CHILD YOU AND I HAD?
LET'S! GET BACK! TO THE TOPIC AT HAAAND!
—I HAVE NO IDEA WHAT YOU MIGHT MEAN BY THAT.
I HAVE NO MEMORY OF ANY SUCH THING.
... YOU'RE ANGRY, AREN'T YOU?
THAT DAY, I DRUGGED YOU, AND YOU FELL ASLEEP.
THEN, I GAVE BIRTH TO A CHILD...

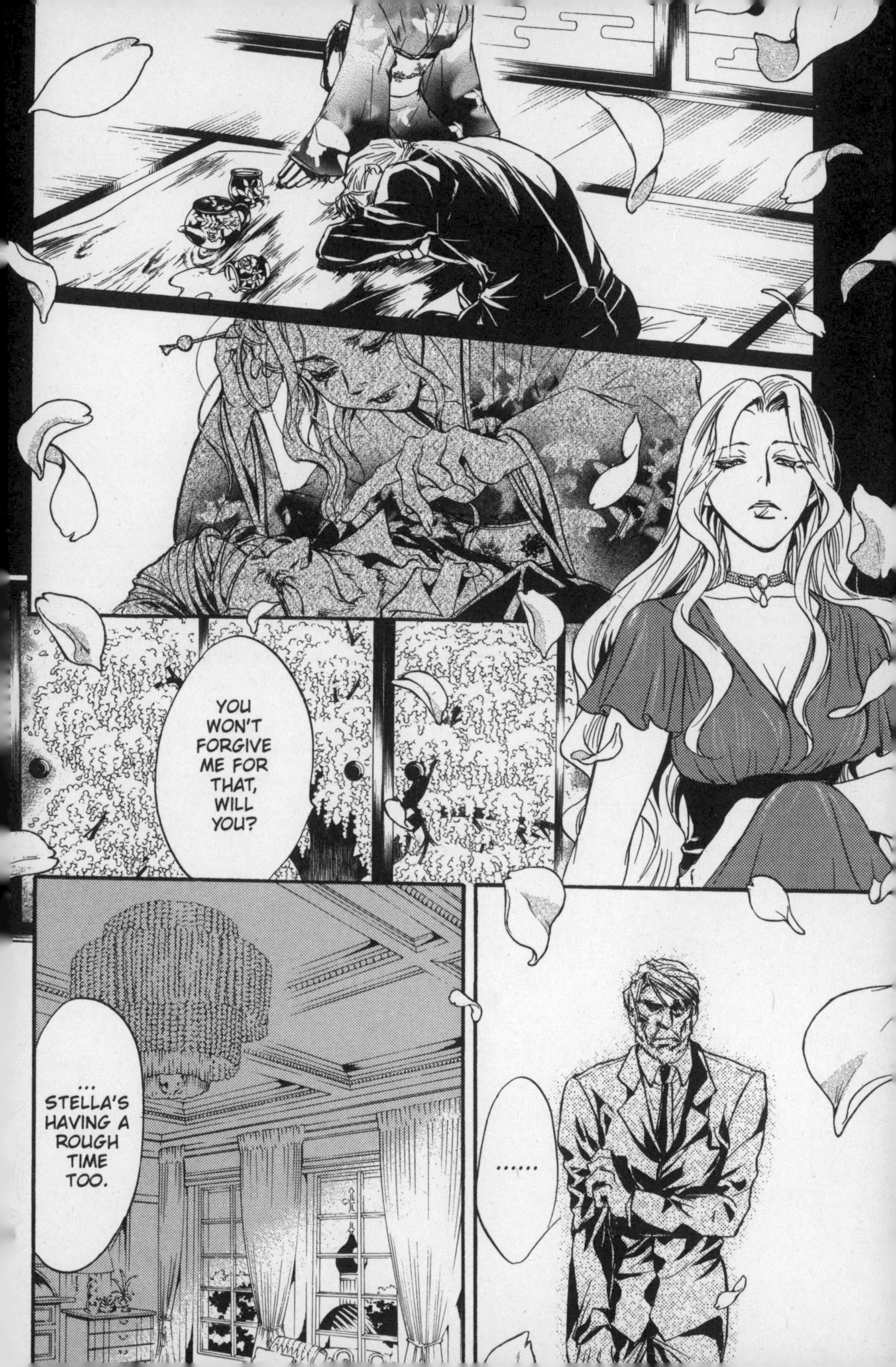
YOU WON'T FORGIVE ME FOR THAT, WILL YOU?
......
... STELLA'S HAVING A ROUGH TIME TOO.

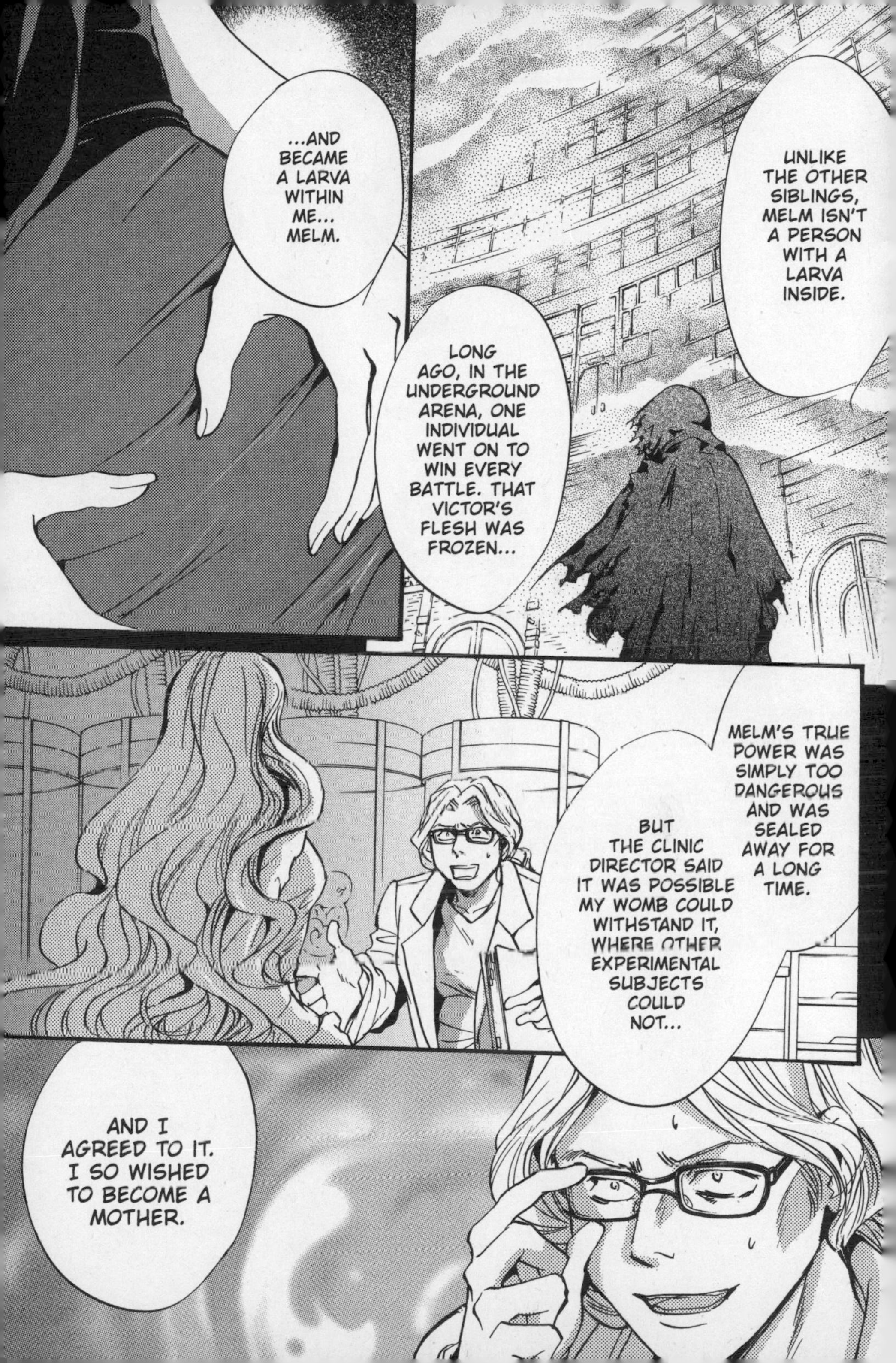
UNLIKE THE OTHER SIBLINGS, MELM ISN'T A PERSON WITH A LARVA INSIDE.
LONG AGO, IN THE UNDERGROUND ARENA, ONE INDIVIDUAL WENT ON TO WIN EVERY BATTLE. THAT VICTOR'S FLESH WAS FROZEN...
...AND BECAME A LARVA WITHIN ME... MELM.
MELM'S TRUE POWER WAS SIMPLY TOO DANGEROUS AND WAS SEALED AWAY FOR A LONG TIME.
BUT THE CLINIC DIRECTOR SAID IT WAS POSSIBLE MY WOMB COULD WITHSTAND IT, WHERE OTHER EXPERIMENTAL SUBJECTS COULD NOT...
AND I AGREED TO IT. I SO WISHED TO BECOME A MOTHER.

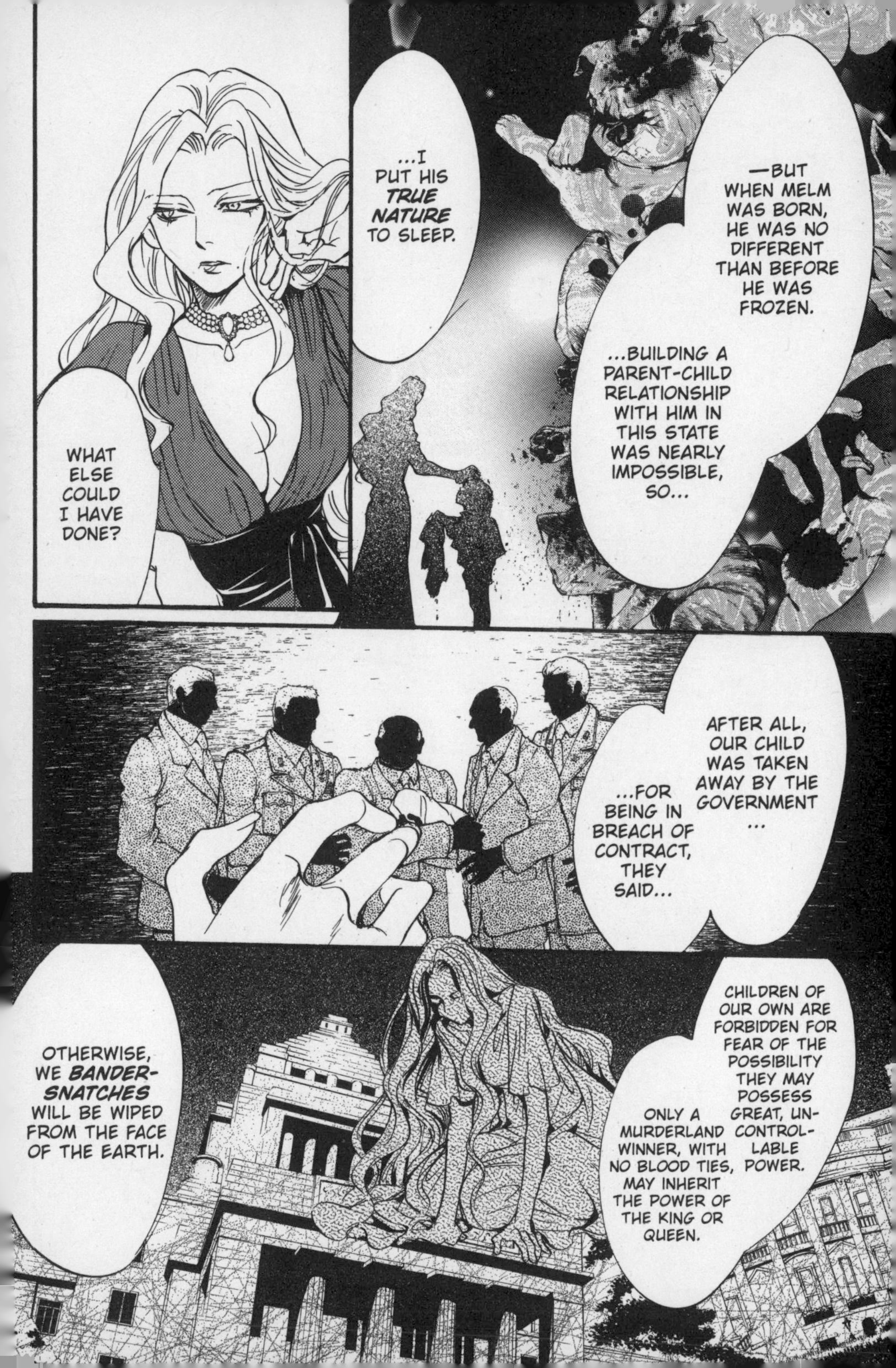
—BUT WHEN MELM WAS BORN, HE WAS NO DIFFERENT THAN BEFORE HE WAS FROZEN.
...BUILDING A PARENT-CHILD RELATIONSHIP WITH HIM IN THIS STATE WAS NEARLY IMPOSSIBLE, SO...
...I PUT HIS ***TRUE NATURE*** TO SLEEP.
WHAT ELSE COULD I HAVE DONE?
AFTER ALL, OUR CHILD WAS TAKEN AWAY BY THE GOVERNMENT...
...FOR BEING IN BREACH OF CONTRACT, THEY SAID...
CHILDREN OF OUR OWN ARE FORBIDDEN FOR FEAR OF THE POSSIBILITY THEY MAY POSSESS GREAT, UNCONTROLLABLE POWER.
ONLY A MURDERLAND WINNER, WITH NO BLOOD TIES, MAY INHERIT THE POWER OF THE KING OR QUEEN.
OTHERWISE, WE ***BANDERSNATCHES*** WILL BE WIPED FROM THE FACE OF THE EARTH.

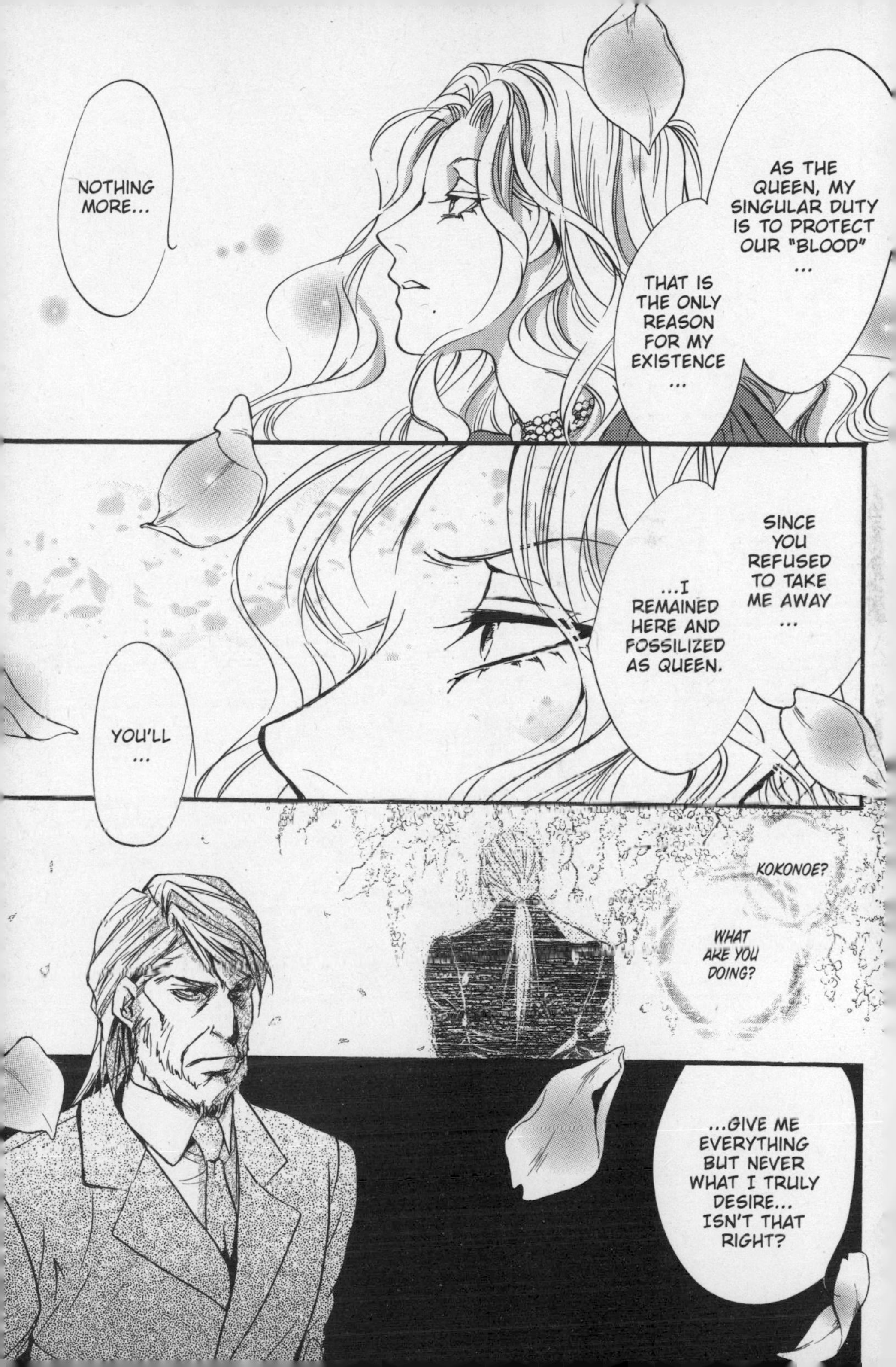

AS THE QUEEN, MY SINGULAR DUTY IS TO PROTECT OUR "BLOOD" ...
THAT IS THE ONLY REASON FOR MY EXISTENCE ...
NOTHING MORE...
SINCE YOU REFUSED TO TAKE ME AWAY ...
...I REMAINED HERE AND FOSSILIZED AS QUEEN.
YOU'LL ...
KOKONOE?
WHAT ARE YOU DOING?
...GIVE ME EVERYTHING BUT NEVER WHAT I TRULY DESIRE... ISN'T THAT RIGHT?

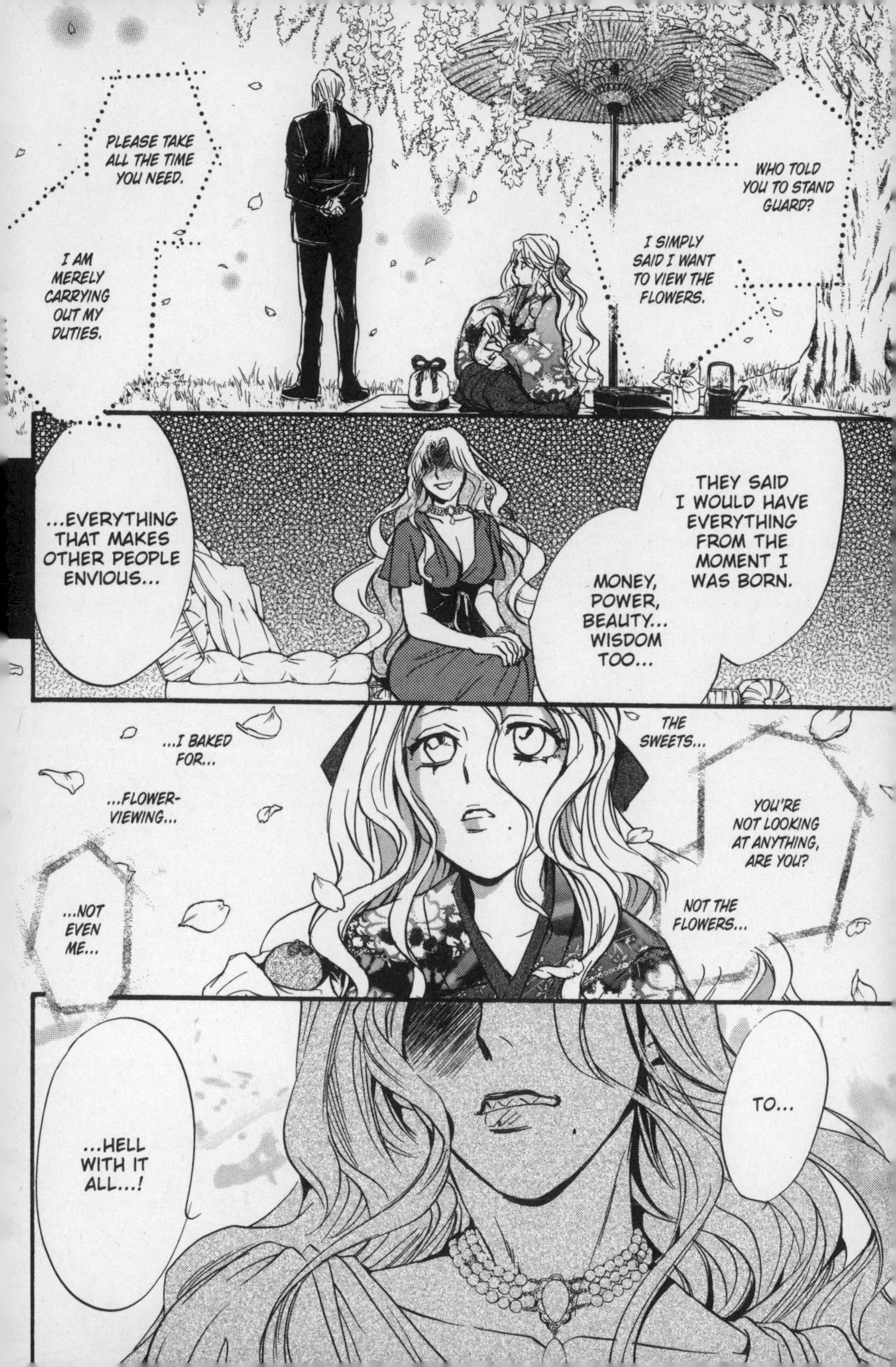
WHO TOLD YOU TO STAND GUARD?
I SIMPLY SAID I WANT TO VIEW THE FLOWERS.
PLEASE TAKE ALL THE TIME YOU NEED.
I AM MERELY CARRYING OUT MY DUTIES.
THEY SAID I WOULD HAVE EVERYTHING FROM THE MOMENT I WAS BORN.
MONEY, POWER, BEAUTY... WISDOM TOO...
...EVERYTHING THAT MAKES OTHER PEOPLE ENVIOUS...
THE SWEETS...
...I BAKED FOR...
...FLOWER-VIEWING...
YOU'RE NOT LOOKING AT ANYTHING, ARE YOU?
NOT THE FLOWERS...
...NOT EVEN ME...
TO...
...HELL WITH IT ALL...!

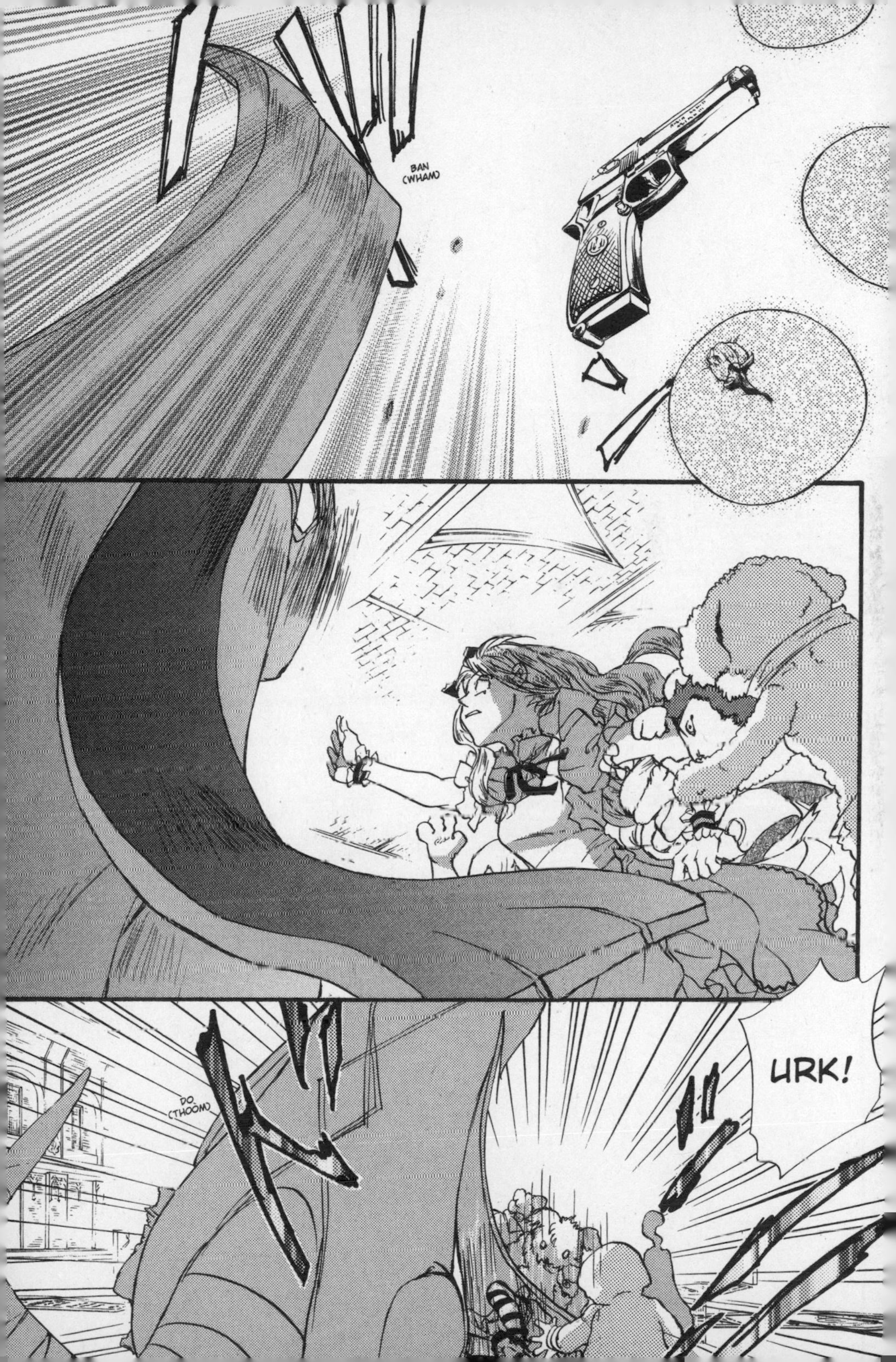
BAN
(WHAM)
URK!
DO
(THOOM)

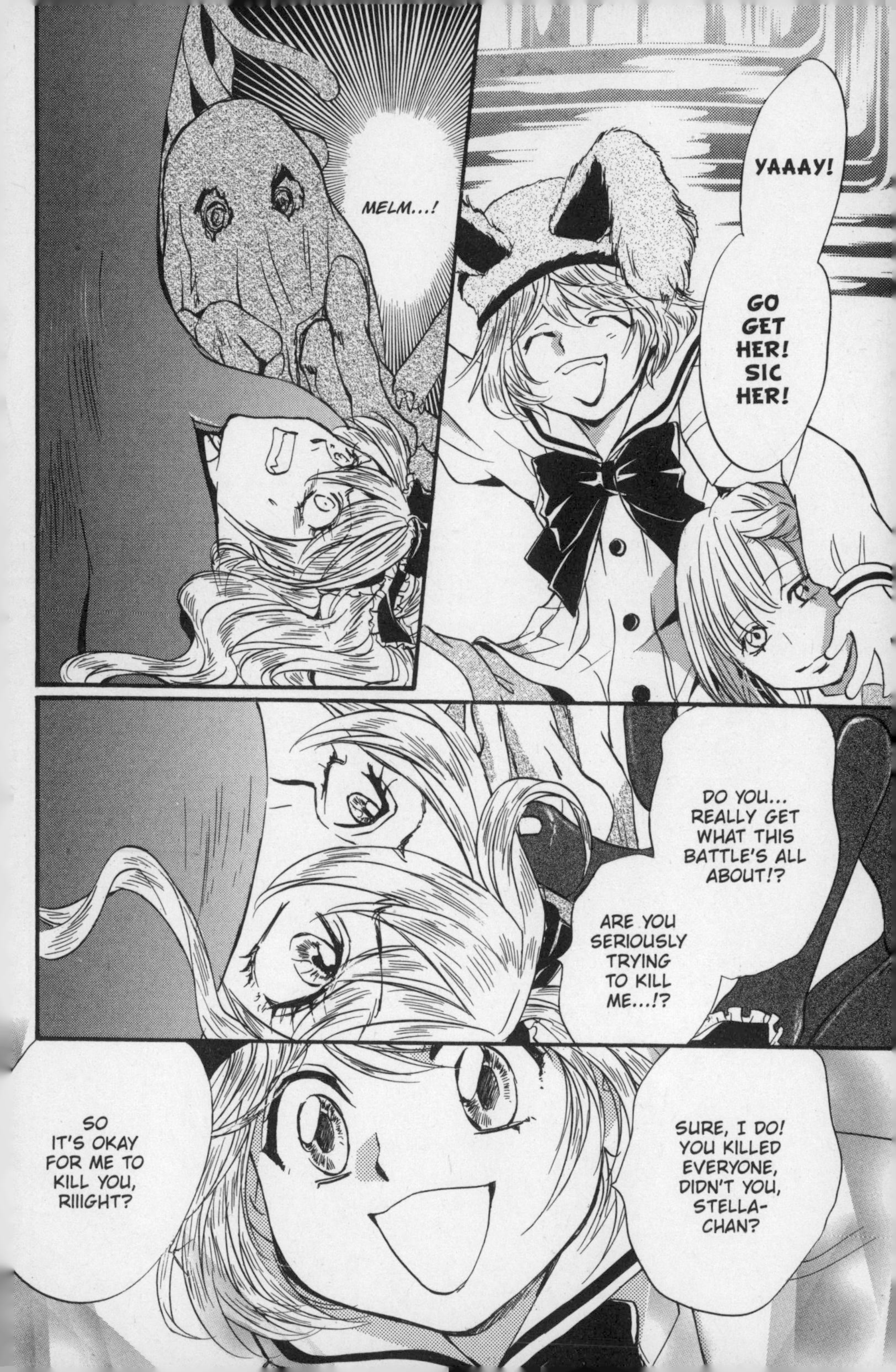
YAAAY!
GO GET HER! SIC HER!
MELM...!
DO YOU... REALLY GET WHAT THIS BATTLE'S ALL ABOUT!?
ARE YOU SERIOUSLY TRYING TO KILL ME...!?
SURE, I DO! YOU KILLED EVERYONE, DIDN'T YOU, STELLA-CHAN?
SO IT'S OKAY FOR ME TO KILL YOU, RIIIGHT?

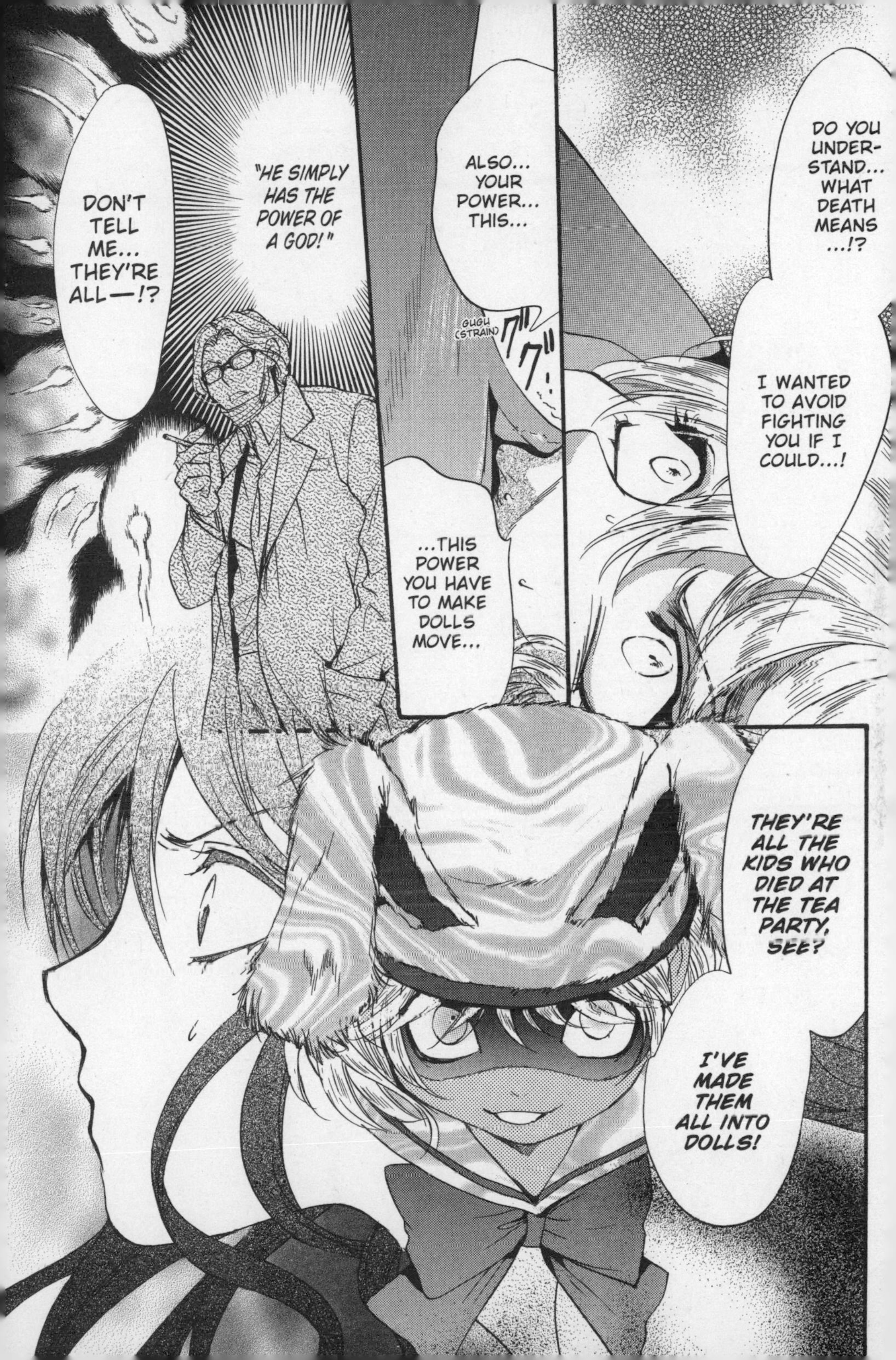
DO YOU UNDERSTAND... WHAT DEATH MEANS ...!?
I WANTED TO AVOID FIGHTING YOU IF I COULD...!
ALSO... YOUR POWER... THIS...
GUGU (STRAIN)
...THIS POWER YOU HAVE TO MAKE DOLLS MOVE...
"HE SIMPLY HAS THE POWER OF A GOD!"
DON'T TELL ME... THEY'RE ALL—!?
THEY'RE ALL THE KIDS WHO DIED AT THE TEA PARTY, SEE?
I'VE MADE THEM ALL INTO DOLLS!

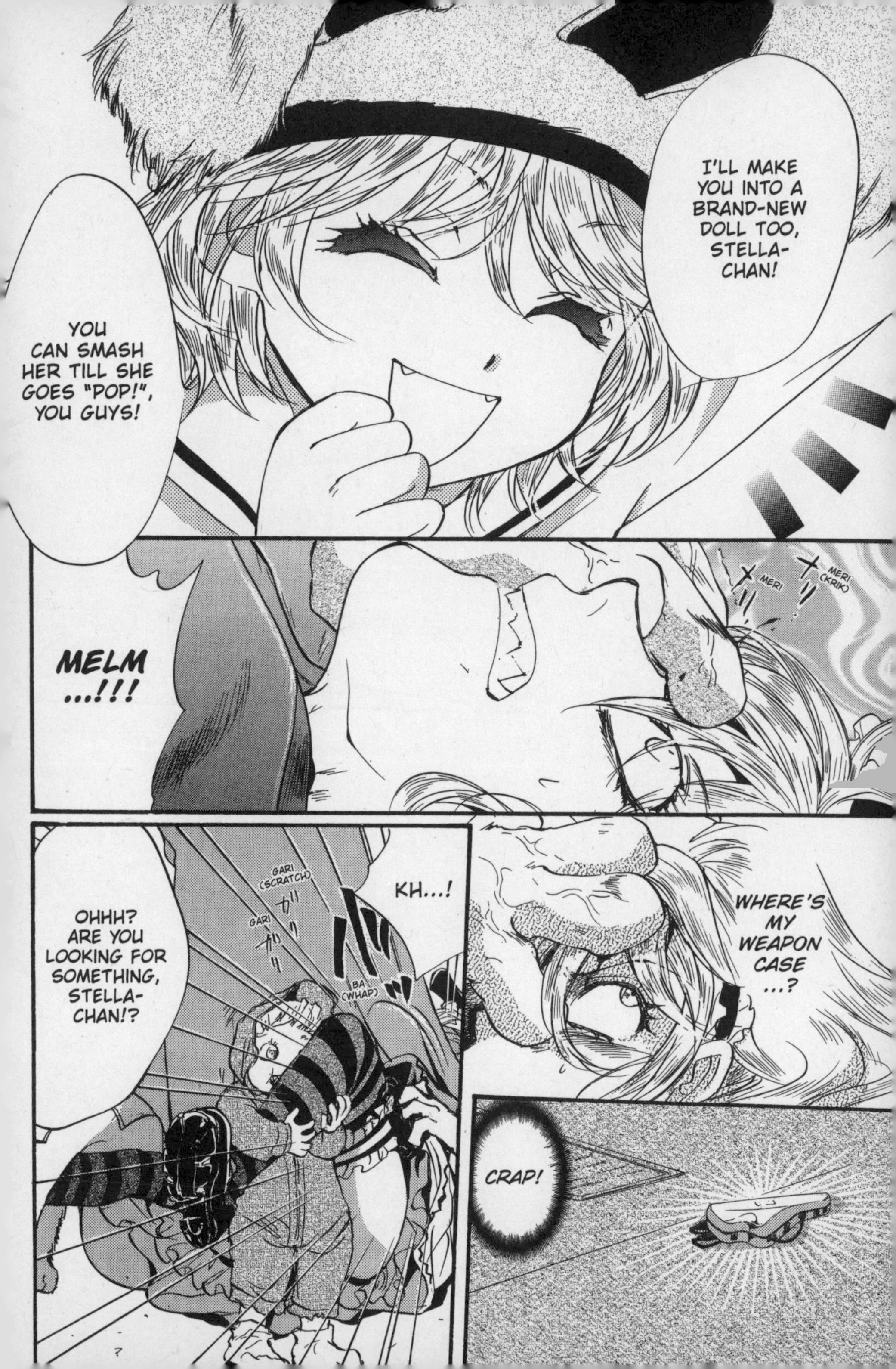
I'LL MAKE YOU INTO A BRAND-NEW DOLL TOO, STELLA-CHAN!
YOU CAN SMASH HER TILL SHE GOES "POP!", YOU GUYS!
MERI
MERI (KRIK)
MELM ...!!!
WHERE'S MY WEAPON CASE ...?
CRAP!
KH...!
GARI (SCRATCH)
GARI
BA (WHAP)
OHHH? ARE YOU LOOKING FOR SOMETHING, STELLA-CHAN!?

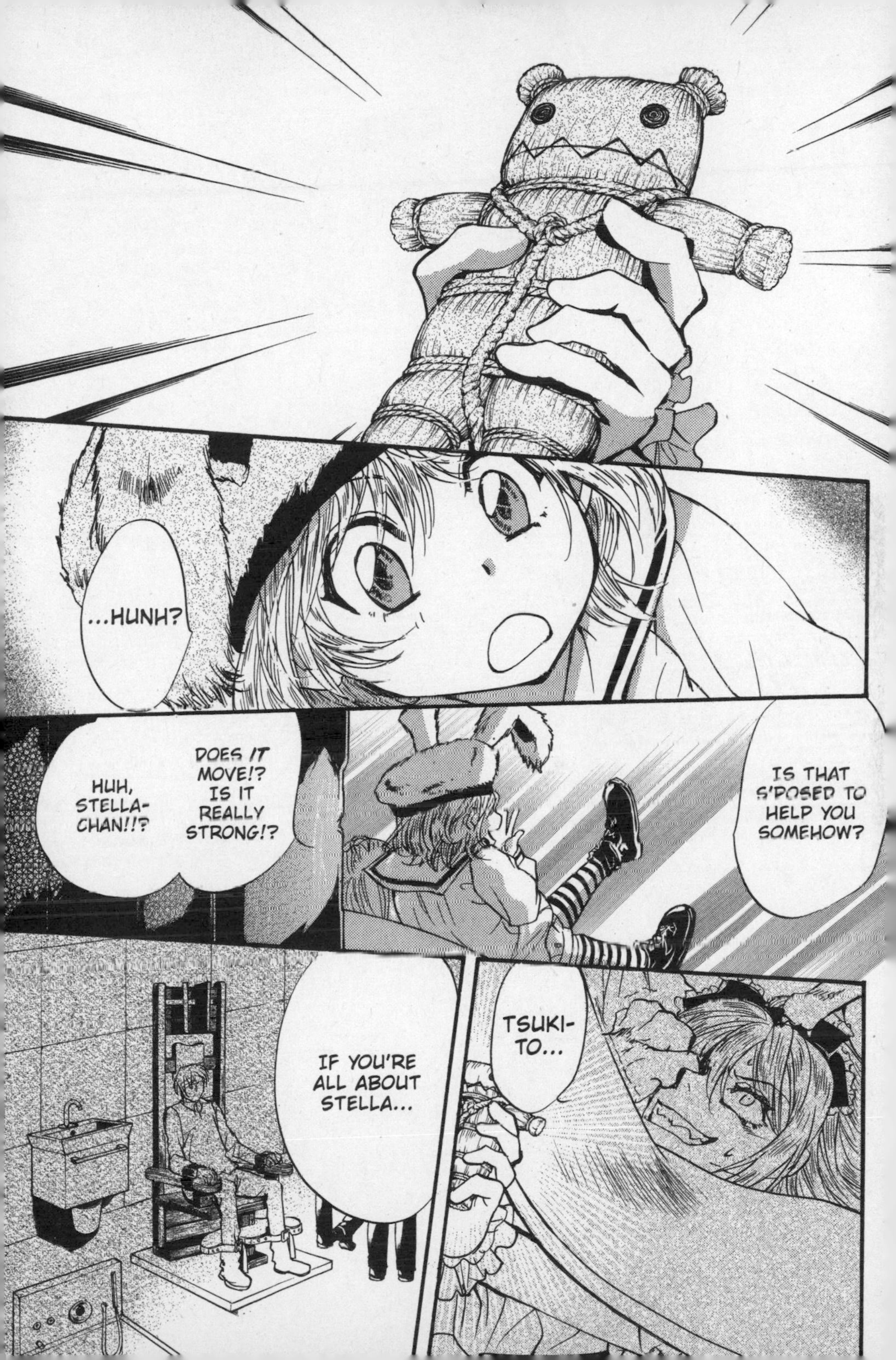
...HUNH?
IS THAT S'POSED TO HELP YOU SOMEHOW?
DOES *IT* MOVE!? IS IT REALLY STRONG!?
HUH, STELLA-CHAN!!?
TSUKI-TO...
IF YOU'RE ALL ABOUT STELLA...

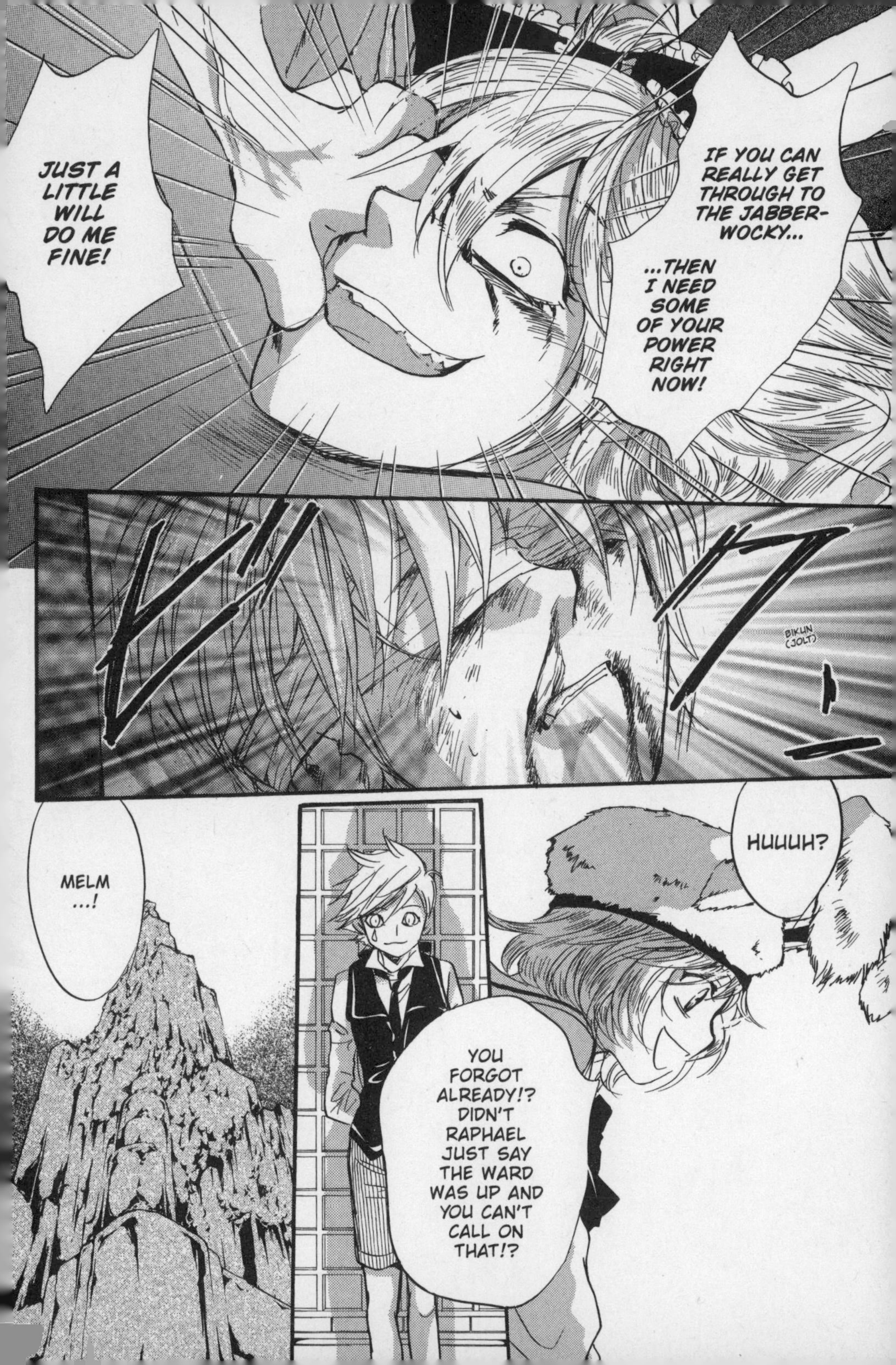
IF YOU CAN REALLY GET THROUGH TO THE JABBER-WOCKY...
...THEN I NEED SOME OF YOUR POWER RIGHT NOW!
JUST A LITTLE WILL DO ME FINE!
BIKUN (JOLT)
HUUUH?
YOU FORGOT ALREADY!? DIDN'T RAPHAEL JUST SAY THE WARD WAS UP AND YOU CAN'T CALL ON THAT!?
MELM ...!

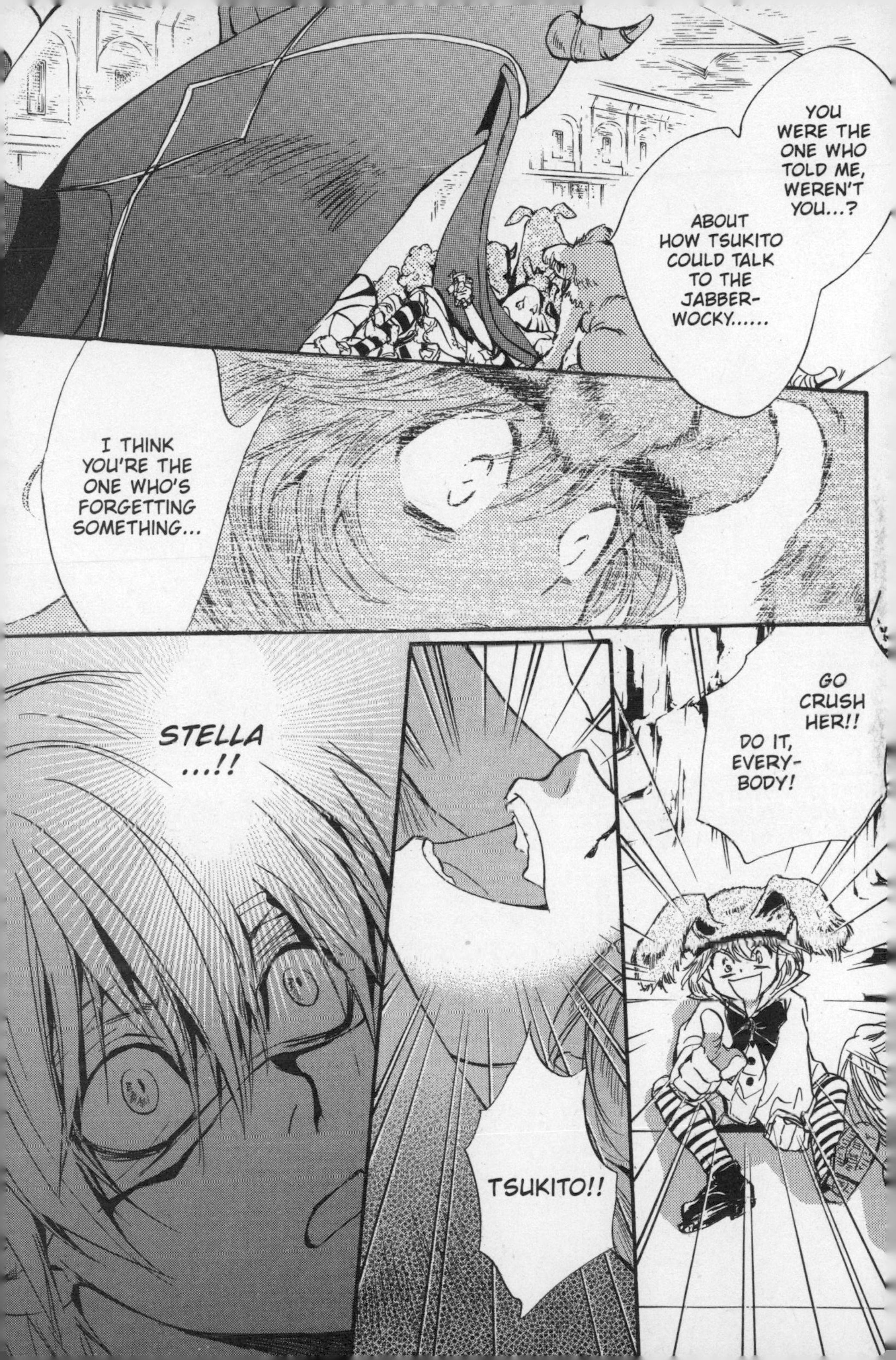
YOU WERE THE ONE WHO TOLD ME, WEREN'T YOU...?
ABOUT HOW TSUKITO COULD TALK TO THE JABBER-WOCKY......
I THINK YOU'RE THE ONE WHO'S FORGETTING SOMETHING...
GO CRUSH HER!!
DO IT, EVERY-BODY!
TSUKITO!!
STELLA ...!!

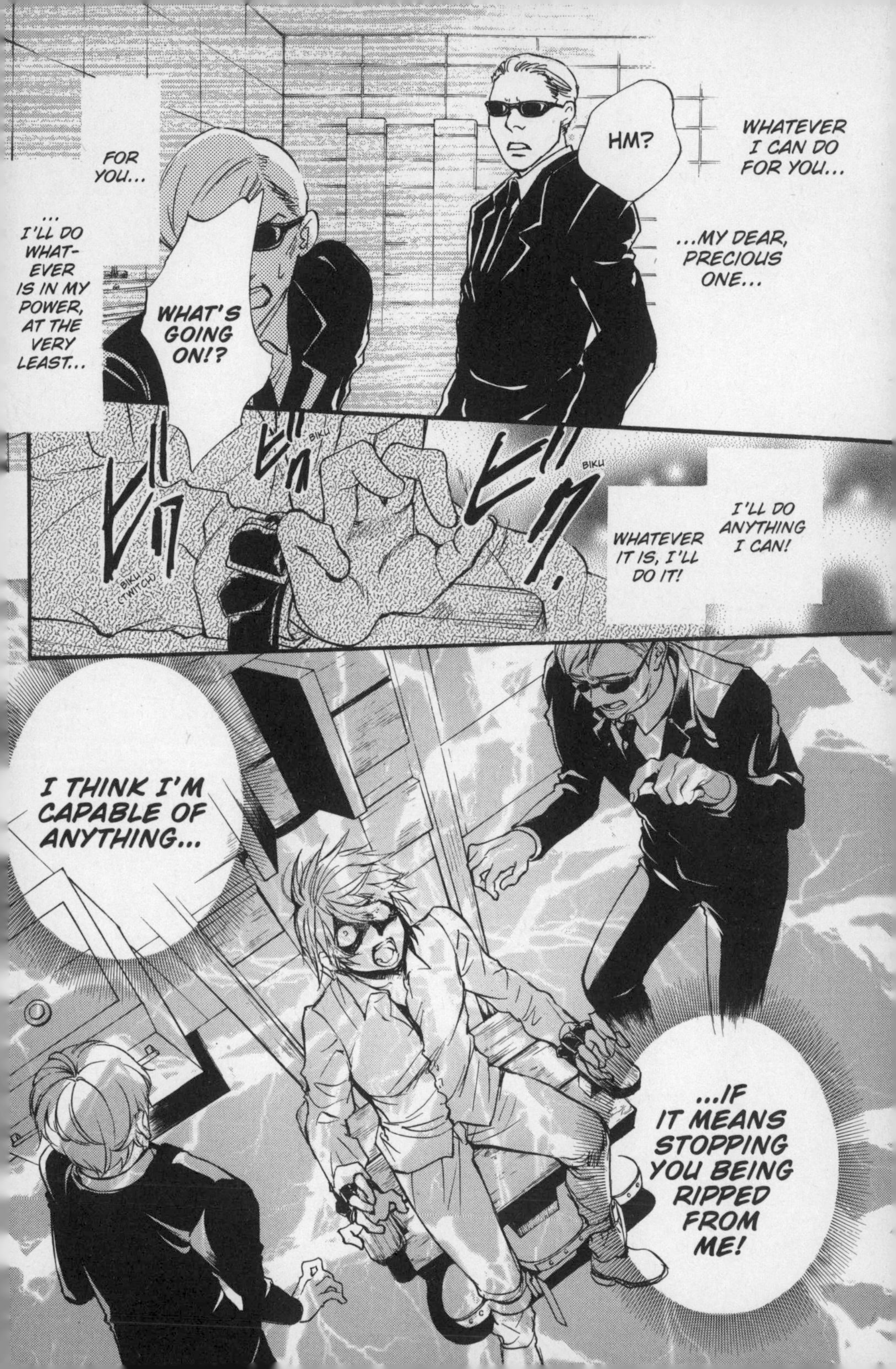
WHATEVER I CAN DO FOR YOU...
...MY DEAR, PRECIOUS ONE...
HM?
WHAT'S GOING ON!?
FOR YOU...
...I'LL DO WHAT-EVER IS IN MY POWER, AT THE VERY LEAST...
I'LL DO ANYTHING I CAN!
WHATEVER IT IS, I'LL DO IT!
BIKU
BIKU
BIKU (TWITCH)
I THINK I'M CAPABLE OF ANYTHING...
...IF IT MEANS STOPPING YOU BEING RIPPED FROM ME!

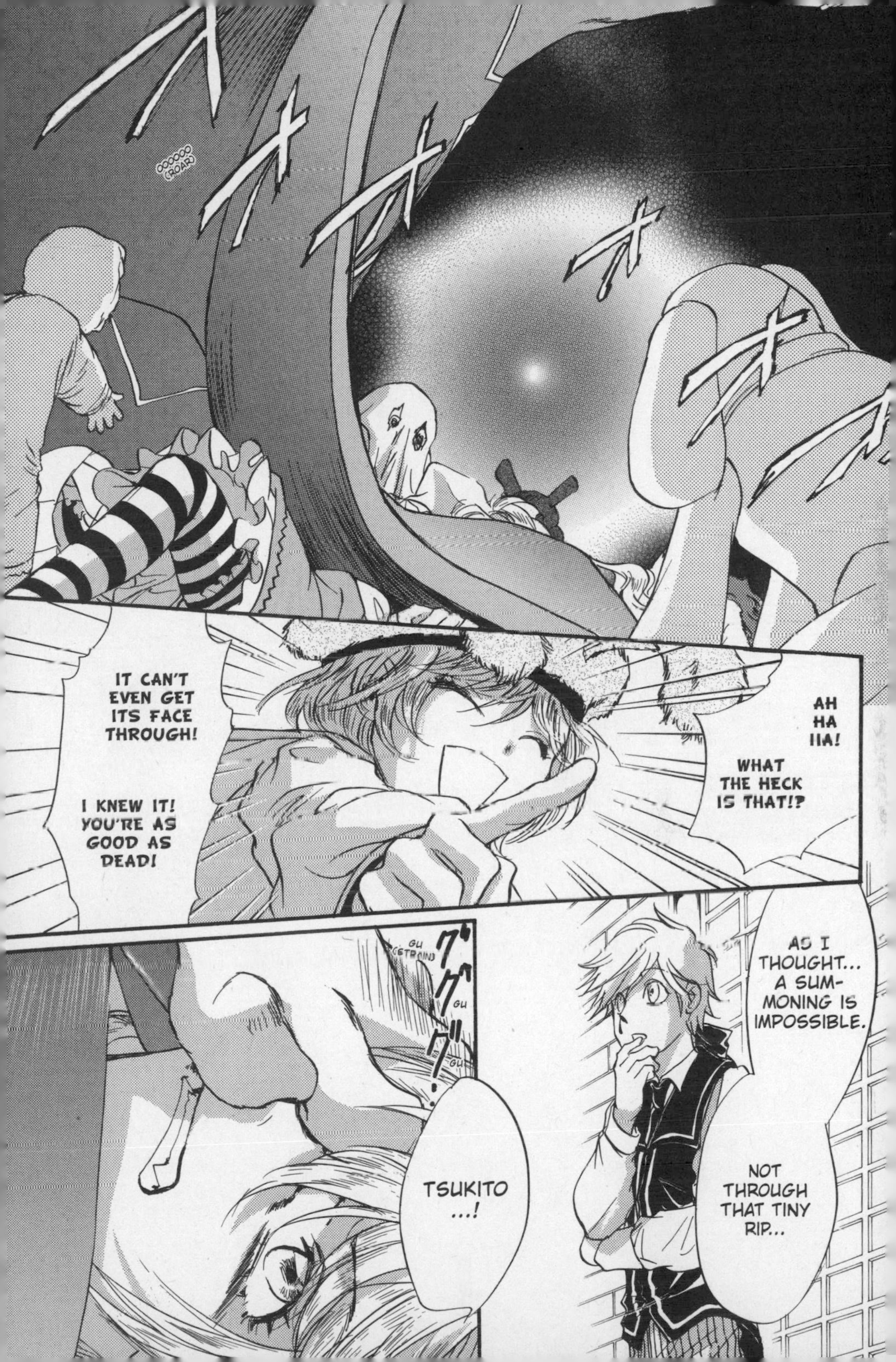
OOOOOO
(ROAR)
AH
HA
HA!
WHAT
THE HECK
IS THAT!?
IT CAN'T
EVEN GET
ITS FACE
THROUGH!
I KNEW IT!
YOU'RE AS
GOOD AS
DEAD!
AS I
THOUGHT...
A SUM-
MONING IS
IMPOSSIBLE.
NOT
THROUGH
THAT TINY
RIP...
GU
(STRAIN)
GU
TSUKITO
...!

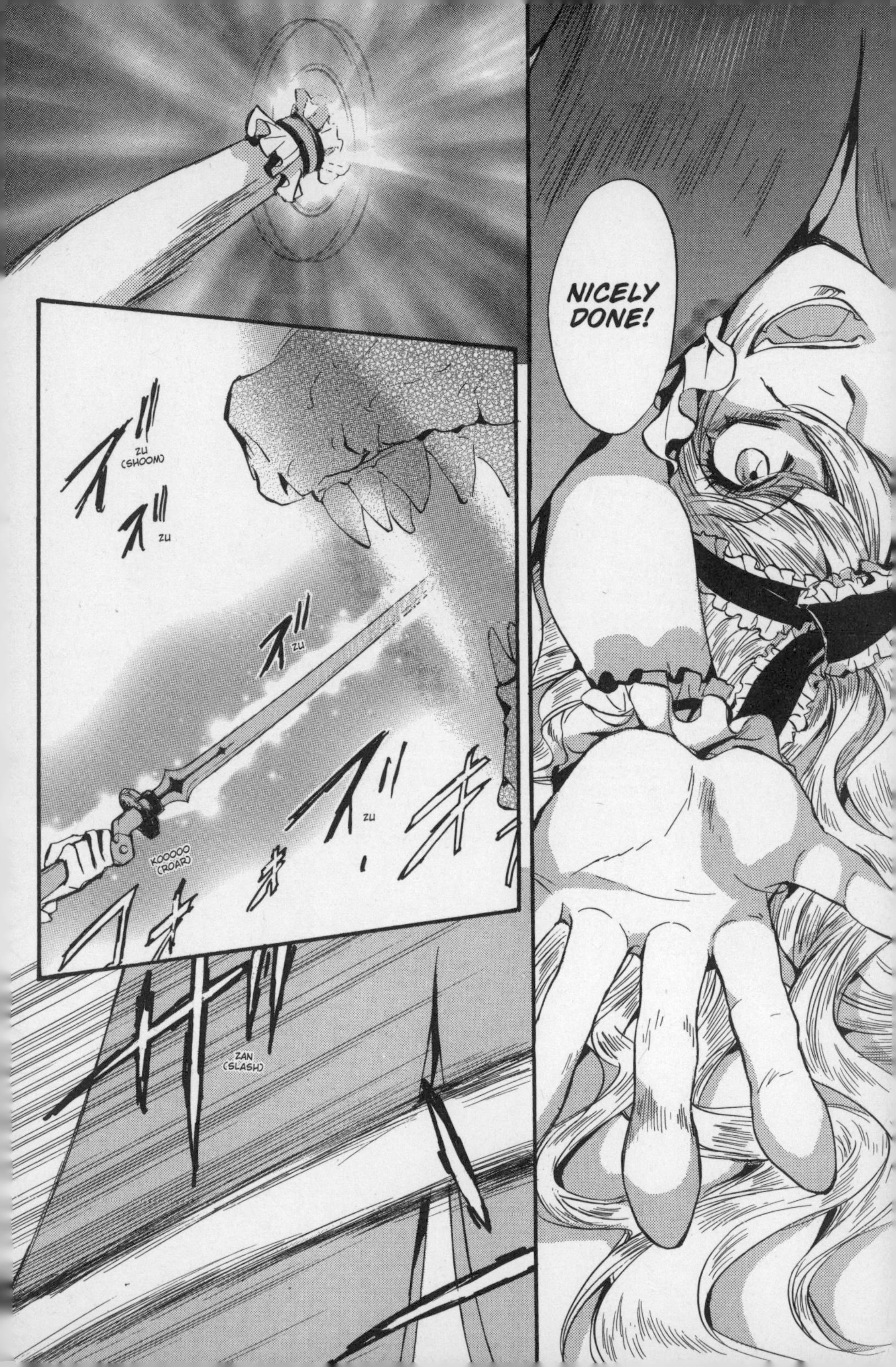
NICELY DONE!
ZU (SHOOM)
ZU
ZU
ZU
KOOOOO (ROAR)
ZAN (SLASH)

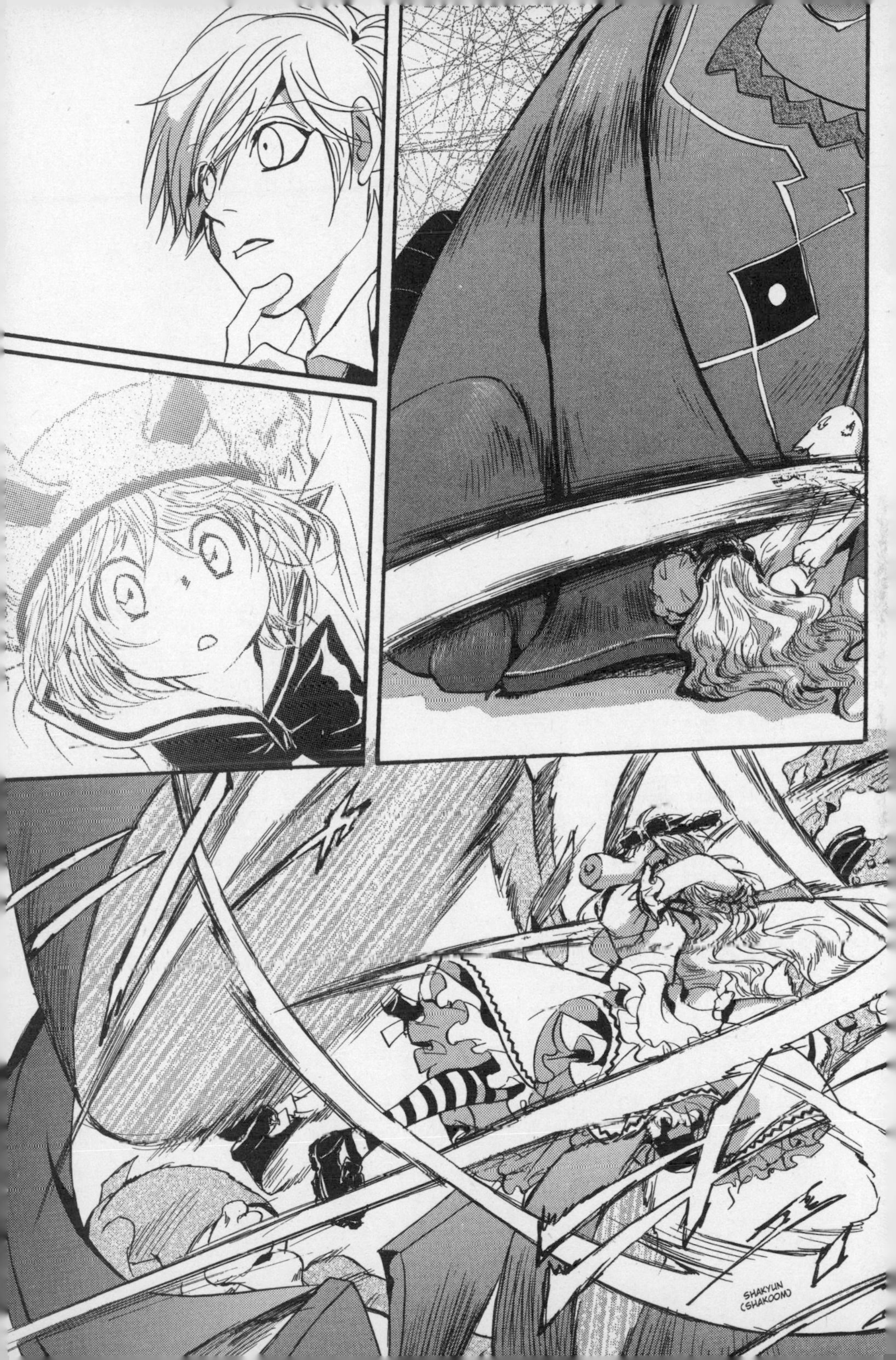
SHAKYUN
(SHAKOOM)

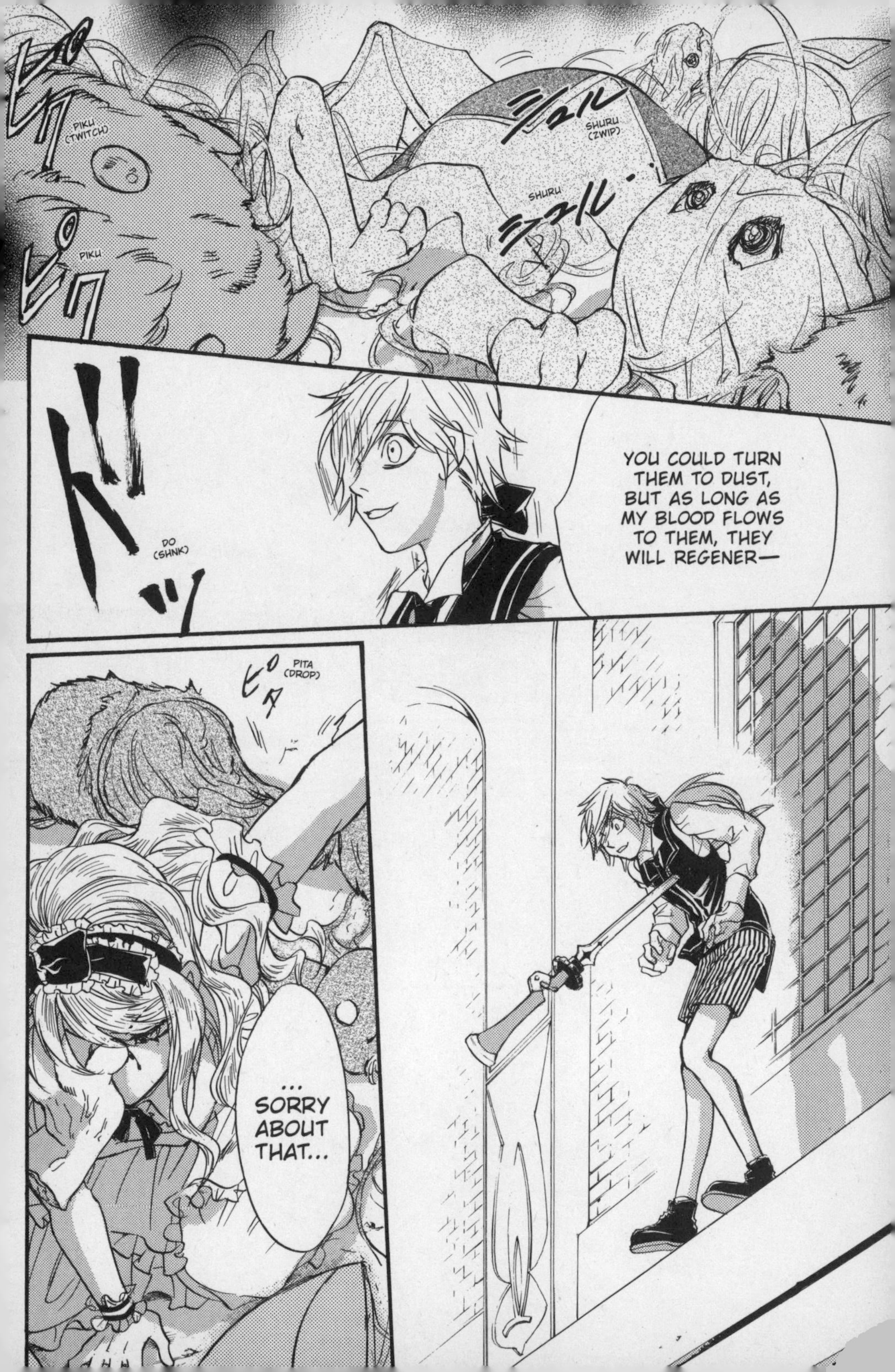
SHURU (ZWIP)
SHURU
PIKU (TWITCH)
PIKU
YOU COULD TURN THEM TO DUST, BUT AS LONG AS MY BLOOD FLOWS TO THEM, THEY WILL REGENER—
DO (SHNK)
PITA (DROP)
... SORRY ABOUT THAT...

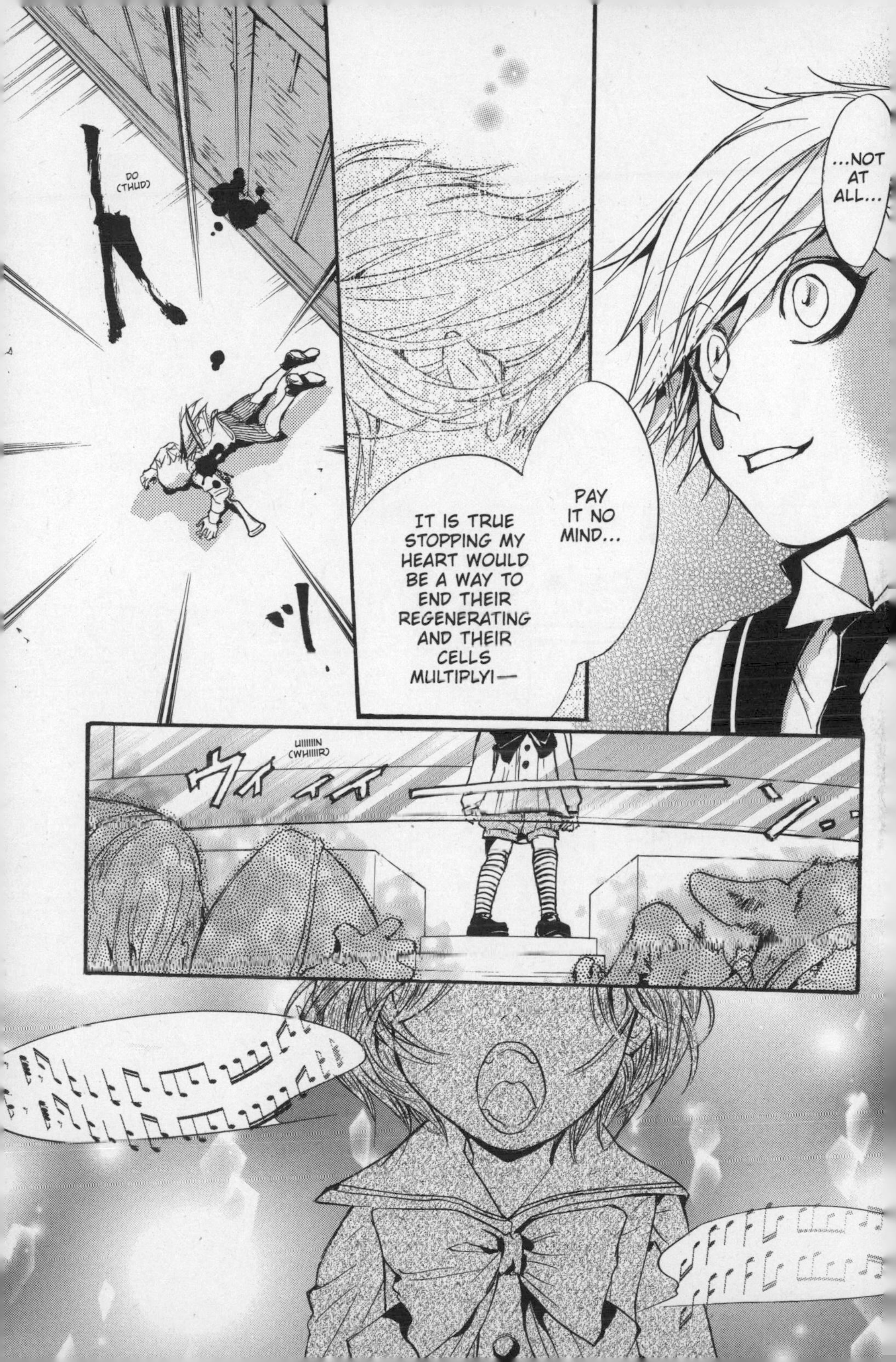
...NOT AT ALL...
PAY IT NO MIND...
IT IS TRUE STOPPING MY HEART WOULD BE A WAY TO END THEIR REGENERATING AND THEIR CELLS MULTIPLYI—
DO (THUD)
UIIIIIN (WHIIIR)

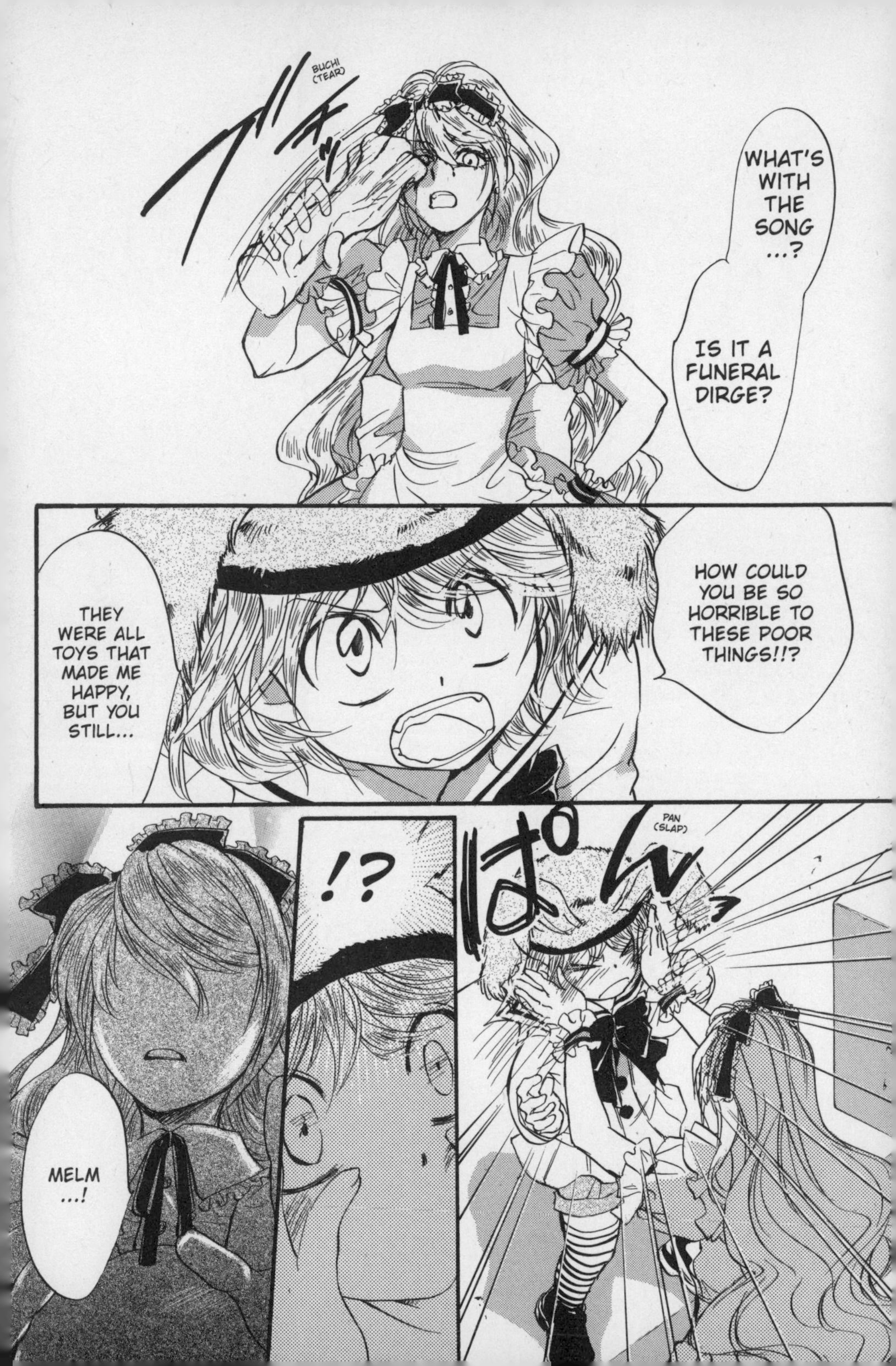
BUCHI (TEAR)
WHAT'S WITH THE SONG ...?
IS IT A FUNERAL DIRGE?
HOW COULD YOU BE SO HORRIBLE TO THESE POOR THINGS!!?
THEY WERE ALL TOYS THAT MADE ME HAPPY, BUT YOU STILL...
PAN (SLAP)
!?
MELM ...!

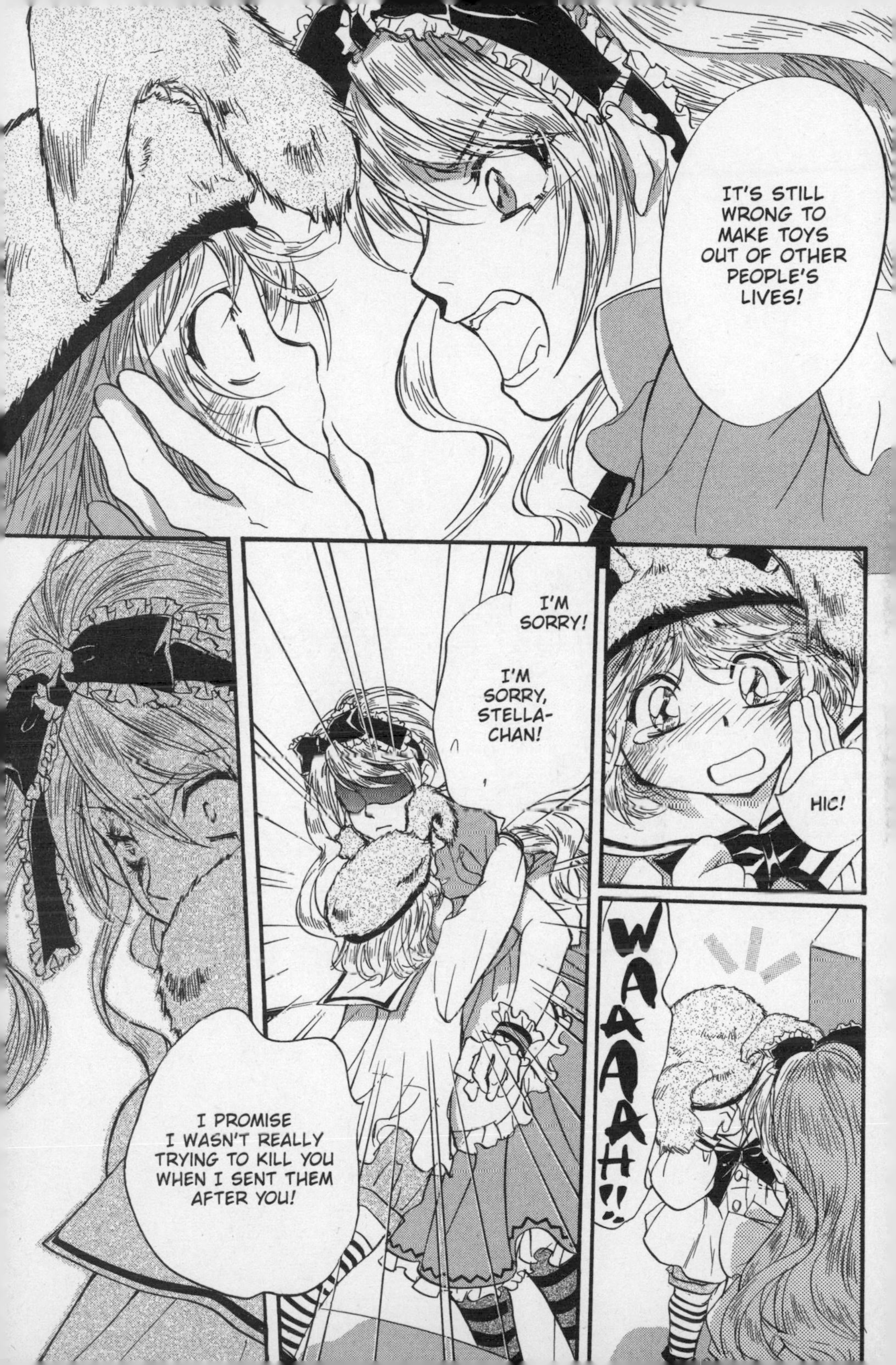
IT'S STILL WRONG TO MAKE TOYS OUT OF OTHER PEOPLE'S LIVES!
HIC!
WAAAAH!!
I'M SORRY!
I'M SORRY, STELLA-CHAN!
I PROMISE I WASN'T REALLY TRYING TO KILL YOU WHEN I SENT THEM AFTER YOU!

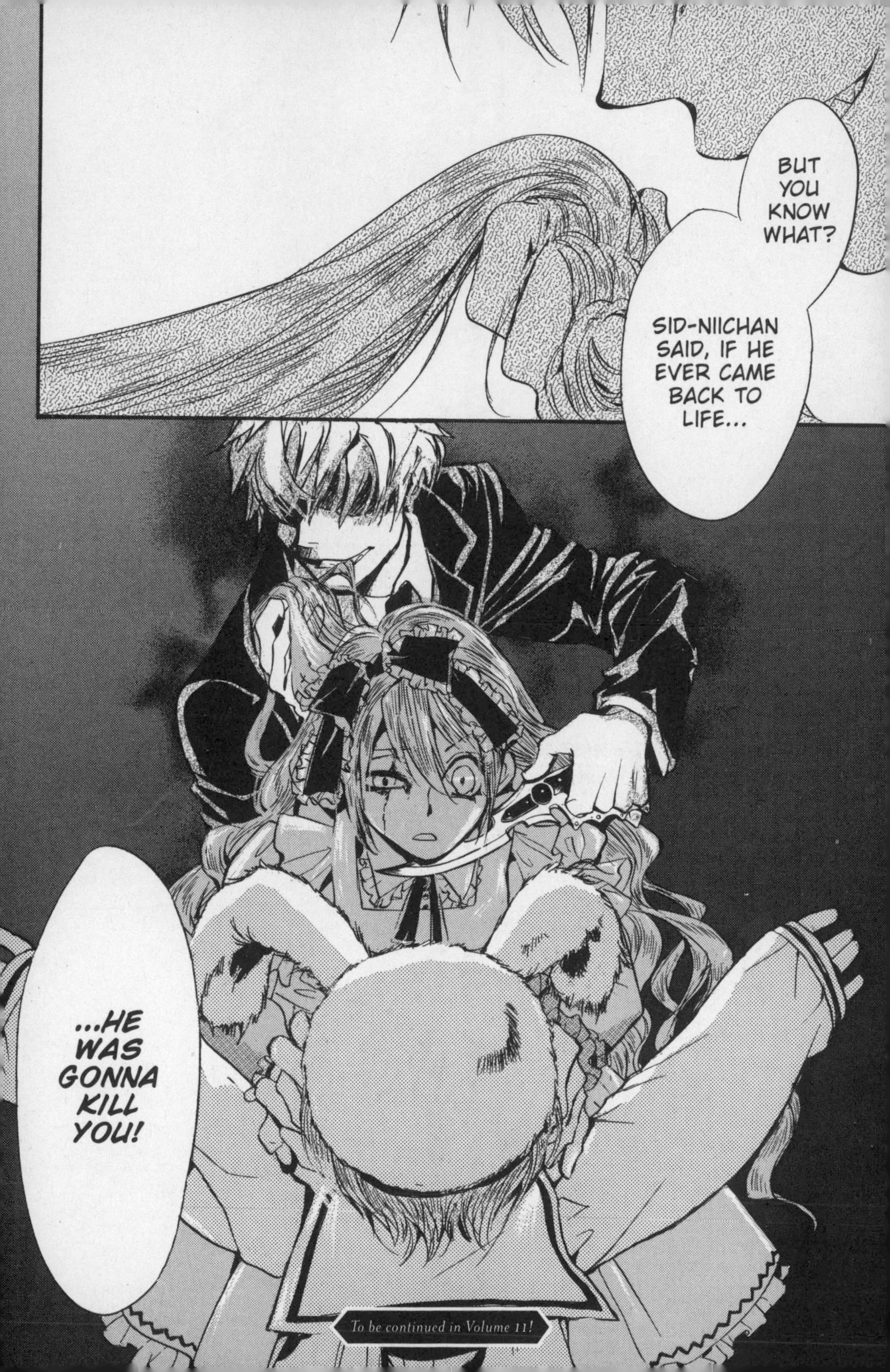
BUT YOU KNOW WHAT?
SID-NIICHAN SAID, IF HE EVER CAME BACK TO LIFE...
...HE WAS GONNA KILL YOU!
To be continued in Volume 11!

Alice in MURDERLAND

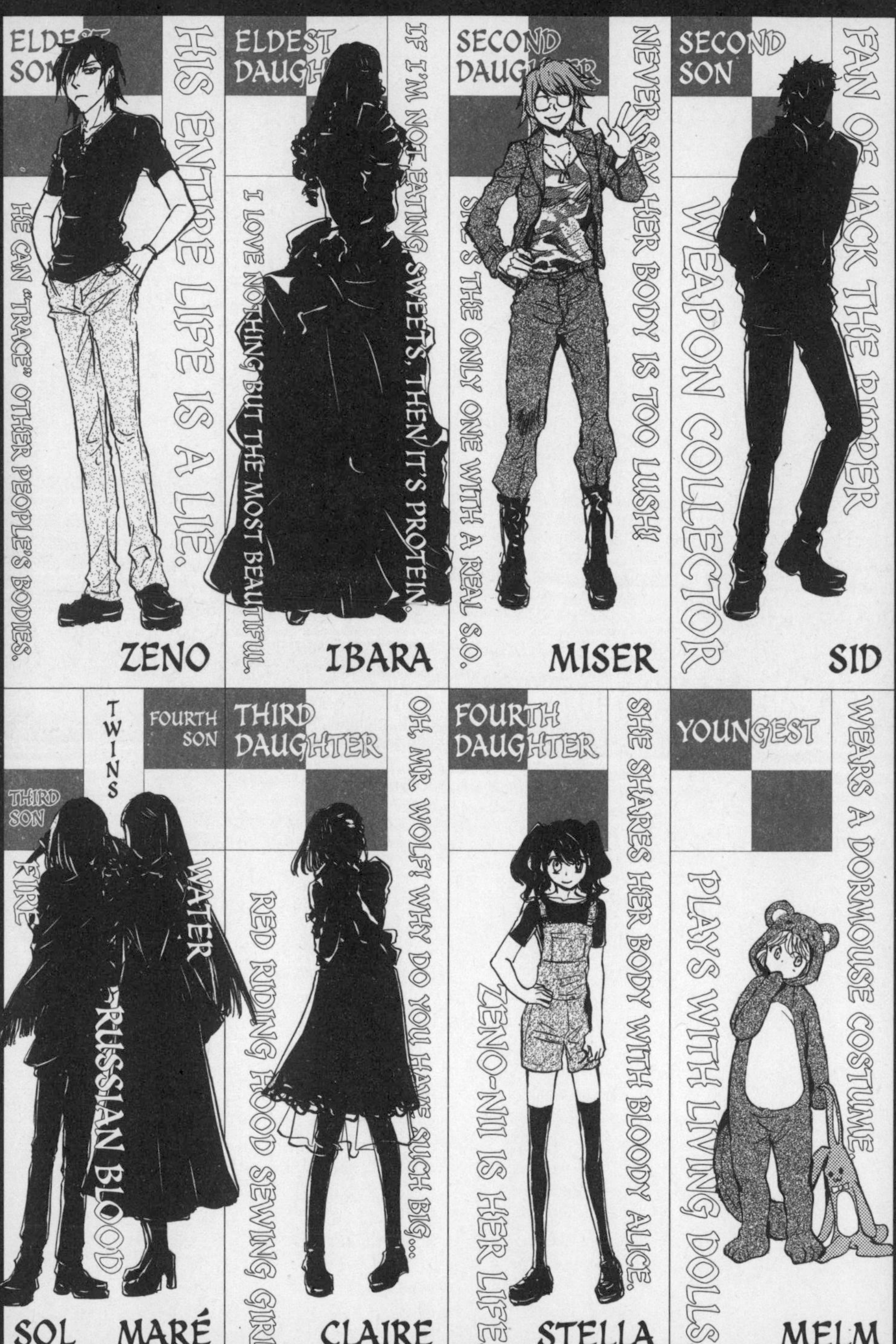
SECOND SON
FAN OF JACK THE RIPPER
WEAPON COLLECTOR
SID
SECOND DAUGHTER
NEVER SAY HER BODY IS TOO LUSH!
SHE'S THE ONLY ONE WITH A REAL S.O.
MISER
ELDEST DAUGHTER
IF I'M NOT EATING SWEETS, THEN IT'S PROTEIN.
I LOVE NOTHING BUT THE MOST BEAUTIFUL.
IBARA
ELDEST SON
HIS ENTIRE LIFE IS A LIE.
HE CAN "TRACE" OTHER PEOPLE'S BODIES.
ZENO
YOUNGEST
WEARS A DORMOUSE COSTUME.
PLAYS WITH LIVING DOLLS.
MELM
FOURTH DAUGHTER
SHE SHARES HER BODY WITH BLOODY ALICE.
ZENO-NII IS HER LIFE.
STELLA
THIRD DAUGHTER
OH, MR. WOLF! WHY DO YOU HAVE SUCH BIG...
RED RIDING HOOD SEWING GIRL
CLAIRE
FOURTH SON
TWINS
THIRD SON
WATER
FIRE
RUSSIAN BLOOD
MARÉ
SOL

Le LOIr

Now that Stella is up against her last opponent,
you can't help thinking "Finally!"
The battle with the youngest, Melm, is here.
It's quite possible the next volume will close out the series.
Looking back, it seems like it's gone by in an instant.
But if you think about it, we've been doing this for years.
It's a little late to be saying this, but
I'm struck by how fun it is to draw this series.
You don't know how grateful I am to *Aria* for serializing it (in Japan)!
Having a little kid like Melm become the boss character...isn't all that odd
for me, but killing kids is something that shakes me to my core.
That said, I'm also against resolutions that are too sappy,
so I'm conflicted about this...It's hard.
And so, the next volume will be the climax!
I'll be working very hard on it, so
I appreciate your continued support!

Twitter (Japanese): @angelaid
Kaori Yuki

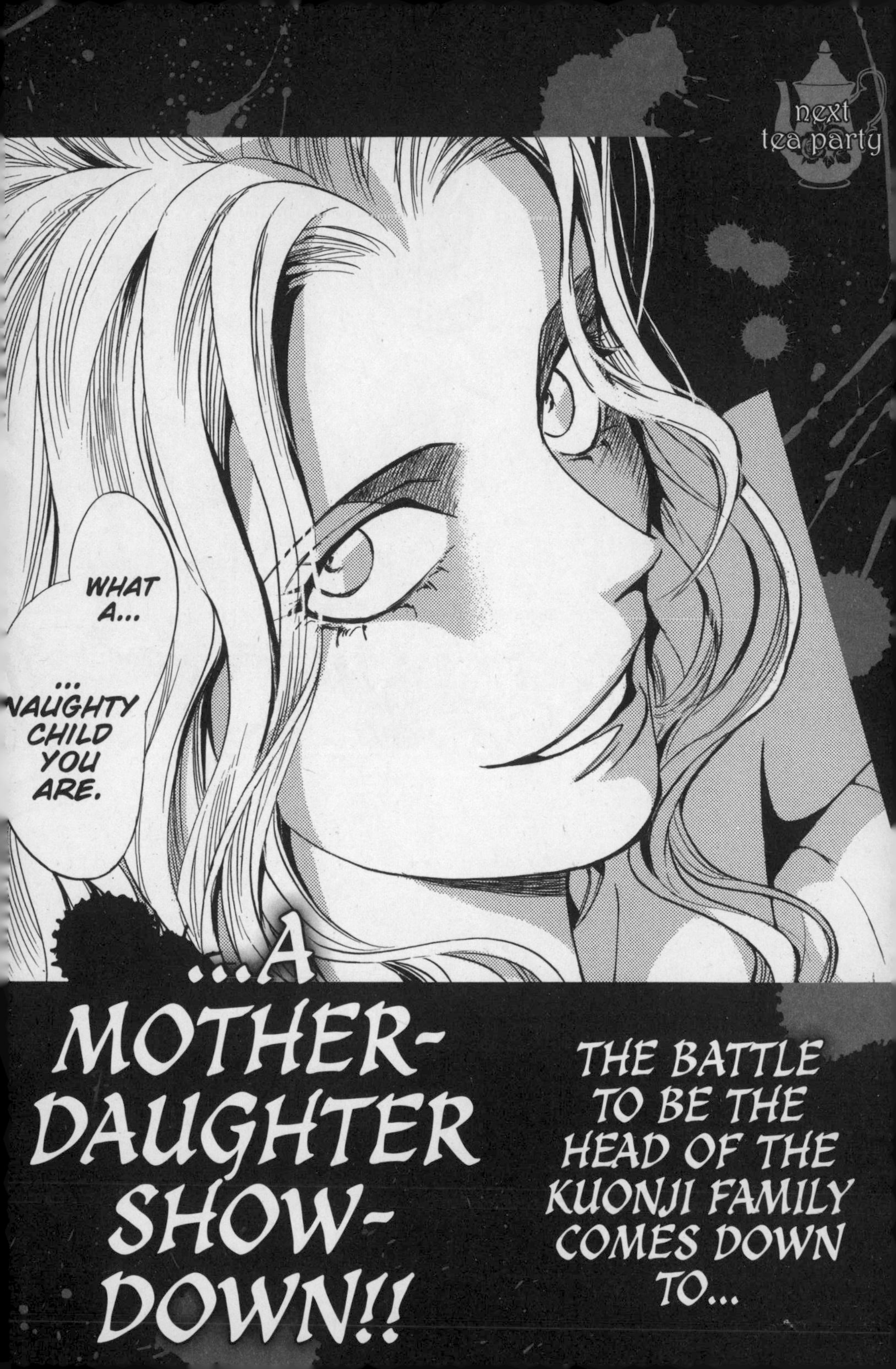
next
tea party
WHAT A...
...NAUGHTY CHILD YOU ARE.
THE BATTLE TO BE THE HEAD OF THE KUONJI FAMILY COMES DOWN TO...
...A MOTHER-DAUGHTER SHOW-DOWN!!